Ominous Whoosh

Ominous Whoosh:
A Wandering Mind
Returns to *Twin Peaks*

JOHN THORNE

Library of Congress Control Number: 2022914382

John Thorne, Dallas, TX

ISBN-13: 978-0-9971081-2-5

FOR LAURA

MY LAURA

(TRULY, THE ONE)

"If mankind was put on earth to create works of art, then other people were put on earth to comment on those works, to say what they think of them. Not to judge objectively or critically assess those works but to articulate their feelings about them with as much precision as possible...even if those feelings are of confusion, uncertainty or—in this case—undiminished wonder."

– GEOFF DYER, *ZONA*

"Our endless and impossible journey toward home is in fact our home."

– DAVID FOSTER WALLACE

Table of Contents

PRELUDE:

THE DARKNESS OF FUTURE PAST

A WOMAN SCREAMS.

WE SEE HER AT DISTANCE, framed through the window of the Twin Peaks high school, fleeing through a courtyard. Shrieking and sobbing, her hands clutch her face, hiding her identity. Who she is doesn't matter. What matters is what she represents. She is trauma made manifest, a visceral response to tragedy. She is the young woman who appears early in the *Twin Peaks* pilot just before Laura Palmer's death is announced to the high school population.

David Lynch chooses to show us this grief-stricken woman in the opening moments of the third season of *Twin Peaks* because her distress instantly reminds us of the tragedy of Laura Palmer. She also reminds us that *Twin Peaks* has never satisfactorily concluded, that for decades it has been suspended in time, open to speculation but never certainty. This long-awaited and unexpected third season—this return to *Twin Peaks*—is full of promise. In fact, we're hopeful for resolution to the many mysteries left dangling by the cancellation of the original *Twin Peaks* in June of 1991.

But wait. Are we really expecting resolution? Do we think a third season will answer our questions? Or will we end up like the anonymous woman in the courtyard, forever running toward an unknown, impossible destination? David Lynch is nothing if not deliberate, and here, at the beginning of the new *Twin Peaks*, he shows us a powerful scene from the old, reminding us that some questions

1

may never be answered. He has chosen the perfect sequence to restart *Twin Peaks.*

FRANZ KAFKA WROTE: "We ought to read only books that bite and sting us. If the book we are reading doesn't shake us awake like a blow to the skull, why bother reading it?" Channeling Kafka, David Lynch and Mark Frost (the co-creators of *Twin Peaks*) shake viewers awake with *Twin Peaks: The Return*, a profound and challenging work that asks more from audiences than most film or television. If you've seen *The Return*, then you already know: It can bite, and it can sting. It doesn't matter if you're a long-time fan or completely new to *Twin Peaks*, *The Return* can hit you like a blow to the skull.

Twin Peaks: The Return is an abstraction, a piece of art that defies the very medium on which it lives. Not surprisingly, reactions vary when we are confronted with such art. We might process it quietly, letting it steep in the recesses of our minds. We might dismiss it entirely, rejecting it as too demanding, too obscure. Or we might devote ourselves to it, sifting *The Return* in hopes of finding patterns. Of finding shapes within the shadows.

Taking that last approach is not easy. *The Return* can be overwhelming, and not everyone has the time to watch eighteen hours of *Twin Peaks* again (and again). Hopefully, that's where this book will help. If you've wanted to dive deep into *The Return* but don't know how to start, you've come to the right place. I don't promise answers to every question in *Twin Peaks*, but I do promise some compelling theories. Maybe I can offer some salve against the stings, some balm to ease the bites. Maybe I can cushion a few of the blows from this bewildering work.

I NEVER EXPECTED TO SEE *Twin Peaks* return to television—or to any medium—again. As a longtime and dedicated fan of the 1990-91 television series and its 1992 follow-up feature film, *Fire Walk With Me*, I took David Lynch at his word when he stated *Twin Peaks* was "gone" and "as dead as a doornail." This was tough to accept because *Twin Peaks* was incomplete. The series had ended without resolving its major storylines and had left many of its characters in perilous situations. *Twin Peaks* had been the victim of cruel cancellation, and, despite the hope it might one day be resurrected, one of its primary creators had publicly stated the property was dead.

I had made peace with the idea that *Twin Peaks* would be forever incomplete. I accepted that it would only ever comprise a fragment of some larger, indefinite whole, eternally suspended in cliffhangers and perpetually poised at revelation. And that was OK. Because it had to be.

Naturally, like any devoted fan, I pondered the "what ifs." What if David Lynch decided to return to the work and make a new series or film? What if a new story showed us what happened after Season 2? These were questions Craig Miller and I frequently discussed in the pages of *Wrapped In Plastic* in the years immediately following the show's cancellation. After thinking about it at great length, Craig and I concluded that any new Lynch-directed *Twin Peaks* project, as unlikely as it might be, would ultimately leave us as perplexed as we already were. We knew that if Lynch ever did return to *Twin Peaks* it would be under his own conditions. That if, somehow, Lynch could be convinced to explore his and Mark Frost's fictional world again he would create something other than what *Twin Peaks* fans wanted.

Craig and I wrote an editorial about just such a scenario in *Wrapped In Plastic* number 35 in June of 1998.[*] In it, we warned fans that a new *Twin Peaks* might not meet their expectations. Here is what we said:

> Ever since we began publishing *Wrapped In Plastic*, readers have asked us one question over and over. They've asked us at comic conventions. They've asked us at *Twin Peaks* festivals. They've asked us on the phone. They've asked us in letters.
>
> "Is David Lynch going to do any new *Twin Peaks* project?"
>
> "Is David Lynch going to do any new *Twin Peaks* project?"
>
> "Is David Lynch going to do any new *Twin Peaks* project?"
>
> And over and over we respond, "Nothing new has been announced. If he ever returns to *Twin Peaks*, it probably won't be for a very long time."

---

[*] Nineteen (!) years before *Twin Peaks* returned to TV for a third season.

3

While preparing last issue's *Fire Walk With Me* article, we began to ask ourselves: "Do *Peaks* fans *really* want what they say they want?"

Fans are frustrated with what they perceive as the "unfinished story" of Dale Cooper and the rest of the characters. But consider that Lynch has already had two opportunities to provide an unambiguous conclusion to the story at hand, once during the second season finale, and again during the feature film. Both times he rejected such a path in favor of more open-ended stories. Why do fans believe that, given a third chance, Lynch wouldn't do more of the same?

As we prepared the *FWWM* material, we remembered the anticipation that preceded the film. After all, the final television episode showed a possessed Cooper stuck in the bathroom at the Great Northern. With ABC's cancellation of the series, *Twin Peaks* appeared to have ended on a note of triumphant evil. Surely such a negative, pessimistic, defeatist moment would not be the final image for a story that provided glimpses into the wonders of a transcendent union with the natural world and beyond. Surely Lynch would "explain" what had happened in that final scene.

But *Fire Walk With Me* turned out to be primarily a prequel (time was not exactly linear in the film), and the fans' questions remained mostly unanswered—or at least not answered in the way they wanted.

Fire Walk With Me has aged well, and it is gradually gaining its deserved place as one of Lynch's finest films. But imagine the response if Lynch announced that he had begun scripting a second *Peaks* movie. Many fans would want him to *answer the questions* and *explain everything* and *not leave anything hanging or unresolved.*

But of course, Lynch wouldn't write such a script. *Lost Highway* shows that, if anything, a second *Peaks* movie would be even more obscure than the series finale or *Fire Walk With Me*. It would open new plot lines, introduce new characters, and leave lots of issues unresolved.

Then the fans would be *really ticked off.*

Lynch is not going to do another major *Twin Peaks* project. Mark Frost is not going to, either. We'd love it if they did, even if they left questions unanswered and introduced new ones. But that's not the story many fans really want to see.

The prophetic words of *Wrapped In Plastic*! Though we were ultimately wrong about a new *Twin Peaks* (David Lynch and Mark Frost *did* return to create the eighteen-hour third season which aired on Showtime between May 21 and September 3, 2017), we were right about almost everything else. The new series radically departed from the structure and themes of its earlier incarnation; it introduced new characters, ideas and storylines; and it concluded without a clear and definitive denouement.

Not surprisingly, many fans were dismayed by how Season 3 turned out and felt betrayed and abandoned by what David Lynch ultimately gave them.[*] Even if they had read what Craig and I wrote all those years ago (and few probably had) they likely expected *Twin Peaks* to, at the very least, provide an explicit answer to the fate of Dale Cooper. Alas, that was not to be in Season 3.

I understand that *The Return* didn't give many fans what they expected, and I respect some of the considered, honest criticism they have levelled at the show. *The Return* is not immune to criticism. Indeed, there are many aspects of it that can be quite frustrating.

Notably, *The Return* leaves few of its characters better off than they were at the end of Season 2. Many are lost souls, living in the confusion of what one character describes as a "dark, dark age," and almost everyone is either mentally or physically suffering. In fact, many characters are in so much pain or in such anguish that they can barely cope with their day-to-day lives. With the exception of Big Ed and Norma (and a few others such as Andy, Lucy, and, eventually, Nadine) most of the characters in *Twin Peaks* have found little peace or reward in their lives. This is hardly what longtime fans wanted to see when returning to that curious and alluring world depicted in the first two seasons of *Twin Peaks*.

Many characters in *The Return* came off as puzzling rather than sympathetic or relatable. Even with the rich history of folks such as Ben Horne, Bobby Briggs, and Deputy Hawk (and many, many others), the

---

[*] I say David Lynch here because while Mark Frost was a vital creative force behind the new *Twin Peaks*, Lynch continued to expand and alter the script after Frost left to write his book, *The Secret History of Twin Peaks*. What's more, it has been confirmed by various cast members that Lynch was revising the script even while in the midst of shooting.

new season often failed to connect with its characters in meaningful ways. Most of them were simply on display rather than intimately involved with the larger story. That, plus the fact *The Return* provided only glimpses into their lives (with few satisfying conclusions), left many fans cold.

Some favorite characters from the original series were missing altogether. We never learned the fate of Annie Blackburn, whose condition was the subject of the original series' most enduring cliffhanger: "How's Annie?" We don't know "what happened to Josie" after her baffling death and curious supernatural resurrection. And what of Windom Earle, the malevolent, absurd arch-nemesis of Dale Cooper? Although he was perfunctorily dismissed at the end of the original series, he dominated much of that story and might have been a prominent player in the new season. And perhaps no character demanded a presence in a new *Twin Peaks* more than Sheriff Harry S. Truman, who, unfortunately, remained entirely off-screen in *The Return* (despite his story taking a precarious and unresolved turn). Fans were hoping to see Harry Truman and all those others again, but *The Return* barely addressed them.

Unlike many successful and acclaimed series of the past decade, *Twin Peaks: The Return* moved slowly. It lacked forward momentum as it meandered into peculiar subplots and lingered on isolated, irrelevant sequences. It was also stingy, persistently withholding crucial revelations while erratically, sometimes notionally, advancing the plot. The experience of watching *The Return* could be frustrating, and many fans grew uneasy as the final episode approached and the story continued to wander. Ultimately, *The Return* ended with as many questions as it had when it started. Maybe more.

As a result, a great many invested fans believed *The Return* did not deliver the emotional payoff they were owed. Many also felt that the ambiguous, inconclusive nature of the story damaged the existing narrative, rendering all that came before as inconsequential, or, worse, counterfeit. For those fans *The Return* was a major disappointment. You might say they were *ticked off*, just as we predicted all those years ago in *Wrapped In Plastic*.

But not everyone felt that way.

When I heard that a third season of *Twin Peaks* was happening, I was ecstatic, but I also knew it would be unlike anything that had come before. Yes, I wanted to see how the story might play out twenty-five years later, but I didn't assume a new David Lynch-directed *Twin Peaks* would neatly address the many questions left open in the original. I knew it would be confusing, contradictory, and confounding. In that regard *Twin Peaks* Season 3 was exactly what I expected.

I was ready for *Twin Peaks* to challenge me, and I was careful not to have any preconceived notions. I understood that Lynch and Frost could do whatever they wanted. Lynch has never been tied to traditional storytelling conventions (*Fire Walk With Me* proved that he was willing to take liberties with existing backstory), and Mark Frost had already confounded fans with his book, *The Secret History of Twin Peaks*, which ostensibly discarded many established "facts" about *Twin Peaks* and told a story that deviated from what had come before.

So, I was on guard. Especially after Frost said, "The thing that folks have to remember is that we created the mythology. We dreamt it up, so I think that gives us a certain amount of license to take it wherever we choose." And: "If we want to change it, we are going to change it and that's our prerogative. And that also reflects reality. Reality is fungible."

It was clear to me that to appreciate any new *Twin Peaks* we needed to approach it on Lynch and Frost's terms. They weren't negotiating—they were offering a "take it or leave it" proposition. Still, I felt they were serious about their endeavor. Take it or leave it? I was ready to take it.

Twin Peaks: The Return is not merely a new chapter in a larger story, not just an account of heroes and villains, or a superficial melodrama powered by surprise twists and unexpected revelations. It is something far more profound. If we limit ourselves to seeing *The Return* as simply an appendage or extension of the earlier work, we are denying its unique power.

The Return is an ambitious work that explores weighty, complicated themes. It does not promise answers (far from it!) to big existential questions about life and death, but it does provide an honest, sometimes uncomfortable, study of these ideas.

The Return is about the struggle to connect, to clearly and precisely communicate with one another. It posits that perfect communication is impossible because no two people can ever see the world the same way. If our perceptions of reality differ, then we lack a reliable, shared foundation on which to converse. In other words, if we all inherently perceive the world according to our individual, idiosyncratic frames-of-mind, it becomes impossible to convey to one another nuance, feeling, and belief. (In fact, the very core of *The Return* is about Dale Cooper believing his way of seeing the world supersedes all others—a topic I'll expand upon as this book progresses.)

As I mentioned, *The Return* is about pain and suffering. Almost everyone in the story is struggling to overcome some sort of hardship, whether it be physical, mental, or spiritual. Pain is part of life, and *The Return* reminds us that how we deal with our pain and how we cope with hardship defines us. What's more, how we deal with the pain of others is equally important. We see people in need everywhere we look. What do we do when someone needs our help? Do we turn away, or do we offer aid, even if it means sacrifice? *The Return* looks at this idea again and again across its eighteen hours.

Most importantly, perhaps, *The Return* is about memory. It's about growing old, about how we perceive our own pasts and about what we hold precious in life. As such, *The Return* becomes a *reckoning*—a story that confronts its older self, interrogating and challenging it in order to evolve beyond the constrictions and stale notions of an earlier form and to metamorphose into something new, astonishing, and potent.

Throughout *The Return* we see Dale Cooper struggling with the past, attempting to make peace with memory. Late in the story Cooper confidently states, "The past dictates the future," and then sets forth to change history. Cooper wishes life had gone differently, that he could have prevented the suffering of others, and so he convinces himself he can go back in time and change things. This hubris is Cooper's biggest failing—he refuses to accept that the past cannot be changed, that it is fixed and unalterable.

What Cooper doesn't understand is that while we can't change the past, we have a choice in how we interpret it. We decide how we let the past inform our present, and that, in turn, gives us power over our future. If we are lost in the past—pining for it, regretting it—then we become stagnant, incapable of fully embracing our lives as they are now. Our memories become traps holding us back from true joy. Only when we deny the past its hold upon us, when we liberate ourselves from nostalgia and regret and become fully engaged with the present, can we see the world for what it is—and is not.

So, Cooper is wrong: The past does not dictate the future. What we do with the present does.

What I choose to do with the present is to come to terms with *Twin Peaks: The Return.* To make peace with it, if you will. No matter how confounding *Twin Peaks* is, there is something immensely satisfying about it. Something transformative. We will never completely understand the whole of *Twin Peaks*—pieces of it will endlessly elude us—but struggling with the mystery of the work is a worthy endeavor in itself. Engaging with *Twin Peaks* can be revelatory, not only about what we see in it, but also about what we ultimately see in ourselves.

Yes, some argue that it's pointless to interpret David Lynch's work, that *The Return* resists analysis. In fact, some critics explicitly advise us to avoid trying to decipher *Twin Peaks* altogether and simply let the work wash over us. While there may be some merit to this argument, I believe such an approach encourages surrender to, rather than engagement with, the art, and when it comes to *Twin Peaks*, I don't see any value in remaining passive.

When someone asks why I've spent so much time and so many words on *Twin Peaks*, my answer is, "Why do you sing along with your favorite song?" I believe each of us wants to participate in the art we love. If the art is special—if it touches us like nothing else—we can't merely sit still; we must express ourselves. We sing and we dance. *Twin Peaks* is my favorite song, and I am compelled to sing along with it.

David Lynch once said, "It's hard to believe that someone looks at your films so closely. But then I turn around and *I* look at *other* people's films so closely." (Emphasis added.) Lynch understands that people enjoy paying attention, that they want to study art and offer interpretation. "Somebody has got to intellectualize stuff and put things into words," Lynch explains, "and if you do it well, then that's peachy keen." I can't say if I've put *The Return* into words well, but I've tried to offer some insight and suggest some reasons for how and why

The Return works the way it does. Hopefully, this book will evoke new ways of seeing *Twin Peaks*. Maybe it will spark some ideas that I never even considered. If it does, well, that's just "peachy keen."

YES, I SYMPATHIZE WITH THOSE FANS disappointed with the new *Twin Peaks*. The original series held a special place in many hearts and memories. But if we are not careful, our view of *Twin Peaks* can be as much a burden as a joy. For many, expectations for *The Return* were rooted not only in what *Twin Peaks* was but in what many thought it had to be. Like Dale Cooper, some believed the past would dictate the future, and, like Cooper, many were left in the dark when the show was over, abandoned and baffled by a world that operated according to an unexpected and unpredictable logic.

But nothing about *The Return* changed the original series. It remains every bit as mysterious and captivating as it ever was. It did not lose its charm when the third season came along; those things we loved about the original series—its humor, its mystery, its sense of wonder—have not been undone or rendered any less potent.

And if we wanted *The Return* to answers questions, well, it did. It also gave us a bundle of new questions to ponder. That's as it should be. *Twin Peaks* began with a question: "Who killed Laura Palmer?" and that question spawned countless others. Questions keep *Twin Peaks* alive. They keep us going back to the story again and again. Decades from now, audiences will still be debating and dissecting *Twin Peaks*. Many will be celebrating it, while others will be cursing and, yes, indicting it. *Twin Peaks* evokes strong emotions, and that won't ever change.

Love it or hate it, *Twin Peaks* is a kind of magic. And all of us who spend time with it—whether we be critics, fans, detractors, or devotees—are under its spell.

Act I

"Listen to the sounds."

PART 1:
MY LOG HAS A MESSAGE FOR YOU

WE BEGIN IN A TIMELESS, black-and-white space—an otherworldly parlor where Agent Dale Cooper and a figure we will come to know as The Fireman* sit facing one another. Between them, an old-fashioned gramophone emits odd, chirruping sounds. The Fireman, wearing a smoking jacket (of course), regards Cooper for a long moment. "Listen to the sounds," he says; "It is in our house now." Cooper obediently listens. The Fireman tells Cooper to remember a few cryptic clues: "Four three zero, Richard and Linda, two birds with one stone." Cooper confidently replies, "I understand," and vanishes, as if venturing forth to complete an assignment—a mission given to him by The Fireman.

The opening scene of *The Return* is disorienting. We don't know where or when it takes place, and we don't know why Cooper is receiving orders from this supernatural figure. The scene implies deliberation, a straightforward journey upon which the hero of the story, Dale Cooper, is about to embark, but we have no context, no meaningful way to decipher such a puzzling preamble. And so, as the story moves on, and our attention is distracted by other, earthly happenings, we are likely to forget what happened here.

---

* Credits for Part 1 of *The Return* hide the identity of this character (played by Carel Struycken) as "???????." In the original series he was referred to as The Giant, but for simplicity's sake—and to avoid confusion—I'll refer to him as The Fireman from here onward.

That would be a mistake. The Fireman/Cooper scene is important, and David Lynch has put it here for a reason.

Opening scenes in David Lynch's films are always significant. They provide allusion, impetus, and thematic context for the stories that follow: In *Blue Velvet*, the hidden world of insects implies forces writhing beneath an everyday order; in *Mulholland Drive*, the point-of-view of someone falling into bed suggests dreams about to begin; in *INLAND EMPIRE* a "lost girl" is trapped in a hotel room, subjected to a multitude of alternate realities visible on a television screen; and in *Eraserhead*, a "Man in a Planet" pulls levers, triggering events on the mortal plane. Though obscure, each of these opening scenes informs a larger narrative.

As *The Return* opens, The Fireman—a godlike figure who monitors and modifies the earthly realm—is setting in motion pieces of a grand plan. It is not at all obvious, but he is programming Dale Cooper, installing in him instructions that Cooper must follow. Arguably, The Fireman's phonograph contains this programming, and the sounds it emits are being implanted in Cooper's mind, encoding him for a crucial role. The Fireman needs Dale Cooper to find Laura Palmer and deliver her to a certain time and place. Some of this plan will become clearer as the story progresses, but it will never be obvious. The Fireman's cosmic scheme is not the primary story of *The Return*. That story belongs to Dale Cooper.

Although Cooper believes he understands his mission, he's really a lost soul, incapable of moving forward until he resolves the various conflicts within himself. "You are far away," The Fireman cautions, but Cooper either doesn't hear or doesn't understand this warning.

The Fireman is right; Cooper *is* far away—he has lessons to learn and struggles to endure before he can assume the awesome responsibility of guiding Laura to her destiny. As the story begins (or, more accurately, as the story *resumes*) Dale Cooper is diminished and incomplete and needs to be rehabilitated. That rehabilitation won't be easy, nor is it guaranteed. In the meantime, as we wait for him to right himself, Cooper's psychological flaws will take him on a journey full of false turns, dead-ends, and detours. Dale Cooper has a long way to go.

IN THE WOODS SURROUNDING the tiny northwest town of Twin Peaks, Doctor Jacoby emerges from his dilapidated trailer to receive a shipment of shovels. Jacoby is looking worse for wear; his hair is disheveled and he's wearing grubby overalls. Given his appearance and hermit-like habitat, he's probably no longer practicing psychiatry, which is a good thing; Jacoby's advice was often rather dubious. We last saw Doctor Jacoby in the final episode of the second season of *Twin Peaks*, where he escorted Sarah Palmer into the Double R Diner so she could channel an otherworldly message to Major Briggs about the whereabouts of Dale Cooper. Jacoby seemed to be in the supernatural loop back then, but now seems far from that old life. (Still, why does he need all those shovels?)

WE'VE BEEN IN TWIN PEAKS less than three minutes before the story shifts to a nighttime view of New York City. Brightly lit skyscrapers stretch out below us. The image dissolves to a darkened, windowless building. In the vast space of the top floor, a young man sits on a couch staring across the room at a large glass chamber that is connected by wires to all sorts of monitoring equipment. Cameras and lights surround the box, and open cardboard boxes, which once likely contained all the equipment, are scattered around the room. For a few moments nothing happens, but then a disembodied voice prompts the man, Sam, to change a memory card in one of the cameras.

Despite the lack of action, this scene with the glass box is charged with tension. Lynch, in collaboration with his editor, Duwayne Dunham, uses a series of static images to build suspense. He shows the glass box in close-up and then slowly pans out to establish its placement in the room. The box dominates the physical space, insinuating power and menace. Lynch cuts to Sam's face watching the box. Then he cuts back to the box again and again. This simple technique ratchets the tension and charges the inanimate box with sense of dread. Adding to the scene's uneasiness is a heavy, ambient sound permeating the room, a low hum, part sound-effect and part non-diegetic music.

The glass box and its attendant high-tech equipment are an overt science-fictional element in the story and recall some of the visuals from Lynch's third feature film, *Dune*. The genre of science fiction is often concerned with defining and making sense of the seemingly inexplicable, and we get the sense that the glass box is designed to do these very things—to capture and record and perhaps even catalog. *Twin Peaks* has in the past resisted a science fiction template; its supernatural elements defied the forensic work of the FBI and the Airforce, and there is a feeling here, early in the narrative, that this is still true. Whoever built and funded the glass box device may have underestimated the forces they are trying to record.

A voice on an intercom calls Sam to receive a delivery. Outside the room, a security guard sits at his desk while a young woman, Tracey, stands holding two coffees. She asks Sam if she can go into the room, but he tells her no, she's not allowed. Tracey watches as Sam taps in the code to regain access to the room. Sam notices what she's doing and playfully tells her she's a "bad girl." Tracey plays right back with not-so-subtle innuendo: "Try me." No doubt, there's sexual tension between these two.

Sam returns to the room and resumes watching the box. He sips his coffee, and we plainly see, thickly scrawled on each of the coffee cups he took from Tracey, a black letter "Z." Presumably these Z's were put there by some attentive barista in order to identify the cups as Tracey's. But they could signify something else. We will see the letter Z pop up frequently in the story, usually around moments when Dale Cooper needs protection. Perhaps Tracey is one of these protective forces. She clearly wants access to the room, so it's safe to say she has some ulterior motives, but, like so much else in the story, whoever Tracey is will remain a mystery.

AT THE GREAT NORTHERN HOTEL in Twin Peaks, Ben Horne informs his assistant Beverly to refund two-night's stay to a skunk-startled guest who is part of a wealthy New York coterie that "keeps The Great Northern Spa running." Ben's reference to New York teases a potential connection between the glass box we just saw and Twin Peaks, but, alas, there is no connection, merely coincidence.

Jerry Horne watches with amusement and reminds Ben of his past penchant for infidelity (the implication being that Ben is attracted to Beverly, who is married). For the first time, *The Return* feels *exactly* the *Twin Peaks* of old. Ben and Jerry's brotherly banter mirrors the time we first met Jerry when he barged into the Horne dining room to share with Ben baguettes he brought from France. What's more, Jerry describes Beverly as "the new girl," a characterization that startlingly recalls Jerry's long-ago discussion with Ben about "the new girl" at One Eyed Jacks, the Canadian brothel. Ben and Jerry haven't changed much in twenty-five years, and their scene here together brings back vivid memories of the *Twin Peaks* of old.[*]

Over at the Sheriff's station an insurance agent arrives and asks receptionist Lucy Brennan if he can speak with Sheriff Truman. Lucy asks, "Which one?" and so begins a perplexing back-and-forth in which the insurance agent does not understand what Lucy is trying to convey.

So, what *is* Lucy trying to convey? On one level she is reminding us, the audience, that there is more than one Sheriff Truman in *Twin Peaks:* There's Harry Truman, whom we all remember, and there is Frank Truman, Harry's brother, currently serving as sheriff. But there could be more going on in this odd scene, depending on how deeply (or obsessively) you want to analyze it. The idea of two Trumans parallels the idea that there is more than one Cooper (a concept that will be introduced soon). There's some symmetry at work here, and it invites us to wonder at the possibility of more doubling in the narrative. Could other characters have parallel selves? For that matter, is this whole new *Twin Peaks* narrative simply an alternate take on an old story? Although it may seem absurd at first glance, the concept of parallel timelines is hinted at more than once later in the story.

Having an insurance agent looking for Truman is clever, because it foreshadows the Lucky 7 Insurance Agency, a business which is soon to become a major part of the story. But sneakier is the agent's line, "it's about insurance," which essentially sums up the whole story. Everyone seems to have insurance in *The Return.* The bad Cooper (whom we meet in the next scene) has a myriad of backup plans to ensure his survival; the good Cooper, as we just discussed, is unfailingly protected by "insuring" forces associated with the letter Z (whenever he is in trouble a *deus ex machina* event always seems to help him); plus, there's Major Briggs' complicated, convoluted plan to make sure the bad Cooper is stopped and the good Cooper succeeds. And, most importantly, The Fireman has insurance—a backup plan that includes Lucy herself (although she has no inkling of the vital role she will play). *Twin Peaks: The Return: It's about insurance.*

---

[*] Speaking of memories, there's a stuffed animal displayed on a shelf to Ben's right. It looks feline, but it's hard to be certain. Could it be a Pine Weasel, that endangered species Ben was so desperate to save in Season 2? Some irony here if it is.

A CAR DRIVES DOWN A DIRT ROAD at night, its headlights starkly illuminating trees and weeds. Loud, heavy music ("American Woman" by Muddy Magnolias, as remixed by David Lynch) accompanies its movement through the dark. The car comes to a stop, and the bad Dale Cooper emerges. Stony-faced and black-eyed, this Cooper is an inexorable force, an embodiment of violence and greed. He approaches an armed man outside a cabin and suddenly, effectively, dispatches the guard and enters the house. Inside, he greets some associates, the drunken Otis and the proprietor, Buella.

The bad Cooper tells Buella to fetch "Ray and Darya," and soon two young people emerge from the dark. The bad Cooper has come to collect them, but before Ray and Darya leave the cabin, they approach two misshapen figures sitting in a dark corner. Ray and Darya each hand the first figure a small white card, and then each dutifully acknowledges the second shadowy form. We'll never know who these bizarre creatures are or what importance they have in *The Return*, but they appear to belong to a gallery of arcane "watchers" who populate the *Twin Peaks* narrative, figures such as the gnomish woman who intruded upon Agent Chet Desmond in Teresa Banks's trailer in *Fire Walk With Me*, or the "drugged-out" mother who lives in an empty house in Rancho Rosa, or the mocking drunk who inhabits the Twin Peaks jail. All these beings are observers—dwellers upon thresholds—surveilling the world as if crude agents put in place by higher powers, sent to Earth to audit mortal affairs. Only after Ray and Darya perform their creepy ritual of "checking out" can they leave with the bad Cooper. (Oh, and he's not simply the "bad Cooper" anymore; he's got a name: He's *Mr. C*—a *nom de guerre* bestowed upon him by Otis.)

IT'S ANOTHER NIGHT IN NEW YORK CITY, and Sam again leaves the glass box room to get coffee from Tracey, only to find her alone in the anteroom, the guard nowhere to be seen. Sam checks the bathroom, but it's empty. "Weird," he says. Tracey jumps at the opportunity and asks if she can go inside the room with Sam. Not wanting to pass up a chance to be alone with Tracey, Sam agrees.

When Tracey enters the larger room, she is astonished by the glass box. Sam explains that some billionaire has funded the project and he,

Sam, has to watch the box in case anything appears inside. He's never seen anything, but the guy who had the job before him did.[*]

Sam and Tracey sit and look at the box. Sam turns and stares long and hard at Tracey. She can feel it and turns to look back at Sam, and when she does a distinct low rumble is audible for a moment, underscoring the energies building between them. They start to kiss, and things quickly get heated. Tracey starts to undress, and, for a fraction of a second, we see on her lapel the exact same Z pattern visible on the coffee cups, reinforcing the idea that Tracey is aligned with the mysterious forces that frequently appear in the narrative.

Soon Sam and Tracey are having sex, but the box is watching—or so it seems: As Sam and Tracey go at it, energies surge in and around the chamber. The interior goes dark, and an indistinct figure appears. Sam notices, and he and Tracey stare in horror as the figure resolves into a ghastly visage: an emaciated nude female with a grotesque, deformed head. The figure (aka "Experiment," according to the end credits) bangs against the side of the box. Then, in a sudden explosion of glass, Experiment breaks free and moves rapidly toward Sam and Tracey, violently slashing at the couple until there is nothing left but bloody pulp.[†]

The appearance and escape of Experiment raises many questions: First, what happened to the guard in the other room? If we assign agency to Tracey and assume she wanted access to the glass box room, then perhaps she, or the forces she represents, found a way to remove the guard. Playing on Sam's lust, Tracey gets into the room, but the narrative never gives us a full explanation about why she wanted to be in there. If the "Z forces" I alluded to earlier really do protect Dale Cooper, it's possible Tracey (as part of those forces) distracted Sam long enough for Cooper to pass through the glass box (which we will see Cooper do during these exact moments in Part 2).

---

[*] Which raises some questions: Who was the guy before Sam, and what did he see?

[†] I first saw this scene in a movie theater. The woman sitting next to me (who, like I, was invited to the screening) struck me as someone unfamiliar with the style and content of David Lynch films. She gasped when Experiment attacked, as if a cruel prank had been played on her. As the scene ended, she quietly moaned: "Jesus Christ."

One thing I don't believe is that Tracey is trying to "summon" Experiment. Some fan theories suggest that Sam and Tracey may have roused Experiment through "sex magic"—the idea that supernatural energies can be harnessed or unleashed through the act of sexual intercourse—and this was Tracey's goal. I'm doubtful. Yes, it's possible that Sam and Tracey's passion lured Experiment to the box, but it is equally possible that Experiment was simply pursuing Dale Cooper and became distracted by the couple. (Maybe that was Tracey's primary goal, to keep Experiment from following Cooper, to protect him from being caught.) Either way the result is the same: Experiment breaks free and is loosed in the world. But where did it go after killing Sam and Tracey? We know Experiment escaped, but we never see it again in the present-day story. If it freed itself, *where did it go?* I believe Experiment knew it could find purchase somewhere else in the world, that it could house itself inside one of the narrative's longest-suffering and profoundly injured characters, Sarah Palmer, who, desolate and alone, is home watching a brutal animal documentary on television at the same moment Experiment breaks free in New York. (But more of this later.)

One more note before we move on: The image of Experiment inside the glass box looks as if it came straight out of a Francis Bacon painting. Many of Bacon's works depict hazy, agonized figures inside a "spaceframe," a type of scaffolding that encases an occupant and "intensifies" the image.[*] David Lynch (a great admirer of Bacon) frequently adopts this style in *The Return*, framing characters within stages, platforms, boxes, or staircases. "There's nothing like a beautiful, contained space," Lynch explains. "Without architecture everything's just open, but with it you can make a space, and you can make it beautiful, or you can make it so hideous that you can hardly wait to get out." Lynch's spaces imply containment and exhibition, stasis and solidity. When characters break free from these spaces (as they often do), there is a release of powerful energies, and stability devolves into chaos, just as it did here with Experiment.

---

[*] Examples include *Study for Portrait* (1949), *Pope II* (1951), *Portrait of a Man* (1953), and *Man in Blue* (1954).

THE STORY MOVES to the small (and fictional) town of Buckhorn, South Dakota, the next morning. Alarmed by a smell in her next-door apartment, Marjorie Green calls the police to check on her neighbor, Ruth Davenport. The police arrive and, hoping to get a key to Ruth's apartment, briefly speak with the apartment handyman, Hank, who is visibly nervous. Marjorie remembers she has a spare key, and when the police check inside the dwelling they find the remains of two dead bodies—the head of Ruth Davenport, shot through the eye, and the headless body of a middle-aged man. It wouldn't be *Twin Peaks* without a murder mystery, and now we have two: Who killed Ruth Davenport? And who is the dead man in her bed?

And what about Hank? Does his story connect in any meaningful way with the Davenport murder? Hank is a suspicious character, and he's clearly worried about the police. Stressed, Hank calls someone named Harvey and says that he, Hank, has "all of it." (We don't know what "it" is, but the implication is something illegal.) Here, we get a glimpse of a shady operation involving Hank, Harvey, and another man named Chip, in a subplot that seems like it's about to gain momentum. In fact, we expect this subplot to develop as the story continues, to possibly inform the larger mystery surrounding Ruth Davenport. But it won't. *The Return* will never return to Hank and his dubious endeavors. "Fragments of things are pretty interesting," Lynch tells us, "You can dream the rest." Hank's story is simply that, a fragment, the first of many tangential subplots in *The Return* that briefly intersect the narrative but are never seen again. The rest of Hank's story is up to us.

And that brings us back to Marjorie Green, who, although a minor character, represents a fundamental theme of *The Return*: Memory. The undependable, variable nature of memory will be referenced again and again as the story progresses. Some characters will remember things they long forgot; some will be lost in memories and trapped by their pasts; still others will question their memories and worry about the capricious nature of reality.[*] The very fabric of *Twin Peaks: The*

---

[*] Here's a real-world example: Early in the first season of *Twin Peaks* a distraught Leland Palmer (Ray Wise) dances with a framed photograph of Laura Palmer. Sarah

Return is arguably one long, inconsistent, inexact memory—the reflection of Dale Cooper's troubled mind.

LATER THAT NIGHT, in Twin Peaks, Margaret Lanterman (The Log Lady), calls Deputy Chief Hawk to tell him her log has a message: Something is missing regarding Dale Cooper, and Hawk has to find it. The way Hawk will find it has something to do with Hawk's heritage. The Log Lady is terribly ill and struggles to complete her call with Hawk. We see the pain in her face, the suffering she has to endure. This emotional, gut-wrenching scene is made all the more powerful because we know that Catherine Coulson—the actor who plays The Log Lady—was suffering from late-stage cancer when she filmed her scenes for *The Return*.

Coulson[*] was supposed to reprise The Log Lady on-set and had planned to fly to Washington State to shoot scenes with other actors on location, but when the time came to travel north, she was too ill to make the trip. Despite the severity of her illness, and knowing she had perhaps only days to live, Catherine was determined to be part of the show and agreed to shoot her scenes from home while David Lynch directed her through Skype. All of her sequences were shot in a single night. Catherine Coulson died five days later.

Palmer (Grace Zabriskie) attempts to wrest the photo from Leland's grasp, and while the two struggle, the glass in the frame breaks. Leland cuts his hand and spreads his blood over the photograph. The blood, in fact, was real—one of the actors cut themselves during filming. Zabriskie says it was she: "I cut myself. David [Lynch] saw that I was wounded, and he came and got me, sat me down on the couch, sent for ice, and—I swear to God—he sat there for twenty minutes holding my hand above my head." But Wise claims it was he who got hurt: "I cut my hand; I still have a scar. I saw the blood and I started finger-painting with the blood. It was very strange." So, who's right? Was it Wise, or was it Zabriskie who cut their hand? We may never know because both remember the scene differently. Zabriskie and Wise each claim they were bleeding, and neither mentions that the other actor was injured. Unreliable memory makes the truth elusive. (My guess is that both actors cut themselves, but each remembers only their wound.)

[*] I can't say that I personally knew Catherine Coulson, but I was lucky to interview her many times for *Wrapped In Plastic* and equally lucky to meet her in person on three occasions. What struck me about Catherine was how welcoming and giving she was. She supported the work Craig Miller and I did and often advocated for us. What's more, she took a personal interest in our lives: Whether on the phone or meeting face-to-face, she always remembered to ask me about my kids. She genuinely wanted to know how my family was doing, how my life was going. It made me feel good. I think she was the same way with everyone she met. Speaking for all fans who had a chance to meet Catherine I say: She was special, and she is missed.

The Log Lady was a peaceful, positive presence in *Twin Peaks*, and Catherine Coulson understood how important she was to that universe. What she gives in her final performance is both heart-breaking and inspiring. So close to death, Catherine Coulson brings The Log Lady to life one last time. She is, in these final moments, a liminal soul, poetically imparting to Hawk—and to all of us—reassuring messages about the magic and mystery and meaning of life. Never has there been such a brave performance by an actor in film or television. Despite her suffering, one of Catherine Coulson's last acts is to fearlessly and honestly guide us from one world to another.

After taking The Log Lady's call, Hawk resurrects files from the decades-old Laura Palmer case and explains to Lucy and Deputy Andy Brennan that The Log Lady told him something was missing. Lucy remarks that Agent Cooper is missing, too; they don't even get a Christmas card from him (which seems like a legitimate concern, sending a Christmas card is just the thing you'd expect Cooper to do). This bit of dialog tells us that Cooper's old friends in Twin Peaks don't know what really happened to him twenty-five years ago; they don't know that Cooper's bad self fled Twin Peaks, while his other self remained trapped in the Black Lodge. Lucy also mentions that she and Andy have a son, Wally, whom Cooper has never met, and who was born on the same date as the American actor Marlon Brando.[*]

BACK IN BUCKHORN, Detectives Constance Talbot and Dave Macklay discover that the fingerprints found in Ruth Davenport's apartment belong to Bill Hastings, the mild-mannered principal of the local high school. Macklay visits the Hastings home and places Bill under arrest. Bill's wife, Phyllis, is worried and not a little miffed; she has guests due for dinner that evening, and Bill's arrest is certainly going to put a kink in their plans.

At the police station, Macklay asks Hastings straightforward questions about his whereabouts on Thursday evening, the night of Ruth Davenport's murder. Hastings says he was at a faculty meeting, left

---

[*] Attentive viewers (OK, yes, *Twin Peaks* fanatics such as myself) noticed a possible error here: In the original series, Lucy learned she was pregnant in early March of 1989, which means she likely would have had her baby in late November or early December of that year. Marlon Brando was born on April 3, so the timing of Wally's birth makes no sense—unless, of course, Wally is the result of a later pregnancy.

around 9:30, and got home around 10:15. Macklay may seem slow but he's sharper than he looks. "Just how long does it take you to get home?" he asks. Bill knows he's in trouble, and what little composure he has falls apart. He grasps for an explanation and then "remembers" he had to take his assistant, Betty, home after the meeting. At this moment—as Bill Hastings revises his story to keep the truth hidden—a menacing bass rumble can be heard. There was no music in the scene up until this point, but Lynch adds it now to signal potential danger. Something was afoot Thursday night. In fact, many things were afoot. Thursday night seems to be when destructive, supernatural energies were released in both South Dakota and New York City. Ruth Davenport was likely killed around the same time Cooper appeared in the glass box and when Experiment broke free. The release of these energies may also have alerted The Log Lady and motivated her to call Hawk the next day. (The humming sound in the Great Northern—which we will hear in Part 7—also probably started around this time.)

The police return to search the Hastings home, while Macklay and Detective Don Harrison search Bill's car. They open the trunk and peer inside, and Macklay's broken, blinking flashlight illuminates a grotesque chunk of flesh, pulsing under the strobe of the intermittent beam. Whatever that ugly piece of meat is, it doesn't bode well for Bill. (We won't discover what this fleshy blob is, but it's probably related to the decapitation of Ruth Davenport.)

PART 1 OF *THE RETURN* ends here, but let's back up a few minutes for a final, important observation. As the police knock on the front door of the Hastings house, we can glimpse through the window a portrait hanging on the wall. It's a photo of the author Franz Kafka, which seems like a strange thing to find in the mundane, suburban home of the Hastings.

I mentioned earlier in the book that David Lynch is nothing if not deliberate. We know that by its very provenance *The Return* will be Lynchian, but David Lynch wants us to see it also as Kafkaesque.[*] There's something off-kilter about this new *Twin Peaks*, something

---

[*] Which, according to *Merriam Webster's Collegiate Dictionary* means, "having a nightmarishly complex, bizarre or illogical quality."

ineffable, as if rooted in Kafka's style and themes. Franz Kafka wrote about characters whose deep psychological flaws often manifest in surreal, sometimes horrifying imagery. His characters' inner selves—their lives of quiet desperation—leak into the world as impossible, impassable instantiations.

Dale Cooper is a character straight out of Kafka's pantheon. He's Gregor Samsa in *The Metamorphosis*, he's Josef K in *The Trial*, he's the myriad unnamed narrators who struggle to navigate Kafka's uncertain worlds. Like all these characters, Cooper is a "powerless individual who is burdened by the tragedy of his own loneliness and insignificance." The story in *The Return* is a reflection of Cooper's innermost self, his churning, restless mind manifesting the surreal. When Dale Cooper looks out into the world, he sees his own estranged psyche staring back.

This Kafkaesque storytelling strategy is not obvious at first. Cooper's observing presence won't overtly intrude upon the narrative for another 16 hours (in Part 17), but David Lynch is already dropping hints of a deeper mechanism at work.

Lynch wants us to keep Kafka in mind, wants us to identify a style and sensibility that will inform much of what we are about to see. Lynch has expressed his admiration for Franz Kafka: "He thrills me with every sentence…. I love his thinking." Kafka, whose classic story, *The Metamorphosis*, Lynch adapted into a screenplay and hoped to eventually film; Kafka, who once attended a theosophical lecture by the spiritualist Rudolf Steiner and thereby encountered the concept of thought-forms; Kafka, about whom Lynch once said, "[He's] the one artist that I feel could be my brother;" Franz Kafka haunts the very fabric of this new *Twin Peaks*. The same Franz Kafka who, in describing himself in his diary, eerily foreshadowed the schemata of *The Return* when he wrote: "I am memory come alive."

<INTERLUDE 1>
DAMN! THIS IS REALLY SOMETHING
INTERESTING TO THINK ABOUT

A VALID AND COMMON CRITICISM of *Twin Peaks: The Return* is that it doesn't feature enough of Dale Cooper. Yes, there are prominent roles for the evil Cooper (Mr. C) and the good Cooper (Dougie Jones), but the Cooper we remember from the original series is mostly absent, appearing in only five of the eighteen parts (and even then, only for about two-and-a-half hours of screen time). When *The Return* first aired, fans were understandably disappointed by how little they saw of the eccentric and endearing Special Agent.

But what if Cooper *is* there? What if he is a constant presence, haunting the entirety of what we see?

Years ago, I wrote an essay for *Wrapped In Plastic* entitled "Dreams of Deer Meadow," in which I argued that the first 30 minutes of *Fire Walk With Me* was actually Dale Cooper's dream. I made a case that "Almost all of . . . the dream is based on Cooper's own memory," and that the dream was, in part, wish-fulfillment. Cooper "re-lived" events of his earlier trip to Deer Meadow, WA, where he investigated the murder of a young woman named Teresa Banks. In Cooper's dream, he reworked the case in ways that opened his subconscious to new possibilities and new information. In this way, Cooper was able to grow and change. His story arc was not immediately evident, but it was there. Dale Cooper was a resonant, albeit hidden, presence in *Fire Walk With Me*.

Does such a dream theory have any value when we look at *Twin Peaks: The Return*? Does it provide any insight into the narrative workings of this new season? I believe it does, but we've got to rethink what we mean when we use the word "dream." Cooper's role in *The Return* is more nuanced and complex than how I perceived it to be in *Fire Walk With Me*. And the story we see in *The Return* is hardly a dream.

Of course, it would be easy to excuse the entirety of *The Return* as existing entirely within Dale Cooper's imagination. Such a reading would explain much of the odd and perplexing nature of the story. As compelling as this kind of interpretation might be, however, I believe it ultimately damages *The Return*, drains it of consequence and renders it impotent. If the story is simply a dream, all the characters (and their rich world) are nothing but figments of Cooper's subconscious mind. And if the people and places of *Twin Peaks* are simply fabrications, they lose their diversity, openness, and innate enigmatic qualities. Essayist Tim Kreider (who has made a persuasive case that all of *Twin Peaks* is Cooper's dream) acknowledges that such a reading "threatens to render all the characters and their dramas…moot, mere illusions. All the show's moments of pathos and wonder, surreal horror and cornball humor…seem obviated."

I reject the idea that *The Return* is merely the fantasy of one specific character. I propose a different way of looking at it.

I contend that the story in *Twin Peaks: The Return* is grounded in an objective reality. It's a world where Mr. C is attempting to amass power, where a good Cooper is deposited in Las Vegas to serve as a beacon of hope, where Sarah Palmer is possessed by a demonic entity, where the FBI searches for answers to the mysteries surrounding Bill Hastings and Major Garland Briggs, and where the deputies of Twin Peaks are revisiting the Laura Palmer case to piece together the fate of Dale Cooper. All of this is real, but we are seeing it filtered through a specific point-of-view. The story of *The Return* is being *encrypted* by a potent, eccentric personality.

I believe that what we see in *The Return* is mediated through the mind of Dale Cooper. That he is, in fact, *translating* events from the way they really happened to the way he *thinks* they happened.

27

What we see is a not a dream, but a story refracted through the prism of Dale Cooper's psyche. As I proposed back in my *Wrapped in Plastic* essay, "Cooper is a critical player in the narrative [whose] presence is far more profound if we recognize him as a consciousness that governs [the story]."

IF THERE IS ONE CRUCIAL line in *The Return*, it is this: "We live inside a dream." No matter how much you may want to ignore it or explain it away, this line is the defining principle of the narrative.

We first hear the line when Gordon Cole recounts one of his "Monica Bellucci dreams" in Part 14. In the dream, Bellucci recites what Cole calls "the ancient phrase": "We are like the dreamer who dreams and then lives inside the dream"—a phrase that originates from the Hindu text, the Upanishads.

Hindu philosophy permeates *The Return*, which is not surprising given David Lynch's adherence to Hindu theology, especially as it is conveyed through the teachings of Maharishi Mahesh Yogi and his practice of Transcendental Meditation. What seems confusing or con-tradictory in *The Return* makes more sense when seen through the lens of certain Hindu beliefs and its foundational text, otherwise known as the Vedantic texts. Once we orient our reading to encompass these ideas, we can more clearly see why the story works the way it does.

The Log Lady's advice to Hawk in Part 10 about "the dream of time and space," and "all that is and is not," echoes passages from the Hindu text, the Bhagavad Gita. Janey-E's observation in Part 6 about living in a "dark age" evokes the Kali Yuga, an era of moral decline and evil ascendance (the fourth and final age in the Hindu cycle of time). The Fireman's creation of Laura Palmer in Part 8 suggests the coming of the tenth avatar of Vishnu who will descend to Earth on a white horse to destroy evil and restart the cycle of time. And the narrative's central conceit about living inside a dream is explored in the Yoga Vasistha, which scholar Paul Corazza calls "One of the most important scriptures of Vedantic philosophy."

Monica Bellucci's reminder to Cole about living inside a dream is only part of her message. After quoting the ancient phrase she asks, "But who is the dreamer?"—a critical question that both the audience and Cole must ponder. *Who is the dreamer?* And yet, the question is redundant because Bellucci essentially answers it: "We are like the dreamer." Monica Bellucci stares straight into the camera and tells us that *we* are the dreamer. All of us. Each of us lives inside our own dream.

So why even ask the question?

Because, in this case, Bellucci is telling Cole that he is tapping into someone else's dream—someone else's personal view of the universe. This story—this dream—is bleeding over into Cole's perceptions.

So, the question again: Who is the dreamer?

Well, it's Dale Cooper, of course.

In Cole's dream Cooper is standing nearby; Cole can see Cooper's body but not his face. Cole soon remembers a long-suppressed memory of Cooper in Philadelphia speaking of a dream he once told Cole about. (This sequence, from *Fire Walk With Me*, occurs moments before Phillip Jeffries makes his return to the FBI to announce, "We live inside a dream.") These few bits of data are enough to identify Cooper as the dreamer.

Later events in *The Return* almost certainly confirm Cooper's function, especially in Part 17 where Cooper's looming face appears superimposed over the action taking place "underneath" to announce, "We live inside a dream." In these scenes the audience can see Cooper's face, but the characters (including Cooper, himself) are completely unaware of it. Cooper's ghostly face implies a second, overlapping narrative, one which occurs either above or behind what's unfolding on the screen. Cooper is watching just as we are, and his presence suggests that we are seeing the story from his point-of-view, that everything is being mediated through his mind.

Cooper's account recalls the mindset of another Lynch protagonist, Fred Madison, from the film *Lost Highway*. There, Madison famously states, "I like to remember things my own way...how I remembered them, not necessarily the way they happened." This line is crucial to understanding *Twin Peaks: The Return*. What we see transpire through most of the eighteen hours are events presented the way Dale Cooper mentally processes them, but *not necessarily the way they happened.*

Cooper is the dreamer, but he is not dreaming in the obvious sense. Most people when they hear the term "dreaming" immediately think of an imaginary landscape concocted by a sleeping mind, but in the cosmology of David Lynch films, "dream" has a more evocative and complex meaning. Quoting the Maharishi Mahesh Yogi, Lynch reminds us, "The world is as you are. Every person perceives it his own way." Lynch returns to this idea—"the world is as you are"—again and again when discussing his philosophy. He expresses it to Martha Nochimson when talking about human consciousness and perception. He says it to interviewer Richard Barney when discussing the journey of the main character in *INLAND EMPIRE*, using the analogy, "If you have dark green dirty glasses and you look out, that's the world you see, that's the world you experience." For Lynch, the phrase, "the world is as you are," is another way of saying: "We are the dreamer who lives inside the dream." Our personal view of the universe is a dream, and no two dream worlds can be the same because we each see a reality that reflects our unique psychologies.

The idea is not unique to Lynch or to Transcendental Meditation. Immanuel Kant explained it like this: The "real" world—what Kant calls the *noumenal* world—can never be truly known. Every human being views the noumenal world through their own psychological filters, and the world they see is what Kant calls the *phenomenal world*: "That which is rendered by the senses and the mind's tools of understanding." In *The Return*, the "tools" of Cooper's mind render a unique world for him. He perceives the world as only he can, with all his idiosyncrasies and biases at work. As author George Saunders tells us, "There is no world save the one we make with our minds, and the mind's predisposition determines the type of world we see."

And what is the predisposition of Cooper's mind? In the first and second season of *Twin Peaks* Cooper believed himself to be a champion, a moral upholder of the law and a protector of those defenseless and vulnerable. But, in truth, Cooper was frightened and uncertain, someone who masked his failings with a façade of bravado. His confrontation with Bob at the end of Season 2 laid bare the flaws in his character. *The Return* implies that the real Cooper is searching for something but unsure of what he seeks. He is arguably blind to those who genuinely care about him (like Diane) and handicapped by his sense of duty to do what is right (like saving Laura). Torn asunder by the forces of The Black Lodge, Cooper is lost and confused, unable to know himself or the world in which he lives. This is the Cooper who looks out into the world. This is the mind that processes the story of *The Return*.

Confused, vexed, regretful, Cooper interprets the universe accordingly. He is puzzled by a world that left him behind, anxious that he cannot return to set things right, saddened that he may have hurt or abandoned people who were close to him. And perhaps most significantly, Cooper is impotent. Lacking physical control of his two material selves (Mr. C and Dougie), Cooper can only watch and hope for the best. The added stress of this passivity further impacts the way he perceives the world. Through Cooper, *The Return* becomes a story of uncertainty and distress. *The world is as he is.*

This is not the first time David Lynch has designed a narrative in such a way. Essayist Brian Rourke argues that *INLAND EMPIRE*, Lynch's last major project before directing *The Return*, is a narrative composed of "overlapping deliria of a single character." This character (whom Rourke labels "a woman in trouble") has "withdrawn from view, persisting only in cerebral images...." To properly decipher *INLAND EMPIRE*, Rourke explains, viewers must remain aware of the mind behind the story: "Remembering that the images [on screen] are produced from a particular perspective is ... necessary for basic understanding of the film."

TO GROUND THIS CONCEPT in theory, what we are seeing in *The Return* is Dale Cooper acting as a covert narrator, which scholar Seymour Chatman defines as "someone who speaks of events, characters and setting...but remains hidden in the discursive shadows." A covert narrator can be omnipresent but is not necessarily omniscient. He can relate events from any place or from any time in the story but does not necessarily know how the story will end. More importantly, he can relay pieces of the story in a non-linear way, jumping back and forth in time on a whim. (David Lynch has suggested, perhaps facetiously, that episodes of *The Return* can be viewed out of order, referring to how, in movie theaters, "Projectionists once in a while would make a mistake and put reel four before reel two or something.... People still made sense of it.")

A covert narrator picks and chooses what he will convey. Chatman tells us: "Mental entries [into the minds of characters] seem matters of chance, reflecting the randomness of ordinary life." Cooper can move from character to character and watch what they're doing, but he does so notionally, as if he's surfing a real-world internet, bouncing from link to link, post to post, tweet to tweet, reading what interests him, sometimes just the headlines, sometimes scrolling deeper, his attention caught by an influx of new images and data. The world appears before Cooper as a cascade of overlapping windows, tabs, and screens—a "virtual" landscape that is, in fact, reality. Cooper rarely follows any one thread to completion. He is constantly distracted, pulled in a dozen directions at once. (It wouldn't surprise me if Mark Frost and David Lynch deliberately designed *The Return* to be fragmentary and inconclusive in order to comment on how social media has transformed society. The style and structure of *The Return* mirrors the impermanent, erratic, impulsive way most of us connect with the larger world. We are, all of us, Dale Cooper watching the world from our own Red Rooms.)

As the following chapters of this book will show, Cooper's presence exerts itself throughout *The Return*. His point of view will probe into various corners and recesses of the narrative, exploring, seeking answers, trying to make sense of a baffling world he's watching from a remove. His explorations may not cohere into any logical plot, but that doesn't matter. Plot is not necessarily the purpose. With a covert narrator, Chatman explains, "Thinking is itself the plot." If there is one single concept to understand about *The Return*, it is this: the "plot" is about the psychological journey of Dale Cooper. On the surface we may see a story Cooper is relating, but the deeper, more important story concerns *how* Cooper is relating it. In other words, the real story in *The Return* is about the workings of Cooper's mind. Is he in crisis? Is his mind breaking down? Is he confronting or overcoming mental obstacles on a journey toward enlightenment? This is the story of *The Return*, and, despite getting a glimpse of this concept in Part 17 (when Cooper's superimposed face appears over the action), it is not at all obvious.

YOU MAY BE ASKING, "Is all this discussion about mediated narratives versus dreaming minds just a distinction without a difference? After all, isn't a dream its own form of mediated story?" My hope with this chapter is to explain the difference between two theoretical approaches to *Twin Peaks*. In a dream, what we see exists entirely within the mental landscape of a character, even if it is based on real-life memories (an argument I made in my original dream theory essay in *Wrapped In Plastic*). The *mediated narrative* is something else. It may be as unreliable as a dream, but it remains an account of a true story, told with embellishment, imperfect recall and varying emphases on what the teller thinks is important. A mediated story is not a fantasy, it is point of view. We've all heard the saying, "No two people see things the same way." It's an idea David Lynch has expressly reiterated: "I think people's memories are different. Sometimes their memories are flat-out wrong, but mostly they're just different." What we see in *The Return* is Cooper's different way of seeing things. Had the story been mediated by another character, say Deputy Hawk or Lucy Brennan, we would have seen something different—the same basic facts but remixed through another mental filter. That's the difference: A dream is imaginary; a mediated narrative is a *translation*.

And what a mediated narrative does is allow us to restore consequence to the characters and their stories. It allows us to take some satisfaction that the outcomes in their various dramas had meaning and were worth our investment. Ed and Norma really do get back together! Audrey's therapy succeeded, and she woke from her self-imposed fantasy. Andy and Lucy are happy! Albert has found a soulmate! It feels good to know these things happened and were not merely the quirks of a dreaming mind.

Of course, this theory does not explain everything in the story; some curious elements of *Twin Peaks* will contradict (or arguably refute) the idea of a mediated narrative. This shouldn't be surprising. *Twin Peaks* will never fit satisfactorily into one easy box; the text will continue to confound and provoke for as long as it has an audience. But that's the beauty of it. As David Lynch has said of *Mulholland Drive*, "Even if you get the whole thing, there would still be some abstract elements in it that you'd have to kind of feel-think."

ONCE UPON A TIME I wrote an essay about Dale Cooper and dreams and how part of what we saw in *Fire Walk With Me* was a subjective telling of events. It was a rudimentary attempt at deciphering a complex and nuanced approach to storytelling, but I think I got close to what David Lynch was up to. Now, after studying *The Return*, I have reevaluated what "we live inside a dream" means. I realize that the story of Dale Cooper and the worlds of *Twin Peaks* are too complex to be simply a dream.[*]

Near the end of the essay, I wrote that in *Fire Walk With Me*, David Lynch "positioned story material to function as the reflection of a specific consciousness, in this case, Dale Cooper's." I'm confident I got that part right, and *The Return* seems to confirm it. Cooper's observing presence conveys the story and shapes it according to his specific mindset. He may seem a distant, unfathomable figure throughout most of *The Return*, but he is closer than we realize. When we watch *Twin Peaks,* we don't just sense Cooper, we become him. Full of confusion, hope, despair and duty, Dale Cooper is there throughout.

---

[*] Some readers will want to know if this means I think Chet Desmond, the FBI agent investigating the Banks case in *Fire Walk With Me*, is a real character rather than a figment of Cooper's dreaming mind. My short answer is: It doesn't matter. I'm not trying to evade the question; it's just that *Twin Peaks* is ultimately about Laura Palmer and Dale Cooper. The *Fire Walk With Me* prologue, no matter how much it features Desmond, is Cooper's story. This is what David Lynch originally envisioned and what he wrote and intended to film. Last minute changes in Kyle MacLachlan's availability made that impossible, so Lynch found another way to make the prologue work. Chet Desmond's presence is negligible and doesn't add anything to the deeper connections between Laura and Cooper. If it makes you feel better to think Chet Desmond is real, fine, but that won't make the story any more (or less) meaningful.

PART 2:

THE STARS TURN AND A TIME PRESENTS ITSELF*

IN THE BUCKHORN JAIL, Bill Hastings grasps at his head over and over, trying to make sense of the predicament he's in. A heavy ambient sound permeates the scene, accentuating his fear. Phyllis arrives, and the two spouses sit facing each other, their heads only inches apart. Bill insists he wasn't at Ruth Davenport's apartment, but he confesses to having a dream he was there. Phyllis is having none of it; she confronts Bill about his affair with Ruth, claiming she's known about it for some time. This angers Bill who counters with his knowledge of Phyllis' affair with George (their lawyer), and maybe someone else. At long last these two tortured souls are exposing their secret lives to one another, a situation Lynch highlights by carefully framing both characters in profile, suggesting that each has kept a hidden side from the other.

It's hard to know if Bill is telling the truth about not being at Ruth Davenport's, but he's convincing when he claims to having had a dream about being there, as if he's trying to understand exactly what happened that night. Bill doesn't realize it yet, but he's been played by forces beyond his comprehension. As he moans in despair, the camera

---

* Technically, the second hour of *The Return* is considered "Part 2," even though the first two hours of the story were originally broadcast as a single chapter. These first two hours were also shown theatrically at the Los Angeles premiere of *The Return* and at the Cannes Film Festival in 2017. (Also, the Blu-ray release of *The Return* allows for the option of watching the first two hours as a "combined feature-length" presentation.) An argument could be made that Part 1 and Part 2 were envisioned by David Lynch and Mark Frost as a single introductory chapter to a longer story. In interviews, Mark Frost has stated that he and Lynch completed the script for the first two hours, and there was "a long period" before they scripted the rest.

slowly pans to the right to reveal, two cells down, a blackened, bearded man staring vacantly into the distance. The man fades from view and his disembodied face floats up and out of the frame. This creature is a Woodsman, one of many malevolent beings that haunt the narrative and one of those forces beyond Bill's understanding. Bill's been played, alright; in fact's he's already been taken off the board.

Phyllis arrives home and is pleased to see Mr. C, but her pleasure is short-lived when she sees he's holding a gun. She flees, but Mr. C shoots her in the back, killing her. Phyllis is just another loose end Mr. C needs to tie up.

IN LAS VEGAS, DUNCAN TODD sits in his chic office and gives his assistant, Roger, two stacks of cash. Though not explicit, Todd is directing Roger to hire a woman named Lorraine to arrange the assassination of a local insurance agent named Dougie Jones. Todd is part of Mr. C's operation, but he's fearful of Mr. C's ruthlessness (the kind of behavior we just saw Mr. C inflict on Phyllis). Todd warns Roger to never get involved with a man like Mr. C.

To emphasize the power and threat of Mr. C, Lynch cuts to a nighttime shot of a railroad crossing. Warning lights flash, barriers drop, and the dopplering sound of a locomotive intensifies. A train blasts across the screen, freight cars strobing in a spotlight's glare. That's Mr. C: An unstoppable force barreling through the night.

BACK IN BUCKHORN, Ray, Darya, Mr. C, and a new accomplice, Jack, sit in a diner and discuss their plans. Ray watches in amusement as Jack chows down on his third plate of spaghetti. He carries this amusement into his conversations with Mr. C, probing him about his plans and his potential "worries." Mr. C is not worried and directs Ray to get him the information he wants from Hastings' secretary (presumably, Betty, whom Hastings mentioned in his interrogation with Detective Macklay).

Mr. C makes it clear that he "wants" the information; he doesn't need it: If there's one thing you need to know about Mr. C, it's that he doesn't *need* anything.[*] Ray says he'll get the information and glances at Darya. Mr. C notices this exchange and grimly stares at Ray. A train horn blares in the distance.

The beginning of a much deeper plot is unfolding here. We know that Mr. C has been involved in the Hastings matter, and now we learn he is seeking information from Bill Hastings and his secretary, Betty. Mr. C wonders why Betty will only give this information to Ray. We should wonder about that, too. Ray is a tricky character and his role in the narrative is never made clear. We learn later that Ray is an inform- ant for the FBI, reporting on Mr. C's dealings to Gordon Cole. But Ray is probably working for other forces as well, possibly an entity that claims to be the long-lost Phillip Jeffries. As an agent for this entity, Ray's job is to kill Mr. C, but the story never makes clear why Ray must do this.

Ray Monroe's story will remain murky. In fact, the logic of *The Return*'s backstory falls apart when you start to examine it closely, a criticism many fans levelled against the show. (This episode will delve heavily into this backstory, and I'll address some of its contradictory, confusing nature shortly.)

IN THE EERIE PSITHURISM of the nighttime forest, Hawk hikes toward Glastonbury Grove, the place where, twenty-five years earlier, Dale Cooper left this world and entered the realm of the Red Room. Hawk speaks on his phone with The Log Lady and tells her he believes something is supposed to happen. The Log Lady simply responds with *The Return*'s most poetic line: "The stars turn, and a time presents itself."

Moments later, Hawk sees red curtains materialize among the trees, and the night becomes charged with possibility. We're on the verge of something momentous, an overlapping of worlds, the emergence of Dale Cooper from his decades-old trap. But then, just as this potential is about to be realized, the scene ends. If anything did happen in Glastonbury Grove, we don't see it. Hawk never refers to his excursion

---

[*] Mr. C, here, is a reminder of those disappointed fans who complained that *The Return* didn't deliver what they "wanted" from *Twin Peaks*. (David Lynch, however, gave fans everything they needed.)

again, as if he forgot ever hiking into the forest (which is apt to happen when you visit the spooky woods surrounding Twin Peaks).

It is tempting to think that Dale Cooper was supposed to emerge from the Red Room at this moment, but Cooper does not return this night. His fate will follow a far more complicated and convoluted path.

AND NOW WE COME TO THE RED ROOM, the core of *Twin Peaks*,[*] a place of power, possibility and portent, a "free zone" (according to David Lynch) where "anything can happen." The Red Room exists outside time as we know it. As Sheryl Lee tells us, it's a place where "Time doesn't exist. It is not in linear time." Or, in other words, The Red Room is *timeless*.

The next few scenes in the Red Room (and those to come later in Part 2) are some of the most important in the story. They are, in effect, the blocks upon which the narrative foundation of *The Return* is built. Still, when it comes to The Red Room, it's almost impossible to decode everything that happens there. The Red Room is an abstraction, a reminder that, according to David Lynch, there are "some elements in [his work] that you'd have to kind of *feel-think*."

So, let's start "feel-thinking" about the Red Room.

We open with a static shot of three chairs, sitting empty on the chevron floor. Behind the chairs we see the Greek statue, Venus de Medici. Suddenly, Cooper is sitting in a chair, as if blinking into existence. Phillip Gerard[†] sits across from him and asks, "Is it future or is it past?" (That's a trick question, because in the Red Room it is both future *and* past at the same time. It is also neither. As far as Cooper is concerned, it is always the present.)

Gerard disappears, and Cooper watches a woman who looks like Laura Palmer walk across the room and sit. She tells Cooper he "can go out now." Cooper asks if the woman is Laura Palmer, and she responds, "I feel like I know her but sometimes my arms bend back" (a repeat of a line Laura first told Cooper way back in episode 2 of the original

---

[*] Lynch: "It's the pilot and the Red Room and where they led—put those things together and you've got the real *Twin Peaks*."

[†] Gerard was also known as Mike, "the One-Armed Man" in the original series; in *The Return* he will only be referred to as Phillip Gerard, but, as we'll see, Mike is an important identity to keep in mind.

series). Cooper directly asks, "Who are you?" and the woman tells him she is Laura Palmer.

Cooper is a bit confrontational and definitively states: "Laura Palmer is dead."[*] To this, Laura replies, "I am dead, yet I live," and "detaches" her face, opening it to reveal a white light within. Laura walks over to Cooper, kisses him and whispers in his ear. Cooper is startled, but before he can ask any questions, Laura violently screams and is whisked away. The curtains of the room blow back, and the camera zooms into a black void, passing a white horse. For a moment there is only darkness, and then Phillip Gerard is again sitting across from Cooper asking, "Is it future or is it past?"

Cooper's encounter with Laura is cryptic and confusing, but if we carefully "feel-think" about what happened here we can make some guesses about who Laura is, and what she's really trying to tell Cooper.

When Laura opens her face, she reveals her numinous essence, a pure white energy that glows inside, implying that she is more than human. (Later events will show that, indeed, Laura was created in an otherworldly realm by The Fireman and dispatched to Earth.) Laura tells Cooper she is both dead and alive, suggesting that she returned to life after she was killed. (She hints at a new identity when she says, "Sometimes I feel like I know her," a possible allusion to her existence as Carrie Page, the alternate Laura who won't appear until Part 18.) Finally, when Laura screams, she is foreshadowing the end of the story and revealing her purpose for being sent to Earth.

None of what Laura says or does is decipherable right now, but her scene with Cooper in The Red Room provides important clues about Laura's grander role. Cooper might not be able to make sense of it, but he's receiving important information about Laura's deeper identity and purpose.

COOPER AND GERARD walk to another room where they meet "The Evolution of the Arm," the same being Cooper once knew as The Man From Another Place and then later as The Arm, the embodiment of

---

[*] This critical line repudiates one of Cooper's apparent motives for journeying into The Red Room, his desire to reverse the death of Laura Palmer. If Cooper asserts that Laura is dead (as he explicitly does here), then he never expected he could change her fate. *It was not part of his plan.* (I'll speak more about this in Part 17.)

Phillip Gerard's missing arm (or, more precisely, the embodiment of *Mike's* missing arm—Mike being the alter-ego of Gerard). This new "Arm" appears as a lump of flesh sitting atop a leafless tree whose branches sway dreamily in an absent breeze.

The Arm speaks in a breathless whisper[*] and asks Cooper if he remembers his doppelganger. The scenes cuts to a flashback from the original series in which Cooper confronts his evil half—the "bad Cooper"—who shares a ghastly laugh with Bob, the demonic entity who had possessed Leland Palmer. The good Cooper races for the Red Room exit only to be overtaken by the bad Cooper, who escapes into the world, leaving Cooper trapped in this timeless realm. The flashback ends, and, back in the "present," the Arm explains that Cooper cannot leave until the bad Cooper comes back in.

The first time I saw this scene I thought to myself, "Yes, that's exactly right; those are the rules." I had written about the division of Cooper in an essay I published in *Wrapped In Plastic* in which I argued that only one Dale Cooper could exist in the real world at any time. This wasn't a groundbreaking conclusion: Annie Blackburn essentially confirms the idea in *Fire Walk With Me* when she states, "The good Dale is in the Lodge and he can't leave."

But is it really the "good Cooper" who is trapped in the Red Room? I'm not sure it's that simple.

Dale Cooper, as we know him from the original series, was someone who believed in the rule of law, who cared for those less fortunate. He was, for sure, a good man, but he wasn't *purely* good. Cooper was flawed and sometimes made choices that skewed toward his own self-interest: He refused to sign Albert Rosenfield's official complaint against Sheriff Truman after Truman punched Albert; he acted outside the law when he enlisted Truman's help to illegally cross into Canada to rescue Audrey Horne; and he once had an illicit affair with Caroline Earle, the wife of his partner, Windom Earle. Cooper made all these choices because he felt they were the right thing to do, but a *purely good* Cooper would not have made them.

---

[*] This new iteration of The Arm resembles Kafka's "Odradek," a creature which "once had some sort of intelligible shape and is now only a broken-down remnant." Odradek had a "kind of laughter that had no lungs behind it…like the rustling of fallen leaves."

Like all human beings, Cooper had a darker side. Like most human beings, Cooper kept this darker side in check and did not act on purely selfish wants. Cooper found a way to balance his two sides. By acknowledging his darker impulses, Cooper could better appreciate the power of good.

But Cooper's failure in the Red Room at the end of Season 2 shows that he had not fully succeeded in balancing his two selves. When Cooper allowed fear to get the better of him, his bad half took control and freed itself.

The Cooper who *understands* the power of good became trapped, while his bad side, allied with Bob, escaped. The Cooper in the Red Room is still the "good Dale" (as Annie calls him) but he's an impotent soul, searching for answers.

BACK IN THE REAL WORLD, Darya is alone in a motel room, speaking with Ray on the phone. She hears Mr. C approaching and hurriedly ends the call. Mr. C asks who she was talking to, and Darya lies and says she was talking to Jack. Mr. C puts his arm around her and says he killed Jack two hours ago. Darya struggles to break free, but Mr. C holds her tight and plays a recording of the call she just had with Ray.

On the recording, Ray explains he got a call from "Jeffries," who, it turns out, hired Ray and Darya as assassins. Indeed, Ray says that Darya must kill Mr. C "tomorrow night." Mr. C ponders this information and says, "The game begins tomorrow." He knows someone is working against him and that there's an element of chance at play. He's part of a "game" with no guaranteed winner.

Mr. C's careful strategies (and those of his opponents), resemble the gameplay of expert chess players. Each is setting traps, anticipating his opponent's moves, arranging and removing pieces. While no overt mention of chess is ever made in *The Return*, Mr. C's "game" is perfectly symbolized by chess.

Chess, as we all know, was a major plot point in the latter half of the original *Twin Peaks*, where Cooper played a deadly match against his old partner, Windom Earle. The Cooper/Earle chess game was never completed, but the chess metaphor (black versus white, good versus evil) perfectly suited the themes of *Twin Peaks*. Now, chess, with all its elaborate strategies, gambits, traps, and false traps, is a perfect schema for the larger narrative at work in *The Return*, where unseen powers manipulate players in order to win a desperate "game."

Part of that game involves a set of coordinates that Mr. C is trying to get from Bill Hastings' secretary. Mr. C believes these coordinates will lead him to Experiment, the apparition that appeared in the glass box in New York City. (Mr. C is almost certainly the "billionaire" who funded the glass box project.) Mr. C shows Darya a playing card depicting a distorted ace of spades, an image that looks very much like Experiment, and this probably seals Darya's fate. Mr. C would never show Darya this image and allow her to live. Indeed, after showing her the card, Mr. C shoots Darya through the head.

The murder of Darya is tough to watch. Mr. C punches her in the face and knocks her head against the wall, a scene that recalls the brutal murder of Madeleine Ferguson by Bob in the original series. Like Maddy, Darya is helpless against the relentless strength of her killer. Mr. C is remorseless, a creature totally stripped of emotion or empathy. It's hard to believe this being is an aspect of Dale Cooper.

Mr. C uses an arcane electronic device to place a call, and a voice Mr. C assumes is Phillip Jeffries answers. When the voice claims to know Mr. C met with Major Garland Briggs, Mr. C realizes he's not talking to Phillip Jeffries, at least not the Jeffries he assumed. The voice declares, "You are going back in tomorrow, and I will be with Bob again," and the connection is cut.

Who was behind the voice Mr. C was talking to? Was Ray taking orders from this "imposter" Jeffries? (Ray's dialog in Part 13 almost certainly confirms that, yes, he had been talking to the imposter Jeffries all along, but this again begs the question: "Who is this imposter?" The murky backstory of *The Return* continues to elude us.)

The voice on the phone claims that he will be "with Bob again," which narrows his identity down to a handful of candidates who have been associated with Bob in the past: Leland Palmer, Mike (the one-armed man), and The Arm. If I had to pick a name from this list, I would choose Mike, the ill-defined, often inexplicable Black Lodge spirit from the original series.[*] Mike once explained that Bob was his

---

[*] Leland and the Arm simply don't have the agency to mount the kind of plan Mr. C is up against.

"familiar" and that he and Bob worked as a team (presumably gathering pain and sorrow on which to feed). Mike had a change of heart (when he saw the face of God) and reformed his ways. Since then, Mike has been trying to capture and contain Bob.

According to Mark Frost, the voice on Mr. C's device belonged to someone "pretending to be Phillip Jeffries [in order] to gain access to more information about someone else's location." Though extremely vague, Frost's comment implies that the impersonator is Mike, the only being who would likely want to "be with Bob again."

If all of this sounds confusing, though, I totally understand. *It is confusing!* As I write this, I'm trying to piece together the role of Mike in the narrative so I can explain it to you, and I find myself getting bogged down by vague and contradictory details about who or what Mike is. And you know what? I think David Lynch and Mark Frost are just as confused. They don't really know who or what Mike is either. From the start, they never fully developed the character or found a way to logically integrate him into the story. If you asked either Lynch or Frost, they'd be hard-pressed to explain Mike.

In the end, though, it doesn't really matter who was on the phone, or who Mike really is. As I've mentioned before, *The Return* is less about plot and more about the psychologies of its characters, particularly the psychology of Dale Cooper.

IN THE RED ROOM, the Evolution of the Arm provides Cooper with more cryptic clues. It says, "2-5-3, time and time again," and then thrice repeats Bob's name. A rumbling sound grows, and The Arm commands Cooper to "Go now!"

Cooper follows Phillip Gerard to the room's exit but emerges alone into the accompanying hallway. Gerard is gone. Cooper walks in slow-motion and then regains his normal speed and moves to the other end of the hall. When he tries to part the curtains to pass into the next room, he encounters a barrier he can't push through. An "ominous scratching noise" is audible. Cooper tries again to push through but fails. Confused, he looks around and walks back down the hall the way he came.

At this moment a trap is being sprung: Cooper has been blocked from leaving the Red Room and been forced back along a path that will ultimately snare him. (Meanwhile, Phillip Gerard and The

Evolution of the Arm know something is wrong. The Arm quickly identifies the culprit: the Arm's doppelganger has interfered with Cooper's exit.)[*]

Cooper passes through an empty room, pausing for a moment to note the absence of The Evolution of the Arm. He passes into the next room and finds Leland Palmer sitting alone. Leland looks dismayed, as if he has found himself here quite unexpectedly. This Leland is not a doppelganger—the being Cooper encountered in the final episode of Season 2—this is the true Leland, the one Cooper guided into the afterlife as Leland was dying.[†]

Moments earlier, Laura was whisked away, and Cooper's point-of-view raced into the void to follow her. Now, here's Leland Palmer, sitting right in front of Cooper, telling him to "Find Laura." Cooper studies Leland, who looks as if he's on the verge of tears. Something grabs Cooper's attention, and he swiftly turns and leaves.

Cooper walks to the corner of the room and sees a flash of white light (accompanied by an "ominous scratching noise"). Instead of parting the curtains to exit (as he's done *every* time before), Cooper *phases* through the curtains, as if he's a ghost passing through a wall. Once on the other side, Cooper sees an image of two overlapping Red Rooms, one room "sliding" over the other—two paths diverging in front of him.

And it is here, I believe, that Cooper comes to one of the most important junctures in *The Return*. It is here that the story splits onto two paths. In one, Cooper's mind remains in the Red Room, helpless to observe events as they unfold before him. (The close-up image we see of Cooper's face as he watches the two rooms separate is almost the same image we see later, in Part 17, when Cooper's face materializes over the action.) On the other path, Cooper's physical self follows a path where he will emerge in the real world in the form of a man named Dougie Jones.

---

[*] What might have happened had Cooper avoided the trap and been able to pass through the curtains? Would he have emerged into Glastonbury Grove to find Hawk waiting to receive him? Hawk knew something was "supposed to happen" the night he saw red curtains shimmering among the trees. Perhaps Cooper was behind those curtains, trying to get through.

[†] See episode 16 of *Twin Peaks*.

These two distinct storylines unfold simultaneously but are still entwined. Cooper in the Red Room becomes the observer, watching the story of the other Cooper as he makes his way through the real world. This observing Cooper (the "dreamer") watches all that transpires in the real world and conveys it to us (the audience) through his unique psychological filter.

The physical Cooper exits into another hallway and sees an armless statue (The Venus of Arles). He parts curtains and peers into the real world. His point-of-view is high above a lonely desert road. A car that Mr. C is driving approaches in the distance. Just as the car is about to pass "under" Cooper, the statue in the hallway transforms into the doppelganger of The Arm.

Chaos erupts. The floor beneath Cooper oscillates wildly. The doppelganger screams, "non-exist-ent!" and Cooper drops through the floor and is hurled through a furious void of light and sound. The trap has been sprung. Cooper is caught.

Cooper has encountered the Arm's doppelganger before (in the last episode of Season 2), but it was not nearly as powerful then as it is now. Somehow, this evolved doppelganger has found a way to banish Cooper to a realm of nonexistence, which, according to some Hindu texts, is a place beyond cosmic law, possibly a realm of death. That's where the Arm's doppelganger is sending Cooper.

Luckily for Cooper, powerful protective forces (The Fireman, and possibly Major Briggs) have anticipated the Arm doppelganger's plans and taken precautions to steer Cooper away from banishment. Before Cooper goes fully into that dark realm, he finds himself slamming onto the roof of the glass box in New York City. He phases through the glass and floats into the box and stares out into the room that Sam just left. (At this very moment, Sam is talking with Tracey in the anteroom and looking for the missing guard.) Cooper is shifted and shuffled within the box and disappears before Sam and Tracey re-enter the room. Shunted onto a new path, Cooper is thrown back out into the chaos of the void, where he once again falls through space.

In this supernatural game of chess, The Fireman has predicted the moves of his opponents and strategized accordingly. Dale Cooper has avoided a trap and been moved across the board with deliberation.

IN TWIN PEAKS, Sarah Palmer sits in her dark living room watching a violent nature documentary on television. Brutal images of lions tearing into water buffalo play across the screen. As Sarah watches, Lynch's camera carefully moves around the room to show mirrors on the wall behind Sarah. By framing the scene this way, Lynch allows us to see both the brutal imagery on the television and Sarah Palmer as she watches it.

A lion bites bloodily into a buffalo's neck. The buffalo shrieks in pain as blood pours from its wounds. Sarah's face goes still. Her eyes widen. Something is happening.

Sarah Palmer watches television at the same moment chaos is erupting in New York City—the exact instant Experiment is violently, *bloodily,* killing Sam and Tracey. Experiment disappeared after it killed the two young people, but where did it go? The answer, I think, is right here in Twin Peaks, inside the darkness of the Palmer house. Experiment went to the one place where it could safely reside in the real world. It went to Sarah Palmer, who was made ready for this moment fifty-eight years earlier, when, as a teenage girl, she was infested by a horrible entity. This entity has been hibernating inside Sarah for decades, waiting to serve as host for Experiment. Loose in this world at last, Experiment targets Sarah Palmer and finds refuge.

We will soon learn that Sarah Palmer is a looming evil that haunts both the Palmer house and the surrounding environs of Twin Peaks. But was she always this dreadful? Was she always a monster?

Look at Sarah sitting there in the dark: She is in pain, she is despondent, she is the victim of decades of suffering. Her daughter was murdered by her own husband, a kind of tragedy that seems impossible to bear. Before the murder, before the tragic loss of Laura, Sarah's husband, Leland Palmer, abused and tormented Laura for years. Are we to believe that all while these awful events transpired, all while Laura suffered and Leland raged, Sarah was as evil and depraved as Bob, the demon who drove Leland to madness? Are we to believe that Sarah was a victim thrice over: her daughter murdered, her husband crazed, and she an evil entity gleefully basking in all this pain?

No. It's too much to believe, too much to accept that Sarah Palmer was the true villain of *Twin Peaks.*

So, I choose not to believe. I don't accept that the Sarah Palmer of *Fire Walk With Me*, the Sarah who was drugged by Leland so he could molest Laura without fear of discovery, the Sarah who winced while Leland demanded Laura tell him where she got her necklace, the Sarah who insisted Leland leave Laura alone, is the same horrible creature we see in *The Return*. I don't accept that the Sarah Palmer of the first two seasons of *Twin Peaks*, the Sarah who moaned into the phone when she learned of her daughter's death, the Sarah who screamed at Leland for ruining Laura's funeral, the Sarah who sat in mourning and was comforted by the wise words of Dale Cooper, is the monster that haunts the Palmer house twenty-five years later.

And yet the Sarah Palmer we see in this new story is a potent figure of evil, of darkness personified. Something happened to her to make her this way, something changed inside. I believe this change happened the night she sat alone in a dark room, while a terrifying blue light played across her face. The same night, a continent away, a demon vaulted into the world.

I choose to believe that Sarah was a good person who harbored a latent kernel of horror which could not bloom until infused with evil. That happens this awful night as Sarah Palmer becomes yet another piece in a powerful, unfathomable game of supernatural chess. Poor Sarah, again a victim as Experiment blossoms within. But before this terrible night of transformation, Sarah Palmer was human, she was heartbroken, and she was innocent.[*]

IT IS NIGHT, AND THE ROADHOUSE IS FULL. A band, Chromatics, plays on stage, and people dance and drink. Shelly Briggs is enjoying the scene, but confesses to her friend, Renee, that she's worried about her daughter, Becky. Shelly fears that Becky has made a bad choice in a man named Steven, but Shelly's a fine one to talk; her track record with men is pretty sketchy, especially when it comes to her first husband,

---

[*] Sarah Palmer was a victim not only of a demon, but also of her creators. Mark Frost explains that Sarah's role in *The Return* was the result of new creative impulses on the parts of Lynch and Frost: "I think the show, given that it spans so much time, really operates on a continuum. We knew what we knew when we made the pilot. We knew what we knew when we made the final episode. All of that was informed by what you know in the moment, and [...] that's constantly changing, so I think, in that sense, each episode is a reflection of [...] your evolution as a creative person. Those things change as you go through life."

Leo Johnson. And now, she makes eye contact with a man across the bar, Red, another thug whom Shelly has fallen for. The past repeats itself.

James Hurley admires Renee from afar. He gazes across the crowded room, full of longing and possible regret. With but a few glances and some faraway stares, James exhibits a deep sense of sadness and loss. Shelly feels it and tells her friends that James was in a motorcycle accident, but he's still cool. James has always been cool.

There's something in the air in the Roadhouse this night. A wave of nostalgia, a mood of memories unspoken. But there's something else, too: The observing mind of Dale Cooper watching from an other-worldly plane. Like James, Cooper is sad and lost and confused. As his dream unfolds, those emotions color everything he sees.

On the Roadhouse stage, Chromatics play, and lyrics from their ethereal song, "Shadow," speak to the mystery of *Twin Peaks* and all who inhabit it: "Now you're just a stranger's dream…. You're nothing like you seem."

PART 3:
CALL FOR HELP

COOPER HURTLES THROUGH A MAELSTROM of light and sound and falls onto a large stone balcony, a section of a much larger edifice that reaches high into a black sky. He's in a shadowy, unearthly realm, a liminal space between one world and another. A purple hue saturates the environment. When Cooper peers over the balcony he sees an ocean extending deep into a purple darkness.

Cooper pushes through glass doors and steps into what David Lynch calls "the Mansion Room," a wide space framed by a low, curved ceiling and textured walls. The room's deep shadows and minimal décor recall paintings by American artist, Edward Hopper.* Lynch has expressed great admiration for Hopper's art, and the painter's influence can be seen in several places throughout *The Return* (including later this episode).

An oversaturated purple glow permeates the Mansion Room, just as it did outside. A woman, Naido, sits on a couch, a fireplace burning brightly before her. Naido is blind—swollen flesh covers her eyes—but she senses Cooper and turns her head.

Cooper walks toward Naido and is suddenly caught in a turmoil of stuttering "time jumps." He rapidly shifts back and forth like a record skipping and re-skipping a groove. Stuck in this intractable temporal mess, Cooper cannot move smoothly forward. He progresses spasmodically, as if shaking off fragments of time that cling and pull him back.

---

* See Approaching a City (1946) and The Sheridan Theater (1937).

Eventually, Cooper puts his hands in Naido's, and she becomes alert and excited. She reaches out and touches his face. When she feels Cooper's features, she recognizes him. She knows this man is Dale Cooper. She wants to communicate with him, but all she can do is utter breathy, incomprehensible noises.

Cooper doesn't realize it, but Naido is a manifestation of his one true love and confidante, Diane.[*] How she got to this ethereal realm will never be fully explained, but she's here for a reason. She's waiting to steer Cooper to a specific time and place.

Naido is an overtly Kafkaesque figure in *The Return*. She is Diane "metamorphosed." Like Kafka's Gregor Samsa in *The Metamorphosis*, Diane, whose eyes are entirely encased in flesh, has transformed into something unnatural. Like Gregor, Diane cannot communicate with any precision. When Gregor tries to speak, he can only make animalistic sounds (what another character describes as "no human voice"). So it is with Naido, who can only communicate with chitters and squeaks.

Has Diane really changed physically, or is her distorted appearance simply the result of Cooper's misperception? In the past, Cooper rarely gave Diane his full attention. She was the faceless, voiceless presence on the other side of his tape recorder. If Cooper still thinks of Diane this way, he might not be seeing her as she is. He masks Diane as Naido, morphing her into something distant and obscure because his mind is not ready, or able, to see the true Diane.

A loud pounding erupts from behind a metal door.[†] Cooper is alarmed, and Naido urgently presses her finger to her lips, imploring him to keep quiet. Cooper notices an oversized socket on the wall labelled with the number 15 and, sensing he is on the cusp of escape from his decades-old confinement, moves toward it.

Alarmed by his proximity to the socket, Naido intercepts Cooper and leads him through a door and up a ladder. They climb through a hatch and emerge onto the roof of a metal box, floating in space.

---

[*] The name "Naido" phonetically resembles the name "Diane" in reverse (if you pronounce Diane backward it sounds like "Naid"). In Japanese, you must add an "o" sound to make a proper name; hence, the phonetic "Naid" becomes "Naid-o." (Notably, Naido is played by the Japanese actress, Nae Yuuki, and when we meet the "real" Diane she will be wearing Japanese styles of clothing.)

[†] We'll see this door again, fleetingly, in Part 17.

In a masterful, beautiful shot, Cooper and Naido stand on the metal box, adrift in a vast field of stars, their tiny existences put carefully into perspective. The purple lighting glows brightly, even out here in the starry void.

A large, bell-shaped protuberance dominates the roof of the box, and Naido makes her way around it to reach for a long metal lever. Before she pulls it, she gives Cooper a look of farewell and then yanks the lever down. The harsh purple lighting vanishes. Powerful forces jolt Naido, and she writhes helplessly, trying to withstand the energy coursing through her. The forces overwhelm her, and Naido is flung into space. Dress flapping, she plummets away from Cooper into the void.

Cooper looks around, trying to make sense of this strange place he's found himself. He peers over the edge of the box and sees the distorted, ghost-like face of Major Garland Briggs float across the stars. Staring back at Cooper, Briggs slowly speaks the words, "Blue Rose," before drifting away.

Naido has done her job; she pulled a "reset" switch and stabilized the environment. Where there was once turmoil, now there is calm. But more than that, by pulling the lever Naido has subtracted the red from the purple. When Cooper arrived from the Red Room, he brought with him the unstable, anachronous properties of that realm. Contaminated by the Red Room, Cooper's presence threw the Mansion Room into chaos. Nothing there could work correctly until Naido "degaussed" Cooper and removed the "Red Room" field clinging to him.

When you remove the red from the purple you get blue. Indeed, as soon as Naido eliminates the red, Major Briggs arrives to announce, "Blue Rose." Cooper now stands at a threshold into the real world. A blue zone.

Cooper is unsteady on his feet; the metal box shudders and shifts like a ship tossed by waves. Seeing no other option, Cooper descends the ladder back into the box. When he returns to the Mansion Room, he no longer suffers from the stuttering time jumps. Everything is smoother. Quiet. The purple hue is gone. Cooper glances over to the socket and notices it is now labelled with the number 3. A vase holding a blue rose stands on a side table, but Cooper doesn't notice it.

A woman (identified as American Girl in the credits) sits on the couch. She looks at Cooper and checks her watch. The digital display changes from 2:52 to 2:53, and when it does, a small desk lamp illuminates next to the number 3 socket.

A humming sound begins, and Lynch's camera slowly zooms toward the socket. As it reaches the opening, the scene cuts to a desert road where Mr. C is driving. His dashboard clock shows the time to be between 2:52 and 2:53. Mr. C's vision blurs and his head drops. His car's cigarette lighter emits an intense electrical crackling.

As Cooper steps closer to the socket, an invisible force mildly shocks him. American Girl says, "When you get there you will already be there," a warning that when Cooper gets back to reality his doppelganger will still be out there—he will not have exchanged places with his double. Cooper is about to enter very dangerous territory, and American Girl wants him to be prepared. Cooper faces the socket yet again and is blasted with electricity. His eyes go wide, and he sways from the shock.

Back out on the road Mr. C struggles to stay conscious. His car swerves wildly across the road.

As Cooper stares at the socket, the loud banging recommences on the metal door. American Girl tells Cooper to hurry, her "mother" is coming. Cooper moves closer to the socket. Electrical forces grab hold and pull him entirely within (save for his shoes, which drop from his feet and remain in the Mansion Room).

And that's the last we'll see of this bizarre, transitional space, this borderland between the Red Room and the real world. Dale Cooper has exited the Mansion Room (aka, the Blue Zone, or what I like to think of as the *Blue Rose* Room) and moved on to another realm.

THE FIRST 14 MINUTES OF PART 3 contain some of the most striking imagery we've seen in the *Twin Peaks* narrative. David Lynch again proves his mastery of the medium through a singular combination of editing, sound and lighting. The "stuttering" Cooper encounters when he first enters the room, for example, illustrates his temporally untethered state, his inability to move smoothly through time.

Cooper's initial frustrations in the room are exacerbated by the trouble he has talking with Naido. His efforts to converse with her foreshadow the difficulty he will have communicating later in the episode. Lynch has always been fascinated with failed communications. Naido's chirps and squeaks recall the way the grandmother speaks in *The Grandmother,* or the way Jeffrey's hospitalized father attempts to talk in *Blue Velvet.* For these characters, human language is impossible.

When Cooper descends back into the Mansion Room, he encounters American Girl (played by Phoebe Augustine, the actress who portrayed Ronette Pulaski, Laura Palmer's neglected friend, in the original *Twin Peaks*). It would be easy to dismiss American Girl as just another curious observer, one of Lynch's many threshold dwellers (she literally dwells upon the threshold that is the Mansion Room), but her designation as "American" girl is curious. It's the kind of label we often see associated with Laura Palmer, who, for many, is the archetypal American woman. As Todd McGowan observes, Laura "embodies the ideal of contemporary American female beauty." Siobhan Lyons expands on this idea, saying that Laura "symbolizes the exact traits of the American Dream." (Lynch acknowledges Laura's "Americanness" in *Fire Walk With Me,* when Albert Rosenfield, responding to Dale Cooper's vision of Laura, says, "You're describing half the high school girls in America.")

Could American Girl be an avatar of Laura Palmer, sent to advise Cooper as he passes through the Mansion Room? She cautions Cooper about his doppelganger (or at least the idea of multiple Coopers) and explicitly warns him that her "mother" is coming, a reference, perhaps, to Sarah Palmer (and the demon that inhabits her). The possibility that American Girl is Laura Palmer is tantalizing, especially when we recognize her purpose in the Mansion Room is to counsel Cooper, whose ultimate mission is, of course, to "find Laura."

Before we move on, a few comments about the numbered sockets in the Mansion Room: Some observers have noted that the second socket number (3) corresponds to the episode number (i.e., Cooper passes through socket 3 in Part 3) and so it stands to reason that if Cooper had passed through socket 15, he would have emerged into the storyline of Part 15. I have my doubts about this. As I mentioned earlier, I think that when Cooper arrived in the Mansion Room, he was simply not ready for passage through socket 15 because he was contaminated by his exposure to the Red Room. By pulling the lever, Naido restored Cooper to a "safe state" and made it possible for him to continue his journey.

It's tempting to think the socket numbers hold a deeper meaning, that they correspond to Cooper's place in the story and provide alternate paths for him depending on which socket he went through, but I think the socket numbers are less important than they appear. Yes, Cooper will have another "shocking" encounter with a socket in Part 15, but here, in Part 3, "socket 15" merely foreshadows those events. I don't think it holds any deeper meaning than that. (Personally, I like the idea that the socket numbers serve as a call-back to Cooper's room number at the Great Northern Hotel in the original *Twin Peaks*, which was, of course, room 315.)

BACK IN THE REAL WORLD, Mr. C's car careens from lane to lane and veers onto an embankment. It rolls through the air and crashes back onto the road. Inside, a shaken Mr. C clasps his hand across his mouth and struggles to keep from vomiting. He stares wide-eyed through his shattered windshield and sees the curtains of the Red Room shimmer into view. He is on the threshold of being pulled back in.

In an empty house in the desolate housing development of Rancho Rosa, Nevada, a man named Dougie Jones (a dumpier, longer-haired version of Dale Cooper) reclines in bed with a prostitute named Jade. Something is wrong with Dougie's left arm; it feels tingly, and Dougie struggles to pull it through his jacket sleeve. As it turns out, Dougie is wearing the Owl Cave Ring on his left hand.

First seen in the film, *Fire Walk With Me*, the Owl Cave Ring was a powerful talisman used by supernatural predators to ensnare victims. The demon Bob killed ring-bearers and extracted from them a substance called *garmonbozia*, a horrid "creamed corn" upon which Bob and other denizens of The Black Lodge fed. Garmonbozia was more than just food, however, it was the physical manifestation of human "pain and sorrow," emotions which energized Bob and his ilk.

(How is it that Dougie has come to possess this dreadful object? The Owl Cave Ring last appeared in *Fire Walk With Me*, when Laura Palmer placed it on her finger before being killed. Deleted scenes from *Fire Walk With Me* shed light on the ring's possible chain-of-custody after that. In one, the Arm explains to Cooper that "someone else has [the ring] now," implying that he, the Arm, has set the ring loose into world. In another, Annie Blackburn, whom Cooper rescued from the Red Room in the original series, is shown wearing the ring at Calhoun Memorial Hospital. A nurse sees the ring and takes it. Where did it go from there? In Part 7 of *The Return*, we learn that Mr. C visited the hospital shortly after Annie's admittance. Though it's never explicitly shown, we can assume Mr. C took the ring from the nurse.[*])

Jade leaves to take a shower, and Dougie is overcome by pain in his stomach. He collapses to the floor and vomits a creamed-corn-like substance (likely purging himself of his pain and sorrow). With a thunderous clap, Dougie is yanked out of this world and into the Red Room.

Out on the road, Mr. C sees a vision of Dougie through red curtains. The image fades away, and Mr. C vomits a vast amount of creamed corn and passes out. A highway patrol car pulls up to Mr. C's car, and two patrolmen get out. The first officer looks inside the wreck and violently gags.[†] "Something awful is in there," he manages to say before falling to the ground. Mr. C's noxious garmonbozia is too much to withstand.

Dougie finds himself in the Red Room. He sits in a chair, no shoes on his feet, and sees Phillip Gerard standing before him. "Someone manufactured you," Gerard says. "For a purpose, but I think now that has been fulfilled." Dougie's left arm shrinks, and the Owl Cave Ring falls to the floor. Dougie transforms into a charred ember, which emits a viscous goo. The ember vanishes, and all that remains on the chair is a small gold sphere.

Poor Dougie. He's enjoying a visit with a prostitute, and the next thing he knows he's vomiting on the Berber carpet. If that's not enough, he passes out and wakes up in Reality's purgatorial backstage to learn he's been "manufactured," his miserable life nothing but a ploy

---

[*] In *The Final Dossier*, Mark Frost suggests that the Owl Cave Ring fell into the possession of Twin Peaks resident Doug Milford and then found its way out of Twin Peaks with Doug's widow, Lana, but no explanation is given as to how Doug Milford got the ring in the first place.

[†] Identified as "First Trooper" in the credits, the officer is referred to as "Billy" by his partner. This probably means nothing, but it's worth noting because an absent figure named Billy will become a significant, albeit marginal, presence later in *The Return*.

in some cosmic game. It's a lot to take in, but Dougie simply responds, "That's weird." An understatement, to be sure.

Gerard retrieves the ring and the sphere and grimly walks away, knowing for certain that something has gone wrong. Cooper has fallen into a trap. Worse, Cooper's doppelganger has found a way to remain in the real world.

Now we know what Mr. C was talking about when he told Darya he had a plan to keep himself out of the Black Lodge. That plan had a name, and its name was Dougie Jones. Dougie was almost certainly a tulpa, produced, as Gerard explains, for a purpose. Mr. C manufactured Dougie to serve as a proxy, a human designed to take his place in the Red Room while Mr. C remained in the real world.

We don't know how Mr. C manufactures tulpas, but from the way Dougie disintegrates, it seems tulpas are composed of nothing more than basic raw materials. Dougie is reduced to a mere ember (with a gooey core), which quickly dissipates, leaving only the gold sphere behind—the soul of Dougie Jones.

BACK IN THE EMPTY HOUSE in Rancho Rosa, an electric socket begins to glow. A distended image of Dale Cooper emerges from the socket, and his body is soon deposited on the carpet. Jade returns to the room and is surprised to see "Dougie" lying on the floor, wearing different clothes. Cooper doesn't respond to Jade's inquiries; he simply stares at the ceiling.

Jade manages to get Cooper out of the house and notices he's not wearing shoes. She questions him about it, but Cooper continues to stare into the distance. Mildly exasperated, Jade retrieves Dougie's shoes and puts them on Cooper's feet. (Cooper is now literally walking in another man's shoes.)

What's wrong with Cooper? Why can't he put his shoes on or respond to Jade's prompts? It appears that he entirely lacks agency. And yet, despite his inability to do anything for himself, Cooper has become a compelling presence. Without any deliberate effort, he holds sway over Jade. Up until now, Jade's relationship with Dougie has been transactional; she expects payment for a service rendered. But something inside her has softened. She retrieves Dougie's shoes and bends down to place them on Cooper's feet. Then, after she realizes Cooper has lost his car keys, Jade takes pity and offers him a ride. Perhaps Jade has always been this kind, but more likely she is changing, becoming a nicer person just by being in the presence of Cooper.

After Jade and Cooper drive away from the house, another car pulls up. The driver, Gene, radios another man, Jake, to tell him Dougie just left. Gene can't be sure, though, because Dougie's car is still in the driveway. Jake replies that if Dougie is in Jade's car, he'll "get" him.

As Cooper rides out of the neighborhood with Jade he notices a sign for "Sycamore Street" and speaks for the first time: "Jade give two rides." Cooper retrieves his old Great Northern room key from his jacket but is jostled and drops the key at his feet. He bends down to retrieve it just as Jade drives past Jake, who is watching through the scope of a rifle.* Jake radios Gene and tells him Dougie was not in the car.†

Gene attaches an explosive device to Dougie's car and hastily leaves, but his actions don't go unobserved. In a house across the street, a young boy watches Gene's suspicious movements. Down the hall from the boy, a woman yells, "One-one-nine!" again and again. Identified as "drugged-out mother" in the credits, this woman is clearly not well. She sits at a card table, liquor and pill bottles spread out before her. A red balloon sits on the floor (the first of many red balloons we will see in the narrative). The woman carefully takes a pill and washes it down with a shot of whiskey.

RANCHO ROSA IS A CRAZY PLACE. And yet much of what we see in this bizarre setting likely has more to do with Cooper than with the actual world in which he's found himself. Cooper emerges from the socket into a nearly empty house, and, as he assumes the Dougie persona, he seems to have an empty mind. This conflation of mind and home is a theme David Lynch has explored before, specifically in *Lost*

---

* If you look closely at the car's side-view mirror as Cooper bends down, you will see the reflection of a figure sitting in the back seat. Just like the famous shot of Frank Silva in the *Twin Peaks* pilot, here is another unintended reflection of a crew member (possibly David Lynch) in a mirror.

† When Jade drives out of the Rancho Rosa development, a woman can be seen pushing a shopping cart along the sidewalk. This figure could be an homage to Edward Hopper, who more than once painted scenes featuring women burdened with heavy bundles or pushing carts along streets. See *Day After Funeral* (1925) and *New York Pavements* (1924). The woman from Rancho Rosa (or one very much like her) will appear again in Part 9.

Highway, but the idea can also be found in his earlier work. When describing a concept for the unproduced film, *Gardenback*, Lynch said, "In this story...this man's attic was like his mind.... The house was like his head." Houses and homes figure prominently in many of Lynch's paintings, too. One, entitled, "Here I am – Me as a House," shows a spectral figure emerging from a house and into the sky. For Lynch, the mind and the house are often connected, so it's not surprising that an empty mind would originate from an empty house.

When Cooper emerged from the socket he was still dressed in his black suit, but something is missing (besides his shoes): Cooper is no longer wearing his official FBI lapel pin. When Cooper entered the socket, his pin went in with him, but when he made it to the other side, the pin was gone. (Notably, Cooper's wristwatch does not disappear; it stays on him as he passes from the Mansion Room to Rancho Rosa.)

The pin is a critical part of Cooper's identity. It symbolizes Cooper's role as a man of law and as an "agent" of enforcement. The fact that the FBI pin is missing suggests that a piece of Cooper's identity is also missing, a fundamental aspect of his psyche has been erased. Indeed, this newly emerged Cooper is markedly different than the Cooper we have seen so far.

All of what we're seeing, of course, is being filtered through the mind of Dale Cooper, who is still trapped in The Red Room. From the moment Cooper re-enters this world we see evidence of the observer's unique psychological modifications to reality, signs that the world is reflecting the memories and musings of Dale Cooper.

The absent pin is one of these modifications. Another is the Sycamore Street sign. Years ago, in the deep woods surrounding Twin Peaks, Cooper passed through a circle of sycamore trees before entering the Red Room. For Cooper, this is a strong (and probably recent) memory. Newly emerged into the world, Cooper's mind brings with him remnants of his past and projects those remnants onto the world he observes. (The Great Northern key is yet another such remnant; it should not exist as Cooper perceives it. I'll discuss the key in greater detail when we get to Part 5.)

COOPER IS NOT THE ONLY CHARACTER experiencing a fungible reality. At the Twin Peaks Sheriff's station, Hawk, Andy, and Lucy lay out all the old evidence from the Laura Palmer case. Andy and Lucy don't know how to determine what is missing, but Lucy notices the small box of chocolate bunnies[*] on the table and gasps. She ate one of the bunnies long ago, and that means one of the bunnies is missing. Andy suggests that the missing bunny may be what they're looking for, but Hawk insists: "It's not about the bunny." But then Hawk pauses and questions his own certainty, wondering: "*Is* it about the bunny?"

While this scene is absurd on the surface, a piece of bizarre comic relief, it supports the idea of a malleable reality. As we will see in later episodes, Lucy often questions the nature of the universe and her influence on it. Here, in Part 3, we get our first glimpse that Lucy might have some sway over her surroundings. As she worries about her culpability in eating the bunny, Lucy's distress shifts the world around her—and around Hawk. Things become hazy, and Hawk is caught in the wake of Lucy's fluid reality. He loses his certainty. He doubts his perceptions. Maybe it *is* about the bunny.

JADE AND COOPER ARRIVE at the Silver Mustang Casino, and Jade gives Cooper five dollars so he can call someone for help. Cooper enters the casino and approaches a cashier to make change for his five-dollar bill. When the cashier asks Cooper if he is going to play a game, he responds, "Call for help," and when he does, something subtle and profound happens. The cashier pauses before handing Cooper his money and gently places her hands on his. Then, as Cooper walks away, she puts a hand on her chest and follows him with her eyes. Emotions sweep through her. The cashier deals with scores of unusual and eccentric people every day and has probably hardened herself to the sad, sometimes pathetic behavior they exhibit, but here comes Cooper, and she is confounded. She feels for him. She is moved. Cooper has sparked in her a compassion for her fellow human beings. First Jade, and now the cashier: Cooper's goodness radiates.

Cooper enters the game room and watches a man place a coin in a slot machine and pull the lever. The machine hits a winning combination, and the man excitedly yells, "Hello!" as his winnings pour forth.

Cooper looks across the room and spies a shimmering image of the Red Room, a mirage hovering over a slot machine. He places a coin in

---

[*] The same box of bunnies Cooper described to Diane in the *Twin Peaks* pilot.

the machine and pulls the lever. Cooper yells, "Hello!" and the machine hits the jackpot. Alarms blare and torrents of coins spill out. Cooper sees another twinkling image over a second machine and inserts a coin. The machine wins big, and more coins pour out.

An old woman watches Cooper and is astonished. Savvy to his good luck, she warns him away from the next machine he approaches. After Cooper leaves, she inserts a coin and hits her own jackpot. Overcome with joy, she raises her hands in celebration.

If there's any doubt that Cooper is being shepherded by other-worldly powers, his lucrative foray through the Silver Mustang casino removes it. Some entity or higher power is guiding Cooper from winning machine to winning machine, bestowing upon him riches, money that will secure Cooper in the hazardous world he will soon encounter. He's being protected by uncanny forces.

AT FBI HEADQUARTERS IN PHILADELPHIA, Gordon Cole's crack FBI team is reviewing a strange case. A man claims he's innocent of the brutal murder of his wife but says he knows the identity of the real murderer. He can't reveal the killer's identity because doing so would breach national security. In order to help the FBI find the real killer, the man has provided a series of clues: a picture of a woman promiscu-ously posed in a bikini, a pair of pliers, a picture of two women sun-bathing, a picture of a young boy on a beach wearing a sailor's uniform, a semi-automatic gun with a silencer, and a jar of chickpeas. Cole takes it all in and assigns the case a curious label: "The Congressman's Dilemma." As Cole studies the various clues, we're led to believe that everything he needs to solve the case is laid out before him.

Wouldn't it be great if that were true? Wouldn't it be wonderful if the clues really did lead to some solution to The Congressman's Di-lemma? That's not going to happen, though, because The Congress-man's Dilemma is a red herring. The meeting between Cole and the rest of the FBI team is a meta-textual signal from David Lynch that clues don't always add up, that mysteries are not always solved by clever analysis and codebreaking. Lynch is essentially saying, "Here's a series of random images. Go ahead, try to make sense of them!" all while subtly mocking us, the over-attentive viewer, for trying to do this very thing with the mysteries and puzzles of *Twin Peaks*.

In *The Secret History of Twin Peaks*, one of Mark Frost's characters says: "A real mystery can't be solved, not completely. That's what gives it value: It can't be cracked, it's bigger than you and me, bigger than everything we know." David Lynch, of course, has spoken many times of the power of mystery: "That there's a mystery is a huge thrill. That there's more going on than meets the eye is a thrilling thing." Mystery and the wonder of the unknown are at the very core of Lynch and Frost's story-telling philosophy. They designed *The Return* to be an open text, to be an active viewing experience that engages each viewer uniquely.

We all bring part of ourselves to *Twin Peaks* when we watch it. Each of us is our own detective, assembling clues and finding answers that please us. Those answers are subjective, of course, and may not make sense to other fans, but that's the beauty of *Twin Peaks*. It's not reducible to one exclusive "answer." It is open to any number of satisfying possibilities.

This book is my effort at piecing together elements of *The Return* to advance tenable, plausible explanations for many of the odd happenings in it. I find great joy in studying *Twin Peaks* and in trying to make sense of it. No other television series offers such richness and potential. I don't mind if Lynch and Frost are teasing obsessive fans with "The Congressman's Dilemma," because I get the joke and know that it's pointed at viewers like me. (Yes, I spent some time trying to work out an answer to The Congressman's Dilemma. It's begging for a solution.)*

---

* With all that in mind, this seems like as good a place as any to address a comment that appears in David Lynch's biography/memoir, *Room to Dream*. Kristine McKenna (who writes the biographical sections of the book) makes a categorical statement about *The Return* which I found mildly alarming. McKenna says, "Many dots can be connected to create many different scenarios, but those who truly love and surrender to the show have no interest in deconstructing the narrative. It's a work of art, and that's not what it's for."

I was surprised when I read this because McKenna's statement carries with it a prejudice against certain audiences. It explicitly states that those who "truly love *Twin Peaks*" have no interest in deconstructing the narrative. What is the purpose of this claim? Why does Kristine McKenna seek to deter analysis and interpretation of *Twin Peaks*? David Lynch, himself (in the very next chapter of *Room to Dream*), says, "Everybody has theories about what the show is about, which is great." Of course, it is! There nothing wrong with deconstructing the narrative or attempting to map clear pathways through the story. Analyzing *The Return* in no way diminishes it or makes

AFTER COLE DISMISSES HIS TEAM, Agent Tammy Preston summarizes a new case involving the gruesome deaths of Sam and Tracey in the glass box room in New York City. Tammy describes the box and the cameras, and she mentions that the guards in the building are missing. She says that a few hazy images were visible on video recordings but little else could be discerned (which might explain why they have no images of Cooper in the box). Before Tammy can provide more details, however, Cole's intercom beeps, and an excited voice tells him he's received a call pertaining to Agent Dale Cooper. Cole rushes to his office to take the call, and when he hangs up, he tells Albert Rosenfield they must fly to South Dakota in the morning.

Part 3 ends here, appropriately, in the office of Gordon Cole, the seasoned FBI agent who knows far more about the world than meets the eye. Behind Cole's desk hangs a massive black-and-white photo of a nuclear explosion.[*] It dominates the space and evokes feelings of power and danger. On the opposite wall hangs a large portrait of Franz Kafka (similar to the one hanging in the Hastings home in Part 1). Like the mushroom cloud across the room, Kafka is an overt presence in Cole's office. David Lynch wants us to think of Kafka as we process what we've already seen in *The Return* and speculate about what is yet to come. To underscore this Kafkaesque atmosphere, Albert turns to Tammy and says, "The absurd mystery of the strange forces of existence."[†]

Strange forces, indeed. They've been building in this episode, maneuvering, taking action. And here we are, participants in this bizarre and baffling story, moving within its peculiar rhythms, striving

---

it any less a work of art. If anything, such involvement enlivens *Twin Peaks*. Enhances it. We don't have to completely surrender to it to discover its value.

What gives McKenna authority to draw boundaries around *Twin Peaks*, to tell us what it's "for"? In my mind only two artists—Mark Frost and David Lynch—can truly speak to the design and function of the *Twin Peaks* narrative. Lynch chooses not to, while Frost supplies a few answers in his book, *The Final Dossier* (essentially "connecting some dots"). And that make me wonder: Who is Kristine McKenna really speaking to when she says *Twin Peaks* is not something to be decoded or explained?

[*] The photo is of Shot Hood, the sixth nuclear test in the United States' Operation Plumbbob atmospheric weapons testing series, detonated on July 5, 1957. This is not a picture of the Trinity detonation of July 16, 1945 (an event which becomes of particular interest in Part 8).

[†] The subtitle to the unproduced David Lynch film, *Ronnie Rocket*.

to make sense of its "absurd mystery." We are the blank mind of a newly returned Dale Cooper. We are the citizens of Twin Peaks, awakening to a world altered by shadowy forces. We are the FBI, struggling to decode The Congressman's Dilemma. We are, as Kafka observed, "in the confusion of our senses...we have nothing but monstrosities and a kaleidoscopic play of things that is either delightful or exhausting."

<INTERLUDE 2>

SOUL SURVIVOR

IN THE SHOCKING, TRAGIC ENDING of *Twin Peaks* Season 2, Dale Cooper enters the Black Lodge and emerges as an entity of evil and chaos. When he returns to Room 315 of the Great Northern Hotel, he sees his reflection in a bathroom mirror and gleefully lashes out, smashing his head against the glass. Violence and torment—even to his own physical being—are what define him.

And he is not alone. Upon his escape from the Red Room, "Cooper" has brought with him a stowaway, the demon Bob, now lodged within him and serving as a catalyst for terror and brutality. Bob is a contaminating influence, and while he does not "possess" Cooper, he festers deep inside, a foul, rotting presence.

This transformed Dale Cooper is often referred to as the "bad Cooper," the shadow self who bested the "good Cooper" and escaped from the Red Room (the so-called "waiting room" of the Black Lodge). David Lynch confirms this reading in *Fire Walk With Me* when Annie Blackburn tells Laura Palmer, "The good Dale is in the Lodge and he can't leave." Ostensibly, there are two Coopers: A good one trapped in the Black Lodge/Red Room, and a bad one loose in the world. This was for 25 years a simple way of explaining it.

In *The Return*, the bad Cooper is known as Mr. C, and he is, as Kyle MacLachlan describes him, "almost inhuman, lacking any remorse whatsoever." If Mr. C is pure evil with no redemptive qualities, then the "good Dale," the one supposedly trapped in the lodge, should be his exact opposite—a being of total and complete goodness, a self-assured, confident man who could never harm another. And yet that's not quite what we see. For all intents and purposes, the Cooper of the Red Room is the one we've always known, the FBI agent who dutifully came to Twin Peaks to investigate a murder. Yes, he is a *good* Cooper, but he's good because he chooses to be that way. He is someone who rejects evil, someone who knows how to control his darker, baser nature. He is assuredly a whole being, not some half-of-Cooper who embodies only good.

It is insufficient, then, to say that at the end of the original series Cooper had been reduced to two opposing entities, that he had been divided into good and bad. *The Return* supports a more complex reading. The original Cooper (the one who entered the lodge in Season 2) remains intact through most of *The Return* but trapped within the Red Room. Meanwhile, two independent aspects have manifested and escaped. Cooper is still Cooper, but a pair of different beings in Cooper-form roam the real world.

The Red Room is impossible to fully define, but it is safe to say it is as much a psychological realm as it is any kind of physical space. What happens inside the Red Room is a reflection of (or a reaction to) the deeper psyches of those who find their way into it. The Red Room is a place where nightmares take form and where the turbulence of the mind's primitive impulses break free and find purchase in the physical world. That's what happened at the end of *Twin Peaks* Season 2. Cooper didn't divide. His evil self was birthed from the dark recesses of his mind and became a corporeal being that was independent of, and in opposition to, Dale Cooper. Then it broke free and left Cooper behind, trapped.

As the decades passed in the real world, the bad Cooper amassed power and wreaked havoc. Meanwhile, Cooper in the Red Room went into a kind of stasis, his mind effectively put on hold. Suspended on the threshold of the Red Room's event horizon, Cooper does not experience any passage of time. (David Lynch confirms this reading when he tells Kyle MacLachlan "No time has passed for you," when directing the actor in Part 17.) When Cooper re-enters the story in Part 2, he literally pops back onto the scene, and time starts flowing again. Phillip Gerard's cryptic question, "Is it future or is it past?" has no definitive answer because the answer is *both*. No time passed in the Red Room, but in the real world twenty-five years have come and gone.

Cooper's experiences after reappearing in the Red Room are fraught with peril and confusion. He is guided by Phillip Gerard (who has apparently shed all connections to his past persona of Mike, the Black Lodge being who, along with his "familiar," Bob, sowed chaos in the real world); he encounters a transcendent being who takes the form of Laura Palmer; he is instructed by the bizarre creature known as The Evolution of the Arm; and, finally, he is caught in an elaborate trap set for him by the doppelganger of The Evolution of the Arm. This trap hurls Cooper out of the Red Room to a supposed death. But Cooper is somehow saved, first by being rerouted to the glass box in New York City, and then by accessing the Mansion Room of Naido and American Girl.

From the Mansion Room Cooper finally exits and returns to the real world, but the Cooper who emerges is far different than the one who entered. This Cooper is an empty vessel, a being without personality or affect. He is essentially an automaton, relying on others for guidance and direction. Weak, vulnerable, lost, what good is this new Cooper?

What good? *All* good.

Where Mr. C (the "bad" Cooper) is purely evil with no redeeming qualities, the newly emerged Cooper (who has taken the place of a man named Dougie Jones) is purely good. He has no negative qualities whatsoever. These two entities are exact opposites. Dale Cooper's yin and yang.

Perfect Courage

DURING THE YEARS between *Twin Peaks* Season 2 and *Twin Peaks: The Return*, I often pondered how to define a "purely good" Dale Cooper and questioned whether such a being would be superior to a "whole" Dale Cooper, a Cooper composed of his two opposite selves. In *Wrapped In Plastic*, Craig Miller and I debated the merits of a whole Cooper versus a divided Cooper. I believed that a "purely good" Cooper would be a weak individual. I called him "diminished" and said a good Cooper "would only be half-a-person; he would, in all likelihood, be incapable of comprehending the human condition, of understanding the impulses and emotions and weaknesses that contribute to the full essence of human behavior. What's more, his abilities as a detective would be immediately impaired." Craig saw it differently. He believed a good Cooper would be "a sort of super-being, able to understand the lessons he learned while 'whole,' but never giving in to base temptations; it would represent a spiritual maturity of Cooper who, far from lacking in crime-solving ability, would be the perfect incorruptible cop."

Turns out, Craig and I were each half right (or half wrong, depending on your perspective). We couldn't comprehend the scope and limitations of absolute goodness, and we certainly didn't have the imaginations of Mark Frost and David Lynch. Neither of us could predict "Dougie/Cooper," a character who is both impaired *and* a super-being.

In *The Return*, Lynch and Frost posit that a purely good being would be a passive figure who *radiates* goodness. Every action we take as human beings brings with it the possibility of some unforeseen negative side-effect, and therefore a purely good person would never act. He or she would merely drift through life following a route dictated by time and tide. We see this with the Dougie aspect of Cooper. He lacks any kind of agency, lacks the capability of understanding the most basic human needs. He cannot communicate, eat, walk, or even use the bathroom without guidance from another.

Any action that Dougie takes of his own accord is prompted by otherworldly forces. Visions of the Red Room steer him through the Silver Mustang casino; flashes of light alert him to the untrustworthiness of co-workers and potential fraud in his insurance case files; unseen powers impel Dougie to defend himself against the threat of Ike "The Spike." Without these forces to prompt him, Dougie remains a static character, a still presence among the lives of his friends, family, and co-workers.

But just because he takes no action doesn't mean he's powerless. On the contrary, this version of Cooper may be the most formidable being in *Twin Peaks*. Craig Miller was right when he described a purely good Cooper as a "super-being." That's what Dougie is, a supernatural figure akin to the angels that appear to Laura Palmer in *Fire Walk With Me*—angels that bring with them the power of hope, optimism, joy and strength. To encounter one of these beings is to be changed for the better. In Laura Palmer's darkest moments of doubt and despair, when all hope is gone, and she is about to succumb to her worst impulses—when she sees herself as nothing but worthless—Laura encounters an angel, and hope is restored. She finds faith in herself again. She rejects evil and embraces good. The angel does not *make* Laura good, it shows her the light, restores her self-confidence, reminds her that the power of decency and virtue have always been part of her.

Like Laura with her angel, every person in *The Return* who meets Dougie becomes a better person. He brings out their best, inspires and elevates them. "Oh, but when I saw the face of God I was changed," Phillip Gerard exclaims early in the original *Twin Peaks* (a line David Lynch added while shooting the pilot). This message resonates in *The Return*. The power of good is the power of change, and Dougie represents this power. His very presence is transformative.

Look at all the people Dougie positively impacts: Jade shows pity on Dougie and drives him to the Silver Mustang Casino; the cashier in the casino is moved by her brief encounter with him and reaches out to help; Janey-E courageously confronts the loan sharks who have been targeting Dougie and enforces her own conditions of payback; Bushnell Mullins becomes protective of Dougie and ultimately grateful for his work; the Mitchum Brothers (who want to kill Dougie before they meet him) become his fast friends, bringing him gifts and making sure his family is provided for; Anthony Sinclair, who sets out to kill Dougie (and almost succeeds), has a dramatic change of heart and confesses all his crimes. He wants to "make things right" and declares that "Dougie saved my life." Sinclair won't be the first to make that claim: The slot-machine lady has her fortunes change, literally, after she wins big at Dougie's slot machines. Later, her personal life improves when she is reunited with her estranged son. She sums up Dougie's influence when she says, "You changed my life. I have my life back again. You *saved* my life." She turns to the Mitchums and says, "I hope you realize what a special person you have with you." Dougie is indeed special, he improves lives—he saves lives—just by his positive presence.

Still, despite all his powerful positivity, Dougie is a cipher. He is not a whole person. He has no character, independence, or ambition. He cannot choose direction. He lacks intuition and comprehension. His purity has erased all the quirks and traits and complexities of a fully rounded, "warts-and-all" human being. By being superhuman, Dougie ends up being less than human.

Dougie is an amplified, idealized half-of-Cooper. He is pure goodness (and, as such, an impossibility). The same is true of Mr. C, who is the amplified, contemptible half-of-Cooper. Like Dougie, Mr. C is super-powered. But where Dougie is an angel, Mr. C is a demon who corrupts everyone he meets. Otis, Beulah, Chantal, Hutch (all of whom are already loathsome creatures) fall easily under his spell, while others, like Mr. Todd and Warden Murphy, are compelled to do bad simply because they come into contact with him. When Mr. C superhumanly kills a gang-leader, the rest of the gang immediately shifts allegiance. One member (Muddy) refers to Mr. C as "boss," while another (the mild-mannered accountant) falls under Mr. C's thrall and offers to procure money. Everyone who encounters Mr. C quickly surrenders to his power. They fall to the touch of the "devilish one."

I am a Lonely Soul

HOW DO WE RECONCILE the existence of two extreme versions of Dale Cooper? As I mentioned, the ending of Season 2 suggests that Cooper divided into two beings, something I described in *Wrapped In Plastic* when I argued that Cooper "literally comes apart...the imbalance in his psyche results in his division into two physical beings: Cooper has been reduced to mere rudiments, distilled into components of 'good' and 'bad.'"

But what we see in *The Return* complicates things. Dougie and Mr. C are not simply halves-of-Cooper waiting to be reunited, they are *aspects* of him, avatars in Cooper-form that embody extremes—pure good and pure evil. Could these two beings recombine to make a full being, a "complete Cooper," a balance of his opposite identities? I have my doubts.

These vastly different Coopers could never recombine to reconstitute the original Cooper because they would cancel each other out. They would obliterate one another, leaving a void where Cooper should be.

Like all human beings, Dale Cooper is more than the sum of distilled components, more than a "good Dale" and a "bad Dale" recombined. His spirit comes from somewhere else, a deeper essence. It comes from his soul.

That's it exactly. Cooper's *soul* remains in the Red Room, while avatars of Good Coop and Bad Coop are loose in the world. Way back at the end of Season 2, Cooper was willing to sacrifice his soul when Windom Earle asked for it in exchange for Annie Blackburn's life. Cooper didn't hesitate; he agreed to the exchange. But when Earle attempted to take Cooper's soul he was stopped by Bob and subsequently killed. Hawk had earlier warned Cooper that if he faced his shadow self with imperfect courage, his soul would be annihilated. But this did not happen. Cooper's soul survived its confrontation with Earle (and Bob) but was doomed to stay trapped in the Red Room.

In *The Return*, the doppelganger of The Arm recognizes the power of Cooper's soul and seeks to finish the job Bob started. It tries to annihilate Cooper's soul by banishing it to a place called the Nonexistent. The Arm's doppelganger fails. Cooper's soul remains in the Red Room, while another avatar—the Cooper that eventually becomes "Dougie"—is freed.

DALE COOPER IN THE RED ROOM is not a half-Cooper. He is weakened, yes, enervated and imprisoned, but he is still a whole Cooper waiting to return to a more meaningful existence. He is, quite obviously, a lost soul.

And his is a passive existence. He can only watch from the Red Room as two aspects of himself attempt, each according to their abilities, to outlast the other. Neither of Cooper's selves will be triumphant, however, because Mr. C cannot destroy Dougie, just as Dougie cannot act against Mr. C. These two beings co-exist in the world, equally balanced, with no power over the other.

Things will stay this way until Cooper can be rehabilitated. Eventually this happens, thanks in part to a plan put in place by The Fireman and Major Briggs. The demon Bob, who, for Cooper, may simply be a figment of Cooper's darker impulses ("the evil that men do") is exorcised, and balance is restored, a balance that comes not from physical reintegration, but from a psychological *recalibration*. If Cooper had truly divided into two separate beings, it stands to reason that the reunion of those beings would restore him. But this never happens. Mr. C fades away, and Dougie disappears, and there's just Cooper in the Red Room made whole again.

Whole, but not perfect. Cooper, in the Red Room, finally accepts he is not the paragon he thought himself to be. He's a composite of good and evil, light and dark. "In order to appreciate one, you have to know the other," Lynch tells us. "The more darkness you can gather up, the more light you can see too." Once Cooper accepts his flaws and failings, he is ready to move on to another story.

He still has a job to do. The Fireman's mission awaits.

PART 4:

...BRINGS BACK SOME MEMORIES

LOST IN THE LABYRINTH of the Silver Mustang Casino, Cooper hits big on every slot machine he plays.* The casino supervisor, Mr. Burns, watches with dread, realizing how much Cooper's winnings are costing the casino and what price he, Burns, will have to pay for it. Nearby, the lady slot-addict is humming with excitement, energized by the riches flowing around her. She asks Cooper to choose a machine for her, and Cooper, seeing a Red Room avatar hovering nearby, points. She plays the machine and hits big. Alarms blare and coins cascade, and the lady turns to Cooper and thanks him joyfully, profusely. Cooper stares and smiles.

A man, Bill Shaker, recognizes Cooper as Dougie Jones and, sensing Cooper's distress, reminds Cooper he lives in Lancelot Court, near Merlin's Market, in the house with the red door. These King Arthur references are no mere coincidences. In Season 2, Cooper left Twin Peaks through a portal in Glastonbury Grove, a location named after the mythical resting place of King Arthur. Cooper's mind remembers this connection, and the King Arthur mythos continue to manifest in his filtered reality.

Mr. Burns orders a limousine to bring Cooper home. A short while later, Cooper sits in the limo with his bag of winnings while Smithie,

---

* Note that some close-up shots of the machines are "mirrored," the slot machines shown in reverse (the lettering on the machines is clearly backward).

the driver, circles Lancelot Court searching for a house with a red door. He finds it, stops the limo, and helps Cooper out. They stand together in the dark staring at the house. Suddenly, Cooper flinches and looks down, as if aware something is about to happen. An owl hoots, and Cooper and Smithie look up to see it fly overhead.

Ostensibly, the owl is a call-back to the original series, a reminder that owls once figured prominently in the narrative. Owls don't play any significant role in *The Return*, but this one is still important. This owl is not at all what it seems. Remnants of memory swirl deep in Cooper's subconscious, and, once again, one surfaces and installs itself into the world. (Sycamore Street and the King Arthur locations are other examples.) The owl is but another vestige of memory, appearing as it does because Cooper continues to see the reality he wants to see. Indeed, Cooper somehow sensed the owl before it even made a noise.

The red door opens, and Dougie Jones's wife, Janey-E, walks out. She strides toward Cooper, slaps him across the face and rebukes him for being gone three days without a word. He missed work, he missed their son, Sonny Jim's, birthday party. She grabs Cooper by the neck and marches him into the house, forcefully placing him in a chair and asking where he's been and why he didn't call. Birthday decorations, including a prominent red balloon, adorn the house.

Janey-E opens Cooper's bag and is stunned to see the money inside. She is angry and suspicious, but she softens when she sees all the money. She sighs with relief, realizing this windfall will be enough to, in her words, "pay them back." Janey-E is so relieved she kisses Cooper on the head and tells him she is glad he is home. Cooper, looking around absently, repeats the word, "home."

GORDON COLE ARRIVES at the office of the FBI Director and exchanges a few words with a clerk named Bill Kennedy. Cole asks if Martha (presumably Bill's wife) has "fixed that thing with Paul." Bill replies, "Good of you to remember. Paul is now in the North Pole." Cole processes that information and says, "Well, there you go!" and claps Bill on the shoulder. A whole story exists within this brief exchange, and, like so much else in *The Return*, the viewer is left to imagine what it's all about. Who is Paul? Why does his presence in the North Pole fix things with Martha? By extension, how does this make things better for Bill? We'll never know. Frost and Lynch refuse to deliver a punchline because the set-up is enough. We can fill in the blanks and concoct our own outlandish scenarios surrounding Bill, Martha, and Paul.

Cole waits, and after a moment Denise Bryson enters the room. When we last saw Denise in Season 2 of *Twin Peaks*, she was an agent of the Drug Enforcement Agency and an associate of Dale Cooper. Once identifying as a man named Dennis Bryson, Denise found that wearing women's clothes relaxed her, and she started identifying as a woman. All these years later, Denise has risen to the top of the hierarchy in a very progressive, open-minded, FBI. She is the chief of staff of the entire agency.

Cole tells Denise he is going to see Cooper, but Denise already knows about the trip. When Cole asks how she knows, Denise deflects and asks if Cole is bringing Agent Tammy Preston with him. Cole senses Denise's suspicion and assures her he is "old school." He reminds her that he has always supported Denise and her life choices. In the past, he protected her against close-minded co-workers, telling them to "fix their hearts or die." This strong, positive statement from Cole speaks to an idealized atmosphere in the agency, one that arguably allowed Denise to claim the agency's top spot.

Denise appreciates the compliment but circles back to Tammy, commenting to Cole that Tammy is beautiful. Denise is getting a bit personal here, and her comments suggest she finds Tammy attractive and that she has been projecting her desires about Tammy onto Cole. She may even be jealous. There's an implication that Tammy may have told Denise about the trip and that there may be more between the two besides a professional relationship, but, as with Paul in the North Pole, we'll never know. Cole exits the office, and this is the last we see of the curious, campy, strong-willed Denise Bryson.

Denise is unique among the gallery of *Twin Peaks* characters. Played by David Duchovny with a bit of flair and a hint of pageantry (watch as she sways, ever-so-slightly, when she first hears that Cooper's been found, or when she fans herself with her hand after Cole leaves), Denise is a figure both of command and comic relief. In *The Return* she embellishes the story exactly the way she did in the original series, an eccentric, perfectly suited to the environment she inhabits. Her appearance in *The Return* is welcome, if disappointingly brief.

AT THE TWIN PEAKS SHERIFF'S STATION, Lucy Brennan speaks on the phone with Sheriff Frank Truman about the station's thermostat. She's confused about how the device functions and worried it doesn't work when there's no one in the office to observe it. (She's had a repairman look into the problem, but she's still no closer to understanding how and why the heat turns on.) Lucy's nonsensical digressions are easy to overlook, but Lucy is pondering profound metaphysical concepts such as Observer Effect and the Uncertainty Principal. Lucy genuinely wants to know: Does her presence affect the thermostat? "What happens when no one is here?" she asks. "Would the heat still be on then?" These questions speak to the conceptual framework of the story being told. Is reality altered by the presence of an observer? Are we seeing a reality shaped by Cooper's watching presence?[*]

Cooper can't help but see a world distorted by the limitations of his mind, a concept rooted in the science of quantum mechanics, where "Observer Effect" postulates that observation of phenomenon changes that phenomenon. Specific quantum experiments, such as the 1998 Weizmann Experiment, suggest that "the greater the amount of 'watching,' the greater the observer's influence on what actually takes place." These are difficult concepts to grasp, but physicists and philosophers take them seriously. We might dismiss these ideas as ephemeral notions when Lucy raises them, but we shouldn't. Lucy, however unwittingly, is probing the nature of reality. More importantly, she gives us a glimpse into the underlying mechanisms that drive the *Twin Peaks* narrative.[†]

Lucy loses connection with Truman, who has been standing outside talking on his cell phone. Truman enters the station, startling Lucy, who screams and falls over backward in her chair. Exasperated, Truman tells Andy he couldn't stay outside and continue the charade. Once the connection was lost, he had to come in.

---

[*] The Log Lady, herself, asks the same question in the Lynch-scripted introduction to episode 9 of the original series: "Does our thinking affect what goes on outside us? I think it does."

[†] Such a reading also implies that each of us watching *The Return* alters the story according to our own mindsets. I don't think that's too far-fetched. Opinions on *The Return* vary wildly because different viewers bring different expectations to the story. *The Return* speaks uniquely to each viewer because each viewer speaks uniquely to it.

Andy consoles Lucy and tries to explain how cell phones work. "I just don't understand how this keeps happening over and over again," he says, indicating that Lucy's problem with cell phones is a chronic issue. Lucy behaves as if trapped in time, unable to grasp the concept of a basic technology. Maybe she won't be trapped forever—maybe something will happen to break Lucy free of her stupor—but for now she's stuck in place. Cell phones simply don't fit with her perception of reality.

Frank Truman, meanwhile, has made his way deeper into the station. Frank is a new character in the *Twin Peaks* ensemble, and his presence is a stark reminder that Sheriff Harry S. Truman (played in the original series by Michael Ontkean) is not part of the new story. David Lynch and Mark Frost could have recast the role of Harry Truman (a similar thing was done for the character of Donna Hayward in *Fire Walk With Me*, when Moira Kelly replaced Lara Flynn Boyle), but they chose instead to add a new character, Frank Truman (Harry's brother). This was the right choice. Although some fans were disappointed Harry Truman was not in *The Return*, they would have been more disappointed (perhaps even "ticked off") had Harry been played by a different actor.

Robert Forster, the actor playing Frank Truman, brings a grounded and earnest quality to his character. His Truman is a commanding presence who, by the very way he walks through the station, conveys authority and control. Truman is world-weary but dutiful, gruff but kind. He respects his officers, and they (for the most part) respect him. This new Truman is a solid presence in an otherwise quirky setting and a welcome addition to the world of *Twin Peaks*.

Truman greets Deputy Bobby Briggs in the hallway and shares his suspicion that "Chinese designer drugs" are making their way into Twin Peaks from across the Canadian border. Truman asks if Bobby has seen anything on his surveillance cameras, but Bobby has nothing new to report.

It's a surprise to see Bobby Briggs dressed as a Sheriff's deputy. In the original series, Bobby was a punk teenager with destructive habits and criminal tendencies. Back then, it was Bobby who bought and distributed drugs; it was Bobby who defied the police. As the series progressed, however, Bobby got better. He matured, reformed, and planned to make a life with Shelly Johnson, the woman he loved, apparently taking to heart what his father, Major Briggs, told him so many years ago: "I have a tremendous feeling of optimism and confidence in you and your future." Still, despite having navigated away from his criminal past, Bobby remains a haunted soul.

In the conference room, Hawk has laid out much of the evidence from the decades-old Laura Palmer case. Andy, Lucy and Deputy Chad Broxford listen as Hawk explains to Truman The Log Lady's message about something being missing. Truman takes Hawk's story seriously. He does not dismiss or question the odd nature of the case; he ponders it, weighs it, and puts his trust in Hawk. This, despite Deputy Chad's mockery of The Log Lady's eccentric reputation (Chad refers to The Log Lady as a "10-96"—police code for a person exhibiting crazy or psychotic behavior). Truman scolds Chad and dismisses him, but Chad delivers one last parting shot at The Log Lady, infuriating Andy and drawing sharp stares from Hawk and Truman. Clearly, nobody likes Chad.

Just then, Bobby walks into the room and stops short at the sight of Laura Palmer's picture. Overcome by a cascade of memories, Bobby starts to cry. The image of Laura is like a punch in the gut.[*]

This isn't the first time Bobby has cried over Laura. In episode 5 of the original series, Dr. Jacoby forced Bobby to confront difficult truths about Bobby's relationship with Laura, and when Bobby admitted to himself that Laura had never really loved him, he broke down sobbing. Twenty-five years later, Bobby is still overcome. Memories of Laura Palmer overwhelm, no matter how much time has passed.

Deputy Jesse Holcomb interrupts the meeting to announce a man, Wally Brando, is waiting outside and wants to speak with Truman. Andy and Lucy gasp with joy and rush out of the room. Their son has come home for a visit.

There he is, Wally Brando, sitting on his motorcycle in the dark parking lot of the Twin Peaks Sheriff's station. He's dressed exactly like

---

[*] It wouldn't be *Twin Peaks* without a crying deputy. Recall that Andy cried when he encountered the corpse of Laura Palmer back in 1989.

Marlon Brando in the 1953 film, *The Wild One.*[*] He's wearing Brando's same tilted cap, monogrammed leather jacket, and white T-shirt with black neckline. But his similarities to Brando go further than that. Wally speaks with a noticeable cadence, as if mimicking the style and delivery of Brando's performance in *The Godfather.* He reinforces a connection to that film when he twice mentions that Harry Truman is, in fact, his godfather.

Frank Truman has apparently met Wally before and endured similar protracted performances. He suffers Wally's visit kindly and delivers the perfect valediction: "May the road rise up to meet your wheels." This delights Wally, who agrees that the road is, undeniably, his "dharma." Then, with an expansive gesture, he indicates that the Sheriff's station—and all of Twin Peaks—is Truman's.

Wally Brando is an enigma. Part comic-relief, part conjured spirit, Wally briefly passes through town to deliver a message to his parents. Where did he come from? Why is his visit so fleeting? I find it curious that Wally manifests from the darkness shortly after Lucy fainted in the station. It's as if her distress summoned Wally from some other plane, drew him back to serve as a constant, a grounding presence in her life. ("He came in unannounced," Lucy says.) Wally ostensibly releases his childhood bedroom to Lucy and Andy ("such sweet people") so that they may convert it into a study, but maybe Wally is really freeing Lucy, helping her break free from her fugue. ("That's such beautiful news," Lucy exclaims.)

So ends the one and only scene featuring Wally Brando, son of Andy and Lucy Brennan. Wally's appearance is curious and inexplicable, but I take comfort in the idea that Wally pointed his parents toward a brighter, enlightened future and may have—*may have*—opened them to their own unique dharma, one that will help them find courage in dire times.

---

[*] An early script to the *Twin Peaks* pilot describes an opening scene straight out of *The Wild One*: "A flying wedge of motorcycle riders driving Harleys rides into view; seven young men, all between seventeen and twenty-one, clean-cut, wearing leather jackets.... ride through various parts of the city." And perhaps it's only coincidence, but in *The Wild One* the biker gang encounters a local sheriff named Harry Bleeker, who has a brother named Frank.

MORNING IN LAS VEGAS. Phillip Gerard contacts Cooper to say he, Cooper, has been tricked, and that "one of you must die." This ominous message introduces a sense of urgency to the story. Gerard is essentially explaining that two Coopers cannot co-exist in the real world. There was supposed to be an exchange—Mr. C for Dale Cooper—but that didn't happen, and now there is an imbalance. One Cooper will have to die to set things right.

But is that correct? Gerard isn't savvy to the larger game at play. While it's true both Coopers are in danger, the real threat is that one of them will die before Cooper in the Red Room can rehabilitate his psyche. If either Mr. C or Dougie were to die, pieces of Cooper's personality would forever be erased, leaving only a diminished Cooper in the real world. (The *true* threat to Cooper is Bob, who must be eliminated (literally or metaphorically) before Cooper can reintegrate his two selves.)

Cooper can't pay attention to Gerard because of his intense need to urinate. Janey-E finds Cooper in distress[*] and marches him to the bathroom, where Cooper protractedly, "aggressively," relieves himself. After he's done, Cooper notices his reflection in the mirror and stares at it with a dim sense of recognition. This scene is striking because it recalls the shocking final shot of the original series where the bad Cooper smashed his head into a mirror and saw the fractured image of Bob staring back. Perhaps in this moment Cooper faintly senses that Bob is still a threat.

A moment later, Sonny Jim appears in the hallway. Cooper sees the boy for the first time and reflexively puts his hand on his lower stomach. When I first saw this, I thought Cooper was remembering being stabbed in the stomach by Windom Earle (which happened in the last episode of Season 2), but that makes no sense. Why would Sonny Jim provoke such a reaction? Now, I think Cooper is acknowledging his identity as a father. Cooper intuitively grasps that Sonny Jim is the "fruit of his loins," that he, Cooper, is a biological source for Sonny Jim's existence. Cooper places his hand on his body to acknowledge a genetic connection. There is a sense of wonder in Cooper at this mo-

---

[*] Janey-E here refers to Cooper as "Mr. Dreamweaver," perhaps because she believes Cooper is daydreaming (which explains her dismissal of his distant behavior). But the reference is also a hint that Cooper is an observing presence.

ment. Sonny Jim smiles, and Cooper responds with a smile of his own, wide and genuine.[*]

AT YANKTON FEDERAL PRISON in South Dakota, Inspector Hollister and Warden Murphy update Gordon Cole on the Cooper case: When they found Mr. C, he was vomiting a poisonous substance, which they have sent to the lab for analysis. (The poison is almost certainly garmonbozia, the physical form of "pain and sorrow." Unfortunately, the results of the toxicology analysis will never be revealed.) Hollister shows Cole what the police found in the trunk of Mr. C's car: a package of cocaine, a machine gun, and a dog leg (in effect, a whole different kind of Congressman's Dilemma).

Cole, Albert and Tammy enter an interrogation room, and Cole pushes a button. A shutter rolls up revealing the shackled figure of Mr. C staring through a glass partition. Mr. C sees Cole and feebly pretends to be Dale Cooper. He smiles mechanically and gives an awkward thumbs-up and says, "It's *yrev*, very good to see you again, old friend." Cole immediately realizes something's wrong, but he is confused. He can't reconcile the man he sees with the Dale Cooper he remembers.

What is Mr. C up to here? Did he mean to mispronounce the word, "very," or did he simply make a mistake? Mr. C seems far too clever for such an obvious gaffe, so it's more likely he is trying to throw Cole off his game, trying to rattle Cole to force him to take a certain action. Always playing a long game, Mr. C's efforts to confuse Cole are part of a plan to bring Diane Evans, Cooper's long-ago assistant, into the mix. This is who Mr. C wants. He wants Diane.

Mr. C speaks robotically and repetitively, explaining he has been secretly working with Phillip Jeffries all these many years. He was on his way to report to Cole before being waylaid by the car accident. As he talks, he shows no affect or concern for his predicament. Mr. C believes he is in control, but his guise weakens when he stares hard at

---

[*] David Lynch often reuses names in his works, and "Sonny Jim" probably originates from Lynch's short film, *Pierre and Sonny Jim* (or from a character named Sonny Jim in *The Elephant Man*). But here's a strange thing: In the early 1900s, a child actor named Bobby Connelly starred in a series of short silent films in which he played a character named Sonny Jim. Like that long-ago character, Sonny Jim of *The Return* is essentially a silent player. That's a tenuous connection, I admit, but also consider this: Before playing Sonny Jim, Connelly appeared in another film where he played a boy named Bobby Briggs. As Carl Rodd would say, "Weird, huh?"

Albert and mentions the messages, he, Mr. C, sent. Albert can't find the courage to return Mr. C's stare and looks away. Cole notices all this, realizes secrets have been kept from him, and ends the interview.

Outside, Cole, Albert, and Tammy assemble in a courtyard in a scene that is tinted heavily with blue. The blue is so dark it's as if the agents are standing in deep twilight (or even underwater). This is no mistake; blue pervades the scene because the world of the FBI agents has changed. Something supernatural has seeped into their lives. Cole knows it, but he's not ready to admit it.

Tammy explains that Mr. C had been driving west before the accident and could not have been on his way to report to Cole. She also reveals that people who have encountered Mr. C have become ill (again, a subplot that will not be addressed again). Tammy wants to know who Phillip Jeffries is, but Cole dismisses her, ostensibly because she is wearing a wire (but really because he wants to speak privately with Albert).

Tammy is offended and reluctantly walks away. As she does, the camera stays focused on her rear-end. Albert and Cole watch her go, and Albert makes a comment about the effect Tammy has on him. Here, David Lynch's framing and dialog overtly objectify Tammy and emphasize her physicality over her other qualities. If the scene was supposed to remind us of what Denise said earlier about Tammy and Cole, it provides little insight into the dynamics between the two agents. Tammy has so far been positioned as an important character with something to contribute, but her portrayal here is at odds with what we've seen of her so far. (For what it's worth, this is the only time Tammy Preston will be objectified in such a way.)

At Cole's prompting, Albert humbly admits he spoke with Phillip Jeffries years ago. Jeffries told him that Cooper was in trouble and needed urgent information. Albert provided Jeffries with the identity of an agent in Colombia, and a week later that man was killed.

Albert may not realize it, but he probably spoke with the imposter Phillip Jeffries, who I theorize is Mike, the Red Room being who pledged to "stop" Bob. It's likely that Mike wanted to kill Mr. C in South America and managed to fool Albert into providing the name of someone who could perform the task. The plan failed (like Mike's plans are prone to do), and the agent was killed. Once again, Mr. C managed to stay a step ahead of Mike.

Cole is stunned by what Albert has revealed. He stares at Albert carefully, deliberately, and says Albert's name. Then he says it again. And again. Cole says Albert's name three times, evaluating Albert in some imperceptible way, measuring the truth of what Albert is telling him. The third time Cole says Albert's name, a high-pitched squealing noise becomes audible. It lasts a long moment while Cole stares at Albert, and then it stops. Once it does, Cole seems subtly satisfied, as if he has made an assessment and concluded that Albert is, in fact, telling the truth. Cole's evaluation provides the merest hint that Cole possesses paranormal abilities (which he probably does). Cole has lots of secrets, not least of which are his uncanny powers of perception.

Convinced he can still trust Albert, Cole expresses his worry about Cooper and mentions the unusual greeting Mr. C gave them: "Something is very wrong," he says and asks if Albert understands the situation. Albert pauses and then declares: "Blue Rose." Cole agrees: "It doesn't get any bluer." (And, literally, the scene is so saturated with blue it's hard to imagine it could be bluer. David Lynch, not always known for subtlety, drives his point home here in the most overt way possible.)

Blue Rose: The enigmatic phrase uttered by Major Briggs in Part 3. Blue Rose: The label for a special kind of mysterious FBI case. Cole and Albert both know they are dealing with something very unusual, something beyond the normal forensic scope of most investigations. They know supernatural forces are at work.

Cole believes the next step is for someone else ("one certain person") to evaluate "Cooper." Albert agrees and says he knows just where to find her. And here, perhaps, Mr. C's plan is set in motion: Diane is about to be drawn into the story.

Part 4 concludes on an ominous note in a dark and brooding setting. David Lynch's exaggerated Cole turns quiet and contemplative, while Miguel Ferrer's caustic Albert becomes sober and remorseful. For the first time, Cole and Albert are allowed nuance. They become real, flawed, rounded beings. Albert has made a mistake keeping secrets from Cole, and his regret is palpable. Meanwhile, Gordon Cole is deadly serious and unsteady in a way we've never seen. Although determined to get to the bottom of things, he appears genuinely flummoxed. His line, "I don't understand this situation at all" is rather stunning. If Gordon Cole is worried, then all of us should be.

Cole is attuned to a wavelength few other characters in *The Return* can access. He sees through the illusions of the everyday to a deeper reality. Cole is beginning to grasp that he might be subject to someone else's Observer Effect. He doesn't yet know Cooper is the observer, but he knows something, or someone, is interfering with his perceptions.

Cole is off-balance, lacking the language to even frame the right kind of questions. But that will change. Once Cole gets deeper into this case his mind will open, and he will know enough to ask: "Who is the dreamer?"

PART 5:
CASE FILES

IN THE GHOSTLY NIGHTTIME of Rancho Rosa, Gene and Jake sit in a car watching the house Cooper had earlier exited with Jade. Gene calls Lorraine, the woman Duncan Todd hired to orchestrate the hit on Dougie Jones, to explain they have yet to find Dougie. This news puts Lorraine into a panic, and she hangs up and texts a single character (the number "2") to a receiver in Argentina. Somewhere, in a dusty, abandoned crawlspace, a simple electronic device receives the signal and beeps twice.

Why is Lorraine contacting unidentified forces in Argentina? Given her desperation, you would assume she would contact Mr. Todd to apprise him of the delay in killing Dougie, but instead she sends a coded signal to Argentina. We might assume Lorraine is making contact with Phillip Jeffries, whose backstory suggests he's in Argentina (a deleted scene from *Fire Walk With Me* shows Jeffries staying in a fancy hotel in Buenos Aires before mysteriously vanishing and reappearing in the Philadelphia FBI offices[*]), but this seems unlikely. Jeffries, as Gordon Cole tells us in Part 17, "doesn't really exist anymore."

Lorraine is probably sending a message to Mr. C, who, the story tells us, has been ranging all over South America—from Colombia (where he killed an agent), to Brazil (where he owns a home in Rio de

---

[*] This scene can be found in *The Missing Pieces*, a home video feature David Lynch composed for release on Blu-ray Disc. Ostensibly, the scene exists outside of *Twin Peaks* continuity, but Mark Frost's book, *The Final Dossier*, explicitly establishes Jeffries in Buenos Aires.

Janiero), to Buenos Aires, Argentina, (where, according to page 109 of Mark Frost's *The Final Dossier*, Mr. C also has a residence). No wonder Lorraine is so terrified when she makes her call; she is making direct contact with Mr. C.

IN BUCKHORN, CONSTANCE TALBOT extracts a wedding ring from the stomach of the headless male victim (whom, we soon learn, is Major Garland Briggs). The ring is inscribed: "To Dougie, with love, Janey-E." How and why the ring ended up in the body will remain a mystery. Maybe Mr. C put it there, or maybe Major Briggs swallowed it. Either way, this curious development is a plot point that doesn't really make sense.[*]

IN THE SHADOWS of Yankton Federal Prison, Mr. C stares into a mirror and remembers his long-ago alliance with Bob. Mr. C's reflection subtly alters, transforming into the visage of Bob. "You're still with me," Mr. C says, confirming what David Lynch said long ago about the relationship between Bob and Cooper's evil half: "Coop wasn't occupied by Bob. *Part of him was.* The one that came out was with Bob." (Emphasis added.)

IN AN OFFICE SOMEWHERE in Twin Peaks, Mike Nelson meets with a prospective employee, a young man named Steven Burnett. Mike is appalled by Steven's résumé and disgusted by his lack of preparation and gives Steven a good dressing-down. Steven, blind-sided, makes a hasty exit.

There's irony here. Mike Nelson was once a high school hooligan (a loser just like Steven) palling around with his best friend, Bobby Briggs, and getting in (or near) serious trouble. Now, Mike has found himself squarely in American middle-class middle-age. We don't know what Mike's job is (he could be a financial advisor, a real-estate

---

[*] It's not the only one. Some parts of *The Return* remain confounding and contradictory no matter how much you try to unpack them. Your best bet in grasping the backstory is to read Mark Frost's book, *The Final Dossier*, but even there you'll come away scratching your head. Nowhere in the book does Frost address the wedding ring mystery. And try as he might to make sense of the roles of Ray Monroe and Phillip Jeffries, or how Bill Hastings and Ruth Davenport obtained the coordinates, Frost eventually writes himself into a corner.

developer, an accountant[*]), but he's stuck behind a messy desk, dressed in a suit and tie. And he's dealing with a young punk who can't get his act together. The past echoes.

At the Sheriff's station, Frank Truman's wife, Doris, complains to Frank about a variety of domestic problems including a leaking pipe, her dad's dilapidated car, and other chaotic incidents going on at home (apparently, the twins are coming this weekend, and Dwight has diarrhea). Frank takes it all in calmly and reassures Doris that everything is being tended to. Still distraught and certainly dissatisfied, Doris marches away.

Doris Truman is a reminder of the many unhappy marriages in *Twin Peaks*, most of which are tragic, unstable unions. To be sure, not all are hopeless. Andy and Lucy Brennan are happy; they genuinely respect and honor one another. And the marriage of Garland and Betty Briggs was a success, a bond between two deeply connected and devoted people. But these are the exceptions.

Infidelity and violence simmers beneath the surfaces of many marriages in *Twin Peaks*. It's been that way since the original series, where Norma Jennings suffered in her relationship with Hank Jennings, and Shelly Johnson endured a tormented time with Leo Johnson. There was more: Ben and Sylvia Horne lived a mockery of a marriage. So did Pete and Catherine Martell. The Hayward marriage seemed solid, yet even it suffered from secrets and mistrust. (And, of course, pain and anguish dwelled at the core of the Palmer marriage, where Leland and Sarah Palmer endured an unearthly torment. Theirs is a union in its own horrific category.)

In *The Return*, we learn that the marriage of Shelly and Bobby Briggs did not last, the marriage of Beverly and Tom Paige is stressed to the breaking point, the marriage of Becky and Steven Burnett is abusive and harrowing, and the perverted marriage of Chantal and Hutch, successful though it may be for each partner, embraces infidelity and thrives on violence. These and other marriages in *The Return* are troubled, stressful loci.

Which brings us back to Doris Truman. On the surface, Doris inhabits a troubling cliché: the hectoring wife. Such a character (usually

---

[*] Mike is probably an insurance agent (after all, it's about insurance).

oriented in the narrative through the viewpoint of the husband) is a nuisance, a complainer, an obstacle a husband must navigate. We see this in other marriages. Sylvia Horne still hectors Ben, threatening legal action if he fails to reimburse her for the theft she's suffered. Janey-E Jones fits the pattern, too, scolding "Dougie" and delivering ultimatums. The classic hectoring wife in *Twin Peaks* is Nadine Hurley, who, in the original series, relentlessly insults, threatens and dominates her husband, Ed.

But look deeper at these characters and you'll see more complicated stories: Sylvia endures the pain of multi-generational trauma. Janey-E justifiably responds to the self-indulgent behavior of Dougie Jones. And Nadine, poor Nadine, suffers from decades of emotional disorder. Nadine does not seek to punish Ed Hurley; she simply has not learned how to love him. She carries scars both physical and psychological and deserves sympathy and devotion, and that's exactly what Ed has given her for over a quarter of a century.

Like Nadine, Doris Truman is also unwell, having suffered a devastating personal loss. Doris is a victim, not a perpetrator. And Frank Truman remains steadfast by her side.

Marriages in *Twin Peaks* are unhappy, yes, but the partners in these marriages are struggling against an unfair world. Rather than failures, these marriages are successes. They exemplify the for-better-or-worse commitment, one partner shouldering the burden of the other's troubled state. Spouses in these marriages are resolute and true, recognizing that the union of two souls is larger than the separate lives of either single partner. If there are heroes in *Twin Peaks*, they are Frank Truman and Ed Hurley and even Janey-E Jones, each suffering in their own way, each providing patience and understanding and love to someone in need.

OUTSIDE THE JONES RESIDENCE in Las Vegas, Sonny Jim waits in the family car to be driven to school. Cooper stares at the boy and is overcome with sadness. A tear rolls down his cheek, and he manages a weak smile. Cooper is still adjusting to the physical reality of his son, and, like he did in the hallway when he first laid eyes on Sonny Jim, he's responding in a profoundly visceral way. Moved that he has a child, Cooper feels regret that he's missed out on the boy's life. The world

Cooper now inhabits is not truly his, these are not his wife and child, and he mourns all that he's lost.

Janey-E drives Cooper to Dougie's office building. A large object draped in white sheets and covered in red balloons occupies the plaza outside the building. (The object under the sheet is a sculpture titled, "Triumph" by artist James Thomas Russell, but David Lynch chose not to show the work in *The Return*.) As Cooper crosses the plaza, his attention is drawn to a bronze statue of man holding a pistol in his extended arm. (A curious object, the statue is a tribute to David Lynch's father, Donald Lynch, who once worked in the Forest Service. According to Lynch, his father "managed to take a picture of himself holding a pistol out with a stance, and that was the impetus for the statue…. It doesn't even look like him really, but it's the pose.") Cooper mimics the statue's pose, perhaps dimly remembering his own time as a lawman.

Cooper wanders the plaza until Phil, one of Dougie's co-workers, leads him into an elevator. Phil greets Cooper with a rhetorical question: "Off in dreamland again, huh, Dougie?" (Another hint that Cooper is an observing presence.) Phil is carrying a tray of coffee cups, and Cooper grabs a cup and greedily slurps. Phil chuckles and says, "Damn good joe, huh?" To which Cooper reacts with the ultimate of Cooper lines: "Damn good joe."

Phil and Cooper exit on the seventh floor and into the lobby of the Lucky 7 Insurance Agency.[*] Phil leads Cooper into a room where other insurance agents are preparing for a meeting with the head of the agency, Bushnell Mullins.[†] Phil, already under the influence of Cooper's radiating goodness, shepherds Cooper to a chair. Moments later, Anthony Sinclair updates Mullins on his various cases, explaining that the agency will have to pay on one of the claims. As Sinclair speaks,

[*] The number seven appears throughout *The Return*, possibly because David Lynch is referencing the Maharishi Mahesh Yogi's idea of "seven states of consciousness." The seventh and highest state of consciousness is "total fulfilment in infinite bliss," which might describe Cooper's current state of mind.

[†] Another tribute to an important figure in Lynch's life, "Bushnell Mullins" is named after Bushnell Keeler, the father of Lynch's childhood friend, Toby Keeler. Bushnell Keeler was a painter who guided Lynch in his formative years as an artist.

Cooper sees a green light flicker across Sinclair's face and says, "He's lying." Sinclair becomes angry, but Cooper simply stares.

Cooper might be purely good, but his accusation about Sinclair could be construed as harmful. Still, Cooper is stating a truth that Bushnell Mullins needs to hear, and he phrases the statement in the third person ("*he's* lying" versus "*you're* lying"), thereby mitigating confrontation with (and harm to) Sinclair.

After the meeting, Mullins reprimands Cooper and gives him a stack of case files to review. ("Dougie" has apparently missed a few days of work and has some catching-up to do.) A large promotional poster hangs behind Mullins's desk, showing Mullins in his prime—when he was a boxer known as Bushnell "Battling" Bud Mullins. The poster catches Cooper's attention and makes an impression on his deeper, observing mind. (Boxing will surface again later in the narrative.)

At the Silver Mustang Casino, Rodney and Bradley Mitchum—tough men, seething with fury—punish supervisor Burns for allowing Cooper to win so much money. Rodney punches Burns and savagely kicks him (seven times) in the stomach. Across the room, three women dressed in pink showgirl outfits watch passively. Each woman stares into the distance, inured to this kind of rage. One of them, Candie, absently gestures with her hand, slowly making wave motions. Energy is flowing, washing out from the casino, pulsing past Candie into the larger story.

In Rancho Rosa, this energy bursts forth. The young boy ventures past his drugged-out mother and out toward Dougie's car, curious about the device Gene planted there yesterday. As he reaches for it, a black sportscar wildly rounds the corner and squeals to a stop. Three young men chase the boy away and proceed to break into Dougie's car. One of them starts the car, triggering Gene's device. The car explodes, killing the man and hurling metal fragments onto the street. The boy runs back to his house. His mom wakes, bewildered by the commotion. A dramatic music cue surges on the soundtrack, amplifying the negative energy in the air.

The drugged-out mother is another of the bizarre "watchers" populating the story. Like the misshapen figures who oversaw Ray and Darya's exit from Buella's, she is positioned to observe nearby supernatural occurrences. Derelict in her duty, she has surrendered the role to her son, who dutifully watches the empty house across the street.

Ostensibly, this mother and son are squatters who found temporary refuge in an abandoned home. They have little or no money (not after the mom has purchased her drugs, anyway) and very few prospects. They are, in effect, sad reflections of what Janey-E and Sonny Jim Jones might look like if the real Dougie Jones (gambler, philanderer, narcissist*) had abandoned them to an uncaring world. The mom and son are doppelgangers, shadow-selves of Janey-E and Sonny Jim, haunting the modern-day ghost town that is Rancho Rosa.

Across town, Jade finds the Great Northern Hotel key Cooper dropped in her Jeep and reads the phrase, "CLEAN PLACE REASON-ABLY PRICED" printed on the back. In any objective account, this phrase should not be here. The phrase was never a slogan of the Great Northern; it was a line of Cooper's dialog from the *Twin Peaks* pilot. (When Dale Cooper was looking for a place to stay in Twin Peaks, he told Sheriff Truman, "I need a clean place, reasonably priced.") Some-how, Cooper's spontaneous remark has tangibly manifested in *The Return*, printed on the back of his old key fob. If we needed proof that Cooper's observing mind is seeing the reality it wants to see, here it is. The physical presence of the quote confirms that what we see in *The Return* is filtered through Cooper's psyche. The Great Northern key is literally a key to unlocking *The Return*.†

Although Jade drops the key in a mailbox to send it back to the Great Northern, everything we see here is suspect. Does Jade really mail the key? Or does Cooper *imagine* she does simply because he wants his story to play out a certain way? Cooper visualizes the key as a powerful tool, one that will allow him to access a fantasy. For Cooper, the key will literally open a door into another world. He will need the key soon, and so he makes sure it gets to where it needs to be. (Yes, perhaps Major Briggs imbued the key with magic powers so that it can make its way back to Agent Cooper. Perhaps, like the Owl Cave ring, the key pops

---

* Only a narcissist has a license plate that reads "DUGE LV."

† OK, sure, the quote could simply be a cute nod to the original series, placed there by Lynch and Frost as a metatextual joke or conspiratorial wink at long-time viewers. But if so, it disrupts the narrative, because it's just too obviously wrong.

up where it needs to be. I don't entirely discount this theory—magic objects such as rings and coins populate the story, so a magic key is easy to accept—but if Cooper needed the key all along, why was it so easy for him to lose in the first place?)

BACK IN TWIN PEAKS, Norma Jennings is using a Double R Diner booth as her personal office. Norma's old-school and lo-tech. A bulky telephone, a rolodex, and stacks of ledgers litter her "desk." She's also doing the books by hand. Paper, pen and Wite-out are her go-to implements.[*] Like so many others in *Twin Peaks*, Norma's still very much trapped in the past.

Becky Burnett delivers bread from the Sweet Loaf Bakery to a Double R employee named Toad. But this is not the Toad we remember from the original series. There, Toad was played by actor Kevin Young, but here, Toad is played by actor Marv Rosand. I don't know about you, but I experienced a minor buzz of cognitive dissonance when the new Toad popped-up. If Kevin Young couldn't reprise his role (as Michael Ontkean couldn't for Harry Truman), why bother with Toad at all? The role was so minor there was no need to recast it. (OK, maybe "Toad" is a popular name in Twin Peaks. If so, I wonder how many others are hopping around out there.)

Becky needs money and asks her mother, Shelly Briggs (né Johnson), for a loan. Becky assures Shelly that "he" (i.e., her husband Steven, who just got kicked out of Mike Nelson's office) is looking for work. Shelly is hesitant but gives Becky as much as she can.

Like Norma, Shelly Johnson's life hasn't changed much in twenty-five years. She still works at the Double R Diner, still serves coffee and pie to truckers and locals. Shelly has an adult daughter whom she loves, and so her life at some point must have encompassed more than waitressing. Still, if the trajectory of her story managed to escape the pull of the diner, the gravity of life's obligations brought her back. Shelly Johnson remains an inert figure, stuck in place as the world passes by outside the windows of the Double R.

---

[*] Watch closely: Norma's pen changes from a retractable red pen to a disposable white pen between takes.

Becky leaves, and Shelly and Norma watch as she gets in a car with Steven. They are worried about Becky, worried that she has attached herself to the wrong man, a desperate man, someone who cares less for Becky than he does for himself. Shelly and Norma are not merely suspicious, they exhibit an instinctual worry borne from their own poor and violent marriages. They know a bad relationship when they see one, and they are looking at one right now.

Steven backs his car away from the disapproving gaze of Shelly and Norma and offers Becky a line of white powder (possibly cocaine, but also possibly "Sparkle," the Chinese designer drug that has infiltrated the area). Becky snorts it, and her mood rapidly changes. Vaulted into a state of euphoria, she throws her head back as Steven drives away, all her worries dispelled by a chemical high.

David Lynch masterfully conveys Becky's blissed-out state by tilting the camera up, framing Becky's face from above as she is whisked away in Steven's convertible. The wind blows, and she smiles in rapture. It's a scene distinctly similar to how Lynch once framed Laura Palmer in *Fire Walk With Me*. Laura, of course, was another young woman addicted to drugs and involved with the wrong men, and the connection between these two characters seems deliberate. Becky's situation is more evidence of the cyclical nature of events in *Twin Peaks*. Drugs are still coming in from Canada, and young people are still succumbing to the same vices. There's nothing particularly unique about what's happening here. It happens everywhere. People suffer and make bad choices and suffer even more. Among the many evils haunting *Twin Peaks*, this particular evil is mundane, the pathetic malady of ennui in wasted lives.

Anger and frustration find release atop White Tail Peak as Doctor Jacoby dons his alter ego and begins his webcast as Doctor Amp, champion of the downtrodden and advocate for everyday victims of global capitalism run amok. Doctor Amp works up a head of steam, growing red in the face as he angrily rebukes a society that poisons its population in the pursuit of profit. Doctor Amp is channeling Howard Beale from the film, *Network*. We almost believe he's "mad as hell and not going to take it anymore," until he breaks for a commercial to sell his gold-painted shovels. Turns out, the shovels are a scam, a "magic" totem he hawks to gullible viewers so they can "shovel their way out of the shit." Amp uses a classic fire-and-brimstone spiel, alarming his viewers about imminent dangers and then offering a simple, exclusive solution: Doctor Amp's Gold Shovel.

A crazy old hermit living in the hills, Jacoby rails because he's *off* the rails. Still, he's caught the attention of some familiar faces: Jerry Horne watches Amp with amusement, while Nadine Hurley watches with awe. Amp may be crazy, but he's connecting with people. Maybe he's doing some good, after all.

At the Roadhouse, a young man named Richard Horne sits in a booth defiantly smoking under a "No Smoking" sign. When Deputy Chad walks past the booth, Richard hands him a cigarette box filled with cash. (No surprise, Chad's a bad guy, taking money from some punk in a bar.)

A young woman asks Richard for a light. When she approaches, Richard roughly grabs her and places his hand around her neck. Richard is no mere thug, he's a psychopath. He's *The Return*'s equivalent of Frank Booth (the relentless villain of *Blue Velvet*), flouting society's norms and razing all who cross his path. Richard, we will eventually learn, is the son of Audrey Horne and Mr. C. Apparently the evil that inhabits the father has passed to the child. Although Richard deserves no pity, the story implies he's helpless to an inherent cruelty. He is the product of a dark age.

PART 5 HAS BEEN ROILING with explosions, savageries and screeds. It all started with a phone call, and it ends with one, too. At Yankton Federal Prison, Mr. C is allowed to make a call. He rapidly enters a series of numbers into the phone. Alarms suddenly blare, lights strobe, and the whole of the Yankton electrical system is sent into overload. At the center of the chaos, Mr. C manages to speak a simple message into the phone: "The cow jumped over the moon." He hangs up, the alarms cease, and Mr. C stares calmly into the security cameras.

Moments later, the device we saw in Buenos Aires at the beginning of the episode receives a message and *implodes*, crumbling into a kernel of twisted metal. Mr. C is covering his tracks, removing any incriminating evidence. His coded message has rendered the device in Argentina useless.

He may be shackled and confined, but Mr. C is hardly a prisoner and certainly not at the mercy of the authorities. He's in control, occupying space at the federal prison because he chooses to be there. Mr. C has a plan, and he is executing it. There's no need for him to leave yet. First, he must reacquaint himself with a certain someone. Once he does, he can collect Ray and make his way back out into the world.

THE WORKDAY IS OVER at The Lucky 7 Insurance Company. Cooper, carrying stacks of case files, is ushered out of an elevator by a group of impatient people ready to get home. He exits the building and stands in the darkening plaza, staring at the statue of the man holding the gun. A security guard gently urges Cooper to move on, but Cooper has nowhere to go. Darkness has fallen, the plaza is abandoned, and Cooper remains transfixed. Unlike Mr. C, Cooper wants nothing. He's content to remain spellbound by the moment, while around him the world spins.

PART 6:

DON'T DIE

IN THE TWILIGHT OF THE OFFICE PLAZA, Cooper struggles to pull his left arm into the sleeve of his jacket, suggesting he's dimly aware of how Dougie's left arm shrank into his sleeve in the Red Room. Cooper's mind is a blank slate, seeking some identity to hold onto. Neither Dougie nor the true Cooper are available, and Cooper is helpless to wander the night.

The police officer returns and asks where Cooper lives. Cooper sees the officer's badge and says, "Lancelot" (which, yes, answers the question, but can also be interpreted as Cooper equating the badge with the duties of a knight-errant: keeping order, helping the needy, rescuing those abandoned in the dark). The officer, responding to Cooper's pure goodness, gently leads Cooper away. Not once does he raise his voice or challenge Cooper or unduly impose his authority; he simply performs his duty to protect and to serve. In so doing, he ensures that Cooper is delivered safely into the custody of a worried Janey-E, waiting at home in Lancelot Court.

After dinner, Janey-E directs Cooper to say goodnight to Sonny Jim, who waits upstairs in his room. Sonny Jim may be a twenty-first century kid, but his room comes straight out of the 1950s. Images of cowboys are everywhere—on the wallpaper, the drapes, even on the lampshade. Dinosaur toys and model rockets perch on shelves. Piles of *The Hardy Boys* books crowd the nightstand. There's an old-fashioned wind-up alarm clock and even a View-Master, too.

This isn't Sonny Jim's bedroom. This is David Lynch's. In the mid-1950s Lynch would have been about Sonny Jim's age, and what we see in the boy's room comes right out of that era. In fact, Sonny Jim's View-Master is a *1955 Model E* View-Master, the same one David Lynch would have had as a nine-year-old kid.

Downstairs, Janey-E opens a large manila envelope containing a picture of Dougie with Jade. On the back, someone has scrawled, "You're late." Janey-E shows the picture to Cooper, who smiles wistfully and says Jade's name. This infuriates Janey-E, but before she can say anything, the phone rings. Janey-E answers, and a man's voice demands payment of $50,000 to cover Dougie's debt. Janey-E rebuffs the man but agrees to meet the next day.

Despite her anger at Cooper, Janey-E softens after she hangs up and gently kisses Cooper on the head. Even though Janey-E ostensibly sees her husband as "Dougie Jones," she's profoundly influenced by all the good emanating from Cooper. It's impossible for her to stay angry.

Later, Cooper reviews his case files and places a finger on the Lucky 7 symbol. Ominous music swells, and the scene cuts to a nighttime shot of the traffic light in Twin Peaks, swaying in the wind. According to Lynch, "When you see this red light, or a light turning to red, it gives you the willies!" The traffic light symbolizes danger. Indeed, as soon as we see it, the scene dissolves to the Red Room where an agitated Phillip Gerard wanders about. Gerard appears before Cooper and says, "You have to wake up. Don't die." Cooper simply stares, and Gerard's image fades.

As I've mentioned before, Phillip Gerard's role in the story is almost impossible to pin down. Sometimes he's confident and in control, other times he's confused and adrift. Although Gerard is correct when he says that Cooper is in danger, he seems unaware that otherworldly forces are protecting Cooper.

According to Kyle MacLachlan, Lynch had originally planned to have Gerard and Cooper communicate with deliberation: "There were moments where Cooper had more lucidity, primarily when he was communicating with the one-armed man.... [they] just didn't make it into the series." Gerard's scenes (like this one and the one in Part 4) are remnants of an earlier storytelling approach, one where Cooper was consciously aware of his plight. In the final cut, however, Lynch preferred to keep Cooper a blank slate. In *The Return*, Gerard cannot consult with Cooper, he can only offer warnings.

As Cooper stares at the insurance claims, a bright light shimmers across the papers. Cooper scribbles where he sees the light, scrawling jagged lines that resemble ladders and steps.[*] He makes marks next to Anthony Sinclair's name and vigorously scribbles next to the names of two detectives, Loomis and Stockton.[†]

The same light that alerted Cooper to Anthony Sinclair's lies in Part 4 now highlights irregularities on the insurance forms, pinpointing cover-ups that Sinclair is perpetrating against the Lucky 7 Insurance Company. Cooper performs the automated task of marking this evidence, even though he seems completely unaware of what he's doing. The forces guiding Cooper are revealing a crime, but they are also protecting Cooper. In Part 3, Red Room avatars guided Cooper to slot machines where Cooper won enough money to pay Dougie's gambling loans. Now, these same forces are helping Cooper avoid trouble at work and establish him as an asset to the agency. They are preparing Cooper to remain comfortably within the life of Dougie Jones (complete with rewarding job and happy family). When a later version of Cooper returns to Las Vegas to continue his life with Janey-E and Sonny Jim, he will be financially secure.

IT'S COLD AND RAINING in Philadelphia as Albert enters a nightclub named "Max Von's Bar."[‡] He weaves his way through the crowd and approaches a woman sitting at the bar and says her name: "Diane." The woman turns and, with a level gaze, says, "Hello, Albert." This is our first glimpse of the mythical Diane, the faceless character who lived behind Agent Cooper's cassette recorder so many years ago, the woman who received and processed all of Cooper's notes, ideas, and musings, the woman with whom Cooper shared his deepest secrets. She is, according to Gordon Cole, someone who knows Cooper "extremely

---

[*] Watch closely, Cooper's pencil changes from yellow to red between takes. While this is almost certainly an editing mistake, the change in color eerily resembles the changing color of the traffic light.

[†] Some familiar names also appear on the forms. "Nancy Deren" is one of *The Return*'s set designers. "Jake Cavallo" is an assistant in the art department.

[‡] "Max Von" is probably a reference to the film, *Sunset Boulevard*, which features a character named Max von Mayerling. One of David Lynch's favorite films, *Sunset Boulevard* is also the source of Gordon Cole's name and will play an important role in *The Return* in Part 15.

well." She's been a mystery all these years, Diane has, and she remains one. Diane may have a deep emotional connection to Cooper, but as we'll soon learn, her encounters with Mr. C after Dale Cooper disappeared have shaken her to the core. This Diane, sitting in the bar, drinking and smoking and trying to forget a horrible past, has been broken and hardened again. She's full of secrets, dark and dangerous. And she holds a story as powerful—and perhaps just as vital—as Dale Cooper's.

IN TWIN PEAKS, Richard Horne meets with Red, a dangerous drug dealer whom we briefly saw in Part 2, "shooting" a gesture at Shelly Briggs. Red is recruiting Richard to sell drugs in Twin Peaks[*] and has just given Richard a sample of a highly potent substance called Sparkle (undoubtedly the Chinese designer drug that worried Sheriff Truman and which killed a high school student named Denny Craig).

Flanked by two machine-gun toting thugs, Red is jumpy and erratic. He unsettles Richard with sudden moves and an inexplicable query about whether Richard has ever seen the musical, *The King and I.* Red is making a veiled reference to the song, "Getting to Know You,"[†] and he spells it out for a baffled Richard: "I don't know you yet."

Richard acts tough, defiantly telling Red not to call him "kid," but Red is not some naïve girl in a Roadhouse booth. Red flips a dime into the air, and Richard stares, dumbfounded, as the coin hovers in place. A moment later, Richard softly gags and spits the dime into his hand and then looks up to see Red catch the dime out of the air (the dime in Richard's hand having vanished). Speechless, and not a little frightened, Richard knows who has the real power here.

Red is a mysterious and fleeting figure who appears only briefly in *The Return.* We learn little about him other than that he supplies drugs to street-level dealers. Still, we know enough about Red to see striking parallels between him and Leo Johnson, a character from the original

---

[*] Why does Twin Peaks attract such powerful drug dealers? Does the town's relatively small population really support the kind of drug market Red would want? This was an issue in the original series, too: Why would drug cartels work so hard, for so long, to move product into Twin Peaks?

[†] Coincidentally, Leland sang "Getting to Know You" at the Great Northern Hotel in episode 13 of the original series.

Twin Peaks. Like Leo, Red is in a relationship with Shelly. Like Leo, Red drives a Chevy Corvette. And like Leo, Red is running drugs into Twin Peaks. Red, whoever he is, is a menacing and violent presence. Just like Leo Johnson.

It's worth noting that Red's meeting with Richard eerily parallels Leo's meeting with Bobby and Mike in episode 2 of the original series. Back then, Leo threatened Bobby because of his failure to pay for the drugs Leo was supplying. While Leo never performed a magic trick like Red does, a mysterious figure *did* emerge from behind a tree to startle Bobby. What's more, Bobby and Mike fled from Leo in much the same way Richard drives angrily away from Red. I think it's quite possible that Red is an echo of Leo Johnson, if not Leo Johnson himself, manifesting as a Lynchian double within the narrative.[*]

In fact, Red might be construed as an *entangled identity*, a "spooky" character whom Cooper equates with Leo. We should not ignore the Corvette prominently parked in the warehouse. Lynch's camera lingers over the car as the scene begins. Lynch *wants* us to see it, wants us to know it belongs to Red. He's reminding us that Leo Johnson owned the same kind of car—a bright *red* Chevrolet Corvette. This connection is important, because Red is quite likely an expression of Dale Cooper's jumbled memory, a character so very much like Leo Johnson that Cooper simply nicknames him "Red."[†]

Speaking of doubles, over at the "new" Fat Trout Trailer Park in Twin Peaks, Carl Rodd prepares to drive into town. A resident of the park, Mickey, asks to hitch a ride. As they travel, Mickey explains that "Linda" has received a new electric wheelchair from "the government agencies" (probably The Department of Veteran's Affairs, since Linda is apparently a veteran). Given that the Fireman told Cooper to remem-

---

[*] Some fans have theorized that Red could also be an adult Pierre Tremond, the grownup version of Mrs. Tremond's grandson. Red's magic trick with the dime is strongly reminiscent the way, in the original series, Pierre made creamed corn disappear from a tray of food and then reappear in his cupped hands. (The connection between Red and Pierre Tremond is compelling, but I still see more parallels between Red and Leo.)

[†] *The Return* never explains what became of Leo Johnson, but in *The Final Dossier* Mark Frost reveals that Leo was shot and killed in Windom Earle's cabin. That does not preclude the possibility that Leo is a presence in David Lynch's narrative, however.

ber "Richard and Linda," we assume Mickey's mention of Linda here is important, that whoever Linda is she will be a crucial character in the unfolding story. It turns out, this Linda is merely a red herring, another example of Lynch playing with recurring names (just as he did in the original *Twin Peaks* with characters like "Mike and Bob" and "Mike and Bobby").

David Lynch re-wrote the Mickey/Carl scene on the day he shot it (actors Jeremy Lindholm and Harry Dean Stanton barely had time to rehearse before the cameras rolled, which is why, according to Lindholm, they smile at the end of their scene, having completed their tricky dialog in one take). Linda was a likely improvised element, added by Lynch at the last minute. In fact, the entirety of the "Richard and Linda" subplot (for lack of a better word) was written by Lynch late in the production. As Mark Frost explains, "[Lynch] added the Richard and Linda references later and never explained his reasoning to me."

As he's done in past works, Lynch is exploring the idea of interchangeable identities. In *The Return*, names are not fixed labels but fluid and elusive identifiers. A character might have multiple identities (just as Red might be Leo). Richard and Linda might simply be ciphers, names tenuously assigned to other players in the story. Cooper's restless mind struggles to determine who Richard and Linda really are, not realizing that neither entity may exist, or that one of them might, in fact, be him.

It's great to see Carl Rodd again, but what's he doing in Twin Peaks? Rodd used to manage the Fat Trout Trailer Park in Deer Meadow, Washington, a town in the southwest corner of the state and quite some distance from Twin Peaks. From what we know, it's unlikely that the Carl Rodd we met in *Fire Walk With Me*—the man who complained about being woken before nine a.m., the man who "never touched a goddamn thing" in Teresa Banks's trailer, the man who groused about showing the trailer to the FBI because it meant "more shit I gotta do now," the man who "had already gone places" and *just wanted to stay where he was*—is a man who would uproot himself from Deer Meadow and move hundreds of miles to another park with the same name in Twin Peaks. And yet here he is, and here it is.[*]

No matter how fishy it seems, we have to take the "new" Fat Trout Trailer Park at face value. It's a second park with the same name. (*Two* Fat Trout Trailer Parks. Weird, huh?) This is *Twin Peaks*, after all, and the new trailer park is simply a reflection of the old, an entangled space that forever harbors troubled and troubling residents. The kind of place that would naturally draw Carl Rodd to it.

RICHARD SPEEDS ANGRILY down a nearby road, muttering and yelling because Red humiliated him. He approaches an intersection and, seeing cars stopped at the red light ahead, swerves his truck into the oncoming lane to speed through. Just as he does, a young boy runs into the crosswalk. Richard smashes into the boy, killing him instantly. The boy's mother, still on the sidewalk, screams. Richard races away, but not before a woman on the other side of the road, Miriam, witnesses the impact and makes eye contact.

The mother crouches in the intersection, holding the broken body of her boy and wailing in horror. Carl Rodd approaches and sees a golden light (ostensibly, the boy's soul) emerge from the boy's body and ascend into the sky. For a moment Carl stands in awe and then kneels beside the mother and looks into her eyes. He cannot ease her pain, but he stays next to her, wordlessly sharing her torment. Electricity crackles, and the mother's pain (her *garmonbozia*) courses through the nearby power lines, surging away to feed whatever foul entity would consume such trauma.

Carl Rodd has been places, this we know, and wherever he's been, whatever he's seen, he knows that the world is unpredictable and frightening, that mankind suffers from unrelenting and random anguish. Carl Rodd kneels in the street, silently, soothingly, willing to share this woman's grief because he knows the only thing a person can do in a moment like this is provide comfort in whatever way he can.

---

[*] In *The Secret History of Twin Peaks*, Mark Frost explains that Carl Rodd had been born in Twin Peaks and that the original Fat Trout Trailer Park had always been located just outside of town. This contradicts the facts established in *Fire Walk With Me*, where the trailer park was located in Deer Meadow, WA. (With all due respect, I'm not sure Frost really paid much attention to the details of *Fire Walk With Me*, so we should take all of Carl Rodd's background with a grain of salt.)

IN LAS VEGAS, hitman Ike "The Spike" Stadtler receives orders to kill Lorraine and Dougie Jones. Ike takes his spike (which appears to be an ice pick) and stabs at photos of both his targeted victims.

At the Lucky 7 Insurance Agency, Bushnell Mullins reviews Cooper's marked-up case files. Mullins scoffs at the scribbling, angry at the mess, but then he notices a pattern, a deeper, troubling set of data. Realizing the import of what Cooper has delivered, Bushnell thanks Cooper, who, standing there, has been staring up at the poster of Bushnell in his boxing prime. (Cooper, who has experienced no passage of time since becoming trapped in the Red Room, seems baffled by the image of a younger Bushnell, as if he, Cooper, is trying to grasp the concept of aging.)

At a local playground (in a park near Guinevere and Merlin), Janey-E waits nervously for the loan sharks to arrive. Two sleazy guys approach and explain that Dougie lost a bet of $20,000 and now he owes $52,000. Janey-E is having none of it. She furiously explains that she cannot afford to repay that kind of money. She is part of a middle-class family who can barely make ends meet, and she will only provide a payment of $25,000. To prove her point, she shoves a roll of bills at one of the men and marches away. Cowed by Janey-E's unbending manner, the two men meekly accept her counteroffer.

While the Janey-E scene serves as a short commentary on income inequality in the United States (and mirrors the same thematic frustrations presented in the Doctor Amp scenes), and while it illustrates the strong, no-nonsense qualities of Janey-E as a character, the scene is far more important than it first appears. Janey-E's short speech to the loan sharks is, in fact, a summary of two fundamental themes of *The Return*. In it, Janey-E exposes the very core of the new *Twin Peaks* when she asks, "What kind of world are we living in where people can behave like this? Treat other people this way without any compassion or feeling for their suffering? We are living in a dark, dark age." Indeed, *Twin Peaks* is all about this dark age and all about suffering.

It's no secret that David Lynch is an adherent of Hindu philosophy, specifically the teachings of Maharishi Mahesh Yogi. In an interview shortly after *The Return* aired, Lynch explained a central concept of Hindu belief: "In the Hindu religion, there are [four] different ages. We are in the Iron Age. It's the shortest of the four ages...and it's a dark

age. All who live today are born at this age and deserve to be there."
The four ages (or yugas) comprise a cycle. At the end of the fourth age
(the Kali Yuga) the cycle starts again with a Golden Age, an age of peace
and happiness.

Right now, we live in the dark age, a time of despair and ascendant
evil. That's what we see playing out in *The Return*: characters
struggling against pain and hardship, people bewildered by a pall of
dread that blankets the entire world. Suffering is everywhere, from the
mental distress of Doris Truman to the physical pain of Tom Paige,
from the emotional burden of Big Ed to the psychological collapse of
Audrey Horne. Bobby Briggs suffers as he watches Shelly embrace
another man; Ben Horne suffers as he relives the regrets of his lost
childhood; Becky and Steven Burnett suffer as they endure a violent,
dangerous marriage. The list goes on and on: A girl vomits in a car; a
woman endlessly scratches a painful rash; a distressed Roadhouse
patron crawls across a dance floor; a drunkard bashes his head against
prison bars; a man donates blood just to pay his bills. This is the dark
age Janey-E Jones so urgently evokes.

And if suffering darkens this age, so too does evil. It thrives in these
times. Bob has been loose in the world for decades. Now allied with
Mr. C, he has become more potent than ever. And Experiment has
broken free, finding purchase within the despairing mind of Sarah
Palmer. As Doctor Amp so forcefully reminds us there is other evil, too.
The strong subjugate the weak, and the selfish steal from the needy. We
see it as Red disperses drugs, Richard carelessly murders a boy, Ike
prepares for assassinations, and Anthony Sinclair cheats those who
trust him most. In this last age of the Hindu cycle, a banal evil
permeates the world. Compassion (like what we saw from Carl Rodd)
is rare. "It is a dark time," says David Lynch, "We can hope that it lights
up, but for now it's very dark." *Twin Peaks: The Return* charts a course
through that darkness, seeking a light that may never come.[*]

EVIL DEEDS ARE IKE "THE SPIKE'S" SPECIALTY. He arrives at
Lorraine's office amid screams of terror and, brandishing his ice pick,

---

[*] But there may soon be an end to this dark age and a return to something Golden—a
cleansing scream to end one cycle and begin another.

confronts a terrified Lorraine and savagely kills her. As Ike stabs at Lorraine, blood sprays on the walls. A horrified witness watches from the hallway, and Ike, somewhat frustrated by this unforeseen bystander, pursues her and presumably kills her as well.

The murder of Lorraine is quick and bloody. It is terrifying to watch, but it happens fast. So fast, you might not notice the odd item hanging on the wall behind Lorraine's desk. It's a piece of cardboard similar to the boxes we saw in the Glass Box Room in New York City. This piece of cardboard is crudely duct-taped to Lorraine's office wall, and a cylindrical object, resembling the lens of a camera, protrudes from the center. Whatever this thing is, it hardly seems to belong here. It's not art (not really), and it's not decoration. So, what is it?

The object is most likely a whim of David Lynch, whose painterly eye saw the need for compositional balance in his shot and found that the cardboard box made the room "look right." Even so, I don't think that's all there is to it. If, indeed, Cooper's interpretive mind is conveying the story, he may associate the blood-splattered killing of Lorraine with the bloody slaughter of Sam and Tracey in the Glass Box Room. As he conflates one bloody murder with the other, Cooper projects the boxes (and the many camera lenses) from the Glass Box Room into Lorraine's office. That's why this strange object hangs on the wall. David Lynch did not place it there simply for aesthetics (even though aesthetics may have been the motivation). He placed it there because it also fit with his conceptual discourse of *The Return*.[*]

IN TWIN PEAKS, spattered blood clings to the front of Richard's truck. Richard stops in a remote area and parks under power lines (we see them reflected in his truck's front window) and washes the blood off the fender, erasing the evidence of his heinous act. Electricity crackles, suggesting dark energies coiling nearby.

In the men's room at the Sheriff's station, Hawk examines the door of a bathroom stall and discovers a gap in the door's metal seam. He pries the door apart and finds a few pieces of paper hidden within. They appear to be diary pages.

---

[*] Honestly, I like this answer. While I may be stretching things to sensibly explain the cardboard on Lorraine's wall, I believe (for Lynch, at least) this odd object could easily be the mental embellishment of Dale Cooper.

Diary pages can only mean one thing: Laura Palmer's missing pages from her "secret" diary. We won't know what these pages reveal until the next episode, but their discovery here provides a direct link to the plot of the original *Twin Peaks*. Back then, Hawk discovered a few torn pages from Laura's diary near where Laura had been killed. The pages revealed many of Laura's secrets, but, even so, critical clues about Laura's fate (and other secrets she may have kept) remained lost. No one knew that Annie Blackburn had visited Laura in a dream and conveyed to her crucial information about the fate of Dale Cooper. Annie urged Laura to write this information in her diary, and Laura did.[*] Now, Hawk's discovery of these long-hidden pages (which, if examined in a high-definition freeze-frame thrillingly reveal the name "Annie") promises to bring decades-old mysteries back into the light. What's more, the pages provide a much-needed narrative jolt to *The Return*, dramatically, dizzyingly, connecting the past to the present.

Elsewhere in the station, Doris Truman rages into a room where Frank Truman is reviewing paperwork with deputies Chad Broxford and Jesse Holcombe. Doris continues her protests from her last visit, complaining about her father's car and Frank's lack of support. Truman attempts to soothe Doris and walks her gently back to his office.

Chad makes a crude comment about Doris, which exasperates Maggie, the station's dispatcher. Maggie explains that Doris wasn't always this way; she only fell into despair after her son's suicide. Chad doesn't care. He mocks the Trumans' dead son, who, he dismissively claims, "couldn't take being a soldier."[†]

Chad may lack empathy, but Maggie's explanation about Doris contextualizes Frank and Doris's relationship and helps us understand why Doris is the way she is. Doris and Frank Truman have endured the tragic death of their son, who, himself, likely experienced a devastating trauma from something that happened during his military service. Unlike Chad, we sympathize with the pain of the Trumans. They, like

---

[*] "I know that Laura wrote that down, in a little side space in her diary," Lynch said in 1997, in a rare moment of explicitness.

[†] This is the second reference to soldiers and/or the military in Part 6. Recall that Carl Rodd laments about Linda because she was injured in the "fuckin' war."

countless others in *The Return*, are suffering, but they carry on with their lives, shouldering pain and coping with trauma.

As Part 6 ends, Deputy Jesse Holcombe stares into the distance, moved by some unknowable, ethereal notion. He's a curious character, Jesse is, one of the few souls in *Twin Peaks* who seems satisfied with his place in a wider universe. Jesse likely belongs to that small group of inexplicable observers who watch the tumultuous lives of others and yet remain unruffled by the trauma of this dark, dark age.

As Jesse stares, music swells, and we transition to the Roadhouse where a band plays and people dance. Sharon Van Etten sings a song titled, "Tarifa." Mournful and mysterious, it contains tantalizing lyrics that speak to larger concepts in the story and to Dale Cooper's struggle to make sense of who he is and where he belongs: "I can't remember, I can't recall, I can't remember anything at all."[*]

---

[*] Plus, there's the puzzling line, "Send in the owl," which is just cool.

<INTERLUDE 3>

LEAVE HER OUT OF IT

IN *TWIN PEAKS: THE RETURN*, Mr. C and Agent Cooper, two fundamentally different beings, are both on the same quest. Each wants to locate the mysterious entity known as Judy. In Part 15, Mr. C aggressively demands that Phillip Jeffries tell him Judy's identity, and Agent Cooper, we learn, has been looking for Judy since 1989 (when he and Major Briggs developed a plan to find Judy). Despite their efforts, neither Cooper nor Mr. C will succeed. They've each contextualized Judy through a naïve understanding of the universe, convinced themselves that she (or it) is a tangible entity, a being that can be confronted or attained.

Cooper and Mr. C are grasping at shadows. Judy is not a demon. She has no "alter ego." Judy is something far more complex and nuanced. She is a condition. She is a premise. She is the antecedent of pain and sorrow.

Judy is trauma.

Let Me Write It Down for 'Ya

THE RETURN IMPLIES Judy is a character, someone we might recognize. When Phillip Jeffries explains that Mr. C has "already met Judy," Mr. C assumes he's encountered Judy's alter-ego, and he repeatedly asks: "Who is Judy?"

That's a good question, and just like "Who killed Laura Palmer?" it begs for an answer.

The story of *Twin Peaks* contains many potential candidates for Judy. She could be Diane or Sarah Palmer. She could be Laura Palmer or Audrey Horne. She could be Naido, American Girl, Lil, or the Bosomy Woman. Judy could be anyone.

The identity of Judy has been a mystery since *Fire Walk With Me*. There, Phillip Jeffries explicitly told his fellow FBI agents he wasn't "going to talk about Judy." More curious was a second reference, late in the film, when a monkey emerges from the darkness to utter a single word, "Judy." With only these two brief mentions, there wasn't much data from which to assign an identity, but clues outside the main text of *Fire Walk With Me* shed some light on who or what Judy might be. In an essay I wrote for *Wrapped In Plastic*, I described a few theories about how Judy might fit into the story.

In the first theory, Judy is another dead girl, perhaps the first in a series of victims that later included Teresa Banks and Laura Palmer. "She fits into a cyclical pattern—a girl is killed, and an FBI agent (Cooper, Chet Desmond, Phillip Jeffries) is assigned the case. The case is never solved because the assigned agent ends up missing." Although this was a popular interpretation for some time, the theory has no substantive evidence to support it. Plus, it fails to explain why the monkey appears later in the film and says, "Judy."

In the second theory, Judy, as *originally scripted*, was an associate of Phillip Jeffries, perhaps Josie Packard's sister. This is almost certainly what David Lynch and co-writer, Robert Engels, intended. In scenes Lynch deleted from the final cut, Phillip Jeffries explicitly discusses Judy as if she were simply another person. He asks a hotel concierge about a letter from a "Miss Judy," proclaims that "Judy is positive about this" ("this" being whatever Jeffries is trying to convey to Cole) and mentions that he found something "in Seattle at Judy's." All this dialog points to Judy being a flesh-and-blood character (someone who writes letters and lives in her own home). Robert Engels confirms this interpretation: "[Phillip Jeffries] was down there [Buenos Aires], and that's where Judy is. I think [Josie] is there, and I think Windom Earle is there.... *It's really as simple as that.* In our original planning of the prequel there is a whole other section about all this—a whole other set of mythology that was going to be around Judy and Josie and where Windom Earle ended up." (Emphasis added.) In the end, however, much of this backstory was eventually discarded, and Judy didn't make the cut. Literally.

In the third theory, Judy is Laura Palmer. David Lynch was contractually forced to edit *Fire Walk With Me* to a runtime of two hours and fifteen minutes. As a result, many scenes were deleted, including those where Philip Jeffries speaks about Judy. Still, there was no easy way to delete Jeffries' *first* mention of Judy, that indelible sequence when Jeffries strolls into Gordon Cole's office and declares, "We're not going to talk about Judy. In fact, we're not going to talk about Judy *at all*." This line stayed in the movie, and Judy became a loose end, a character with no identity.

To clear up this loose end, Lynch inserted a new scene, late in the film, of a monkey saying the name, "Judy," a scene that immediately precedes a close-up of Laura Palmer being unwrapped from plastic. In my earlier essay, I argued that the juxtaposition of these shots was deliberate, that the monkey was *introducing* Judy to us. Perhaps I was susceptible to the Kuleshov effect, but I confidently concluded that Laura was Judy and believed this association made sense to Lynch: "In Lynch's mind, there is some deeper meaning—some substantive connection—between Laura and Judy. Perhaps [...] Judy simply becomes a 'code word' for Laura, a symbolic representation of the *idea* of Laura Palmer."

Now that I've seen *Twin Peaks: The Return*, I still think this makes sense. I think Laura and "Judy" are profoundly connected; Judy informs the very essence of who Laura is and what she's been through.

But, as with everything in *Twin Peaks*, it's complicated.

Who Do You Think That is There?

WHEN DAVID LYNCH AND MARK FROST developed the backstory for the third season of *Twin Peaks*, they monkeyed around with the concept of Judy, refining and re-orienting what she was and what she meant to the larger *Twin Peaks* milieu.

In his book, *The Final Dossier*, Frost expounds upon Judy, explaining that she/it is an ancient Sumerian demon known as Joudy, who walked the Earth long ago and "fed on human suffering." Frost goes further, essentially confirming that Joudy inhabits Sarah Palmer (he links the two characters together when he reveals that Sarah's full name is Sarah *Judith* Novack Palmer), and that Sarah was, indeed, the young girl in Part 8 of *The Return* who was infested with an otherworldly parasite.

Though Frost is explicit and substantive, there's no way to know how much of this characterization David Lynch subscribes to. As Gordon Cole, he corroborates that there is an entity of "extreme negative force" named "Jowday,"* and in interviews Lynch claims that he always envisioned Judy to be a "bad entity," but despite this latter claim, it seems Lynch is remembering Judy the way he wants to remember her and not necessarily the way she "happened."

It's hard to reconcile the demonic Jowday with the Judy implied in the Phillip Jeffries scenes from The Missing Pieces and in the "whole mythology" Engels talks about. That's because Judy started out as one thing in *Fire Walk With Me* and developed into something more complex and disturbing for *The Return*. Martha Nochimson notes the same evolution, suggesting in her book, *Television Rewired*, that Lynch changed his thinking about Judy over time. During one of their conversations (years before Lynch started work on *The Return*), Lynch asks Nochimson if she knows what the monkey says in *Fire Walk With Me*: "He never explained why he asked, but I do not think it was because he knew then how important Judy would become…. I suspect that when Judy appeared in *Fire Walk With Me*, it was a beginning, *of which he was not conscious at the time*, of an evolution that yielded Judy a critical place [in *The Return*]." (Emphasis added.) Nochimson is right, Judy was a nebulous idea left undefined in *Fire Walk With Me*— an idea Lynch later expanded upon in *The Return*.

Here's where things get tricky, and where, I think, we plainly see the two creators of *Twin Peaks* approaching the narrative from starkly different viewpoints. It's no secret that Lynch and Frost have distinct story-telling sensibilities. Frost is forensic, plot-driven, interested in a story's concrete internal logic (no matter how uncanny the subject matter), but Lynch, for better or worse, is not tied to the script and is willing to make changes if they feel right to him: "You might think your script is complete, but it may not be. There may be opportunities and ideas coming that are so valuable. You have to stay feeling and focused all the time. It's got to all feel correct to be finished."

---

* This spelling comes from the closed captioning of dialog in *The Return*, Part 17.

While Lynch embraced the idea of Judy as a negative force, that didn't mean he was willing to confine Judy to the boundaries of Frost's specific definition. In fact, Lynch gives himself a lot of wiggle room when it comes to assigning identity to Judy:

- Lynch never provides a name for the girl who is infested with the mysterious "frog-moth" in 1956. Frost, however, unequivocally identifies her as Sarah Palmer. ("According to her parents, they found Sarah unconscious and unresponsive in her upstairs bedroom.") Even if the girl is Sarah Palmer in Lynch's version, that doesn't mean she's Judy (as Frost would define her). Lynch leaves enough ambiguity in the narrative to establish Sarah Palmer as something else entirely.

- Lynch never labels the gruesome apparition that appears in the glass box (and in the heart of the nuclear explosion) as anything other than "Experiment." If he wanted to name this thing "Judy" he could have, but he didn't. (Notably, Mark Frost claims no knowledge of the apparition being called "Experiment," telling David Bushman, "I've never heard that term before.")

- Lynch is careful to say Briggs's plan was designed to lead Cooper to Judy, meaning Cooper was simply trying to locate Judy, not necessarily combat her. Maybe I'm splitting hairs, but it seems like Cooper would want to do more than just find Judy if he was certain she was some world-threatening demonic force. He'd want to destroy her. But in Lynch's story, Cooper is not sure what Judy is. He wants to investigate and leave all his options open.

In *The Return*, David Lynch ensures that Judy remains ambiguous. He refuses to commit to any one limiting definition for what (or who) she might be. Although Judy is defined as an "extreme negative force," this does not mean she is a demon or an entity with a nefarious agenda. She is something far more abstract and complex. Just as the ancient Greeks might personify emotions with names ("Lupe" for pain, "Achos" for grief, "Ania" for sorrow), "Judy" in *Twin Peaks* is a name that personifies suffering. For Lynch, Judy is the evocation of trauma. She is pain, sorrow, and grief all rolled into one.

I'll Find It For You

AND SO, WE COME BACK around to Laura. Cooper is trying to find Judy, yes, but his quest is inextricably tied to his obsession with Laura Palmer. Cooper believes the two are connected, but he can't see past his own limited definitions to make progress toward either. Phillip Jeffries is more perceptive and attempts to help Cooper. When Jeffries opens a portal to 1989, he tells Cooper, "This is where you'll find Judy," even though Cooper never asks about Judy (he only provides Jeffries a date). Jeffries furnishes an all-important clue and then sends Cooper directly into Laura Palmer's path.

In *Fire Walk With Me*, the monkey invokes Judy on the same horrific night Laura Palmer is killed, and that's exactly where Phillip Jeffries puts Cooper. He transports Cooper to the moment when Laura Palmer's identity is crumbling. When, at her lowest level of despair, she tells James Hurley: "You don't even know me. Your Laura disappeared."

Cooper doesn't realize it, but he's just found Judy.

In these final hours, Laura has surrendered, convinced herself that she is worthless. She is willing to endure depredations at the hands of Leo Johnson and Jacques Renault. At this intense moment of hopelessness, Laura is suffering Judy.

Laura's pain will only get worse. She will be captured, bound, and forcibly marched to a place of gruesome death—the train car. There, the demon Bob will attempt to fully possess Laura, eroding her sense of self-worth so completely that she has no choice but to submit to his awful demands. In these moments Judy will exalt.

But Laura has strength even she does not expect, and in her final moments her faith in herself is restored. Laura denies Bob his claim. She pushes back and wrests power from Bob (and his cohort, the Arm), and, though she chooses death, she defeats the dark forces that seek to quash and consume her.

Does she still suffer? Yes, beyond what most people can comprehend. But she faces her torment and refuses to be victim to it. To be sure, Laura doesn't defeat Judy (you can't defeat what is all-pervasive), but Laura learns in these last moments that you can *overcome* Judy. Laura finds her perfect courage, banishes her shadow self, and denies her abusers any further pain. This is why Laura is ultimately the victor and not the victim.

Cooper, Remember

IN *THE RETURN*, Cooper thinks he is doing the right thing when he intercepts Laura in 1989 to keep her from being killed. He meets her in the woods and attempts to lead her home, hoping to save her from the ordeal of the train car. But Laura's destiny lies elsewhere; she cannot be removed from the path she's already on. David Lynch has positioned Laura as a savior, a figure sent to Earth by higher powers to end a pervasive evil. What Laura must accomplish in the train car is far more important than Cooper's impulsive mission. It is her destiny, and, try as he might, Cooper is powerless to stop it. As Cooper leads her through the trees, Laura screams, and the inevitable agony of Judy vaults her back to her original path, her own story.

Blinded by his hubris, Cooper misses an opportunity to simply stand aside and watch. If he could perceive the reality of what happens to Laura in the train car, see the truth in what she endures and overcomes, then maybe he'd finally get the answer he's been seeking. Maybe he'd at last get a glimpse of what Judy really is and understand she cannot be reduced to some simplistic adversary to be stopped or defeated or erased. Judy is a *truth*, a condition to be endured by all human beings. Courage and a clear understanding of one's true self are the only ways to contend with Judy. Laura has learned this truth, but Cooper can't summon the patience (as The Log Lady would advise) to "watch and listen."

Why Don't You Ask Judy Yourself?

I DON'T BELIEVE THAT DAVID LYNCH fully rejected the idea of Laura and Judy being connected. Judy arises in moments of pain and suffering, and when Laura suffers, she effectively becomes Judy—or at least evokes the presence of Judy. Laura is not special in this regard. She is not the only person to encounter and suffer Judy. Everyone experiences pain. Everyone endures some form of sorrow. Over the course of a lifetime every human being inevitably confronts their own private Judy. We see this time and time again in *The Return*: Characters suffering, living with pain, shouldering the burden of grief. This is Judy. And she is everywhere.

Judy is the longing in Bobby Briggs' eyes, the ache in James Hurley's voice, the hurt inside Big Ed's blank expression. She is the remorse that lingers over Carl Rodd and Norma Jennings and Ben Horne. She is regret, and she is anger. Judy is the murky ellipses of Gersten Hayward's life and the fury of Richard Horne's momentum. She's a trespasser in words, clinging to the guilty phrases of Beverly Paige's alibis, basking in the back-van chatter of Hutch and Chantal, exalting in the tortured incantations of Steven Burnett's suicide. She's the bullets in Becky's gun, the drugs that doomed little Denny Craig, a headless body woven with weeds in a wasted field. She's the seven savage kicks at the Silver Mustang Casino. Judy is haunted minds and plagued memory: She's the fraying fabric of Diane's identity, the urgency of Audrey's Zeno-paradoxical refuge. She corrodes, and she corrupts. She's Warden Murphy's woeful bargain, Anthony Sinclair's submissive admissions, Darya's deadly double-cross. Lurking and skulking in all the tortured territories of *Twin Peaks*, Judy is the empty frame on Doris Truman's wall and the half-open door on the outskirts of town, and, most terribly, she's the echoing chamber of an abandoned train car, deep in the forest, resonant still with the howl of murder.

Judy troubles the ailing Harry Truman, the absent Annie Blackburn, the forgotten Donna Hayward. She's the fear that "happened to Josie," and the wounds inflicted upon Caroline Earle. She's bank blasts, exploding cars, drugs, and domestic violence. Judy is a television's cold blue light. She's something in the kitchen. Shattered glass in a picture frame. A ceiling fan. A tainted glass of milk.

Judy is the evil that men do.

It's Slippery In Here

IN *TWIN PEAKS: THE RETURN*, David Lynch refuses to answer the question, "Who is Judy?" He may have initially bought into Mark Frost's idea that Judy is a "Wandering demon that thrives on human suffering," but he shied away from the execution, preferring to keep Judy an open concept and subject to the viewer's interpretive stance. That's not surprising; Lynch has always been careful to preserve ambiguity in his work. When writing *Lost Highway* with Barry Gifford,

Lynch explained, "A lot was left unsaid. We talked, but that can be dangerous. If things get too specific the dream stops."

Lynch and Frost worked long and hard on *The Return*. Frost had specific views on how certain parts of the story, like Judy, should work, but Lynch saw an inherent "danger" in committing to these specifics. For Lynch, it doesn't matter if we, the audience, want to see Judy as a demon or as an idea. Both interpretations are valid. Lynch designed *The Return* to allow Judy's identity to oscillate between aliases.

Years ago, Lynch was careful to keep Judy a mystery in *Fire Walk With Me*, and he is careful to maintain that mystery in *The Return*. Earlier, I mentioned "the Kuleshov effect," the idea that we ascribe meaning from how scenes in a film are positioned. In *Fire Walk With Me*, the monkey says Judy, and then we see Laura, and I connected those scenes and concluded Laura was Judy. But let's go backwards. Let's look at what happens right *before* the monkey appears. The preceding shot is an extreme close-up of the Arm eating a spoonful of garmonbozia, the corporeal manifestation of "pain and sorrow." In effect, the Arm is eating a small dose of trauma, newly supplied to him by Bob. That's right—*trauma*. And right after the Arm eats it, the monkey appears and says, "Judy." From the positioning of these two scenes, we might conclude that David Lynch had a plan all along, that maybe Judy was always a "bad entity." She was "pain and sorrow." She was garmonbozia with a different label.

Curious, isn't it, that in the entire eighteen hours of *The Return* not once do we hear the word, garmonbozia. There's a reason for that. Garmonbozia has simply been exchanged for another word.

A simple name.

Judy.

PART 7:
THERE'S A BODY ALL RIGHT

JERRY HORNE IS LOST in the woods and high. Distraught, delirious, he calls Ben Horne and says his car has been stolen. Ben is confused, not sure what Jerry is trying to say (does Jerry even have a car?). Jerry is just as confused; Ben's replies make no sense. This simple, failed exchange between the Horne brothers illustrates another of *The Return*'s themes: the inability to communicate. Like so many other characters (including the observing presence of Dale Cooper), Jerry and Ben are attempting to make a connection, trying to make sense to each other, but their messages become jumbled and lost in translation. They can't overcome the many impediments to understanding.

The inability to communicate is isolating. When we're not heard we feel alone and abandoned. Indeed, Ben and Jerry are both lost in worlds they cannot convey to others. Ben in his office, Jerry in the woods, their physical environments mirror their inability to relate, to join, to be heard.* Ben listens desperately into the phone, but the line disconnects. There's only a dial tone.

At the Sheriff's station, Hawk shows Frank Truman the three diary pages he found in the bathroom stall. Over the next few minutes, Hawk relates to Frank much of the story from twenty-five years earlier. He mentions Annie Blackburn, Leland Palmer, Harold Smith, and Jacques

---

*And poor Dale Cooper is more isolated than anyone. Trapped in the eternal neverwhere that is the Red Room, Cooper helplessly, wordlessly, watches a world he cannot access, let alone converse with. Muted against his will, Cooper remains a lost soul.

Renault. He discusses the Black Lodge, Laura Palmer's diary, and the possible existence of two Cooper's. For longtime *Twin Peaks* fans, it's a mesmerizing, breathtaking scene.

The most exciting moment happens when Frank Truman reads one of Laura's diary entries in which she describes her dream about Annie Blackburn. Many years ago, Annie appeared to Laura and told her about Dale Cooper (the "good" Dale) being trapped in the Lodge. Annie urged Laura to write that information in her diary, and Laura apparently did. Now, all these years later, Frank Truman and Hawk discover this most crucial of clues. From it, Hawk surmises that the good Cooper is still trapped in the Lodge and a bad Cooper has been let loose into the world. This must all sound crazy to Truman, but he takes it seriously. And it's a good thing he does; Truman's knowledge of two Coopers will help him later, when he comes face to face with Mr. C.

Hawk explains that the three pages came from the same diary the police discovered at Harold Smith's apartment. He further speculates that Leland had possession of these pages and hid them in the bathroom stall when he had been brought into the station for questioning about the murder of Jacques Renault.[*]

Hawk reveals that only three of four missing diary pages have been found, and that the fourth page is still unaccounted for. What might Laura have written on it? We'll never know, but it's tempting to think she might have gained some insight into her larger purpose, had some inkling of The Fireman's grand plan and glimpsed her future as "Carrie Page." (Hawk's focus on the missing "page" hints at Laura's alter-ego. The symbolism is too obvious to dismiss.)

Frank calls Harry Truman to give him an update, but when he realizes Harry's condition has worsened, his face falls, and he responds

---

[*] There's a possible continuity error here. In *Fire Walk With Me*, Laura delivered her diary to Harold Smith before she encountered Annie in her dream. How, then, could the pages describing Annie's message have ended up at Harold's? Some convoluted theories suggest Laura went back to Harold's to write about Annie, and Leland followed her and ripped those pages out. That's a possibility, but why would Leland remove those pages and not take the *whole* diary? Here's a more satisfying (though still inelegant) solution: Laura, herself, removed a few blank pages from her diary (before delivering it to Harold) so she could continue to write in her "secret diary." After Leland killed Laura, he found these extra pages in Laura's bedroom and simply took them.

with short, stunned replies: "Oh. No kidding. Damn." Frank urges Harry to get some rest and adds a final plea: "Do me a favor. Beat this thing." Frank Truman proves again he is a good man. Steadfast with his troubled wife, he is also devoted to his ailing brother.[*]

Andy has traced the truck that killed the boy to a local farmer, who insists he wasn't driving the truck when the boy was hit. Andy presses him to reveal who was, but the farmer is extremely frightened. He pleads with Andy to leave, promising to answer his questions later. Reluctantly, Andy agrees and drives away. Surely, Andy must wonder why the farmer is so frightened (I'm no detective, but this seems like pretty incriminating behavior to me), but Andy never returns to the farmer to investigate the hit and run. Neither does anyone else. Only Cooper shows an interest. Later, after the farmer fails to meet Andy, the story cuts back to the farmer's house. The camera slowly moves toward the open front door as ominous music plays. Curious about the fate of the farmer, Cooper's observing mind returns to find answers. Here, Cooper assumes the role of what critic Jean-Pierre Oudart defines as "the Absent One," a presence "identified with the camera and hence the source of what is revealed."

Frustrated that the farmer has not given Andy any answers, Cooper tries to find them himself but discovers only an aftermath, an empty space the farmer once occupied. Thwarted, Cooper moves on to more important matters. The farmer's fate warrants no further attention.

At the Sheriff's station, Frank Truman invites Doc Hayward to talk via Skype and then enters Hayward's handle ("middleburydoc") into his computer.[†] Truman asks about the last time Doc Hayward saw Cooper, and Hayward recounts a troubling incident at the hospital, twenty-five years earlier, when he saw Cooper emerge from the intensive care unit where Audrey Horne was lying in a coma. (At the end of the original series Audrey was caught in a bomb explosion at the Twin

---

[*]Frank's phone call was another last-minute scene devised by David Lynch. As Robert Forster explained in an interview with *Entertainment Weekly*: "It was a scene that I hadn't seen prior to almost the moment that I shot it. I had maybe 20 minutes of work on it. I consider it a small gem in my career. Something that I said, 'God, I loved doing that shot.' Simple. Quick. It was perfect in every detail."

[†] I'm embarrassed to say that I noticed an error here: Truman types one too many letters on the keyboard, apparently typing *middleburrydoc*. (I know; I can see you rolling your eyes.)

Peaks Savings and Loan. Here, Doc Hayward confirms she survived.) Hayward recalls Cooper looking at him with a "strange face" before walking away. Neither Hayward nor Truman wants to contemplate what Cooper might have been doing in that room alone with Audrey, so Truman changes the subject. After a bit of small talk, Truman says a hearty farewell to Doc Hayward and ends the connection.

Frank Truman's pleasure at seeing Doc Hayward mirrors our own. Doctor Will Hayward was a strong, comforting presence on the original *Twin Peaks*, and it is good to know he has retired comfortably. Still, there are questions surrounding Hayward that have never been answered. Twenty-five years earlier, Doc Hayward struck Ben Horne, causing Ben to hit his head on the edge of a brick fireplace. Obviously, Ben recovered from the blow, but the bad blood between Horne and Hayward about the identity of Donna Hayward's biological father has never been resolved.

Clearly, Doc Hayward has moved away physically *and* mentally from Twin Peaks. Donna Hayward doesn't appear in *The Return*, but another of Hayward's daughters, Gersten, will appear later, and her circumstances are most troubling. Given Doc Hayward's sunny disposition, we can only assume he knows little of what Gersten's been up to. (None of this really matters, though, at least to the observing mind of Dale Cooper, whose interest in the Haywards is notional. Like his glancing attention for the missing farmer, Cooper devotes little time to long-ago Hayward melodrama.)

GORDON COLE WHISTLES in his office, waiting for an update from Albert. The photo of the nuclear explosion dominates the wall behind him, but it's not the only picture we see. Lynch opens the scene on a framed image of a half-shucked ear of corn, floating on a background of gray clouds. Lynch holds his camera on the picture, emphasizing its presence. "There is another picture in the office," Lynch explains in a post-*Return* interview, referring to the corn picture: "Look, you will see." In *Fire Walk With Me*, corn (specifically, creamed corn) is defined as *garmonbozia*, the physical manifestation of "pain and sorrow" (and the sustenance for demonic entities such as Bob). That a dramatic image of corn hangs adjacent to a powerful image of a nuclear explosion is no coincidence. Corn, too, represents a powerful, devastating energy.

Albert informs Cole that Diane is unwilling to help. Cole knows he must see her himself, and soon he and Albert arrive at her front door. Diane is not happy to see them, but Cole explains that her cooperation is extremely important and "involves something that you know about." Though Cole is not explicit, that "something" has to do with a plan Dale Cooper devised long ago.

Before he disappeared into the Red Room, Cooper told Diane about the Blue Rose case he was pursuing. He told her of the plan he was devising with Cole and Briggs to stop a grave threat. Now, Cole reminds Diane of that plan.

To be clear, none of Cooper's plan is explicitly described in the story. Cole's vague comment to Diane regarding "something that you know about" is our first hint regarding Cooper's scheme. (Later hints come in Part 9, when Diane acknowledges Cooper's Blue Rose case, and in Part 16, when Diane remembers crucial information regarding Cooper, but even in these instances Diane does not articulate the plan.) Diane "knows something" about the plan and is privy to secrets Cooper shared with her.

Still, there's a complication. It will later be revealed that this Diane is a *tulpa*, a manufactured replica of the original Diane, designed to do Mr. C's bidding. Decades ago, Diane endured a tragic, violent encounter with Mr. C, but her memories following this incident are hazy. She knows that Mr. C (whom she thought was Cooper) attacked her, but she doesn't know she's a duplicate of her former self. This Diane considers herself the real Diane—her mind, memories and emotions the same as always. (Cole won't learn about Diane's history with Mr. C until she tells him about it in Part 16.)

Poor Diane. She's a victim, and she's a pawn. Both Coopers, each in his own way, have compelled her to participate in perilous schemes. As she sits in her comfortable home, facing Cole and Albert, she knows her inevitable role in this ordeal is about to commence. No matter how much she hates it, no matter how angrily she resists, Diane doesn't have a choice.

A short while later, Diane joins Cole, Albert and Tammy Preston on an official flight to South Dakota.[*] When she gets to the prison, Diane insists on questioning Mr. C alone. Once inside the interrogation booth, she stares hard at the man she calls Cooper, demanding to know if he remembers the last time they met. She's testing Mr. C, trying to determine if he is the same man who assaulted her. Mr. C says he remembers being at Diane's house—he will always remember that night. That's all Diane needs to hear. "Who are you?" she demands, but Mr. C will say no more.

In but a few minutes Diane confirms that the man locked in the Yankton Federal Prison is not the Dale Cooper she knew long ago. Deep down, she knows he's a derivative of Cooper, a distillation of evil in human form. Shaken and distraught, Diane hastily exits the building and emphatically explains to Cole that the man they've captured is not Cooper. Something inside him is missing. Diane is exactly right, the man she spoke with is missing his soul, his sense of right and wrong, his moral compass.

The soulless Mr. C knows he's in control. Now that Diane has been drawn into his scheme, there's no reason for him to remain in prison. Through a carefully orchestrated blackmail, Mr. C compels Warden Murphy to release both him and Ray Monroe, and a few hours later they are escorted to a waiting car and drive away. Mr. C's plan is back on track. If Ray can't (or won't) supply the coordinates, Diane is now in place to get them.

AT THE LUCKY 7 INSURANCE AGENCY, a trio of detectives (all brothers with the surname Fusco) inform Cooper and Janey-E that "Dougie's" missing car was destroyed in an explosion. Stunned by the news, Janey-E agrees to follow-up with the detectives in the morning.[†]

---

[*]When we see the FBI jet in flight, various windows on the plane appear to be "blinking" in and out of existence, as if flashing a code. These blinking windows were deliberate, an effect added in post-production. I have no idea why Lynch chose to do this, nor do I know why certain letters (O, R, D, P) in the Lynch/Frost Productions logo at the end of the episode are also flashing. I find these incidents simply baffling. Another "Congressman's Dilemma."

[†] A nondescript painting hangs on the wall behind Janey-E. This same painting also appears in the television series, Mad Men. David Lynch has expressed admiration for

As Janey-E and Cooper exit the Lucky 7 building, Ike "The Spike" darts from the crowd brandishing a gun. Cooper springs into action. He pushes Janey-E away and forces Ike's hand, still holding the gun, toward the ground. Cooper strikes Ike to get him to release the gun. Suddenly, the Evolution of the Arm appears, wildly screaming for Cooper to "squeeze his hand off!" Cooper maintains his grip and forces Ike to relinquish the weapon. Ike sprints away. Cooper stands, staring blankly into the distance as if nothing happened.

For the first time since emerging into this world, Cooper has taken bold, decisive action. What's more, he has struck another person. If, as I've argued, Cooper is a benign and passive being, how could he take such action? How could he injure another human being?

We've seen instances where supernatural forces guide and protect Cooper. This incident, while quite dramatic, is no different than those others. Cooper is unaware of what he is doing when he defends himself against Ike. As if suddenly possessed, he reflexively protects himself (and, more importantly, Janey-E) and disarms his assailant. Once that task is accomplished, Cooper reverts to his passive self.

Otherworldly forces carefully monitor Cooper, and, like supernatural bodyguards, they fiercely act to keep him safe. If necessary, they can force Cooper into action (even if it's against another human being). Here, such a force was almost certainly The Evolution of The Arm, who materializes to aim Cooper toward his task. The Evolution of the Arm orders Cooper to harm Ike (to "squeeze his hand off"), but Cooper doesn't go that far. He merely applies enough pressure to force Ike to release the gun.

AT THE GREAT NORTHERN, Ben Horne and Beverly Paige try to find the origin of a strange ringing tone that permeates Ben's office. They walk from one side of the office to the other but can't quite pinpoint it. The sound seems to be everywhere, a constant presence, a reminder of the ringing noise that occurs in Franz Kafka's short story, "The Burrow." There, the story's narrator hears an incessant tone in his home

---

Mad Men and once took two of the show's actors, Jon Hamm and Elisabeth Moss, to dinner and referred to them only by their character names (Don and Peggy). Another possible (though tenuous) connection between *The Return* and *Mad Men* is the name, Janey-E Jones, which bears striking resemblance to the name of *Mad Men* actress, January Jones.

but cannot determine its origin: "I don't seem to be getting any nearer to the place where the noise is, it goes on, always on the same thin note…wherever I listen, high or low, at the roof or at the floor, at the entrance or in the corners, everywhere, everywhere, I hear the same noise."

The omnipresent sound in "The Burrow" is a manifestation of the narrator's psyche, an expression of his fear of the outside world. Like the sound in "The Burrow," the sound in the Great Northern is a manifestation of a particular psyche, in this case Dale Cooper's. It's no coincidence that as Ben and Beverly listen to the noise, they discuss Cooper and his Great Northern room key. Cooper needs the key back in Twin Peaks, and, sure enough, it has just arrived in the mail. For Cooper, the humming noise and the key are connected. Later, when Cooper confronts a narrative dead-end in his story, he will devise an exit strategy and follow the same mysterious Great Northern hum to a door he believes the key will fit. Cooper will unlock that door and free himself from one story so that he may enter another.[*]

Ben and Beverly leave the office, but Cooper ("the Absent One") continues to hunt for the source of the sound. A point-of-view shot slowly moves toward the corner of the room, approaching the wall of Ben's office and advancing into the very grain of the wood. Cooper is seeking a passage out of the Great Northern. He knows the key will open a door; he just needs to find which one.[†]

Ben Horne and Beverly Paige are clearly attracted to one another and engage in a mild flirtation as they listen to the odd noise. Beverly is in no rush to get home. She's staying late, "way past quitting time," because she's avoiding her husband, Tom, who languishes at home

---

[*] Jade mailed the key just a day earlier. In a normal timeline there's no way it could have made it to the Great Northern so quickly. Either Ben and Beverly's scene was supposed to take place later, or the key is here because Cooper *needs* it to be here.

[†] For longtime fans of *Twin Peaks*, it's hard not to think of Josie Packard in this scene. In the original series, Josie died in the Great Northern, but her spirit infused itself with the wooden décor of the hotel (her screaming face is famously shown contorting within a wooden drawer pull). In a later episode, Ben Horne stands in his office and senses something behind him. He turns sharply at the sensation, but the scene cuts away before we know what Ben sees. This sequence strongly implies that Josie haunts the Great Northern. Now, twenty-five years later, a strange sound is heard, and Cooper's point of view follows it deep into the walls. But there is no face there, no proof that Josie Packard is still a ghost in this wood.

under hospice care. Tom suffers from a debilitating ailment, likely cancer, and his illness has put a strain on the marriage. When Beverly finally does arrive home, the tension between the couple is palpable. They argue, and it becomes heated. Beverly resents being forced back to work, and Tom is suspicious of Beverly's excuse for being late.

Here, again, *The Return* shows us characters in pain, striving to navigate the hardships of a "dark, dark, world." The Paige marriage echoes the Truman marriage, where one spouse is tasked with the well-being of the ailing other. Beverly Paige may not have the same fortitude and patience as Frank Truman (she reveals a need, perhaps a weakness, when it comes to Ben Horne), but she is still trying to do right for her partner. There are no guilty parties in the struggling Paige marriage, only two regular people shouldering the hardships of an uncaring world and struggling to remain compassionate amid great emotional and physical pain.

PART 7 HAS BEEN FULL of dramatic twists and turns. Mark Frost describes it as one of the most traditional *Twin Peaks* episodes of *The Return*, and it's easy to see why. A number of mysteries from the original story (Laura's missing diary pages, Annie's dream visit, Audrey Horne's fate after the bank explosion) are referenced. Diane has a searing encounter with Mr. C (and we now know her past encounters with him were dangerous and traumatic), Cooper springs into action to defend himself against an assassin, and a strange hum at the Great Northern evokes hauntings past and present.

That's a lot of story. So much, you almost need a moment to catch your breath. Perhaps realizing this, David Lynch provides us time to decompress. At the Roadhouse, a man sweeps peanut shells as the song "Green Onions" by Booker T. & the M.G.'s plays on the soundtrack. The man sweeps and sweeps. He sweeps around a table. He sweeps behind bar stools. He sweeps peanut shells into a pile and sweeps the pile across the floor, adding shells to it as he goes. The man sweeps for two minutes and seventeen seconds. (Why not? If you have eighteen hours to tell a story, two minutes of sweeping is but the blink of an eye.)

The sweeping scene at the Roadhouse (derided by many as a frustrating waste of time) is a respite from the preceding narrative. It's a moment to stop and reset. Maybe that's what Dale Cooper is doing.

Watching from the Red Room, Cooper lets his mind wander for a bit, allows himself a moment of aimless contemplation. We all need to do that from time to time, so why not Cooper? The sweeping scene is a chance to order his thoughts, to clear his head. It's Cooper taking a break. And when he does, we do too.

Cooper's meditative moment is interrupted when the phone rings. Bartender Jean-Michel Renault (twin brother of the dead Jacques Renault, but not to be confused with his dead brother, Jean Renault) answers. We hear only Renault's side of the conversation, but we can deduce what he's talking about. Like his brother Jacques, Jean-Michel is running prostitutes out of the Roadhouse. He's arguing with a business associate about payment for two girls he recently provided and denying he knew the girls were underage. His demeanor and the seedy business he's running are stark reminders that time stands still in Twin Peaks. Renault, like so many others in the town, is an echo of the past, a character living a static life in an unchanging place. The same thing is happening to Cooper in the Red Room. Imprisoned in that anachronic realm, Cooper can only observe the world through a mind trapped in the past. To Cooper, Jean-Michel Renault, perched behind the Roadhouse bar like a petty criminal kingpin, is simply a reflection of a different Renault, a twin brother Cooper encountered long ago.

THE DOUBLE R DINER IS HUMMING with late-night activity. Shelly, Heidi, and the rest of the staff are serving a crowded house, while Norma Jennings busies herself with paperwork. Suddenly a man named Bing bursts through the door and yells, "Has anybody seen Billy?" Someone yells, "No," and Bing runs away.

Bing's interruption is startling. Norma looks up from her work,[*] and Shelly halts for a moment and glances wide-eyed around the room. Things quickly settle back to normal, and the end credits for Part 7 begin to roll, playing over the diner activity in the background.

As the credits roll, the camera cuts from one angle of the diner to another, but something is off. The patrons visible in the first shot are either missing or in different locations in the second shot. What's more, we see Bing get up from a booth and walk toward the cashier—the

---

[*] This shot of Norma is the exact same one we saw in Part 5, recycled here in Part 7.

same Bing who moments earlier shouted into the diner looking for Billy. What's going on here?

When Part 7 first aired, many attentive viewers believed these mismatched shots were deliberate and might imply an alternate, or "braided" narrative—two worlds of *Twin Peaks* running parallel, unfolding side-by-side. As enticing as this theory might be, the reason these edits don't align is simply due to a mistake. Duwayne Dunham, the editor of *The Return*, confirms it: "It's just one of those things you do in movie making. You take whatever footage happened to be shot in the diner and you use it. It could be made up of two or three different diner scenes. That's why those people are moving all around. It's just one of those things."

We know David Lynch is a careful filmmaker and there is meaning in the cryptic nature of his work (or at least there is for Lynch; the "blinking" windows on the FBI jet are a likely example), but in the case of the Double R editing glitch, the obvious discontinuity between shots is nothing more than an accident. Yes, it's noticeable, and *yes*, it's a bit sloppy. But it's not deliberate. At eighteen hours, *The Return* was a major undertaking by all artists involved, and post-production was intense. "We did nine movies in one year!" Dunham explains, "Eighteen hours means nine two-hour movies in exactly one year." Editing errors naturally slipped into the work. On a film this length, mistakes like these couldn't be helped.

In the end, these mistakes don't matter. Throughout *The Return*, Lynch explores the concepts of imperfect recall and misapprehension. He weaves these aspects of the human psyche into the fabric of his *Twin Peaks* (indeed, this very episode began with the failed communication between Ben and Jerry Horne). As a result, and perhaps quite by accident, Lynch found he could tolerate "sloppy" edits by simply interpreting them as misperceptions of an observing mind, the mental malaprops of Dale Cooper's inconsistent and fatigued psyche. Though not deliberate, the many editing mistakes in *The Return* don't necessarily disrupt the narrative, they add to it. The sometimes-erratic flow of *Twin Peaks* is merely the reflection of Dale Cooper's muddled, imperfect mind.

DRINK FULL AND DESCEND

woman screaming distantly soft clicking box cutter slicing distant traffic whooshing distant horns honking atmospheric hum intercom alarm buzzes computer processing softly 8112802685 SD08112802714 elevator lift clicks keypad beeps metal door slides open soft warbling tone stomping chickens clucking distantly shotgun clanks door creaks open soft rumbling very soft whooshing pounds glass Intense otherworldly whooshing glass shatters flesh slicing camera shutter clicking trees creaking line trilling mouse clicks H62499810 lock clatters keys scrape 68N416 flashlight clicks skin crinkling metal clanks softly dog barking distantly gunshot blood running softly bells clanging train horn blaring distantly train whooshing ominous whooshing ominous tone odd reverberations Intense ethereal whooshing whispering indistinctly rumbling wind whooshing eerie electrical sputtering thud echoes metal grating lock clattering thunder booming rain pattering drawer rustling headboard thuds tape rewinding faucet squeaks briefcase latches click radio static clicking lock rattles kdhgw sdl04pcsecprot mkeuouc-q eeuoubp3x 398715015787412 ominous scratching noise intense discordant music electricity crackling engine humming intense rumbling breathy sputtering whooshing structural creaking loud clanking sonic pop intense ominous whooshing wind whipping intensely soft whoosh waves lapping distantly ominous atmospheric hum indistinct breathy noises loud pounding foreboding atmospheric music eerie humming brooding tone soft electrical hiss high pitched static rumbling tone lever clanks dress flapping hatch clanks electrical thud hiss electricity sputtering loud thrumming tires squealing soft electrical scratching stifled gagging birds calling faintly sirens wailing distantly car engine revving distantly shower running heaving stifled vomiting gurgling spittle dripping electric guitar strums flesh squishing softly ring clinking on floor loud ominous pop squelching atmospheric whooshing footsteps departing house alarm beeps locks clicking rifle cocks engine turning over coughing static crackles birds chirping motor creaks softly spray can rattling hissing door clunking steadily buzzer sounds slot machines ringing, coins rattling Indistinct chatter bells dinging coin clinks, machine chimes lever clicks TV beeps knocks table machine beeping camera whirring owl hoots 25140 door slams phone ringing distantly footsteps approaching insects chirping 1171 1507 10-4 16 1007 bird cawing urine splashing aggressively groaning chuckling silverware clatters drawer closes chokes gags sizzling computer whirring airplane engine roaring tires screeching gate buzzing lock buzzes button clicks shutter whirring static whines shoe scrapes against pavement feedback whines line beeping device ringing bright tone beeps keys jangle knob squeaks water running manic laughter ARGENT 159 indistinct chatter elevator bell dings telephone ringing sniffs grunting man speaking indistinctly over radio 37890 engine grinds ER3Z7LL snorting clock ticking alarm ringing bell tolls record player winding up switch clicks fireworks exploding liquid sloshing ringing tone shimmering tones clicks tongue shouting indistinctly dial tone humming doorbell chimes chews potato chips toiletry clinks grating music 0340 -839256 -10045 1384393 004 011 94771 traffic blaring gear shifts neon humming muffled rock band playing machinery rumbling sniffing swallows arm whips coins jingle coin whirring coin clinks soft metallic crunching coin landing train passing distantly truck whooshes traffic passing faintly gear crunches engine rumbling keys clacking motor droning truck bed clanks truck bed motor whirring elevator buzzing children chattering roars spits growls weapon whips furniture clatters NP8B3JD 'beware the thirteenth sycamore' computer beeps buzzer blares handcuffs click panicked breathing chair creaking pen scratching gun cocks choking helicopter whirring overhead sirens approaching indistinct police radio chatter cell door unlocks whirs distant clanking door buzzes lock clicks gate creaking open gate whirring closed window rolls crickets chirping coyote howls distantly revolver clicks trigger clicking gunshots echo distorted moaning explosions booming static sputtering otherworldly exhaling waves lapping alarming metallic clanking ambient vintage music wind whistling ticking shell crinkles crinkling squishing wing flitters light fixtures creaking distorted scream blood spewing body thuds soft groaning soft crunching record scratches record needling crackling radio static humming soft pained groaning metal tool clatters body clumps soft chittering pained gagging soft pained whimpering breathing heavily splat horse whinnying distantly bottles clinking plane droning overhead siren blares bell dings on website distant thump rapid footsteps hinge squeaks device clanging weeping sniffling neck cracking heavy blow lands knob squeaking match fizzes line rings gas hissing panting fly buzzing door handle clatters yelps device humming chewing noisily birds cawing objects clattering drink sloshing frequencies whistling water roaring ball bounces soft moaning pained moaning LK902NL whistle shrieks ZN38YS dishware clinking shells clinking thunderous reverberation ominous rumbling sniffles horn honking gun clicking stammers low gurgling spewing chair creaks slurping muffled pipes flushing ignition beeping seatbelt clicks 778H bandage rips gun uncocks upbeat ditty playing on piano ice clatters champagne fizzing glasses clink wine pouring glass thumps softly dial clicking cell phone chimes buzzes ice tinkling in glass liquid pouring scanner beeps bottles rattling 133.70 boy whistles leaves rustling passing engine hums thunder rumbling fan whooshing bottles rattling faintly indistinct PA announcement footsteps tapping rapid beeping smacks lips dull thumping silenced gunshot fire crackling rotary dial clicking vacuum whirring ambient whooshing neon buzzing garage door rumbling door clanks elevator motor humming scattered chuckling elbow thuds men shouting bone crunching paper rustling clinking echoes siren chirping coffee maker hissing slurps doorbell buzzing cheering on TV liquid trickles touch tones beeping wiper squeaking feedback shrieks glass squeaking man shuffling lighter clicks water rushing bird chittering whimpering shakily faint hissing warbling static sputtering lock clanks blood dripping nut cracks door creaking mechanical rumbling faint cackling billiard balls clacking faintly truck horn honks ice rustling ominous hiss intense ominous clank gargling crowd murmuring car whooshes past gas station bell dinging electric tools clanking NIP633 vehicle rumbles softly high-pitched rewinding light bulb humming erratically ominous humming static clank snorts crowd gasps men grunting song scratching song skipping muffled child screaming terrified wheezing motorcycle revving distantly lips smacking dishware clinking creaking over line wind moaning distantly spotlights whirring SW51 faint beeping continuous tone DSX636 engine clicks off monitor beeping ventilator hissing 93289853-0-224 274JID 458IGR 739L8M flames roar softly blows raspberry glass thuds lightly eerie whooshing odd rattling object whooshing wings flapping odd rumbling snoring lightly intense whoosh motorized device clanks bullets rattling flesh tearing distorted growl sonic thud sonic smacking distorted cackling soft clank clock ticking irregularly stairway creaking distorted whooshing deep rhythmic whooshing electrical hum 7481D2 water lapping reel whirring wailing oddly reverberates static pulsing softly VS2-168R brakes squeal softly turn signal clicking fryer oil bubbling Back away there, Michael. Yeah, back away. Back, back, keep goin' back. There. Perfect, perfect.

PART 8:

GOTTA LIGHT?

THE DETONATION OF THE FIRST ATOMIC BOMB in 1945 was a historic turning point. There was the world before atomic weaponry, and there was the world after. Once the bomb exploded there was no going back. It was a thing that could not be undone.

There was *Twin Peaks* before *The Return* Part 8, and there was *Twin Peaks* after. Once Part 8 aired on June 25, 2017, it fundamentally reshaped a decades-old story. Something new had been introduced into the world of *Twin Peaks*. Its mythology was expanded, its history remade. All that comes after Part 8 is defined by events depicted therein. All that came before is now haunted by a startling new backstory. There is no going back.

RAY AND MR. C RACE AWAY from Yankton Federal Prison. Aware they're being tracked, Mr. C activates a program on his phone, enters the license number of a nearby truck, and hurls the phone out the window. Mr. C once again employs mysterious tech. Whatever arcane app he used, it has deactivated (or diverted) any tracking devices.

Ray says he's memorized the coordinates and expects to be paid for them. Mr. C coolly evaluates Ray and tells him to exit the freeway. They drive onto a dirt road, and Ray stops to "take a leak." After Ray gets out, Mr. C retrieves a gun from the glove compartment, checks to see it has bullets, and exits the car. Holding the gun, Mr. C demands that Ray give him the coordinates. Ray turns and faces Mr. C with a gun of his own. Mr. C pulls his trigger, but nothing happens. His gun is filled with blanks. Ray smiles and shoots Mr. C twice at point-blank range.

The shooting of Mr. C sets in motion ominous forces. Ghostly apparitions of Woodsmen emerge from the darkness. Dirty, ragged, and blackened with soot (or is it engine oil?), the Woodsmen immediately set to work, some surrounding Ray to prevent him from causing further damage, others crouching around the body of Mr. C to perform a bizarre healing ritual. The Woodsmen dig into the dirt and spread Mr. C's blood across his body and face. Mr. C's abdomen swells, and a large cyst, the size of a basketball, emerges. As it rises, the leering face of Bob is visible inside.

As soon as Ray sees Bob, he scrambles back to the car and drives away. On the road, he calls Phillip Jeffries to report that he "saw something in Cooper," and says, "it may be the key to what this is all about." This latter comment hints that Ray knows more about the supernatural than he previously let on. Still, as I mentioned Part 2, Ray's role remains murky. He's working for the FBI, but he's also working for the imposter Phillip Jeffries. Right now, his allegiance seems to be with the imposter, who probably supplied Ray with the gun and (we learn later) the Owl Cave Ring.[*] (Ray was supposed to put the ring on a dead Mr. C, but that didn't happen. Ray still has the ring in his pocket.)

The Woodsmen continue their bizarre ritual over Mr. C's body. They complete their job and fade back into the night, leaving Mr. C unconscious and apparently healed (and still a viable host for Bob). The Woodsmen are Mr. C's insurance. He's impossible to kill as long as they can emerge to repair him.

AT THE ROADHOUSE, the band Nine Inch Nails performs "She's Gone Away." It's a hard song, a loud song, wrought by vocalist Trent Reznor with fury and aggression. Reznor's lyrics speak to the uncertain nature of the narrative: "I can't remember what she came here for. I can't remember much of anything anymore," lines that arguably describe Cooper's tenuous hold on reality. Reznor's lament, "She's gone, she's gone away," surely reflects Cooper's anxiety about Laura Palmer and what Cooper still must do to find her.

---

[*] How did the imposter get hold of the ring? Good question. I'll discuss the curious path of the ring when we get to Part 13.

The performance of "She's Gone Away" knocks us back a bit, throws us off balance. The bruising performance underscores the bizarre procedure Mr. C has just endured. As we reel from the intensity of Nine Inch Nails, the story cuts back to Mr. C lying on the ground. Suddenly he sits up, eyes open, and stares fiercely into the night.

AND HERE THE STORY takes leave of the interpreting presence of Dale Cooper. Up until now, we've been witnessing a story as Cooper construes it, his observing mind looking into the real world. For the rest of Part 8, that changes. The story transitions from color to black and white, signaling a new perspective, an *objective* account. Black and white is "a beautiful medium for going back in time," Lynch tells us. "A beautiful medium for slipping to another kind of world."

What follows is, indeed, another kind of world, a story untainted by the encrypting psyche of Dale Cooper. The facts here are far more reliable.

History is about to unfold.

July 16, 1945

WHITE SANDS, NM

5.29 AM (MWT)

10 – 9 – 8 – 7 – 6 – 5 – 4 – 3 – 2 – 1

Boom

ONE OF THE MOST INDELIBLE and startling images of *Twin Peaks: The Return* is the detonation of the world's first atomic bomb. The scene opens high above the dark New Mexico desert, miles to the northwest of Point Zero, the Trinity Site. Things are quiet at first, almost serene, but that's about to change. A subatomic chain-reaction initiates deep within a man-made gadget. A fraught cascade of neutrons reaches the fury of its own momentum. In this dreadful moment—a "moment of completion" unlike any other—comes a blinding flash of light and heat. A second later, the world's first nuclear mushroom cloud blossoms into the sky.

David Lynch's camera moves smoothly over the desert toward the bomb's expanding shockwave, slipping effortlessly into the heart of the cloud. Once inside, Lynch shows us the roiling energies unleashed by the bomb. Everything is tumult and turmoil and abstraction. Searing anarchies of fire and light. Deafening roars of a universe torn asunder.

Thrashed about, pummeled by conflagration, we are severed from anything recognizable. Only the dissonant chords of Krzysztof Penderecki's "Threnody for the Victims of Hiroshima" provides traction amid the chaos. Lynch's heart-of-the-bomb imagery is awesome and frightful and not unlike Stanley Kubrick's "star gate" sequence from *2001: A Space Odyssey*, a kaleidoscopic barrage of worlds both ominous and magnificent.

From out of the chaos the camera settles on the exterior of an old convenience store somewhere in the desert. At first, all is still, but energies are suddenly unleashed here, too. Smoke pours from the store's entrance. Electricity arcs and sputters. Woodsmen appear, frantically pacing amid bright flashes of light. To emphasize the agitation, Lynch superimposes images of the wandering Woodsmen over one another. Like a nest of ants disturbed by some outside force, the Woodsmen scramble to restore order. After a time, they do, and the Woodsmen enter the store. But something is clearly amiss. A tremor has shaken the foundation of reality.

Did the detonation of the bomb introduce the Woodsmen to Earth, or have they always been here, their agonies merely the result of energies released? It's hard to say, but it appears the bomb shook the Woodsmen out from their realm and dumped them in front of the store. Now, connected to this mysterious place, they are destined to meet "above" it. The store will become known as "The Dutchman's" (named after the fabled ghost ship, "The Flying Dutchman"), an untethered, liminal space straddling realities and providing egress between this world and others. In times to come, Mike (the one-armed man) will live here, and Phillip Jeffries will infiltrate the place to spy on its odd inhabitants.

From the chaos of the convenience store, we move to the quiet of a dark void. A figure emerges from the blackness, floating in infinite space. This is "Experiment," the same creature that broke free from the glass box in Part 1.[*]

Experiment vomits forth a stream of white, viscous gel. Embedded within the gel are hundreds of speckled eggs. One of the eggs breaks free and tumbles off-screen (and falls to Earth, into the sands of the New Mexico desert, where it will incubate for many years). As the spew of vomit extends from Experiment, a cyst-like object containing the image of Bob emerges. The cyst looks just like the one The Woodsmen removed from Mr. C. It clings to the side of the column and then detaches and floats away.

What is Bob doing here? What does it mean that he emerges from the maw of Experiment? Many believe we are seeing the birth of Bob into the world, that this is his beginning. The atomic explosion ripped open a rift in the fabric of reality, and Bob slipped through.

But is this really the *origin* of Bob? Does this moment mark his introduction to our plane of existence?

I'm not convinced.

I'm not convinced because the presence of ancient evil is woven deeply into the *Twin Peaks* backstory. Recall in the original series that Harry Truman tells Cooper: "There's a sort of evil out there. Something very, very strange in these old woods. Call it what you want: A darkness, a presence. It takes many forms, but it's been out there for *as long as anyone can remember.*" (Emphasis added.) Surely Truman is alluding to Bob or something like him, an idea Mark Frost reinforces in *The Secret History of Twin Peaks*, when he describes Bob-like entities that have haunted the environs of Twin Peaks for hundreds of years. The "silent man" Merriweather Lewis describes in his journal is one of them. So is a character named "Denver Bob," who disappeared after visiting Owl Cave. If Bob is a metaphoric symbol for "the evil that men

---

[*] The performer upon whom Experiment is modelled, Erica Eynon, is credited as Experiment in both Parts 1 and 8. Notably, Experiment's "face" resembles the distorted ace of spades that Mr. C showed Darya in Part 2. Note also that Experiment's arms seem to be attached backwards (left for right, and vice versa), which recalls Laura Palmer's strange comment to Cooper in the original series: "Sometimes my arms bend back."

do" (another idea suggested in the original series), then Bob has been on Earth for as long as man has, certainly long before 1945.

In Part 8, Bob is purportedly "born" moments after the Trinity bomb explodes, emerging from whatever goo Experiment disgorges. He is loosed into the world after mankind unleashes unprecedented, transgressive forces. That's what it looks like, anyway.

But nothing Lynch shows us definitively proves this is Bob's beginning. Rather, Bob could be *escaping* from whatever realm he previously inhabited. The cyst containing Bob is not submersed in Experiment's vomit. It appears to be tucked into a crevice on the exterior. Hiding in a fold, riding the stream like a stowaway about to jump ship, Bob detaches from the goo and drifts into the void. He has escaped.

OK, yes, whether Bob "escapes" or is "born" makes no difference, this moment marks the advent of Bob into the world, his "origin" (if you must). Still, it doesn't feel right. A better interpretation (for me, anyway) is that this escape is one of *many* instances where Bob has broken free from wherever he's been trapped. Time and again, Bob gets away, and time and again other beings (such as Mike) follow him into the world to capture and bring him back. This scenario has probably played out for eons. Bob returns again and again. For as long as we exist in this dark age there will be evil, and there will always be Bob.

THE STORY MOVES to the realm Cooper visited in Part 3, the one where he stood upon a balcony of some vast structure and stared across a dark and roiling ocean. Lynch's camera moves across this turbulent ocean until it reaches a tower on an island (likely the same place where Cooper landed). The camera slowly moves up the tower toward a lone narrow window near the top.

Inside, a woman sits on an ornate couch listening to music. Festooned with rings, bracelets, and an elaborate necklace, wearing a long, sequined dress, her head haloed by a delicate collar, this is Señorita Dido. Beside her, a large metallic object (resembling the bell-shaped protuberance Naido climbed to in Part 3) dominates the room.

An alarm sounds, but Señorita Dido barely flinches. She glances to her right, and the Fireman appears from behind the bell. He stares silently at Señorita Dido, communicating to her without speaking. He turns to the bell and pushes a button, silencing the alarm. The Fireman stares again at Señorita Dido. Advanced beyond the limitations of spoken language, The Fireman and Señorita Dido both understand what the alarm means. They both know they have roles to play in what comes next.

The Fireman enters a space that looks like an old movie theater and approaches a screen situated on a stage. When he raises his hand, images flicker on the screen, and he sees the exploding atomic bomb, the Woodsmen outside the convenience store, and the Bob-cyst floating away from Experiment. The image freezes on Bob's leering face. The Fireman does not balk at Bob or at any of the other images. He is prepared for this moment and levitates into the air above the stage.

Señorita Dido enters the room and sees the image of Bob. She climbs the stairs to the stage and stands under the Fireman, who floats on his back above her. The image of Bob on screen disappears and is replaced by stars floating through space.

Golden strands of energy emit from the Fireman's head. With joy and wonder, Señorita Dido watches the strands coalesce into a golden orb. Señorita Dido grasps the orb, peers inside and sees the smiling face of Laura Palmer.[*] Señorita Dido lovingly kisses the orb and raises it above her head. The orb floats up and into a tubular mechanism, which pivots toward the screen. As the mechanism turns, the image onscreen shows the Earth emerging from the stars. The tube deposits the orb into the image, and the orb floats across Earth toward North America.

OSTENSIBLY, THE PRECEDING series of events are straightforward: Powerful beings (the Fireman and Señorita Dido) monitor Earth and when alerted to danger (such as Bob and/or The Woodsmen) generate a force of good to counterbalance the imminent threat.

But it's not that simple. Laura Palmer's unexpected presence in this scene is simply baffling. The idea that The Fireman created Laura and sent her to Earth undermines just about everything we thought we knew about *Twin Peaks*. Rather than Laura being the mortal teenage girl who suffered and died at the hands of Bob, it appears as if Laura was the creation of divine beings, who sent her to Earth to *combat* Bob.

---

[*] The image from Laura's homecoming photo, which appears in every opening credits sequence of *The Return*.

Why else would the Fireman immediately "create" Laura after seeing Bob's image?

But let's be careful. Any assumptions we make now are based on what we thought we knew. We think we know Laura's story, especially having seen *Fire Walk With Me*, but there's much more to come in *The Return*. Laura Palmer's story is far from complete. Suffice to say, what we learn in later episodes (combined with the curious details revealed in Part 2) supports the idea that Laura Palmer was created by the Fireman not to combat Bob, but to restore order to the universe. (In *The Return*, Laura never encounters Bob. The story of that conflict has already been told.)

David Lynch subscribes to the Hindu idea that the universe experiences a recurring cycle of four distinct eras. He has explicitly discussed this belief in various interviews over the years: "There are different ages: the Golden age, the Silver Age, the Bronze Age, and the Iron Age. We are in the Iron Age…and it's a dark age." When we reach the end of the fourth and final age—the Kali Yuga (the dark age we're in now)—the cycle ends and starts again. The story in *The Return* is heading toward this cyclical transition. Indeed, Laura's role is to bring the "dark age" to an end.[*]

FROM THE FIREMAN'S REALM we shift back to Earth, back to the New Mexico desert in 1956. In the dark of night, a speckled egg (almost certainly the one originating from Experiment's gooey column) lies in the sand, having incubated there for the past 11 years. The egg hatches, and an unnatural creature, part insect and part frog, emerges. This "frog-moth" flutters its wings and slowly crawls across the sand.

On a nearby desert road, a teenage boy and girl walk home under the light of a full moon.[†] The girl sees a penny, heads-up in the dirt, and retrieves it. She says it will bring good luck.

Not far away, Woodsmen materialize in the desert. One drops from the air onto the ground (recalling a Woodsman's line from the *Fire*

---

[*] See the next chapter, "Ten is the Number of Completion," for a detailed analysis of Laura's role in *The Return*.

[†] Here's your chance to roll your eyes again: There was no full moon on August 5th, 1956. It was, in fact, a moonless night.

Walk With Me script: "We have descended from pure air"). The Woodsmen stalk onto a nearby road and are illuminated by the lights of an approaching car. The car stops, and the first Woodsman extends a cigarette and asks if the driver has "Gotta light?" The driver becomes immobilized by the Woodsman's hypnotic force, but when the woman in the passenger seat wails with fear, the driver regains his willpower and steps on the accelerator.[*]

The girl and boy continue their walk home, shyly making small talk as they go. They share a tender kiss, and the girl goes into her house.

Out in the desert, a radio station broadcasts the song, "My Prayer" by The Platters. Local residents listen to the song as they go about their lives: A mechanic works on a car, a waitress cleans the counter of a diner, the young girl sits on her bed, smiling dreamily.

The "Gotta Light?" Woodsman enters the radio station and kills a woman working in the front office.[†] He enters the next room, subdues the DJ, and grabs a microphone. The Woodsman then broadcasts an odd mantra to the listening world: "This is the water. And this is the well. Drink full and descend. The horse is the white of the eyes and dark within." All the people listening to the station, including the young girl, hear the Woodsman's chant and collapse into unconsciousness.

The frog-moth crawls across the sand toward the girl's house. It flies into her open window and approaches her face as she sleeps peacefully on her side. The girl unconsciously opens her mouth, and the frog-moth pushes inside and down her throat. The girl swallows and continues to sleep.

---

[*] The "Gotta light?" Woodsman is portrayed by actor Robert Broski, who, in real-life, has had a successful career portraying Abraham Lincoln in film and television. While Broski does not overtly portray Lincoln in Part 8, he does appear immediately after the girl finds the penny and rubs her thumb across the face of Lincoln. There may be no meaning to this sequence other than David Lynch making a subtle, extra-contextual nod to Broski.

[†] This office is staged as an homage to Edward Hopper's 1940 painting, *Office at Night*. The woman working in the station wears the same dress, has the same hairstyle, and stands in the same pose as the woman in the painting. Earlier scenes in Part 8, such as the exterior of a gas station and the exterior of the young girl's home, are also influenced by Hopper's works. See *Gas* (1940) and *Summer Evening* (1947).

Back at the station, the Woodsman kills the DJ by crushing his skull. He ends his hypnotic chant and walks out into the night. A horse whinnies in the distance.

WHAT FOUL PLOT IS HATCHING this dark New Mexico night? Clearly, the Woodsman's chant, its effect on the listening population, and the frog-moth's objective are tied together. Once the creature hatches from its egg, the Woodsmen arrive. One of them finds a radio station and deliberately puts the surrounding residents to sleep, making them vulnerable to the creature. But for what purpose? Why did the frog-moth target this girl and use her as host? Perhaps the penny, the one the girl found on the ground, was bait, marking her as a victim (just like the Owl Cave ring might do). It's curious that Lynch puts emphasis on the penny and includes the girl's ironic comment that it will bring good luck.

The Return never clarifies the identity of the young girl, but outside sources confirm she is Sarah Palmer. Mark Frost identifies her in his book, *The Final Dossier* (providing her full maiden name as Sarah Judith Novack), and Tikaeni Faircrest, the actress who played the young girl, confirms in interviews she was playing "the young Sarah Palmer." And so, the implication is that the frog-moth inserted itself in Sarah, where it festered for years waiting for the right moment to fully corrupt her. Indeed, later episodes reveal that Sarah has become a being of horror and despair, a being Frost identifies as Judy (or Jouday), an interdimensional demon that feeds on the suffering of human beings.

I don't know about you, but I find the idea of a possessed Sarah Palmer far more startling than the idea of The Fireman creating Laura Palmer. As I've argued earlier in this book (see the discussion of Part 2), I don't accept that Sarah Palmer was an evil entity with evil designs. I choose to view Sarah Palmer as a victim, a woman who carries within her an empty vessel waiting to be inhabited. When Experiment finally blasts into the world on a gruesome night in New York City, it finds purchase in Sarah Palmer, whose body was made ready for this possession long ago.

ALL THESE DUELING ENTITIES in *The Return*, playing their long games. Major Briggs devises a plan to find Judy. Mr. C crafts a way to avoid The Black Lodge. Experiment ensures it will someday have a viable host. And the being with the greatest plan of all? The Fireman, who sent to Earth Laura Palmer as the ultimate remedy. Laura has a mission, one that transcends the age-old conflict between good and evil. She is sent to Earth to complete the circle.

Laura Palmer is the cynosure. The moment of completion.

<INTERLUDE 4>
TEN IS THE NUMBER OF COMPLETION

NOW THAT WE'VE LEARNED Laura Palmer shares a connection to the Fireman, how do we reconfigure her role in this revised and expanded *Twin Peaks* narrative? How do we make sense of these baffling developments?

The presence of Laura Palmer in the golden orb, ostensibly sent to Earth to counter the advent of Bob, challenges a story we thought we knew. We thought Laura Palmer was a mere human being, a victim of abuse who endured years of torment but who eventually found the courage to face her abuser and deny him (or it) any further purchase on her soul, a woman who ultimately defied the forces that sought to contaminate her. Laura, who had been deceived into thinking she had no worth, found in the end that she was a good person—righteous and holy—and strong enough to defeat the evil forces working to undermine her.

But now…. Now we are presented with a profound revision to this story. Now we have to rethink everything that has come before and readjust the existing narrative to accommodate an enigmatic new identity for Laura. Where once we might have asked, "Who is Laura Palmer?", Part 8 of *The Return*, with its revelation that Laura is the creation of the Fireman and Señorita Dido, demands we ask a different question, demands we ask, "*What* is Laura Palmer?" A difficult question, to be sure, but I believe the answer is there, cryptically embedded within the text of *The Return*, with clues scattered throughout the eighteen hours. Let's examine these clues and attempt an answer. Let's find out what Laura Palmer really is.

AFTER THE ORIGINAL *TWIN PEAKS* was cancelled in 1991, David Lynch could have made a follow-up feature film that picked up where the story left off. No doubt he would have had the financing for such a project and, quite possibly, the creative cooperation of Mark Frost. But Lynch chose a different direction. He chose to make his sixth feature film about the last week of Laura Palmer's life and fashioned a story that gave Laura Palmer a prominent and meaningful place in the *Twin Peaks* narrative. "I was in love with the character of Laura Palmer and her contradictions: radiant on the surface but dying inside," explained Lynch. "I wanted to see her live, move and talk."

No other character has obsessed Lynch as much as Laura Palmer. After completing *Fire Walk With Me*, Lynch still wasn't done with Laura. He wrote and directed new introductions (featuring The Log Lady) for each episode of the original series and, once again, sought to reorient the *Twin Peaks* text to foreground Laura. In the first introduction, The Log Lady explicitly tells us, "Laura is the one." She is the one character around which all the others orbit. Laura occupies the center; she "is the one that leads to the many." As I wrote in an essay for *Wrapped In Plastic*, these statements show that "Lynch is asking viewers to assess (or reassess) [the original *Twin Peaks*] with a different Laura Palmer in mind—the Laura Palmer who was so vividly brought to life in *Fire Walk With Me*."

Decades later, when Lynch revisited the world of *Twin Peaks* for *The Return*, he ensured Laura would play a part and that her role would be expanded and revised yet again. In *The Return*, Laura becomes a crucial component of the narrative, a role Lynch signals in every opening sequence by showing us an ethereal image of Laura's face, her famous homecoming picture, now a saintly image with a golden halo shining around her right eye.

When we first meet Laura in *The Return*, she has become something more than mortal. The "Laura Palmer" Dale Cooper encounters in the Red Room in Part 2 is transcendent, deliberate, in possession of an intellect vast and vertiginous. She straddles realms both earthly and celestial, and she reveals to Cooper an identity that shines with divine energy. Laura, here, is far more than the flesh-and-blood character of *Fire Walk With Me*, the woman who lived, suffered and died on the mortal plane. Laura of the Red Room is akin to a deity.

She is a cosmic player. And she has a destiny for which she has been *designed*.

NO DOUBT, *THE RETURN* focusses on the intimate stories of its many characters and how they navigate the ups and downs of everyday life. It is a story about losing and finding love, about managing grief in the face of trauma, about dealing with the suffering we encounter every day. *Twin Peaks: The Return* is about trust and faith, memory and regret, life and death. But the larger background against which these stories unfold involves an epic clash between good and evil.

At its core, *The Return* is about the dark age Janey-E describes in Part 6. It's about how evil has manifested in the world and how this evil preys on the souls of human beings. Hindu mythology refers to this dark age as the Kali Yuga, a time of suffering, despair and burgeoning evil. During the Kali Yuga, "moral order will continue to decline, and evil will steadily increase." Fortunately, the Kali Yuga is the last age in a cycle of four ages. When the Kali Yuga comes to an end (and it will) the cycle of ages starts again.

David Lynch is steeped in Hindu mythology. Wisdom from Hindu holy texts (often referred to as the Vedic texts) such as the Upanishads, the Bhagavad-Gita, the Ramayana, and the Yoga Sutras inform much of his worldview. (Lynch quotes liberally from these texts in his short memoir, *Catching the Big Fish*.) So, it's not surprising that Hindu mythology forms the basis of much of *The Return*, particularly the "creation" of Laura Palmer in Part 8.

According to Hindu belief, Vishnu, the god who sustains all of reality, monitors the universe and, over time, sends to Earth a series of ten avatars to maintain order and help humanity during various crises. At the end of the Kali Yuga, when darkness reigns and there is little hope for mankind, Vishnu (along with his consort, Lakshmi, the goddess of wealth and well-being) sends to earth the tenth and final avatar, Kalki. Descending to Earth on a white horse (avatar literally means "descend"), Kalki ends the dark age: Evil is destroyed, moral order is restored, and the cycle of time begins again with the Krita Yuga, an age of purity and creativity (what David Lynch refers to as the "golden age").

With all this in mind, it is hard *not* to see the idea of the Hindu cycle at play in *Twin Peaks*. Man detonates the first atomic bomb and ushers in the final years of the dark age, opening a door for evil to flourish in the form of Bob and the contaminating presence of the frog-moth (which hatches from Experiment's wayward egg). Alarms ring in the realm of the Fireman and Señorita Dido, both of whom monitor the universe, occupying roles akin to the deities Vishnu and Lakshmi. The Fireman recognizes that Bob has escaped (perhaps as Bob has done throughout the ages), but this time there is a dire nature to Bob's freedom. The Fireman realizes his most powerful—and final—avatar is required. And so, he creates Laura Palmer and sends her to Earth to bring an end to the dark age. During her life on Earth Laura will confront Bob, but defeating him is not her true task. Ultimately, Laura must appear in the right place and the right time (one dark night outside the Palmer house) to fulfill her real purpose. She will scream then, powerfully and decisively, so that the dark age can be brought to "completion," and a new age can begin. As a result, Laura Palmer effectively becomes the most crucial player in the narrative, a figure of both termination and renewal—the Omega and the Alpha of *Twin Peaks*.

LAURA'S ROLE AS THE TENTH AVATAR of The Fireman (i.e., Vishnu) is hinted at throughout *The Return*. In the Red Room in Part 2 "Laura" (or someone who looks exactly like Laura Palmer) presents her true self to Cooper. She opens her face to reveal a glowing white light within. This is the divine Laura, the one designed by the Fireman. When this Laura screams and is flung from the Red Room, Cooper sees a white horse manifest in her wake. As Hindu mythology tells us, a white horse is the symbol of Kalki, the tenth avatar.

A white horse has haunted the *Twin Peaks* narrative since the original series. In the second season, Sarah Palmer saw a white horse in the living room of the Palmer house the night Leland/Bob killed Madeleine Ferguson. And in *Fire Walk With Me*, Sarah saw a white horse just after Leland drugged her. In these early iterations of *Twin Peaks*, the appearances of the white horse were exclusive to Sarah, and their meaning was obscure. Some speculated that the horse represented death (the Bible describes Death, one of the four Horsemen of the Apocalypse, as riding a pale horse), while others believed David Lynch had placed the white horse into these scenes because he was fascinated with the French film, *Le sang des bêtes* (*Blood of the Beasts*), in which a white horse is slaughtered. "[Lynch] did tell me about that same movie years ago," Mark Frost acknowledges. "This to him was an indelible, powerful image."

As an artifact of the original *Twin Peaks*, the white horse remained an ambiguous symbol, but when Lynch returned to the story for *The Return*, he saw an opportunity to give the white horse a new and specific connotation. If Laura Palmer represented an avatar akin to Kalki, then a white horse would logically be associated with her. At the end of *The Return*, Dale Cooper travels to Odessa, Texas, to find Laura Palmer living under the guise of Carrie Page, and white horses abound: At Judy's, the diner where Carrie works, a white horse (a coin-operated children's rocking horse) guards the diner's entrance; in Carrie's home, a small statue of a white horse sits atop the center of her mantle; and Carrie, herself, wears around her neck a small horseshoe pendant, a talisman linking Carrie/Laura to an equine presence. Carrie Page is Laura Palmer is Kalki, and the horse is explicitly linked to her. No other character in *The Return* intersects with the white horse. It is Laura Palmer's symbol, exclusively.

But Laura's symbolic connection to Kalki goes beyond the white horse. In Part 10, The Log Lady waxes poetic to Hawk about the nature of reality and the destiny of the universe:

> "In these days, the glow is dying. What will be in the darkness that remains? Watch and listen to the dream of time and space. It all comes out now, flowing like a river. That which is and is not. Hawk, Laura is the one."

Margaret Lanterman, attuned to reality's deeper resonance, knows the end of the dark age is coming. "The circle is almost complete," she says, prophesying the completion of the cycle of ages. She knows Laura will be there at the end, ready to face and eliminate "the darkness that remains." The Log Lady is counseling Hawk about what and how to pay attention. Her words resemble guidance found in the Bhagavad-Gita, a critical passage from which (translated here to English) reads:

What is real never ceases to be.
The unreal never is. The sages
Who realize the Self know the secret
Of what is and what is not.

This kind of Hindu cosmology resonates in *The Return*. And while David Lynch is not deliberately depicting Hindu myths, "his method of telling stories profits from the vocabularies of Vedic texts…and gives him ways to speak about multiple levels of reality." Indeed, The Log Lady's words describe a deeper reality beyond the material world defined by five senses. The soul is eternal, but the physical world is not. The Log Lady advises Hawk to ignore the distractions of the corporeal world. She hints that answers will be found in this deeper reality (where "it all comes out now flowing like a river") and that perhaps Laura has already achieved this transcendence.

And when The Log Lady tells Hawk, "The circle is almost complete," she foreshadows Cooper's remarks in Part 17, where he explains that the numbers, 2, 5, and 3 (or 2:53, as seen on a clock) add up to ten, "the number of completion."* If 2, 5, and 3 occur "time and time again" (as the Evolution of the Arm told Cooper), then "the number of completion" occurs time and time again. Indeed, at the end of every fourth age, Vishnu sends Kalki to restart the Hindu cycle of time: Kalki, the tenth avatar, *the number of completion.*

WE STILL HAVEN'T FULLY ANSWERED the questions, though: How do we accommodate this new identity of Laura Palmer given the existing narrative, the one that precedes events in *The Return*? If Laura Palmer is an otherworldly being designed by gods, doesn't that threaten to undermine her earlier story, especially the one depicted in *Fire Walk With Me*?

Not necessarily.

Hindu theology is clear: The latter avatars of Vishnu "are born into human life—for better or worse. They suffer through all the ills that mortal[s]…experience. They also incur a few very human flaws along

---

* In behind-the-scenes footage from the filming of Part 17, David Lynch quizzes Laura Dern about the sum of 2, 5, and 3. When she answers, "ten," Lynch asks if she knows what that means. "The number of completion," she replies. Lynch is surprised (and delighted), and Dern matter-of-factly says, "I work for David Lynch."

the way." In her mortal life, Laura Palmer was a woman who suffered many ills and developed notable flaws. While she lived, Laura had no idea she had been sent to Earth to end the age of darkness and restore the age of light. Laura was just a human being, born of mortal parents (albeit parents who had been unwittingly contaminated by great evil). She lived an innocent life but fell victim to the horror that possessed her father. Perhaps Bob was an inevitable part of Laura's life. Sensing the threat that Laura posed, Bob knew that if Laura could be defeated—possessed as Leland had been—then The Fireman's grand plan to restore order might be stopped, or at least delayed. The story we see in *Fire Walk With Me* supports this reading: Targeted by evil forces so she might become susceptible to their dark influence—to make her a new host for Bob—Laura is tortured and tormented. "I want to taste through your mouth," Bob tells her, as he inexorably works to weaken her resolve.

But, as we know, Laura Palmer—the flawed and *human* Laura Palmer—found an inner strength and pushed back against the evil pressing upon her. In the end, Laura recognized her inherent goodness and denied her oppressors their grand prize. Laura may have died, but she died triumphant and certain of herself.

But, yes, there's no getting around it, Laura *died*. Her short time on Earth came to an end before she realized her divine purpose, let alone took the action she was sent to Earth to perform.

After death, Laura finds herself despondent and bereft in the Red Room (appearing there, no doubt, because she chose to place the Owl Cave Ring on her finger). In these moments of despair, a new path opens: Dale Cooper appears. A reassuring presence, Cooper places his hand on Laura's shoulder and affirms her new existence. Laura sees an angel floating before her and is suddenly filled with joy. She has found a haven (if not a heaven) from the evil that pursued her. She is happy. She is safe. She is saved.

For decades this was the true and final ending of *Twin Peaks:* Laura Palmer, triumphant over evil and at rest beside Dale Cooper's soothing and knowing soul. It was enough, this ending. Laura was happy. And Cooper had fulfilled his mission. He had welcomed Laura to a holy place.

But, as *Twin Peaks: The Return* moves the story forward again, Laura's ending in *Fire Walk With Me* is no longer a conclusion, but a middle point in a larger narrative. It no longer functions as the final moment of the story. It becomes instead the ending of a chapter.

Yes, time is slippery in the *Twin Peaks* narrative, and there is no way to definitively say one specific scene is the true endpoint in such an Ouroborean (or "Möbius-loopy") story, but there's no getting around the fact that events in *The Return* severely challenge the finality of *Fire Walk With Me*. *The Return* is rather explicit in telling us that Laura's journey is not yet over. "I am dead," the being who calls herself Laura Palmer says in Part 2, *"Yet I live."* If that's true, if Laura Palmer still lives in the real world (and not simply in Cooper's wishful fantasy) then perhaps she returned to Earth after appearing in the Red Room at the end of *Fire Walk With Me*. Perhaps she recognized her true role in the grand scheme of the universe and *chose* to return to Earth (with a new identity) where she would wait for the right time and place to do what she was designed to do. (Perhaps the very title of this new *Twin Peaks* story—*The Return*—is just an overt-but-ironic reference to Laura Palmer's greatest secret.)

Despite the happy and conclusive ending of *Fire Walk With Me*, David Lynch could not leave Laura out of the new story. "Lynch couldn't let go of Laura Palmer as a character," Mark Frost explains, when discussing *The Return*. "There was something about her that just possessed him. That became a little bit more his obsession than mine."

David Lynch had always been revising Laura's role in *Twin Peaks*. He transformed Laura from a mere corpse into an enigmatic spirit, cryptically communicating with Dale Cooper in the "European ending" of the *Twin Peaks* pilot. He highlighted Laura's import to the other characters in an improvised scene in the second season premiere, one where Harriet Hayward reads a poem infused with Laura's spirit: "It was Laura/And I saw her glowing/In the dark woods I saw her smiling/.../It was Laura living in my dreams/It was Laura/The glow was life." He gave Laura Palmer agency and consequence in *Fire Walk With Me*. And he repositioned her as the central component of the story when he had The Log Lady declare in her first introduction: "Laura is the one." Now, returning to the world of *Twin Peaks* again, Lynch saw an opportunity he didn't have in those earlier instances. He saw a way to amplify Laura's importance to the overall narrative. The ending of *Fire Walk With Me* may have been satisfying, but for David Lynch it wasn't satisfying enough. It pointed to a larger story yet to come.

Lynch tells us that "*Fire Walk With Me* is very important to [*The Return*]." Indeed, elements from the film, particularly Phillip Jeffries and the Owl Cave Ring, become critical pieces of the new narrative. But it's the film's ending that hummed with potential, "Things have harmonics," Lynch explains, speaking specifically about *Fire Walk With Me*, "if you're true to an idea as much as you can be, then the harmonics will be there, and they will be truthful. You could come back in ten years and...you may see more in it. You can go back into that world later and get more if you've been true to the basic notes."

David Lynch saw that he could "get more" from the final scene of *Fire Walk With Me*. He realized the ending could be more than just a conclusion; it could provide an avenue for Laura Palmer to return to Earth to fulfill a purpose assigned to her by The Fireman. Yes, the appearance of the angel implies that Laura is in heaven, but why is she in the Red Room, a place fraught with uncertainty? *The Return* hints at an answer, strongly implying that the Red Room was not Laura's final destination, but merely a "waiting room" (as The Man From Another Place once described it). Laura went there after death but passed through to another existence. She tells us as much in the Lynch-directed, *Twin Peaks* short, *Between Two Worlds*: "I knew my life was over. And then there was a time that I cried because I was so happy. Because I saw what it was, and it was so beautiful. I was awake."

Martha Nochimson also sees the angel as an awakening: "The presence of the angel is a reality of the cosmos that Laura cannot see until she moves past the limits of 'normal' reality." To support her argument, Nochimson refers to a quote from author Luce Irigaray, chosen by David Lynch (from among other quotes regarding angels) as being "closest to his intention" in *Fire Walk With Me*: "They [angels] destroy the monstrous elements that might prohibit the possibility of a new age, and herald a new birth, a new dawn." In other words, the angel at the end of *Fire Walk With Me* represents more than heaven, it points toward a new universe and a new role for Laura Palmer.

"Death is just a change, not the end" The Log Lady tells Hawk in *The Return*. This line implies that Laura Palmer, after seeing her angel and recognizing her divine purpose, returned to Earth in the guise of Carrie Page. Returned to Earth in Odessa, Texas where she would wait for the proper time and place to end the dark age. Perhaps Laura reincarnated as a new human being, or perhaps she simply returned to Earth to continue life under a new identity. Either way, Laura's story was not over.

There is enough evidence in *The Return*, from the Hindu mythology David Lynch has incorporated, to Lynch's past patterns of revising Laura's role in the story, to conclude that, indeed, Laura Palmer is "the one," the Fireman's tenth avatar, the being who returned to life to bring the circle of ages to completion, just as The Log Lady foretells. (It's no coincidence that the title to Part 10 of *The Return* is, "Laura is the One." Here, David Lynch cleverly and deliberately encodes Laura's identity as the *tenth* avatar through the title of the *tenth* episode.)

Laura Palmer's powerful role at the end of *The Return* has been pointed out by other critics. In an essay published shortly after *The Return* ended, essayist David Auerbach makes a case that Laura Palmer was, in fact, a weapon used by Dale Cooper to defeat the entity known as Judy. Despite his careful analysis of the text, however, Auerbach resorts to crude terminology to describe Laura, referring to her as a "bomb" and a "capacitor," "storing a huge, accumulated charge of suffering which could then be discharged at the precise moment." In effect, this theory reduces Laura to a mere contrivance. (It's hard to imagine The Fireman and Señorita Dido so lovingly creating another life only to send her to Earth so she can "detonate.") What's more, it ignores all the rehabilitative work David Lynch has done over the years to realize Laura Palmer and reintegrate her into the story. In contrast, the "Laura-as-avatar" theory allows Laura to maintain the agency and victory she achieved in *Fire Walk With Me*. It allows for Laura to have made the conscious choice to return to Earth (either as herself or as someone else) to "awaken" to her larger destiny, the one she hints at in *Between Two Worlds*. As Laura and Dale Cooper drive away from Odessa, Carrie Page mutters, more to herself than to Cooper, "I was too young to know any better," implying that teenage Laura was not mentally or spiritually ready to accept her larger role. She had to come to terms with it. She may have been created by gods to bring forth a new age, but Laura could not—would not—act until she understood it was the right thing to do.

WHILE THE LAURA-AS-AVATAR THEORY is crucial to understanding *The Return*, we mustn't forget that most of the story is about Dale Cooper and his effort to get out of the Red Room, the physical and mental trap he's been stuck in for 25 years. The *Twin Peaks* story makes clear that from the beginning Cooper's identity and motivation is entwined with Laura Palmer. In *Fire Walk With Me*, Cooper becomes preternaturally aware of Laura and explains to Albert Rosenfield that he, Cooper, can sense Laura's presence elsewhere in the world. "She's crying out for help," he says. Later, Cooper appears to Laura in her dream to guide her from what he perceives as a danger. *Fire Walk With Me* clearly establishes a vital connection between these two characters and confirms that Dale Cooper and Laura Palmer are the two central figures in *Twin Peaks*. In *The Return*, Lynch examines this relationship again, this time from Dale Cooper's perspective.

In the first moments of *The Return*, when The Fireman appears to Cooper, a phonograph repetitively emits an odd chirruping sound. Though not shown, a record is likely rotating on the machine, stuck in a groove and forced to repeat the same sound over and over. Like the cycle of ages that The Fireman must maintain, the spinning record needs to be restarted, needs to be set back on track, and so The Fireman assigns Cooper a task. He directs Cooper toward Laura. He cryptically instructs Cooper where and how to find her, effectively making Cooper his proxy. While we have no evidence that Cooper was created by The Fireman (as was Laura) we see that The Fireman needs Cooper to conduct a critical task, to participate in the plan The Fireman began when he sent the Laura avatar to Earth. Cooper must find Laura and deliver her to a certain place.

Even if Cooper is not a deliberate avatar of the Fireman, he sure resembles one. The *ninth* avatar of Vishnu, the one who precedes Kalki to Earth, is Buddha, and in the original *Twin Peaks*, Dale Cooper is specifically positioned as a character who practices a "Buddhist outlook." Essayist Ken Volante carefully examines Cooper's philosophical behavior and concludes that, "Through his deep concern for others, his adherence to the 'no-harm principle,' his attention to nature, and the extra moments he spent appreciating the seemingly minute details of life.... Cooper's Buddhist outlook comprehends the omnipresence of suffering, the interconnection of all beings, and the necessity to appreciate the moment." A character with such a mindset is the perfect candidate to assume the role of Buddha, Vishnu's ninth avatar, the being who must prepare the way for Kalki.

Cooper sacrifices everything human beings most desire—home, love, family and friends—to bring Laura Palmer to the exact place and time she needs to be. Cooper gives up so much of himself that he loses sight of his needs and the needs of others. He fully commits himself to the mission at the expense of his dearest relationships. Although he may not comprehend what it all means when he wakes up in Odessa, Texas, he knows he has a purpose. He finds himself driving Laura into the night toward Twin Peaks, following programming given to him by The Fireman.

And Cooper succeeds. He brings Laura to where she needs to be so she can do exactly what she was designed to do.

LET'S BE CLEAR: David Lynch has not literally adapted the Hindu myths of Vishnu into *The Return*. He is not explicitly dramatizing the stories recounted in Vedic texts. But we must not forget that Vedic texts have influenced Lynch and his art. Hindu cosmology has steered Lynch's work in specific directions, inspiring imagery and narrative foundation: "Lynch's cinematic zeitgeist can be understood in Vedic terms," Martha Nochimson explains. His work is "inflected by exposure to Vedic wisdom."

If we recognize the import of Hindu theology in Lynch's life and acknowledge that he has incorporated many of those ideas into his work, then we can decipher many of the difficult elements of *Twin Peaks: The Return*, specifically the role of Laura Palmer. Hindu cosmology helps us clarify an ambiguous, sometimes contradictory narrative. It provides a map, of sorts, to navigate tricky terrain. It may not be perfect, and it may not explain all the baffling elements contained within, but it points us toward revelation.

At the end of *The Return* Laura Palmer fulfills her destiny, a destiny which originates in Part 8 (and at the end of *Fire Walk With Me*). She screams, and the world goes black. In that uncertain moment of despair and darkness, the wheel of time turns just as it is supposed to. And the potential for a Golden Age shines in the darkness that remains.[*]

---

[*] David Lynch has posited this same kind of ending in earlier works. According to Lynch's memoir, *Room to Dream*, the unproduced screenplay for Lynch's *Ronnie Rocket* (a film he hoped to make after *Eraserhead*) "alludes to the wheel of karma and rebirth." The screenplay ends with a character asking, "When will all the new universes be born?", an overt nod toward the beginning of a new age. Although *The Return* does not show us what happens after Laura's universe-ending scream, the story, just like in *Ronnie Rocket*, implies a Golden Age is about to commence.

Act II

"There are clues everywhere, all around us. But the puzzle maker is clever. The clues, although surrounding us, are somehow mistaken for something else. And the something else, the wrong interpretation of the clues, we call our world."

PART 9:

THIS IS THE CHAIR

FEW CHARACTERS in the *Twin Peaks* universe resonate as strongly as Major Garland Briggs, a figure who, more than anyone else in the original series, defied expectation. In the *Twin Peaks* pilot, Briggs came across as a strict disciplinarian, the personification of asceticism, a no-nonsense military man who had little patience for his son's delinquency. It wasn't long, however, before Briggs revealed a spiritual side. His was a soul in touch with the deeper currents of the universe. Like The Log Lady, Major Briggs was a character who could see beyond the illusory nature of the everyday world.

The untimely death of Don Davis (the actor who brilliantly portrayed Major Briggs) seemed to preclude continuation of his character in the *Twin Peaks* milieu, but as events in Part 9 show, Mark Frost and David Lynch have deftly managed to keep Briggs a vital presence in the new story. Despite having "died" in Twin Peaks, Briggs has still been an active player behind the scenes, pulling strings and making preparations for the imminent threat of Mr. C.

THE BLACK AND WHITE IMAGERY of Part 8 is over, and the story returns to color, signaling the return of Dale Cooper's interpreting presence.

Mr. C trudges up a remote country road, still reeling from being shot and resurrected. Does he have any idea what he just went through? Does he even know what the Woodsmen did? We have to assume he does, that he knows Bob is still "with" him. He may be weak from being operated upon by the Woodsmen, but Mr. C knows Bob's evil energy emanates within.

Mr. C rendezvouses with his primary henchmen, Hutch and Chantal. We met Chantal in Part 2, and now we meet her husband, Hutch, a dedicated enforcer whose simple "aw-shucks" affect masks a brutal proficiency. Mr. C assigns the couple to kill Warden Murphy and to perform a "double hit" in Las Vegas (i.e., kill Duncan Todd and Dougie Jones). Mr. C then "activates" Diane with a cryptic text: "Around the dinner table the conversation is lively"—a code instructing her to monitor Gordon Cole and his team.

ON BOARD THE FBI JET back to Philadelphia, Cole asks Diane if she minds diverting the plane to Buckhorn. Diane complains that she wants to go home, but Cole counters with a curious reply, "It could be of some interest to you, Diane. An old case involving a man Agent Cooper once knew." Diane doesn't hesitate; she responds, "The Blue Rose case." This simple line suggests Diane knows about Major Briggs and the plan Briggs and Cooper put together (the plan Gordon Cole will reveal to Albert in Part 17). As Gordon Cole hinted in Part 7, Diane is savvy to many of Cole and Cooper's secrets.

IN LAS VEGAS, Bushnell Mullins meets with the Fusco detectives to learn more about what happened to Cooper. Bushnell senses a possible connection between the recent car explosion and the attempt on Cooper's life and, stressed by these thoughts, repeatedly makes a fist with his right hand. It's a gesture eerily similar to how Lil (Cole's "mother's sister's girl") made a fist in *Fire Walk With Me*. Back then, Lil's gesture was code, a signal to Chet Desmond that local law enforcement would be belligerent. Here, Bushnell knows the Fuscos are not telling him everything. They're not necessarily being belligerent, but they're holding something back.

Indeed, after Mullins leaves, Detective T. Fusco tells his brothers he can find no records for a "Dougie Jones" from before 1997. This stymies the detectives, and they suspect "Dougie" may be a participant in the Federal Witness Protection Program. We know differently, of course. The original Dougie Jones—the man Cooper replaced—was a tulpa created by Mr. C. The Fusco investigation suggests that Mr. C likely created Dougie as far back as 1997.

At a nearby motel, a despondent Ike makes a call to a "JT" to report that he has failed to kill Dougie Jones.* There's no character in the story with the initials JT, so Ike's dialog is likely a mistake. He was almost certainly calling Duncan Todd ("DT"), who assigned Ike to kill Dougie in Part 6. Ike beats a hasty retreat from his room but is quickly arrested by the Fuscos. His brutal, ugly tale ends here.

IN TWIN PEAKS, Bobby, Hawk, and Sheriff Truman pay a visit to Betty Briggs to enquire about her husband, Major Briggs. Before they ask any questions, Betty says she knows why they've come.† Years earlier, Major Briggs told her that one day Bobby and the others would show up and ask about Dale Cooper. Knowing this, Briggs prepared something important for them. Betty walks to a chair and pulls a lever. Part of the chair's wooden frame unhinges to reveal a secret compartment. Betty removes a cigar-shaped metal tube and gives it to the officers.

When the deputies get back to the station, Bobby throws the tube forcefully on the ground. The tube begins to hum, and Bobby picks it up and throws it again. The tube opens, and Sheriff Truman removes two tightly rolled scraps of paper. The first scrap instructs the officers to travel to "Jack Rabbit's Palace" in two days' time (a place Bobby knows well because he used to play there when he was a boy). The second paper contains an array of numbers in which the name "Cooper" is printed twice. The text looks similar (if not identical) to a print-out Major Briggs showed Agent Cooper in episode 9 of the original series, a print-out that purportedly displayed decoded gibberish received from deep-space monitors. As Hawk looks at it now, he perceives a possible message: "Two Coopers."

For long-time fans of *Twin Peaks*, it is enormously satisfying to have Major Briggs playing a prominent role in the new story. In the original series, Briggs experienced revelatory dreams, knew about the Black and White Lodges, and traveled to other dimensions. In the last

---

* The establishing shot of the motel shows a woman pushing a cart along a sidewalk, a scene similar to the woman pushing a cart outside Rancho Rosa in Part 3. (Both scenes are possibly homages to Edward Hopper.)

† Note that the reaction shot of Hawk, Bobby, and Truman is shown in reverse. Hawk's eyes shift to the side in an unsettling way.

episode of the second season, Briggs was contacted by an unknown entity who, speaking through Sarah Palmer, told him Cooper was in the Black Lodge. This confounding scene apparently spurred Major Briggs to action. At some point, Briggs must have glimpsed the horrible reality of Mr. C (the original series strongly implied Major Briggs could travel through time[*]) and developed a plan to thwart him. Part of that plan was the secret message, hidden in his chair, directing the Twin Peaks deputies to Jack Rabbit's Palace.

AT THE BUCKHORN MORGUE, Diane reads Mr. C's "dinner table" text and looks into the distance, calculating the ramifications of what it will mean. As a tulpa, Diane is forced to follow Mr. C's commands, but Diane is also a player in the deeper plan Cooper put in place years ago (the one she knows "something" about). As she sits alone in the morgue, Diane wrestles with the compulsions of both her distressing roles.

Meanwhile, Constance Talbot updates the FBI on her autopsy findings and shows them the wedding ring she removed from Briggs' body. Neither Cole nor Albert can make any sense of it, but Cole will remember the ring later, in Part 14, when he makes the intuitive leap that Diane might know something about it.

Detective Macklay tells the team that Bill Hastings and Ruth Davenport claimed to have met "the Major" in an extra-dimensional setting called "the Zone." Apparently, Bill Hastings devoted himself to studying other worlds, something he and Ruth Davenport wrote about on their blog, "Into the Zone." Somehow, he and Ruth stumbled into an alternate dimension where they met Major Briggs.

Tammy interrogates Hastings to learn more about this unlikely encounter. Despondent and overwhelmed, Hastings babbles to Tammy about obtaining coordinates, but he doesn't understand what any of it means. That's not surprising. He and Ruth were likely pawns in a far bigger game, steered into the Zone so they would deliver information to Major Briggs. According to Hastings, Briggs said he was "hibernating," which likely means Briggs didn't really die in Twin Peaks but

---

[*] See episode 19 (as well as episode 8, in which Major Briggs recounts his dream "vision" of Bobby's life: "I awoke with an overwhelming feeling of optimism and confidence about you and your future").

went into hiding and waited for the right time to act. The story Hastings recounts implies that the Woodsmen may have interfered with Briggs, beheading him before he could act on the coordinates Hastings delivered. But, as this episode shows, Briggs had insurance in place. He may have ended up decapitated, but Major Garland Briggs was already way ahead of Mr. C.

AT THE GREAT NORTHERN, Ben and Beverly continue to investigate the pervasive ringing tone. After wandering around Ben's office, the two find themselves intimately close. Ben pulls back, explaining that he can't pursue a relationship with Beverly. She responds by calling Ben "a good man."

That's an interesting observation. Is Ben Horne a good man? If we look at the way his story arc resolved in the original series, we'd have to conclude he is. Ben began as a ruthless businessman, someone who stooped to blackmail, forged documents, and hired assassins to get what he wanted, but after his real-estate schemes crumbled, Ben suffered a nervous breakdown and regressed into historical fantasy. When he emerged from this delusion, Ben pledged to lead a better life. From what we've seen so far in *The Return*, he appears to have maintained that pledge. In Part 2, he admonished Jerry for his lewd suggestions regarding Beverly, and soon, in Part 12, he will take responsibility for the damaging actions of his grandson, Richard.

Yes, Ben Horne is still a good man, but he is also a haunted one. His whole world is contained within the walls of the Great Northern, a place where he's retreated to avoid the hardships of his life—his failed marriage, his ailing son, his absent daughter. Ben Horne is a good man but a diminished one. Beverly Paige is his only real connection to the outside world, and he needs her in ways he may not fully understand. She's his vital link to reality, a link Ben fears he could jeopardize if he's not careful. Worse, he might hurt Beverly just as he's hurt so many others.

NOT SURPRISINGLY, PART 9 ENDS at the Roadhouse. Two women sit in a booth, sharing random thoughts about their lives. This is the first of many scenes in the Roadhouse involving characters we've never seen before and will never see again, characters who converse in cryptic, nonsensical dialog. Isolated and insulated, these Roadhouse scenes are flotsam upon the story's flow. They're like remnants of an entirely different TV series that crashed into *Twin Peaks* and scattered debris across the narrative.

Here we meet Chloe and Ella, two listless women adrift in a hazy world of drugs and drab employment. Chloe mentions that "Zebra's out again," and Ella says she was fired from her job because she came to work high. She's troubled by a terrible rash on her armpit and keeps scratching at it. Ella asks Chloe if she's seen "the penguin," but Chloe laughs. Ella keeps scratching.

And that's it. That's all we're ever going to see of Chloe and Ella. We'll never find out what "the penguin" is, never learn the identity of Zebra. (Maybe the penguin is slang for drugs. Maybe Zebra is a friend who just got out of jail. Your guess is as good as mine.)

All the Roadhouse booth scenes feature people in emotional or physical distress. Here, Ella is plagued by the incessant itch of her rash. It's exhausting, it never lets up, and it torments her. In Parts 12 and 14, more characters (almost all of them women) will radiate similar stresses and anxieties. Some will worry about the fates of their friends, one will be frightened by a near-death experience, and one will be haunted by the memories of a violent, bloody encounter. In Part 15, a woman will scream in anguish and despair.

Could there be a connection between these narrative fragments? Could some unifying scheme be at play? Audrey Horne will not show up in *The Return* for another three episodes, but as soon as she does, she will declare she is "going to the Roadhouse." In fact, Audrey's entire story will revolve around whether she can leave her "home" and get to the Roadhouse. She's fixated on the place. Getting there is of the utmost importance.

The anxiety and frustration of the mysterious women in the Roadhouse mirror the distress we see in Audrey. These Roadhouse women are likely aspects of Audrey, pieces of her fractured personality manifesting in a space she desperately pursues. They are reflections of Audrey's troubled psyche, expressions of a mind struggling to secure a stable, reliable identity.[*]

---

[*] I'll explore this theory in detail in the chapter, "I'm Not Sure Who I Am, But I'm Not Me."

Whatever these Roadhouse scenes are, they are not accidents or oversights. They're deliberate. If one thinks of *The Return* as a vast painting constantly in motion (an analogy David Lynch embraces), then these scenes are flourishes to the overall composition. They accent the tapestry, balance the design.

And if, as some will argue, the Roadhouse scenes have nothing at all to do with Audrey Horne, they still have value. They function as humorous asides whose sheer lunacy and exaggeration provide much needed comic relief in a dark, dark story. The scenes in the Roadhouse booth are absurd and delightful, and I wish there had been more of them.

WE'VE ONLY JUST STARTED ACT II of *The Return*, but there's already a sense of leveling-off, the start of a narrative plateau. Dale Cooper is not in control of the story he's watching (not yet) and can only watch as events in the real world unspool at their own pace. Over the next six hours, the FBI will limit their investigations to Buckhorn, South Dakota, Mr. C will weave his way toward his sought-after coordinates, Cooper (in Las Vegas) will slowly transform those around him into better people (and allies for the next stage in his journey), and the deputies in Twin Peaks will make a perplexing mission into and out of the surrounding forest. As Act II progresses there will also be narrative detours, longueurs, and asides (all the Roadhouse booth scenes happen here), and Cooper's frustration will grow as he watches the story wander. Eventually, his impatience will get the better of him, but for now he (and we) can only watch and wait and wonder.

PART 10:

LAURA IS THE ONE

PART 10 IS PROOF the narrative has reached a plateau. The episode features long, drawn-out scenes (Candie trying to swat a fly but instead hitting Rodney Mitchum and then crying endlessly about it, Carl Rodd playing guitar and singing "Red River Valley," Candie slowly retrieving Anthony Sinclair from the gambling floor), and while some scenes promise story progression, they don't really deliver. Jerry Horne is still lost in the woods, and Doctor Amp is still raging on his website (and an ever-attentive Nadine is still listening from home). In Part 10 we check in with a few characters only to find them no further along than last time.

Still, despite Part 10's inertia, the episode is steeped in violence and despair. From its first brutal minutes to its last notes of loss and anxiety, Part 10 writhes under the menace of a dark, dark age.

RICHARD KNOWS MIRIAM told the police that he killed the boy in the intersection. He also learns she sent a letter to the police telling them much more. Angry at this betrayal, Richard brutally beats Miriam and sets fire to her trailer. Then he calls Chad and orders him to intercept Miriam's letter before Truman or any of the other deputies can read it.

Just what, exactly, does Miriam have to do with all of this? Apparently, she was privy to Richard's dirty deals and may have even been helping him sell drugs (she did leave an unusually large tip for Shelly in Part 6). Miriam likely knows Chad is also part of the scheme, but if so, why wait to reveal all of this in a letter? Why not simply tell the police everything when she told them about Richard being the hit-and-run driver? It doesn't make a lot of sense, but in the end it doesn't matter. The Sheriff's deputies have been suspicious of Chad for some time and have enough information to arrest him. They'll do just that in Part 14.

David Lynch doesn't show us Richard's brutal attack of Miriam. His camera remains outside Miriam's trailer as Richard wreaks havoc inside. We hear his vicious blows and see the trailer shudder, but we never actually see what Richard does. That's because we're about to witness a second violent assault inside another trailer across town.

At the new Fat Trout Trailer Park, Steven Burnett rages over his wife, Becky. He leans into her, screaming, "I know exactly what you did!" Vibrating with fury, he raises his fist and barely holds back from punching Becky in the face. We don't know what pushed Steven over the edge, he's a punk and a loser and likely on drugs, but whatever sent him into a rage is beside the point. Like so many other scenes of rage and trauma in *The Return*, it's the energy and emotion that matters. It's a violent world, an angry world, a world of pain and sorrow. Lynch emphasizes it here and elsewhere. People seethe and cry and moan in despair. Agony blankets the world. The cause of such agony is not important. How we deal with it—how we address our pain and shoulder our burdens—that's the crux of Lynch's narrative.

We see here (yet again) a pattern repeating. Becky Burnett is the daughter of Shelly Briggs, who, when she was Becky's age, lived with an equally violent man, Leo Johnson. Now, a generation later, Becky has fallen into the same kind of abusive relationship. Despite looking to her mother for comfort and guidance, Becky still sees in Shelly a woman whose habits haven't changed. Shelly's relationship with her new man, Red, is likely no better than Becky's is with Steven. Becky may also know that, long ago, Shelly chose to fight back against Leo Johnson with a gun. As we will soon see, Becky Burnett is doomed to repeat more than one of her mother's mistakes.

IN LAS VEGAS, Anthony Sinclair riles up the Mitchum brothers with false tales of how Dougie Jones deliberately bilked them out of thirty million dollars. Furious at how Dougie has played them twice, the Mitchums vow a brutal revenge.

Meanwhile, Janey-E finds herself attracted to Cooper and acts on her growing lust. Soon the two are having loud sex (and waking poor Sonny Jim because of it). In the quiet of a post-coital moment, Janey-E tells Cooper (whom she calls "Dougie") she loves him.

Janey-E is, and will remain, a curious figure. On the surface, she is a no-nonsense spouse who guides her family through the trials and tribulations of everyday life, but there's something deeper at work in the character. Janey-E's identity shares its valence with Diane, whom we learn later is Janey-E's half-sister. This relationship seems outlandish on the surface and begs all sorts of questions: Is Janey-E *really* Diane's sister, or does she resemble Diane simply because Dale Cooper, watching from the Red Room, wants to see her that way? More intriguingly, is Janey-E perhaps an *aspect* of Diane, a spirit-self dutifully bound to Cooper so she can watch over him on his journey into the world? The connection between Janey-E and Diane is impossible to decrypt, but whoever Janey-E might be—an avatar of Diane, a surrogate projected by Cooper's needy psyche, or simply a unique character unto herself—Cooper knows she is strong, undaunted, and loyal. He also knows Janey-E deserves love. That's why he makes sure he (or some version of himself) returns to her in Part 18 to return that love in kind.

AT THE TWIN PEAKS SHERIFF'S STATION Chad is on the lookout for Miriam's letter.* As he waits for the mailman, he engages Lucy in some small talk. Lucy recounts an incident in which her clock stopped and neither she nor Andy knew what time it was. It "seemed like forever," Lucy stresses. Just like when she pondered the nature of the thermostat in Part 4, Lucy is probing the underlying nature of reality (and the very narrative framework of *The Return*). Does time flow continuously for Lucy, or does it simply stop when her clock stops, leaving Lucy and Andy trapped in an unending moment? Lucy's comment speaks to Cooper's predicament in the Red Room, a place where Cooper exists both outside the normal flow of time and beyond the physical dimensions of space. In Part 2, Cooper seemingly blinked into existence, as if he had been held in stasis until time started flowing

---

* The letter Chad eventually intercepts is addressed from a Miriam Hodges, but Miriam's surname (according to the credits) is Sullivan. (This mismatch has been confirmed as a production mistake.)

again. Perhaps Lucy and Andy shared a similar experience. They were suspended in time until their clock started. Lucy's dim awareness of this phenomenon hints again at the idea of "observer effect." The more Lucy thinks about time, the more it flows irregularly around her.

Johnny Horne is strapped to a chair in Sylvia Horne's dining room, watching a teddy bear-like toy repeat the same phrase again and again: "Hello, Johnny. How are you today?"[*] Just then, Richard Horne forces his way into the house. Sylvia knows the danger of her grandson's anger and tries to fend him off, but Richard is too strong to stop. He barges in, manhandles Sylvia, and then takes her money and jewelry. Distressed, Johnny topples over in his chair, moaning and squirming as Richard lays siege to the house.

We've seen others suffering in the narrative so far, but few as painfully as Johnny Horne. In the original series Johnny was a cognitively disabled young man with limited mental and social skills. He was being treated by Doctor Jacoby and had once been tutored by Laura Palmer. Twenty-five years later, Johnny is more incapacitated than ever. Restrained in a chair and transfixed by the rote monotone of a primitive toy, Johnny lives a tortured life. Sylvia has obviously tended to him and made his life as comfortable as possible, but Johnny requires extreme care. (In this way, Sylvia is not too different from Beverly Paige, another weary woman caring for an ailing loved one.)

Sylvia likely inherited responsibility for Richard's upbringing (the narrative implies Audrey is elsewhere, perhaps living in a psychiatric facility), and therefore caring for Johnny all these years could not have been easy. Richard is steeped in cruelty, and the burden of managing Richard's behavior while also serving the needs of Johnny have taken an emotional, physical, and psychological toll. No wonder Sylvia is bitter when she reports to Ben what Richard did. She is a broken soul.

IN BUCKHORN, Albert tells Cole they have intercepted encrypted texts from Diane that reveal the team's various activities. Cole is not surprised. He suspected something was wrong with Diane when he

---

[*] Johnny's teddy bear toy resembles Randy, a character in David Lynch's series of animated shorts, *Dumbland.*

hugged her outside the prison. Moments later, Tammy shows Cole a photo of Mr. C taken at the glass box in New York City.

Cole processes these clues, but he's still shaken by what he experienced a moment earlier when he opened his door to Albert's knock. Looming before Cole was an overwhelming apparition of Laura Palmer, sobbing in despair.[*]

Why did Cole see this image? What does Laura's presence here portend?

Laura Palmer is a critical player in this new *Twin Peaks*, and Cole's vision is better understood if we look ahead to the concluding scene of Part 10, where The Log Lady shares more of her wisdom about the nature of reality.

The Log Lady knows the world has fallen deeply into the dark age. "The glow is dying," she tells Hawk, referring to the waning presence of electricity, the life-sustaining medium permeating all of reality. The Log Lady poses a crucial question: "What will be in the darkness that remains?" She already knows the answer, but before she reveals it, she says, "The circle is almost complete," couching in cryptic terms an imminent end (and a new beginning) to all that is.

The Log Lady reminds Hawk about "the good ones" who remain steadfast with him, the friends he considers family. She tells him to "watch and listen to the dream of time and space" and to be aware of what "is and is not." Then Margaret Lanterman, The Log Lady—the gifted seer of Twin Peaks—reveals the most crucial answer of all. She tells Hawk (and all of us watching): "Laura is the one."

It's no coincidence that the title to *The Return*'s tenth episode is "Laura is the One." *The Return* reminds us that the number ten is "the number of completion," that it betokens a transition. And now The Log Lady tells us that Laura Palmer does, too. Although she seemingly speaks in riddles to Hawk, she gives him (and us) enough information to crack her code. Laura Palmer, whom David Lynch once character-

---

[*] This image is taken from *Fire Walk With Me*, a scene where a distraught Laura arrives at Donna Hayward's house seeking solace.

ized as "glowing in the dark woods,"[*] will be present in the darkness that remains. Laura is "the one" who will induce a new age by bringing the circle of time and space to a close.

Manifesting in the doorway of Cole's hotel room, Laura conveys the magnitude of pain coursing through the world. She sobs in distress, and her emotions evoke the many troubled characters we've seen in *The Return*, particularly here, in Part 10: Richard Horne assaults, Steven Burnett rages, and Johnny Horne despairs. They're not the only ones: Part 10 also shows us the anger, grief, and confusion of characters such as Doctor Amp, Jerry Horne, Duncan Todd, Sylvia Horne, and Candie. No wonder Laura is crying when she appears to Cole. She's channeling the anguish of this dark age.

It's worth repeating that The Log Lady's comments to Hawk echo a passage from the Hindu text, the Bhagavad Gita: "What is real never ceases to be/The unreal never is. The sages/Who realize the Self know the secret/Of what is and what is not." This passage (verse 16 of the *Sankhya Yoga*) explains that those who are wise, those who are true to themselves (i.e., are "true men"), can see through the illusions of a superficial world and perceive the larger truths of the universe. Already we've seen in *The Return* certain characters tuned to this deeper reality. Lucy senses it when she ponders time and space. Hawk witnesses it during his nighttime hikes to Glastonbury Grove. And Andy will access it (in Part 14) when he glimpses the underlying mechanisms of reality.

Now add to this list Gordon Cole, who, when confronted with the apparition of Laura Palmer, glimpses the truth The Log Lady gives to Hawk: *Laura is the one.* Cole comes face to face with the most important player in the dream of time and space. He may not fully grasp the magnitude of what Laura represents, but he's starting to access a deeper universe. In this way, Cole resembles the sages the Bhagavad Gita describes. He is a man in touch with his true self.

---

[*] In episode 8 of the original series, David Lynch added an unscripted scene in which Harriet Hayward reads a poem about Laura Palmer. According to the poem, Laura was "glowing in the dark woods," and "the glow was life," suggesting that Laura (the glow) still lived. Given the role Laura plays in *The Return*, this line takes on new meaning. Laura Palmer will bring about new life when she restarts the cycle of ages.

As Part 10 ends—as Rebekah Del Rio sings of a dark and starless night—somewhere in South Dakota, Gordon Cole perceives a vivid truth: Decades after death, Laura Palmer resonates still.

PART 11:
THERE'S FIRE WHERE YOU ARE GOING

THE ILLUSORY NATURE of the world continues to manifest in Part 11. Gaps and fissures in the fabric of reality hint at mysterious truths. As the contours of the universe shift and change shape, characters like Bobby Briggs, Gordon Cole, Dave Macklay and even Bradley Mitchum, reel from a fungible world. Is Cooper faltering too? As he watches from the Red Room, can he tell the difference from what is…and what is not?

MIRIAM HAS SOMEHOW SURVIVED Richard's vicious attack. Battered, bloody, and groaning in pain, she crawls from a thicket of weeds to be discovered by a group of boys playing catch. Miriam still poses a threat to Richard and Chad. What might she say to the police when she's well enough to answer questions? Will she ever get the chance?

OVER AT THE FAT TROUT TRAILER PARK, Becky receives a tip about Steven that sends her into a frenzy. (From what we can gather, Steven is messing around with another woman.) If Becky cowered in Part 10, she thunders in Part 11. Grabbing a gun, she frantically calls Shelly and says that she needs a ride. When Shelly arrives, Becky hijacks Shelly's car and backs away. Shelly jumps on the hood to stop Becky from speeding off, but Becky is blinded by rage and swings the car around, flinging Shelly to the ground. Not looking back, Becky charges out of the trailer park.

Becky arrives at Gersten Hayward's apartment and pounds on the door, calling for Steven. After a neighbor informs Becky that Steven and Gersten have already left, Becky steps back from the door and fires six rounds into it.

When Becky pulls the trigger, her fury courses into the world. It rushes through the corridors of the building, frantic and ragged, an emotion literally outpacing itself. Lynch channels Becky's rage with a point-of-view shot that races down the hall and into the adjoining stair-well, jump-cutting forward until it reaches Steven and Gersten hiding on a landing. They've escaped Becky's wrath, at least for now.

Gersten Hayward's presence here is shocking. She's nothing like the little girl we saw in the original *Twin Peaks*, nothing like the girl who had a life of promise ahead. Back then, Gersten was dressed as a fairy princess and playing piano while her sister recited a poem about Laura Palmer. In that improvised scene, Gersten was an angelic figure who evoked Laura's presence. Like The Log Lady or Major Briggs, she might even have been in touch with supernatural forces surrounding Twin Peaks. Sadly, the grown-up Gersten has lost her way (and her magic). How she came to this lowly existence is left a mystery. She's another victim of a corrosive dark age.

IN BUCKHORN, Cole's FBI team visits "2240 Sycamore," a weedy lot surrounded by dilapidated shacks and abandoned shipping containers. This is where Bill Hastings says he encountered Major Briggs (and last saw Ruth Davenport).

The word, "Sycamore" keeps popping up in the narrative. Maybe it's a codeword for the location of supernatural portals (like the one in Rancho Rosa), or maybe (as I suggested in Part 3) it's simply a quirk of Cooper's observing psyche, an artifact of his subconscious filter. Whatever it is, "Sycamore" signifies this address as no ordinary space.

Hastings remembers little from his first visit to the lot, which is not surprising. At this locus of overlapping worlds, reality bends, and perception becomes suspect. Hastings's mind cannot comprehend what he experienced here. His memories have slipped away.

Cole and Albert, on the other hand, seem to know exactly what they're about to find. As they enter the lot, Cole asks, "Think there's one in there, Albert?" suggesting he and Albert are expecting something specific. Their subsequent actions imply they have a knowledge of portals. Cole and Albert move forward together, but Albert stops, as if anchoring himself should Cole need help. Cole continues deeper into the lot and spies a vortex opening in the sky. Peering into the core of the vortex, he sees three Woodsmen standing on an old staircase. Cole loses his connection to terrestrial reality and begins to fade away, but Albert yanks him back. "Well, I guess we found out," Albert says. Indeed, they did. And they were ready.

Cole and Albert expand their search and find the headless body of Ruth Davenport lying in the tall weeds nearby.[*] Albert takes pictures, particularly of the coordinates written in heavy ink on Ruth's left arm. These are the numbers Mr. C wanted but failed to obtain when his forces attacked Briggs.

Diane, meanwhile, is waiting outside and spies the flickering image of a Woodsman creeping toward the car where Bill Hastings waits. Moments later, there is terrible wrenching sound, and half of Bill Hastings's head is suddenly gone, torn away. Cole looks inside the car and, confirming the obvious, says, "He's dead."

Bill Hastings never had a chance. He's another victim in Mr. C's long plot to get the coordinates. Ruth Davenport and Phyllis Hastings are dead. So is poor Betty, Bill's secretary, killed by a bomb that Jack (also dead) planted in her car. Bill Hastings was the last of the group. That's quite a body count.

AT THE DOUBLE R DINER, Bobby, Shelly, and Becky sit in a booth pondering the ferocious events that Becky set in motion. Becky is a tumble of emotions, claiming at first that she hates Steven and then that she loves him. Bobby and Shelly exchange glances. They know what tumult likely resides at the heart of Becky's marriage. Bobby worries that Steven is physically hurting Becky, and it's obvious he feels helpless to rescue his daughter from her abusive relationship. Shelly, too, is shaken by the events of the day, but when she spies Red through the window, she gleefully runs outside to meet him. Bobby watches in

---

[*] The appearance of Ruth Davenport's decapitated body here is a deliberate reference to the infamous unsolved Black Dahlia murder case, something that has fascinated David Lynch for years. In 1947, actress Elizabeth Short (who posthumously became known as the "Black Dahlia") was brutally murdered, and the remains of her body, which was cut in half, were found in a vacant lot in Los Angeles.

dismay as his ex-wife kisses another man. As Becky gives her father a long look, Shelly returns to the diner in obvious delight.

Poor Bobby. Heartache is rooted deep in the look he gives Shelly. In just these few short moments we can surmise the couple's tragic path. Bobby and Shelly were in love at the end of the original *Twin Peaks*, and their story seemingly ended on a happy note. The two were married for a while, but the marriage didn't last. We can't say for sure what dissolved their union, but it's likely Shelly was the partner who wanted out. Bobby's mournful gape hints that he holds strong feelings for Shelly and wishes he was still with her.

Bobby's life may have travelled a bright path (like Major Briggs foresaw), but it was not without pain and sorrow. He has yet to resolve the aching sadness he carries. It's no wonder his emotions found such easy release when he saw the picture of Laura Palmer in Part 4. He has too often suffered the fate of unrequited love.

Bobby no doubt fears for Becky's safety. He knows what kind of life she's living because he's been there himself. He remembers the ruin that drugs can inflict upon a body and the tragedy that comes from a loaded gun in a frightened hand. Bobby worries that Becky will fall into all the many traps he, himself, once slipped. The patterns are obvious, and the danger around Becky is as real as bullets.

Sitting there in the Double R Diner, watching his daughter's life teeter on a precipice, seeing his one true love welcome yet another thug into her life, Bobby is at a breaking point. In this distressing moment, as his world threatens to spill away, gunshots jolt the night, and bullets pierce the window. Bobby instinctively springs into action. He orders everyone to take cover, and he exits the building with his gun drawn.

Bobby emerges from the diner into a cacophony of blaring horns and screaming people. Cars are stopped in the intersection, and onlookers watch as a woman yells at her husband, furious that their son found a loaded gun and discharged it. The husband silently stares at his wife, exasperated but none-the-less cowed. Their son stands to the side of the family's van, defiantly watching Bobby approach. Bobby notices that the boy and his father are both dressed the same, each wears a camo hunting jacket, blue jeans, and a camo baseball cap.

Horns continue to blare, one from a car behind the van. Bobby pleads with the driver to stop making so much noise, but the driver is distraught and wails about being delayed. "We're late!" she cries, "We have to get home!" Then, looking desperately at Bobby, she yells, "She's sick!", and a girl rises out of the shadows of the passenger seat, drooling a thin stream of vomit. Staring at Bobby, the girl convulses and spews.

The din of honking horns intensifies. The woman screams, the girl vomits, and the camera pushes toward Bobby's dismayed face. The scene ends here, leaving Bobby stranded in the dark in the middle of chaos.

Bobby will not mention this incident again. He won't investigate the gunshots or follow up on the mystery of the vomiting girl. The nighttime bedlam outside the Double R will remain an isolated event within the larger story of *The Return*. What meaning, then, is behind this striking, unforgettable scene?

The chaos outside the Double R reflects Bobby's overwhelmed psyche. Moments earlier, Bobby confronted the truths of Becky's tumultuous life. He knows Becky's reckless driving almost killed Shelly. He knows Becky is in an abusive marriage (and probably doing drugs). He knows Becky fired a weapon into another person's home. These are the actions of a young woman in serious trouble, and they remind Bobby of his own delinquent youth.

Imagine there had been no gunshots. Imagine Bobby said good-night to Shelly and Becky and went home and had a dream. In that dream, Bobby's churning mind wrestles with all he has learned about Becky (and been reminded about Shelly). His anxieties and fears manifest, and in his mind's eye he sees bullets rip through the diner, watches a family fracture around a loaded gun, witnesses a young woman vomit poisons. This is how Bobby's subconscious mind might render his fears.

In Bobby's dream, a boy, emulating his father, fires a gun into a protected space; a woman frantically honks her horn to clear a path through gridlock; and a girl hides her sickness in the shadows. Bobby, a passive observer in the tumult of his own mind, watches in bafflement and despair. Lynch emphasizes Bobby's confusion with a final close-up of Bobby's face and with the amplified sounds of car horns.

We don't know if Bobby went home and dreamed the chaos outside the Double R, but what we see in the intersection is so exaggerated and inexplicable it might as well be Bobby's emotions come to life. Perhaps Bobby, whose fears have risen to such a heightened state, projects his own "observer effect" onto reality and actuates these events.[*] Or maybe Dale Cooper, our observing proxy, is so overwhelmed by watching Bobby's internal conflicts he gives life to them through his own interpretive lens. Either way, it's hard to situate this scene as anything other than stemming from Bobby's subconscious.[†]

Bobby is the dreamer living inside his dream, and his bewildering encounters evoke the absurdity, unpredictability and fear of our current age. Such plot-free moments need not be addressed again because they have a singular purpose. They connect us intimately with a specific character. When Bobby's roiling psyche comes to life in the nighttime street outside the Double R, we don't simply watch Bobby, we become him.

IN THE SHADOWS OF A CONFERENCE ROOM, Hawk shows Sheriff Truman his "very old" map, a piece of parchment illustrated with scenes and landmarks from the surrounding forest. According to Hawk, the map is "always current," it serves as an up-to-date snapshot of the latest supernatural happenings. Truman doesn't blink an eye. He accepts that Hawk possesses a magic map whose symbols shift and shuffle by uncanny whim. Like The Log Lady's log, Hawk's map is a "living thing." It dispenses cryptic advice to guide its observer toward truth.

In fact, the map and the log are likely in contact. After Hawk studies the map's contours and deduces that Major Briggs is directing them toward a sacred place in the forest, The Log Lady calls with a warning: "There's fire where you are going." Hawk listens gravely but refuses to say more about what he and Truman are planning.

At this moment of liminal overlap, when The Log Lady and Hawk both acknowledge a supernatural threat, Deputy Jesse Holcomb knocks on the door. Like a young Carl Rodd, Jesse Holcomb senses the deeper

---

[*] Just as Lucy may have done when she arguably summoned Wally Brando into her orbit.

[†] Note that in later episodes The Double R Diner is still up and running, with no plywood covering the broken windows or police tape cordoning off the booth. Had there really been a violent incident at the diner, one would expect to see some evidence of the aftermath.

currents of reality (and is probably tuned to the same frequencies as the map and the log). At the end of Part 6, Jesse stared into space, piercing the illusions of the everyday. Now, drawn to whatever Hawk and Truman are planning, he interrupts. Maybe he wants to warn the men of their dangerous destination (just like The Log Lady did), or maybe he simply wants to tag along. Whatever his reasons, it's probably no coincidence that Jesse shows up when he does. He asks Truman if he would like to see his new car, and he teases the year of manufacture ("It's a two-thousand and—"), but Truman cuts him off and sends him away. The door closes, and Jesse recedes into the shadows, never to be seen again.

Jesse Holcomb is an enigma. He drifts in and out of the story like a wisp of smoke, a member of the quirky group of "watchers" who briefly dwell in the narrative and then vanish. Truman closes the door on Jesse and gives Hawk a curious glance, as if trying to reestablish his bearings. Jesse's comment about the year echoes, and you can almost hear the question on Truman's mind: "What year is this?"

FRANK TRUMAN IS NOT THE ONLY CHARACTER trying to regain his balance. At the Buckhorn Police Department, Gordon Cole reels from his earlier encounter with the vortex. Hands shaking, he tries to make sense of what happened. Albert is unsettled, too. When he shows Cole a picture of the coordinates they found on Ruth Davenport's arm, he says, "The numbers indicate a small town in the north…," as if he thinks Cole knows nothing about Twin Peaks, as if he's saying, "*There's this small town in the Pacific Northwest called Twin Peaks, Gordon. Maybe we should look into it.*"

Albert, like everyone else in the room, is confounded by the visit to the weedy lot at 2240 Sycamore. He can't put all his facts in order, just like Diane can't be sure she saw a Woodsman get into the car where Hastings was killed. Everyone's memories are muddled. Confusion permeates the room. Tammy Preston feels it, and so does Bill Macklay. Then Gordon Cole suddenly remembers what he glimpsed in the interstitial realm of the vortex ("I saw them in a room. Dirty bearded men in a room."), but it's only a fleeting image. Cole never mentions his vision again. We will never know what sense (if any) he made of it.[*]

BUSHNELL MULLINS IS READY to send Cooper into the lion's den. The Lucky 7 Insurance Agency owes the Mitchum Brothers thirty million dollars, and Bushnell is convinced that Cooper should be the one to deliver the check.

As Cooper and Mullins exit the Lucky 7 building, Cooper sees an image of Phillip Gerard beckoning from inside Szymon's Famous Coffees, a nearby bakery. A few moments later, Cooper carries a large cardboard box toward the waiting limo. Before Cooper gets in, Mullins gives him a pep talk. "Knock 'em dead," he says, tapping Cooper on the chin. Cooper responds by putting his hand to his face, squeezing his cheeks and repeating the word, "Dead." In fact, Cooper squeezes his cheeks just the way Mr. C grabbed Jack's cheeks in Part 2. Does Cooper sense a threat? Is he dimly aware he's walking into a trap? Watching from the Red Room, the mind of Dale Cooper may be equating Jack's tragic fate with an imminent threat to the "Dougie" version of himself.

Out in the desert, Bradley and Rodney Mitchum wait for Cooper, still furious at how Dougie Jones cheated them out of so much money. Bradley is troubled by a dream in which Rodney's wound (the cut Candie so clumsily caused when she tried to swat a fly with a TV remote) had been completely healed. Compelled by the dream, Bradley rips the bandage from his brother's face to reveal that, indeed, the cut is gone. It has totally healed.[†] Bradley knows his dream has import, but, like Gordon Cole in Buckhorn, he can't remember any further details.

Just then, Cooper arrives holding the cardboard box, and Bradley's memories come flooding back. He remembers that if the box contains one certain item, then Cooper is not an enemy. He pleads with Rodney to heed this vision and whispers what he suspects is in the box. Rodney, bursting with impatience and already shaken by the dream's prophetic

---

[*] An awful lot from Part 11 never gets mentioned again: Becky's crazed pursuit of Steven, the gunshots at the Double R, Bobby's encounters in the intersection, Hawk's map, Jesse's car, Cole's vision. All these curious events are simply forgotten, like curls of a dream in a waking mind.

[†] Rodney's healed wound is another reminder of Kafka's *The Metamorphosis*. Gregor Samsa's wounds "seemed to have healed entirely...he no longer felt the least impairment...this was astonishing."

power, turns on Cooper and forcefully demands to know if the box contains a cherry pie. Cooper, parroting Rodney, merely repeats, "Cherry pie."

Bradley opens the box and sees the pie. He can't believe it. He frisks Cooper and discovers the check for thirty million dollars. Stunned and delighted, he prances over to Rodney to show him the check. The brothers howl with glee. They holler into the desert sky. Bradley turns to Cooper and says, "I love this guy."

Inexplicable powers have steered Cooper away from danger and into the good graces of the Mitchum brothers. Once again, Cooper is being protected by forces watching from afar. What otherworldly entity installed in Bradley Mitchum a dream to caution against murdering Cooper? Surely, it was the same entity that steered Cooper to the cherry pie at Szymon's. Maybe these protective forces are The Fireman and Major Garland Briggs carefully maneuvering Cooper past Mr. C's traps. Or maybe Cooper's observing mind steadily manipulates reality to guard and guide him in the real world. Whatever it may be, Cooper exists in a tractable reality, a world that shapes itself favorably around him.

Cooper's radiating goodness is a factor, too. The Mitchums celebrate the return of their thirty million dollars by taking Cooper to a fancy dinner. They smile and laugh and even tolerate Candie's maddening absent-mindedness. In these moments, the Mitchum brothers transform from violent thugs into affable companions. Their brutal days are behind them thanks to their encounter with Cooper. For the rest of *The Return*, they will be nothing but generous and friendly.

The "lady slot addict" from Part 4 enters the dining room and recognizes Cooper as "Mr. Jackpots," the man who steered her to vast winnings at the slot machines. Her change of fortune is obvious. She's no longer dressed in the shabby outfit she wore in the casino. Now, she wears an elegant gown and jewelry. The lady says she has been reunited with her adult son, and she's also bought a house and gotten a dog.*

---

* Dogs appear in every David Lynch work (two appear in *The Return*, one belonging to Marjorie Green, and the other to Cyril Pons). Lynch has an affection for dogs. He

Her whole life has come back to her. The lady profusely thanks Cooper
for all he did and advises the Mitchums to appreciate the special person
that Cooper is. Rodney and Bradley smile enthusiastically, never realizing (or simply not caring) that this woman (like Cooper) recently
won an immense amount of money at their casino. Cooper's goodness
has permeated the setting. The Mitchum brothers have become mag-
nanimous, ready to celebrate and reward their friends with gifts. The
good Cooper has made them better men and, more importantly, allies.

---

once owned a Jack Russell Terrier that he called "the love of[his] life." It's not
surprising, then, that "getting a dog" symbolizes a positive change in the Lady-slot-
addict's world.

PART 12:

LET'S ROCK

IF YOU NEED EVIDENCE that the environs of the Red Room are bleeding over into Dale Cooper's perceptions, look no further than the opening scene of Part 12. Cole, Albert, and Tammy are ensconced in a private lounge at the Mayfair Hotel in Buckhorn. Red curtains separate the room from the rest of the hotel, and Cole brandishes an electronic device, waving it about the room as if to detect any electronic (or perhaps supernatural) eavesdroppers. Albert explains the origins of the FBI's Blue Rose Task Force to Tammy Preston, noting that many members of the force—Phillip Jeffries, Chet Desmond, Dale Cooper— have vanished. Still, despite this potential danger, Cole and Albert invite Tammy to join the Blue Rose team, and she agrees.

A moment later, Diane parts the curtains and joins the group. There's a palpable tension between Diane and Albert. He offers her a drink, but then simply sets a bottle of vodka down for her to pour herself. She does, all while staring daggers at Albert. Despite the friction, Albert explains that he and Cole would like to temporarily deputize Diane into the FBI. (Cole and Albert know Diane is spying on them, and this is part of their plan to "keep her close.") Diane mulls the offer and accepts with an affirmative, "Let's rock!" Cole raps the table in satisfaction.

Diane's declaration, "Let's Rock!" is accompanied by a distinct music cue, an inverted whooshing sound that builds to an abrupt climax. It's an aural jolt, more sound effect than music (what essayist Andrew T. Burt describes as "the sound of doors closing, building to-ward a conclusion that resembles air being sucked from the room").

The same cue is audible in *Fire Walk With Me* when Agent Cooper discovers the phrase, "Let's Rock" written in red paint on the windshield of Agent Chet Desmond's car.

That brings us to the mysterious Chet Desmond, a character who, up until now, more than eleven hours into the third season of *Twin Peaks*, has yet to be mentioned. (More striking, he won't be mentioned again *after* this scene.) Albert and Cole have discussed Phillip Jeffries multiple times but not Chet Desmond. You would think Desmond's disappearance would be an important part of the FBI's current investigation, but it's clearly not. Despite Albert's cursory mention of Desmond now, it's as if the character doesn't exist.

Well. Maybe he doesn't.

Despite repeated suggestions to David Lynch to include Chet Desmond in the new narrative, Mark Frost explains, "[Lynch] didn't pursue it,"[*] which begs the question: Why was David Lynch not interested in Chet Desmond? After all, Lynch went out of his way to ensure Phillip Jeffries was an active presence in *The Return*, even though David Bowie (the actor who played Jeffries) had passed away before production had started. *The Return* explores many mysteries surrounding Jeffries and yet leaves wholly unaddressed one of *Fire Walk With Me*'s most indelible mysteries: The disappearance of Agent Chester Desmond. David Lynch just didn't pursue it. *Why?*

David Lynch didn't pursue it because Chet Desmond is far less important than he seems. Desmond, *as he appears in Fire Walk With Me*, was entirely the fabrication of Dale Cooper's mind. (I still maintain that the first thirty minutes of *Fire Walk With Me* is presented through the dreaming mind of Dale Cooper.[†])

David Lynch always envisioned Dale Cooper as the primary investigator in *Fire Walk With Me*—it's how Lynch originally scripted the film—but when Kyle MacLachlan declined to fully participate, Cooper's role had to be reduced to a cameo. So, Lynch had a problem. How do you preserve your main character when the actor playing him is not available? For Lynch, the answer was simple: *Use a substitute*

---

[*] Mark Frost says he mentioned Desmond to Lynch "a couple of times."

[†] As opposed to my theory here, that *The Return* is filtered through Cooper's very much *awake* mind.

Cooper. David Lynch simply swapped characters, and Chet Desmond became a surrogate Cooper.

Lynch didn't abandon Cooper in *Fire Walk With Me*. On the contrary, Cooper was simply conveyed through another persona. Lynch positioned Chet Desmond as a figment of Cooper's mind, an alter-ego who, after he served his purpose, simply *disappeared.* More precisely, he faded back into Cooper's subconscious, "disappearing" from the narrative just when Dale Cooper emerged as a dominant player. No wonder David Lynch didn't want to bring Chet Desmond back in *The Return.* Doing so would undermine the clever strategy he employed in *Fire Walk With Me.*[*]

Oh, but yes, *I haven't forgotten*, Albert mentions Chet Desmond to Tammy Preston, thereby firmly establishing Desmond within the *Twin Peaks* milieu. Right?

Take a close look at the whole scene unfolding within the red-draped depths of the Mayfair Hotel. What are we witnessing? On the surface, we have a scene that provides backstory to the Blue Rose Task Force, a brief mention of Chet Desmond, and a recognizable piece of dialog (with accompanying music) from *Fire Walk With Me.* The whole scene is highly suspicious. In fact, it's unreliable. Cooper, watching from the Red Room, can't help but impose his troubled memories over the action: Red drapes, Blue Rose, "Let's rock," Chet Desmond—they are all of a piece, a knot of threads tangled deep within Cooper's mind. Reality and memory mix, and the scene in the Mayfair Hotel becomes skewed by a capricious psyche. Once again, the world is as Dale Cooper is.

AT THE GREAT NORTHERN, Ben Horne learns about Richard's violent crimes and laments that Richard never had a father. Though we don't know the specifics, we can surmise that Audrey Horne is Richard's mother and that she was likely the victim of sexual assault. Over the years, Ben may have tried to be a father to Richard and now feels responsible for Richard's wicked ways. As Ben ponders Richard's

---

[*] In *Wrapped In Plastic 75*, I asked David Lynch about the narrative structure of *Fire Walk With Me*, specifically how the opening prologue squared with the rest of the film. He replied that the film had "perfect balance." Of course it does: Cooper in the first part, Laura in the second.

awful behavior, he remembers the bike his father gave him when he was a boy and how much joy it brought. In these moments, there's a real humanity to Ben Horne, a longing for a simpler time and regret that he could not be to Richard what Ben's father was to Ben.

GORDON COLE IS ENTERTAINING A FRENCH WOMAN in his hotel room when Albert arrives with an update on their surveillance of Diane. Cole kindly asks his lady friend to wait in the bar, and she slowly makes her way out, fussily applying makeup and slipping into her shoes. Albert coolly watches her exaggerated exit, and Cole enjoys the moment. Once she's gone, Cole describes to Albert the difficulty of translating jokes into French. "Do you realize," he asks, "that there are more than 6,000 languages spoken on Earth today?" Albert does not respond, and the two men stare at each other for a long moment.

The inefficiency of language has been of interest to David Lynch for as long as he's been making films. Lynch believes that words are poor tools for expressing complicated ideas, or, for that matter, *any* idea: "When you talk about things—unless you're a poet—a big thing becomes smaller."

Lynch described his frustration with language in The Log Lady's introduction to episode 10 of the original *Twin Peaks*: "Even with complicated languages used by intelligent people, misunderstanding is a common occurrence. We write things down sometimes—letters, words—hoping they will serve us and those with whom we wish to communicate. Letters and words, calling out for understanding."

Communication, language, misunderstanding, these are themes that appear time and again in Lynch's work. In almost every film, Lynch features characters laboring to be heard. Some have speech impediments (John Merrick in *The Elephant Man*, Rose Straight in *The Straight Story*), some bark and cackle (Naido in *The Return*, the old couple in *Mulholland Drive*), and some speak with thick, impenetrable accents (Nikki's neighbor in *INLAND EMPIRE*, Valdja Gochktch in *On the Air*). Through these characters, Lynch emphasizes a physical struggle to communicate.

And for every person trying to be heard, there's someone attempting to grasp what is being conveyed. Lynch's characters often listen with bewilderment or simply can't hear anything at all. Slim, a character in *The Cowboy and the Frenchman*, is so hard of hearing it doesn't matter what anyone says, he can't hear it anyway (most of his dialog is simply, "*What?!*"). Slim is a precursor to Gordon Cole, David Lynch's alter-ego in *The Return*. Cole recognizes the inadequacy of spoken communication and masks this knowledge with a feigned deafness. (If it's not feigned, it's inconsistent. Cole's hearing is notional; sometimes he hears things and sometimes not.)

To overcome the barriers of language, Cole attempts a primitive form of mind-to-mind contact (similar to the way The Fireman and Señorita Dido communicated in Part 8). Standing in his hotel room, he silently assesses Albert, wordlessly measuring his friend just as he did at the end of Part 4. For Cole, this kind of communication is more valuable than words could ever be.

Cole, it turns out, dimly understands a fundamental concept of *The Return*: *We live inside a dream* (an idea he'll explore in Part 14). He knows that each person perceives the world through his or her specific mindset. To understand Albert better—to bridge those barriers of language and miscommunication—Cole attempts to see the world as Albert does, but it's not clear if he succeeds. After assessing Albert, Cole says, "Sometimes I really worry about you." He either knows exactly what Albert is thinking, or he finds Albert a complete mystery.

HUTCH AND CHANTAL WAIT in their van outside Warden Murphy's house, casually debating whether to torture Murphy before killing him. Violence and brutality are a normal part of their lives, no different from any other chore they must perform. Hutch and Chantal may be remorseless killers, but they're also simple-minded thugs, wholly corrupted by the evil that emanates from Mr. C. Hutch assassinates Murphy with a calm indifference, oblivious to the anguished cries of Murphy's young son, who sees the bloody body of his father lying on the walk. "Next stop, Wendy's," Hutch announces, shifting easily to the next errand on his list. Hutch and Chantal drive away, pain and sorrow roiling in their wake.

SARAH PALMER GRAPPLES with a burgeoning darkness. At the liquor store, she fills her cart with bottles of vodka and, upon checkout, is suddenly reminded of Laura. Maybe Sarah remembers Laura because the young cashier so strikingly resembles her, or maybe she remembers Laura because she notices the display of turkey jerky behind the counter (Laura once obliquely referred to herself as a turkey). Whatever the reason, Sarah is triggered and, as if speaking to her daughter, says, "Your room seems different." In fact, Sarah seems dimly aware that Laura is alive somewhere in the world (in a "different room"), and she issues an uncanny warning: "Men are coming.... You have to watch out! Things can happen!" In this clairvoyant moment, Sarah Palmer understands that violent men threaten her daughter. Men with guns, loose in the world.[*]

The tragedies of Sarah's life blur. She may be warning Laura of threatening men, but she fears a more imminent threat. Struggling against an interior evil, Sarah's identity wavers. "Something happened to me!" she cries. Distraught, delirious, Sarah abruptly exits the store, struggling to stay in control of her mind and body. If there's any doubt that Sarah is a victim, this scene removes it. Wilting under the pressure of an unremitting evil, Sarah has very little agency. The infestation she carries rots at her soul.

Back home, Sarah Palmer is all alone. She has no family or friends. "No one really knows what I'm thinking—or cares," she says in the *Twin Peaks* short, *Between Two Worlds*. But someone does care. Deputy Hawk, tuned to the supernatural currents eddying around Twin Peaks, visits and offers his assistance. "I want you to call," he tells her, "If you need help of *any* kind." Standing outside Sarah's front door, Hawk hears something rustling deep in the Palmer house and asks if someone is moving about inside. Sarah is dismissive. "It's just something in the kitchen," she says, and Hawk knows he can go no further. He takes his leave, while Sarah Palmer withdraws to the haunted spaces of her home.[†]

---

[*] Loose, perhaps, in Odessa, Texas.

[†] Indulge me, if you will, a short personal anecdote: On July 30, 2017, I was invited to watch Part 12 of *The Return* inside the real-life Palmer house in Everett, WA, the location where the interiors and exteriors of the Palmer residence were filmed. I had never been to this house and was delighted to be a guest of homeowner, Mary Reber (who, as most of you know, will play a part in *The Return* in Part 18). It was surreal, to say the least, to watch Deputy Hawk climb the long steps to the front door of the very house in which I was sitting. I almost turned to the door in anticipation of Hawk's knocks. Later—and I swear this is true—I heard a noise in the kitchen: Someone in the house rummaging for something to eat. It was uncanny. It was *spooky*. I heard "something" in the kitchen while I watched *Twin Peaks* in Sarah Palmer's haunted house.

The Palmer house is but one of many miserable homes in *Twin Peaks*. In *The Architecture of David Lynch*, author Richard Martin observes, "The town's houses are rife with dysfunctional families: adultery, violence, drugs and madness are omnipresent." Indeed, in *The Return* we see evidence of distress inside almost every home we visit: Murder and deception find root in the home of Bill and Phyllis Hastings; violence looms in the spaces surrounding Becky and Steven Burnett; cruelty invades the home of Sylvia and Johnny Horne. There is sickness and addiction, too. Cancer contaminates Beverly and Tom Paige's home, while drugs and alcohol permeate the empty shelter of "the drugged-out mother" in Rancho Rosa. Homes are repeatedly violated in *Twin Peaks*. There is no retreat, and no one is safe.

Only one home in *The Return* has the potential for happiness, and that's the Jones household of Lancelot Court. Happiness flourishes here upon the arrival of Dale Cooper. Not long ago, the faithless Dougie Jones made this a bitter place, but Cooper's presence has transformed it to a place of joy. (We see some of that joy in this very episode, as Sonny-Jim attempts to play catch with a clueless Cooper.)

And yet the Jones home is an exception. Happy households are rare in *Twin Peaks*. Everywhere we look we find despair and anger, from Dr. Amp's forest hideaway to Diane's Philadelphia townhouse. Even the office lodgings of Big Ed Hurley are blanketed with hopelessness. And inside one particular house, confusion rules. We've arrived at last at the cluttered, impossible residence of Audrey Horne.

Has Dale Cooper been avoiding Audrey all this time? Has he been reluctant to check in on her as his mind drifts through the town of Twin Peaks? Although he only knew her for about four weeks, Dale Cooper had a special relationship with Audrey. The two were kindred spirits whose mutual attraction transcended the physical. Cooper no doubt still worries for Audrey, but if he fears she has suffered since he left Twin Peaks—if he knows she was wounded in a bomb blast and then, far worse, sexually assaulted by his escaped evil half—he may be reluctant to look at her now. Still, he can't avoid her forever. Cooper (and we, his partners in spectation) at last turns his attention to Audrey Horne's restless world.

LET'S PAUSE FOR A MOMENT before we dive into this, *The Return*'s most fascinating and difficult subplot. Let's pierce the façade of

Audrey's tale. We know from the shock ending in Part 16 that Audrey's story is not what it appears, that when we first see her at home struggling to take action, trying to solve what she believes is an urgent problem, we are, in fact, peering into Audrey's interior landscape. We are witnessing the delusions of a troubled mind.

Audrey is not at home. She is somewhere else. Maybe she's in a white room. Maybe she lies in a coma in a hospital. Maybe she's sharing her deepest anxieties with a therapist. We just don't know. Audrey Horne will remain a mystery, but there's no doubt her story is a *masked narrative*—a superficial drama concealing a truer conflict....

AUDREY STANDS MOTIONLESS before a fireplace and stares offscreen to her right. The camera follows her gaze, panning across to reveal a short man behind a cluttered desk. This is Charlie, Audrey's apparent husband.

Audrey glowers at Charlie. She has been waiting for him to accompany her to the Roadhouse to look for someone named Billy. Charlie hesitates. It's too late, it's too dark, he's simply too tired to look for Billy. Why don't they get some sleep and wait for the light of day?

Audrey's anger mounts. She lashes out at Charlie, belittling him, scorning him. Audrey says she's really in love with Billy. She's done with Charlie, Billy is all that matters. Still, Audrey needs Charlie to come with her.

Charlie reluctantly agrees to go, but then he has an idea. He can call someone named "Tina," who, as Charlie explains, was the last person to see Billy. Audrey considers the idea and agrees. Charlie should call Tina.

Charlie finds Tina's number in his rolodex and carefully dials his rotary phone. We hear the line ring and click, but when Charlie speaks with Tina, we hear only his side of the conversation; Tina's voice is absent. Charlie asks about Billy and is startled by something he hears. "Oh, my goodness," he replies. "Unbelievable, what you're telling me." Audrey has no idea what Charlie is hearing and motions for him to hurry, to hang up and tell her what's happening. Charlie says a prolonged goodbye to Tina and slowly places the phone back on the cradle. He looks up, face blank, and says nothing. Audrey's is furious at his lack of response, and her anger breaks through. She screams, "You're not going to tell me what she said?!" Charlie remains as still as a statue, staring silently—defiantly—at Audrey, and the scene ends.

Audrey's debut in *The Return* is mystifying. For twelve minutes, we watch a confrontation between two static characters in a scene that spins in place, frustrating us with its lack of resolution. At this early stage, we don't yet know that we are witnessing a ruse, an imaginary landscape existing entirely within Audrey's mind. But while we might be confused, impatient, even *annoyed*, if we look closely, we see clues that betray the artifice:

First, there's a theatrical element that runs through the entirety of the scene. The characters are situated as if posed on a stage, something David Lynch emphasizes by the way he pans the camera across the room.

Second, the "set" which Charlie and Audrey inhabit is filled with anachronisms. A rotary phone, an hourglass and a rolodex clutter Charlie's desk. Papers and books[*] overflow the shelves.

Third, the dialog between the Charlie and Audrey is expository. The two characters talk about "signing papers" and having a "contract," exaggerated reminders about the status of their relationship.

Charlie is a suspicious character. If everything that transpires here originates from Audrey's mind, then Charlie is simply a figment of Audrey's imagination. One part of her mind (the Audrey figure) wants to find Billy, while the other (the Charlie figure) wants to remain safely at home. Charlie continually stalls Audrey. His call to "Tina" is a long tease, a one-sided conversation that supplies nothing of substance. As the scene progresses, Audrey's frustrations mirror those of the viewer, desperate to know more. But there is no more. The scene ends with Audrey (and us) just as confused as when we started.

---

[*] One of the books on the shelf to Audrey's right (our left) is *Four Quartets* by T.S. Eliot. Whole essays could be written about the parallels between this work and *The Return*. The first lines of the first poem (*Burnt Norton*) read: "Time present and time past/Are both perhaps present in time future,/And time future contained in time past." A later passage reads: "Descend lower, descend only/Into the world of perpetual solitude,/World not world, but that which is not world,/Internal darkness..." Also worth noting, the last of the poems (*Little Gidding*) contains these potent lines: "We shall not cease from exploration/And the end of all our exploring/Will be to arrive where we started/And know the place for the first time." A foreshadowing, perhaps, of the end of Part 18.

And we are *supposed* to be confused. That's the point. We are confused because Audrey Horne is confused. She is manifesting a delicate psychosis. Locked in a fugue, incapable of making a decision or gaining any momentum, she has an argument with her "husband" about whether she should leave the house to find the man she loves, or remain safely protected in the bubble of her home. Her troubles are real, but she disguises them as something melodramatic.

As a reflection of Audrey's mental state, the scene is a masterpiece. It is perfectly acted and meticulously designed. The scene's implications cannot be appreciated with just a single viewing, it must be watched again (and within the context of the larger story) to be truly understood.

Audrey's delusory world recalls Bobby's encounter in the intersection outside the Double R. Bobby's fears manifested as terrifying gunshots and sickly apparitions. Similarly, Audrey brings her deepest anxieties to life, her fear of the outside world and her suspicions regarding a long-lost love.* Audrey constructs a world that insulates her from her own truths.

We are witnessing Audrey's imaginings, but what about Cooper? If what we see in *The Return* is a story filtered through Cooper's mind— if he is the observing presence, skewing the narrative to his own predilections (like he does in the opening scene of this episode with the Blue Rose Task Force)—how do we position Cooper in Audrey's fanciful subplot? In other words, when we watch Audrey's story, are we seeing Cooper's *interpretation*, or are we truly peering into Audrey's psychological fantasies?

I believe Cooper shares a special bond with Audrey (in the original series she reached out and contacted Cooper through prayer), one that allows him to interpret Audrey's fraught mental state.† Cooper knows Audrey is not really in a house arguing with Charlie. He's not interested in her physical location; it's her *psychological* conflict that's got his

---

* See the next chapter for a discussion about who Billy really represents to Audrey.

† We know from the original series, specifically the Lynch-directed episode 2, Cooper uses "deep levels of intuition" to "subconsciously gain knowledge." It seems perfectly reasonable to me that Cooper, located in the potent omni-dimension of The Red Room, could peer into the mind of Audrey Horne (just as he probably did with Bobby Briggs in Part 11).

attention. Cooper sees Audrey much the way she sees herself. Sensing her pain and confusion, Cooper reads Audrey's mind and conveys to us the drama unfolding within.

AUDREY WAS DESPERATE to get to the Roadhouse, and that's exactly where we go at the end of Part 12. Again, we eavesdrop on a couple of curious characters sharing gossip and personal drama. Two women, Abbie and Natalie, discuss a mutual friend named Angela, whom they haven't seen in a while. In fact, she's been missing for a few days. Natalie thinks Angela might be seeing someone named Clark, which worries Abbie because she saw Clark with Mary. Now, the two friends become really worried. Angela has already been through so much—she's lost her mother and just got off her medications—how will she respond to Clark's unfaithfulness? As they ponder Angela's messy life, a man, Trick, hurriedly slides into their booth. He's distraught because he was almost run off the road on his way to the Roadhouse. Trick tells the women of his ordeal and rushes off to order a few beers. Abbie watches him go and remembers that Trick might be under house arrest. Natalie explains that Trick has that behind him now. He's a free man again. The women giggle, and the scene ends.

Should we read any meaning to the Natalie/Abbie/Trick scene? Do we dare assign something specific to this seemingly nonsensical digression? It's easy to dismiss all the Roadhouse booth scenes as comic relief* or melodramatic threads invoking a traditional soap opera, but after witnessing Audrey's frantic compulsion to get to the Roadhouse, these curious scenes tease with potent connections. Who is Angela? And who are Natalie and Abbie, really?

Names are fluid in *Twin Peaks*, and identities are often fractured across multiple beings. Audrey is desperate to get to the Roadhouse, impatient to locate a mysterious man, and she dreams of a world outside her confinement. It's not hard to imagine that Audrey's

---

* This conversation may be the funniest one of them all. It's hard not to laugh when we hear just how bad Angela has it. There's that whole thing with Clark, her mom just died, and now she's off her meds. As Abbie tells it, Angela's "kind of on the edge." *Kind of?* That's probably an understatement. And then there's Trick, who frantically relates his near-death experience. He's manic. He never slows down. He's off to grab more beer before Natalie and Abbie can absorb what he's saying. I guess we'd all be a little wired after being under house arrest. *Whoopee.*

troubled dreams conjure the Roadhouse, where (as I mentioned in Part 9) fragments of her uneasy mind acquire different personas—Natalie, Abbie, Angela, Trick (and more to come)—each a reflection of Audrey Horne's fragile psyche.

\<INTERLUDE 5\>
I'M NOT SURE WHO I AM, BUT I'M NOT ME

NESTLED WITHIN the many subplots twining through *Twin Peaks: The Return* lies the tale of Audrey Horne. Hers is the story of a struggle to escape the confines of an impossible space, an anachronistic "home" conjured from the depths of her wounded psyche. At first glance, Audrey's story plays like an afterthought—something parallel, perplexing, potentially irrelevant. Her story is insular, removed entirely from familiar characters and established plots. Her story is fixed, balanced on the cusp of momentum but shying away from meaningful progress. Her story ends with a twist, a shocking image that suggests everything we've seen before has been a masked narrative, the delusions of an injured and troubled mind. And just when we glimpse the supposedly real Audrey Horne, staring unbelievingly at her face in a mirror, we find ourselves at the beginning of a completely new story—one we will be entirely denied.

But what we see of Audrey is enough. In fact, it's a gift. Far more than an afterthought or a remnant, Audrey provides a valuable contribution to the overall narrative of *The Return*. She's on a journey of overcoming. Of awakening and acceptance.

AUDREY'S ROLE IN *THE RETURN* was originally planned as something much different than what ended up on screen. From public comments made by Mark Frost and Sherilyn Fenn, we know Audrey was intended to be a hairdresser who owned a beauty salon in Twin Peaks. In this story, she frequently suffered at the hands of her son, Richard (much the way we saw Sylvia Horne suffer in Part 10). Frost describes some of this scenario in his book, *The Final Dossier*, but (as Frost explained at the Austin Film Festival in October of 2017) when it came to filming, David Lynch abandoned the concept and went in a different direction.

Lynch changed the story because Fenn balked at Audrey's scripted role. "I believe it was the story Mark Frost tells in *The Final Dossier*," she explained. "It was just bad. There was nothing to do." Fenn apparently argued with Lynch and declined to be part of the production, but after Lynch reworked the script and imagined a new story for Audrey, Fenn agreed to reprise her role. As she bluntly puts it: "We got in a fight, and he brought back something new."

What Lynch created was a self-contained work—a story in four acts, complete with rising action and denouement—that he tucked into the folds of the larger tale. Taken together, the scenes Lynch developed might be considered a *de facto* short film, an original piece operating independently inside *The Return*. Yes, aspects of Audrey's story bleed into the Roadhouse, but, as we will see, these occurrences are suspect and likely extensions of Audrey's delusion (especially the last scene). Audrey's connection to the rest of *Twin Peaks* is tenuous. Her story is, in effect, a standalone narrative.

What we see of Audrey is perplexing and frustrating, but a careful analysis, along with a comparison to Lynch's previous works, reveals the story's potency. You need only look at Lynch's *INLAND EMPIRE* to find parallels between that film's protagonist and Audrey. When Lynch unexpectedly found himself reworking Audrey's story, he may have subconsciously (or deliberately) evoked the complex character study he created in *INLAND EMPIRE*.

INLAND EMPIRE's exploration of memory, perception, and re-birth is grounded (as so many of Lynch's works are) in the philosophy of Hindu Vedic texts, particularly the Upanishads and the Bhagavad Gita. The plot of the film is difficult to summarize because it unfolds non-chronologically and shifts dizzyingly from one setting to another. Laura Dern ostensibly plays an actress named Nikki Grace, whose identity yields itself to another persona, Susan Blue, a character Nikki is playing in a film. Neither of these identities is certain, however, because another personality exists beneath the façades of Nikki and Susan, a wounded woman who in various analyses has been denoted as "the Battered Woman," "the abused woman," or "the nameless woman."

I'll refer to this character as "the Monologue Woman," simply because David Lynch describes writing "a fourteen-page monologue" for Laura Dern which became the core of *INLAND EMPIRE*. It was the seed from which the rest of the film sprouted. (Lynch calls the monologue "a standalone thing, but it also indicates something way bigger.")

The Monologue Woman appears late in the film. She climbs a long flight of stairs and sits at a table across from a small, bespectacled man named Mr. K (an overtly Kafkaesque name, recalling Josef K from *The Trial*, or K. from *The Castle*). Over the span of four, lengthy scenes, the Monologue Woman tells her story. She relates to Mr. K incidents where she was the victim of deception, assault, and neglect. She says that after her son died, she lost her grip on reality: "I went into a bad time, when I was watching everything go around me while I was standing in the middle.... I figured one day I'd just wake up and I'd find out what the hell yesterday was all about."

The Monologue Woman serves as the unifying component of *INLAND EMPIRE*. She "holds the key to everything," Lynch tells us. If that's true, all the disparate characters in the film are ostensibly reflections of the Monologue Woman. As Lynch scholar, Greg Olson notes, "Everything in the film [is] part of [her] fragmented mind."

No doubt, the Monologue Woman and Audrey Horne are very much different characters. Each has a unique backstory, and each operates from different circumstances, but the parallels between the two are striking. Studying the Monologue Woman in *INLAND EMPIRE* gives us insight into how Lynch approached redesigning Audrey Horne in *The Return*.

Both the Monologue Woman and Audrey find themselves expressing their traumas to a passive male figure, a mediator who listens and absorbs what each woman is saying. Mr. K and Charlie (Audrey's supposed husband) endure long, anxious confessions. (Mr. K listens quietly, but Charlie is engaged and confrontational.)

Neither Audrey nor the Monologue Woman is entirely certain of their reality. Audrey worries that she is "somewhere else" and "somebody else," while the Monologue Woman says, "I don't know what was before or after. I don't know what's happened first. And it's kinda layin' a mindfuck on me."

Finally, aspects of each woman's personality manifest as other characters in the narrative. The Monologue Woman is Nikki Grace and Susan Blue and quite possibly *all the other* women Laura Dern plays in the film, while Audrey concocts surrogates of herself in the distracted, worried women who appear in the Roadhouse booth.

AUDREY HORNE BEGAN AS AN ENIGMA. A psychologically complex character in the first season of *Twin Peaks*, Audrey rebelled against the oppressive presence of her father and the stifling environment of her dysfunctional family. She sought escape but could not find the intellectual, spiritual, sexual, or, indeed, physical freedom she so desperately needed. Season 1 depicts an intelligent young woman grappling with the onset of adulthood amid one lurid scenario after another. Murder, prostitution, drug-running—these were the fires that stoked the crucible of young Audrey's coming-of-age.

When Laura Palmer died, Audrey saw an opportunity to break free from the confines of her dead-end surroundings. She undertook a risky plan to expose the seedy environments frequented by Laura. Audrey did this, in part, to impress the dashing Dale Cooper, the FBI agent who came to Twin Peaks (and literally into Audrey's home) to investigate Laura's murder. Audrey fell under Cooper's unwitting spell and perceived him as a defining presence in her life. Dale Cooper promised a larger, more exciting world beyond the borders of Twin Peaks, and if Audrey could prove her worth to him, maybe he would take her away from the inevitable despair of a life in Twin Peaks. Audrey describes this fantasy to Donna Hayward: "A tall, dark and handsome stranger falls madly in love with me and takes me away to a life of mystery and international intrigue." Her plan is so simple: "He'll realize I'm the woman of his dreams because I'm going to help him figure out who killed Laura."

Audrey might have been a teenage girl with a crush, but she was a complex, compelling character who saw through the façades of her counterparts and had empathy for those who suffered. These complex characteristics are best exemplified in episode 5, when Audrey laughs at her father's conspiratorial schemes but cries when she sees a distraught Leland Palmer mocked by a crowd at the Great Northern.

Audrey unabashedly expresses her deepest emotions as she struggles to make sense of her place in a nonsensical world.

Sadly, Audrey lost much of her allure in the second season. Where once she was unpredictable, vibrant, and in command of her story, in Season 2 she was flattened by burdensome plots. Audrey's luster faded until she was simply another face in the ensemble, a character diluted by generic storytelling. Her transformation from willful high school senior to part-time executive in the Horne family business verged on the absurd. Worse, it undermined the very essence of what made Audrey so attractive as a character. As Martha Nochimson notes, "Gone was Audrey's original characterization as a young woman resistant to her father's willful stratagems through her visceral spontaneity."

In the end, Audrey became an environmental activist, physically protesting the exploitive practices of the Ghostwood Development Project by chaining herself to the vault of the Twin Peaks Savings and Loan. While this selfless, dramatic act recalled the impetuous behavior of Season 1 Audrey, it still failed to foreground the characteristics that made Audrey so compelling, the psychological tensions that gave her such a unique personality. Throughout Season 2, Audrey was defined solely by external conflict. Her whirlwind relationship with John Justice Wheeler and her struggle to steer the family business through economic and social change were predictable stories in which Audrey went through the motions of plot. But Audrey's fate at the end of the season was far worse than the demotions of reductive storytelling. When a bomb exploded at the Savings and Loan, Audrey ended up as just another cliffhanger, collateral damage in an unrelated, hackneyed subplot. In this moment, all hope of restoring the allusive, transitive charm of Audrey Horne was extinguished.

Or so we thought.

The Audrey Horne of *The Return* is a woman once again in search of herself. Like the Audrey of Season 1, this Audrey is confused but determined, frightened but steadfast. Audrey persistently faces her deepest fears no matter how difficult that confrontation might be.

And it *is* difficult, because this Audrey has not had a chance to lead a meaningful life. Just as she was learning to navigate the dangerous and uncertain world, she had her life abruptly and violently put on hold. Audrey in *The Return* shares the same fate as Dale Cooper, both are suspended in a subjective realm of uncertainty. Like Cooper, Audrey's life has frozen in time.

And so poor Audrey, caught in the static, purgatorial sphere of her mind, seeks shelter by parsing and reliving painful past events. As she does, Audrey finds an unexpected path away from her self-imposed boundaries. Across four distinct acts, Audrey's story charts a journey from confinement to freedom and, ultimately, transcendence.

Act 1

LOOK AT AUDREY HORNE, standing there in an artificial space, provoking her make-believe husband. We join her story *in media res*, as if Audrey has been all-along confronting "Charlie" about her need to search for an enigmatic figure named "Billy." This is Audrey's constant world. She lives forever in asymptotic pursuit of Billy. We don't know where the "real" Audrey is (she could be lying in a coma or merely lost in a state of denial), but wherever she is, her mind has retreated into fantasy, one where Charlie is her husband and where she must locate Billy.

Who is Billy, anyway? Why is Audrey looking for him?[*] Audrey says that Billy is "missing" and that she is "in love" with him. She saw Billy in her dream ("dreams sometime hearken a truth," she explains, hinting at a deeper reality beneath her perceptions), and Billy was bleeding "from the nose and mouth." Who in Audrey's memory might fit this description? To whom has she assigned the "Billy" identity?

The only likely candidate is Dale Cooper.

Think about it. If Audrey's mind churns with memories from her teenage years, then those memories remain strong in a mind that resides so close to that period of her life (especially if her mental fugue dates to the time of the bomb blast). Audrey fell head over heels for Dale Cooper during his brief visit to Twin Peaks. So strong were her feelings and physical attraction, that Audrey offered her naked body to

---

[*] Yes, we see a character named Bing searching for someone named Billy at the end of Part 7, but I chalk that up to a narrative echo, either from Audrey, or from Cooper's interpreting mind. Or it stems from Lynch's artistic impulse to add narrative balance (or imbalance) to the work. (It's worth noting that Billy is the name of the man Susan Blue loves in *INLAND EMPIRE*.)

Cooper. But Cooper rebuffed her overtures and, within weeks, vanished from Twin Peaks and from Audrey's life.

Worse, for all her admiration and infatuation, it's possible Audrey was left with a dark image of Cooper. If she gained consciousness in the hospital after the bank explosion, her last memory of Cooper may have been something devastating. We know that Cooper's doppelganger (his "evil half" that escaped the Red Room) went to Audrey's hospital room; Doc Hayward describes him "sneaking out" of intensive care where Audrey lay. While nowhere is it overtly stated, the horrible truth is this evil Cooper raped Audrey Horne, leaving her pregnant with the child who would become Richard Horne. Could Audrey have been awake at any time during this heinous act? Did she see a wounded Cooper looming over her, his face battered and possibly bleeding from his self-inflicted injury? Only hours earlier, Cooper had bashed his face into a mirror, and his head bled profusely. While his wound was located on his forehead, blood poured down his face past his nose and mouth. This is the visage Audrey Horne might have witnessed when, in wide-eyed horror, she saw the evil Cooper approach her in the ICU at Calhoun Memorial Hospital.

In the haven of her fantasy world, a confused and traumatized Audrey can make no sense of why Cooper behaved the way he did or why he ran off. She wants answers. She *needs* to know. She is desperate to find Cooper, whom, in her insular landscape, she has encoded as Billy. Audrey has assigned a secret name for Cooper so that she doesn't have to confront what he did: She's not really looking for Cooper, she's looking for Billy.

Secret names and alter egos are recurrent concepts in David Lynch's work. From *Lost Highway* to *Mulholland Drive* to *INLAND EMPIRE*, names and identities are always slippery. It shouldn't be surprising to see the idea at play in Audrey's story. Lynch is fascinated by the power and interchangeability of names. As he told Chris Rodley: "Names are weird things. Once a name starts getting certain meanings attached to it, it can be good, or it can be, you know, really bad." He says as much in the lyrics he wrote for the song, "Floating": "When you told me your secret name I burst into flames and burn."

Audrey believes the Roadhouse is the best place to find Billy (even though she says Billy "couldn't stand the place") and getting there has become her fixation. In every conversation, Audrey or Charlie confirm that their destination is the Roadhouse. This location must not be forgotten. It is vitally important. The Roadhouse is a space Audrey needs to access.

And yet Audrey is afraid to go. More precisely, she can't summon the courage to go as herself. In order to get to the Roadhouse, Audrey conjures other identities to safely enter this fraught space.

Like the Monologue Woman in *INLAND EMPIRE*, Audrey's mind fractures into multiple personas. We see her manifest as Abbie, Natalie, Sophie, Megan—characters who visit the Roadhouse and share their various dramas. Audrey is Megan, who remembers seeing Billy "hang his head in the sink" with a strange look on his face.[*] Audrey is Tina, who "had a thing with Billy" and had a "smile on her face whenever his name came up." She is Angela, who is "off her meds" and "on the edge." Audrey is a woman disassembled. "I'm not sure who I am," she tells Charlie. "But I'm not me."

Audrey reels from powerful memories. She recalls the kind and gentle Dale Cooper with whom she fell in love but cannot reconcile him with the terrible acts "Cooper" performed. None of it makes sense.

But she needs it to make sense. And in an effort to *make it* make sense she invokes a bevy of alter-egos who struggle to assemble their murky memories into some coherent whole. But they, too, fail. The truth remains out of reach, and Audrey never lasts long at the Roadhouse. Her alter-egos disappear as she withdraws once more into the dark confines of her "house" and her "husband."

Act 2

AUDREY FEARS she will only ever be a supporting player in someone else's story. Despite her efforts to take center stage when Cooper came to town, Audrey found herself relegated to the wings, watching the spotlight of Cooper's attention follow someone else. No matter how hard she tried, Audrey Horne could never eclipse Laura Palmer. Lying

---

[*] Although Audrey was not there, she might know that after Cooper smashed his head in mirror at the Great Northern, he hung his head in the sink and stared back at himself "real strange and bloody." Audrey might also know that when "Cooper" came to visit her in the ICU he had that "strange look" Doc Hayward so chillingly describes to Frank Truman in Part 7.

naked in Cooper's bed, Audrey heard how determined Cooper was to uncover Laura's secrets, and she realized she would never occupy his attention the way Laura did. Audrey's story was secondary.

As Audrey's mind pushes back against the part of herself that she calls "Charlie," her resentment about Laura rises to the surface. When Charlie threatens to "end" Audrey's story, she rhetorically counters with: "What story is that, Charlie? Is it the story of the little girl who lived down the lane?" In this moment Audrey ruefully admits the truth: The "story" has *always* been about the little girl who lived down the lane, because "the little girl who lived down the lane" is Laura Palmer. *

Laura Palmer is the centerpiece. She's "the one that leads to the many." She's another "little girl who got killed" (as the diner patron in *Fire Walk With Me* describes Teresa Banks, Leland/Bob's first victim). If we look at Audrey's narrative antecedent—the Monologue Woman in *INLAND EMPIRE*—we find an even more striking connection. The Monologue Woman tells her confessor about a crazy town where everyone had "weird dreams" and saw "things that wasn't there." One time, a "little girl" from the town stared into the distance and started screaming. She saw "the end of the world—all fire and smoke and blood rain." David Lynch may have remembered these lines when he was crafting Audrey's story and found new relevance for them in *The Return*. The Monologue Woman's curious anecdote about the little girl vividly describes Laura Palmer, a woman who screams into the night at the end of the story.

Audrey knows she is but a flicker next to the roaring fire that is Laura Palmer, the chosen one (at least by Dale Cooper), the girl who heralds the very end of the world. In her confrontation with Charlie about the "story," Audrey accepts that it has never been about her. As far as Dale Cooper (and everyone else) is concerned, the story is about Laura.

---

* Some viewers assume that the phrase "the little girl who lived down the lane" is a reference to the 1976 film, *The Little Girl Who Lives Down the Lane*, starring Jodie Foster. While it's possible this film informs Lynch's work in *The Return*, I think it unlikely. Lynch has never referred to this film in the past (like he has *The Wizard of Oz* and *Sunset Boulevard*), and parallels between the two works are superficial. The phrase Audrey uses in *The Return* is an old one, a variation of a line from the nursery rhyme, "Baa, Baa, Black Sheep."

This admission is staggering. Audrey is so overwhelmed by her realization that she can no longer stand. For the first time, she finds a chair and sits. Her confidence about Billy and the Roadhouse completely slips away. Charlie notices: "You're the one who wanted to go," he says. "Now you're looking like you want to stay." Audrey surrenders to her indecision: "I want to stay, and I want to go. I want to do both."

Act 3

AS PAINFUL AS AUDREY'S conflicts with Charlie have been, each exchange has nudged Audrey along a path. She's making progress toward breaking free from her confinement and coming to terms with her story. She's not there yet, but as she navigates her jumbled stages of grief (denial, anger, bargaining) Audrey is approaching acceptance.

In Act 1, Audrey is trapped in the deepest part of her mind (the windowless, dark space of Charlie's study). In Act 2, she instantly finds herself in another room, one much closer to the foyer and the front door (the exit from the house). In Act 3, Audrey is now standing in the foyer, next to the door that leads outside. Charlie stands across from her, wearing his coat and ready to leave. Audrey finds herself unexpectedly on a threshold (a term Charlie uses to describe their location), and it overwhelms her. Disoriented by the sudden prospect of leaving the house, Audrey cannot commit to making that final step.

She stalls. She changes the subject from the Roadhouse to Charlie's flaws, calling him a whiner and a "sick dog." To avoid having to leave her "house," she confronts herself, challenging the part of her psyche facilitating her exit.

And, once again, Audrey has a breakthrough. She questions Charlie's identity and seems dimly aware that Charlie is but another aspect of herself, a piece of her mind: "I just never really saw you before the way I'm seeing you now. Like I'm meeting a different person. Who are you, Charlie?" The conflict between the two parts of Audrey's identity reaches a crescendo, and, for the first time, Audrey acts. She screams and pounces on Charlie (who at this point has retreated to the couch). She pummels him with her fists, angrily crying, "How can you be like this? I hate you!" This powerful emotional response—this self-confrontation—triggers a psychological release. At last Audrey can exit her "home" and gain access to the liminal space she calls "the Roadhouse."

Act 4

AT AUDREY'S IMAGINARY ROADHOUSE, a man on stage plays guitar and sings. His lyrics echo Audrey's mental state: "I am who I am/Who I was I will never be again/ . . . Victim or witness, we're gonna get hurt/ . . . There's another us around somewhere with much better lives." These words resonate as Audrey and Charlie enter the Roadhouse and make their way through the crowd. Charlie steers them toward the bar, and Audrey looks around the room, peering past various patrons and straining her neck. Ostensibly, Audrey is looking for Billy, but she could as easily be looking for Megan and Sophie, or Abbie and Natalie. If these aspects of Audrey preceded her to the Roadhouse, then perhaps Audrey believes they might still be there.

Any thought we might have that this Roadhouse is the "real" Roadhouse evaporates the moment the MC announces the house band's next song: "Audrey's Dance"—the same music from the Double R jukebox that Audrey danced to decades earlier and once described as "too dreamy." Indeed, as if in a dream, the crowd drifts off the dance floor, swaying in unison to the music's slow tempo. Audrey takes to the floor and begins her movement.

Audrey's decision to dance marks a moment of tremendous emotional release. For the first time, Audrey smiles, a true, genuine smile, an expression of joy and contentment. She is letting go. Eyes closed, adrift on the melody, Audrey gives herself up to herself. Thoughts of Billy evaporate. Her story is all that matters now. Audrey Horne occupies the center of the dance floor and basks in the gift of the moment. Dancing, she discards the baggage and barriers holding her back.

But Audrey cannot take that final, necessary step. She still can't break free. The past threatens to overwhelm, and Audrey risks slipping back into her mind's hypnotic refuge. Before that soporific realm can claim her, Audrey's psyche shocks her back to life. A man in the crowd hits another man. Everyone gasps, and the music stops. Audrey runs to Charlie (who is just as startled as she is), commanding him to "Get me out of here!"

And Audrey makes the leap. She ends her story. In a flash, Audrey is somewhere else entirely.

The Roadhouse has vanished, and Audrey stares at herself in a mirror. She stands in a white space, wearing a white outfit. Shocked, she is unable to make sense of her new reality.

And that's the last we see of Audrey Horne in *Twin Peaks: The Return*. We learn nothing more after her final distraught moments in front of the mirror. Where is she? Has she woken in a hospital or psychiatric facility? There's no detail in the background, no doors or desks or decorations upon the wall, so there's no way to be sure. Audrey is in a room without definition. White is the only certain element (other than the mirror, of course).

If we cannot identify where Audrey is, we do know that she has *awakened*. Yes, her surroundings might be a physical space (perhaps one she's inhabited for years), but more likely they represent a *spiritual* place, a new state of consciousness. She can't grasp this idea in the first few startling seconds, but Audrey has entered a realm of enlightenment.

As we've witnessed over the four acts, Audrey made progress out of her mind, her "house." She started at the deepest point, moved toward the exit, and then arrived at the Roadhouse. But this was not the final destination. The Roadhouse was merely a borderland, a threshold between Audrey's confinement and her true release. In this expiatory space, Audrey liberates herself from her psychological shackles and transcends.

For David Lynch, the white room is the goal. It's the place where human beings go when they move to a higher state of consciousness: "I picture it like a white room that has yellow, red, and blue curtains covering the white wall. But in the gap between each curtain, you can see the white of the Absolute—the pure bliss consciousness. The white room really is all around you all the time.... You can experience that white wall anytime when you sit and meditate." As Audrey danced to her very own music, on her very own stage, she achieved a moment of profound meditation. Her joyous smile proves it. This meditation, attained after a journey through bad memories and confused identities, opened a door. And when it did, Audrey Horne "passed through a gap" and found the white of the Absolute.

Who I Was I Will Never Be Again

AUDREY HORNE HAS a full and satisfying arc in *The Return*. While it may not have been what most fans wanted or expected, her brief story reveals a deliberate trajectory, grounded in Audrey's unique backstory.

Audrey's psychoses stem from the psychology that defined her in the original series. The fears, desires and motivations that made her such a fascinating character in *Twin Peaks* Season 1 are still here, but masked by a churning, troubled mind. When we find Audrey in a state of distress and doubt, this is exactly the frame of mind we'd expect, given her painful fate at the end of Season 2 and the defilements she experienced at the hands of a demonic Cooper. This Audrey, standing stock-still in the depths of her endogenous retreat, makes sense. *Of course*, Audrey is psychologically damaged. *Of course*, Audrey is spiritually lost. *Of course*, Audrey seeks escape from her perpetual torment. This is who Audrey Horne was and still is.

But there is hope for change. Across four measured sequences, Audrey comes to terms with herself. She learns a difficult truth: To move forward, one must release the burdens of the past. It's a tough lesson and hard-won, but Audrey gets there.

Audrey's journey echoes events in *INLAND EMPIRE*. There, the Monologue Woman tells her Charlie-like confessor that she feels she is watching her life, "like in a dark theater before they bring lights up…. I'm sittin' there wonderin', 'How can this be?'" After confronting her own demons, the Monologue Woman finds herself on a stage, bathed in a bright light. It fills the screen, encompassing the totality of the woman's psyche. In this moment, she transcends, and we see, superimposed over her marveling face, the image of a ballerina dancing on stage. Cheers and applause greet the woman as she glides and pirouettes. This dance is the Monologue Woman's moment of acceptance. Like Audrey's, it's the moment when she frees herself and all her alteregos. And like Audrey, she smiles, and through her joy and wonder receives a new level of understanding, as if the words of the Bhagavad Gita (that guiding text in David Lynch's life and work) have come to pass: "My delusion has gone. Where my life seemed unbearable before, those self-created problems have dissolved. My power and joy have returned to me. I am aware of my true reality and committed to my dharma."

And so it is with Audrey, who dances herself into state of pure bliss consciousness and dispels the self-created problems that have trapped her for so long.

Audrey Horne is *out of there.*

PART 13:

WHAT STORY IS THAT, CHARLIE?

WHETHER BY DESIGN OR BY ACCIDENT, the flow of time has seriously gone awry in *Twin Peaks*, something made quite evident in this episode. After Cooper delivered the thirty-million-dollar check to Rodney and Bradley Mitchum in Part 11, they all went out partying. But in Part 12, we saw Cooper at home playing catch with Sonny-Jim. Now, he shows up at the Lucky 7 offices in the morning, still celebrating with the Mitchums. How could he have been home in Part 12 if he was out all night?[*] None of it makes chronological sense. Neither will many scenes in Part 13. (Three days supposedly pass during the course of Part 13, but if you try to arrange the events into chronological order, the timeline falls apart.)

Anthony Sinclair watches Cooper and the Mitchum brothers (and the showgirls) dance a conga line through the Lucky 7 lobby and into Bushnell Mullins' office.[†] Sinclair is horrified to see Cooper still alive (and, apparently, friends with the Mitchums). He calls Duncan Todd to report this new state of affairs, and Todd implicitly directs Sinclair to kill Cooper.

Thrilled at their recent good fortune, the Mitchums present Bushnell with some expensive thank-you gifts. Meanwhile, at home in

---

[*] The real reason for Cooper's brief appearance in Part 12 is because Kyle MacLachlan was contractually required to be in every episode of *The Return*. He needed to appear in Part 12 in order to earn his end-credits listing.

[†] Anthony is working on a claims form for someone named "Nancy Steiner" (in reality, the costume designer for *Twin Peaks: The Return*).

Lancelot Court, Janey-E is overjoyed to receive a few gifts of her own. The Mitchums have purchased a backyard gym for Sonny-Jim and a brand-new BMW convertible for Janey-E. Later that night, as Janey-E watches Sonny-Jim bounce around on his well-lit circus-like playset, she tells Cooper she loves him. Cooper, sensing the strong emotions coming from Janey-E, silently responds, as if dimly acknowledging that this love, this relationship, has a reality to it unlike anything he has experienced.

MR. C HAS TRACKED RAY MONROE to his hideout in western Montana. Ray has sought refuge with a mob of ruffians who are part biker gang and part prepper militia. Renzo, the gang's leader, challenges Mr. C to a contest of strength: If Mr. C can beat Renzo at arm-wrestling, then Mr. C will become the gang's new boss. If Mr. C loses, Ray will kill him. Mr. C listens incredulously and mocks the juvenile ritual: "What is this, kindergarten? Nursery school?" But he knows his simplest path to Ray is to accept the challenge.

The two men begin to wrestle. At first, Renzo seems to have the advantage but can't quite pin Mr. C's arm to the table. He gets close but can't make that final contact. Just when it looks like Mr. C is about to lose, he effortlessly lifts his arm to the vertical "starting position." Renzo strains with determination, but Mr. C doesn't flinch. After a few moments, Mr. C slams Renzo's arm to the table and then punches Renzo directly in the eye, killing him instantly. The gang watches in disbelief. They have a new boss.

Leave it to David Lynch and Mark Frost to take the stale cliché of dueling alpha males and reimagine it as arm-wrestling. In any other story, we'd see opponents square off in tried and tired competitions—gunfights, knife-fights, boxing matches—but in *Twin Peaks,* power (for this gang, at least) is transferred through arm-wrestling. And why not? There's a simple, civilized element to this form of succession. In normal circumstances, Renzo might have dutifully acquiesced to his superior opponent, but Mr. C is a monster, and Renzo lies broken on a warehouse floor.

Ray tries to run away, but Mr. C shoots him in the leg. Wounded, and laying on the floor, Ray explains he was hired by Phillip Jeffries, who wanted something "inside" Mr. C. Ray also says that when he was released from prison, he was given the Owl Cave Ring and told to put it on Mr. C.

In Part 2, a voice masquerading as Phillip Jeffries said that Mr. C was "going back in." The voice also said it would be reunited with Bob. Earlier in this book, I speculated about whose voice that was and concluded the most likely candidate was Mike, the spirit that once inhabited Phillip Gerard. Ray's revelations about the Owl Cave Ring strongly support this conclusion.

Long ago, Mike and his "familiar," Bob, gathered human "pain and sorrow" in the form of a creamed-corn substance known as garmonbozia. When Mike "saw the face of God" he was transformed and became a figure of good. He purged himself of evil by removing his left arm. His arm then took on a life of its own and became "the man from another place" (who identified himself simply as "The Arm"*). For a while, The Arm allied itself with Bob in order to amass garmonbozia. But Mike was more powerful and (in *Fire Walk With Me*) forced his missing limb to temporarily re-attach. Once restored, Mike castigated Bob for his errant ways. Later, Mike told Cooper he "stays close" to Gerard (inhabiting him, from time to time) for one single purpose: "*To stop [Bob].*"

Mike and Phillip Gerard were—and still are—inextricably linked. This is important because Phillip Gerard dwells within the Red Room and apparently oversees movement of the Owl Cave Ring.

In *The Return*, the ring first appears in Part 3 on the finger of Dougie Jones. Later, in the Red Room, the ring slips off Dougie's finger, and Gerard places it on a pedestal. Technically, the ring next "appears" in Part 7, when Ray receives it from a prison guard. How, then, did the ring get from the Red Room to the prison? Most likely, Mike delivered it—Mike, the inhabiting spirit that "stays close" to

---

* David Lynch may have been inspired by Nikolai Gogol's short story, *The Nose*, when he re-defined "the man from another place" as "The Arm." In Gogol's story, a man discovers that his nose has detached from his face and become an autonomous entity (seemingly with arms and legs). The nose stirs up trouble around town before reuniting with its original body. Lynch has discussed his admiration for *The Nose* and how he was inspired to sketch a "personified nose" in 1971: "I did this drawing based on Gogol's short story. I was into Kafka, and Frank Daniel [the Dean of the American Film institute] told me I should read Gogol."

Gerard, the being whose self-declared mission is to "stop Bob." Mike is almost certainly the imposter Phillip Jeffries.

You might be asking, "Why not simply say the imposter is *Gerard*? Why bring Mike into this at all?"

As established in the original series, Mike and Gerard are separate personalities. The Gerard we see in *The Return* is a passive being. He lacks the commanding voice we hear on Mr. C's call, and he's nothing like the disciplinarian we saw at the end of *Fire Walk With Me*. Indeed, in Part 2, after Cooper falls into a trap, Gerard wanders about the Red Room in confusion, moaning that "something is wrong." Mike never appears in *The Return* (not explicitly, at least according to the end credits), but he is a shrewd presence, working outside the frame to bring Bob to heel, first, by trying to kill Mr. C in Colombia, then later, through an elaborate plan involving Ray. Mike keeps getting outwitted, however, and with Ray lying wounded at the feet of Mr. C, his efforts to "stop Bob" have finally come to an end.

Mr. C demands that Ray give him the coordinates, but Ray resists, asking why Mr. C would trust him. Then, without missing a beat, Ray hands over a slip of paper containing the coordinates. That was a quick turnaround; Ray said he couldn't be trusted and then immediately supplies the numbers. Mr. C recognizes a potential trap and demands that Ray tell him where he can find Jeffries. Ray says Jeffries can be found at "The Dutchman's," a place that may not be "real." Before he can say more, however, Mr. C shoots him in the head. Mr. C is taking no chances; he kills Ray to prevent any potential eavesdroppers from learning where he's headed next.

It's sad to see Ray go; he was played to sly perfection by the inimitable George Griffith. Now that Ray's gone, we'll never know how he learned about The Dutchman's. In fact, there's a lot about Ray we will never know. In Part 17, Gordon Cole reveals that Ray is an FBI informant who supplied tips about Mr. C's schemes, but we also know Ray was working for the imposter Phillip Jeffries (and possibly the real Phillip Jeffries, too). Ray was also apparently a confidante of Bill Hastings' secretary, Betty (but that role might simply have been deception, part of Ray's scheme to infiltrate Mr. C's inner circle). In the end, Ray is a catch-all character.* He provides twists and double-crosses when needed, but his backstory is unclear. A frustrating element of *The Return* who thwarts close analysis, Ray is a piece of the *Twin Peaks* puzzle that never quite fits the larger picture.

ANTHONY SINCLAIR MEETS with Detective Clark to procure a poison to use against Cooper. Clark is angry that Sinclair has gotten so sloppy, but Sinclair pushes back, explaining that he's trying to keep the "whole operation from falling apart." After Sinclair leaves, another detective confers with Clark about Sinclair's recklessness. These detectives are obviously part of Duncan Todd's schemes to undermine the Mitchum brothers, and so you might assume their names to be "Loomis" and "Stockton," the two investigating officers Cooper so vigorously highlighted in the case files in Part 6. But they're not. This mix-up in names is another production mistake. (Either that, or there's a whole squad of crooked detectives in Todd's employ.)

The next morning, Sinclair surreptitiously poisons Cooper's coffee. As Sinclair waits for Cooper to sit and drink, Cooper approaches from behind and gently touches Sinclair's shoulders. This physical contact— this simple touch from the angelic Cooper—overwhelms Sinclair, who breaks down crying. Sinclair whisks Cooper's poisoned coffee away and pours it down a urinal in the men's room.†

The pure goodness of Dale Cooper has fully transformed Anthony Sinclair. Where once he had been willing to bilk the Lucky 7 Insurance Agency for millions and ally himself with the destructive Duncan Todd and even attempt to kill Cooper, now Anthony Sinclair confesses all his sins. He declares his guilt to Bushnell Mullins and says he wants to "make things right again." So powerful is Cooper's goodness that Sinclair proclaims he will either "die or change" rather than continue along his wicked path. Bubbling and sobbing before his confessors,

---

* For example, when Ray's body materializes in the Red Room, Gerard retrieves the Owl Cave Ring. Narratively speaking, Ray functions as a convenient link to get the ring back to Gerard.

† The man standing at the adjacent urinal is played by Mike Malone, a longtime Lynch production assistant. Malone is credited as "on set dresser" in *Twin Peaks, Fire Walk With Me* and *The Return*. He also has a cameo as an FBI agent in *Fire Walk With Me*. (He's the agent who arrests the prostitutes at the school bus.)

Sinclair thanks Cooper for saving his life. In these moments, Cooper becomes more than just a figure of decency, he becomes a savior.

With Anthony Sinclair neutralized, and Sinclair's conspirators exposed, Cooper has, once again, cleared a path for his future. His world in Las Vegas keeps getting better. He has money, friends, a loving family and a valuable job. Threats to his life have been almost eliminated. When Cooper (or some version of him) returns to this life at the end of the story, he will be entering a fairytale-like world, one that is both secure and happy.

TROUBLED AND LONGING MINDS haunt the nighttime setting of Twin Peaks. Audrey Horne doubts her identity as she struggles to find a way out of her fugue. Charlie is of little help, but as he prods her, Audrey sees the dim outlines of a different existence. She's not "the little girl who lives down the lane,"* but she still has value. She's inching toward revelation.

Revelations of a different sort visit Doctor Jacoby and Nadine. Driving through Main Street, Jacoby is surprised to see a golden shovel prominently displayed in the window of Nadine's store, Run Silent, Run Drapes.† He rings the doorbell, and Nadine emerges from the darkness, thrilled to see "Doctor Amp" standing on her doorstep. She explains that her display is a tribute for all he's done. Jacoby is moved, and a memory from seven years ago comes back to him of Nadine looking for a fallen potato in the supermarket. Jacoby says, "There was a big storm that day." At those words, something unlocks in Nadine. "Oh," she says, and she is suddenly unburdened by a weight she did not know she carried.

We don't know what will become of Nadine and Jacoby's newly formed relationship, but their simple, spontaneous meeting is transformative. As they stand looking at each other, a train whistles in the distance, heralding Nadine and Jacoby's powerful connection. This is the last time we see Jacoby in the story, but we sense that all he's been

---

* Cooper, watching from the Red Room, hears this comment from Audrey but probably doesn't recognize its import (as, arguably, Audrey does). He'll be reminded of it again in Part 18 when The Arm nudges Cooper toward a specific goal.

† A play on the title of the 1958 film, *Run Silent, Run Deep*.

striving for finds fruition in his encounter with Nadine. She validates him. As for Nadine, meeting her hero sends her on a new trajectory, a path that will change the lives of many.

One of those people is Ed Hurley, who makes his first appearance in Part 13. Ed sits in a booth at the Double R Diner, making small talk with his one true love, Norma Jennings. Ed has accepted he will never have a life with Norma, and he is content to share whatever time he can with her.

Ed's a moping soul, and so is Bobby Briggs, who arrives at the Double R looking for Shelly, only to learn she has gone home for the night. Sensing Bobby's dismay, Norma and Ed invite him to sit. He does and, during a brief chat, reveals that "today" he and his fellow officers "found some stuff" belonging to his father (referring to the metal tube and secret message Major Briggs secreted away). In fact, Bobby found that "stuff" way back in Part 9, and if we make a quick, back-of-the-envelope calculation, we find that about *seven* days have passed since then. Like the earlier discrepancy of Cooper being out all night but also home with Sonny-Jim, Bobby's scene with Ed and Norma is an editing mistake, something intended to take place much earlier in the narrative (likely, the end of Part 9).

This kind of mistake is noticeable. When Bobby says he found something "today," our alarms go off. This being *Twin Peaks*, we consider the possibility that Bobby's comment is deliberate, that it hints at a disjointed passage of time. In *The Return*, time fluctuates, and it's easy to read Bobby's comment as part of some intentional scheme. But it's not. Bobby's comment is simply a mistake.

And for David Lynch, it's a tolerable one. As I discussed at the end of Part 7 (where the patrons of the Double R Diner change positions between shots), Lynch's exploration of time and perception in *The Return* allows for leniency in the editing. A scene intended for one episode can easily be moved to another. A continuity error doesn't necessarily detract from the narrative flow. Time in *The Return* is circular, unreliable, and a glaring error such as Bobby's can still "make sense."[*]

---

[*] I noted earlier that Lynch tells a story of film projectionists mixing up reels during a screening. According to Lynch, "People still made sense of [the film]."

To emphasize time's erratic nature, Lynch takes us into the dark recesses of the Palmer house, where Sarah Palmer sits slumped on her couch watching a boxing match on TV. As she drinks the last of her alcohol, a clip of the boxing loops continuously: A boxer takes a hit and falls, the announcer becomes animated, a bell clangs, and the crowd cheers. After a sputter of static, the sequence plays again. And again. And again. Sarah doesn't notice. She sits and watches, trapped in a moment that won't move forward.

Time has dramatically slipped in the Palmer household. Like The Fireman's phonograph, it is stuck in a groove, tripping over itself. The creature called Experiment is taking hold, growing stronger, and the world around Sarah Palmer bends to its will.

TIME ETCHES MEMORIES, and memories become burdens. Nowhere is that more evident than at the Roadhouse where James Hurley takes the stage and relives a past he cannot release.

James plays guitar and sings a song from long ago. Two young women share his stage. These are his backup singers. But they are less than that. They are ghosts. Memories made flesh.

Twenty-five years earlier, James Hurley sat in the comfort of the Hayward living room and sang a song ("Just You and I") to Donna Hayward and Madeleine Ferguson. In this indelible moment, James looked deep into Maddy's eyes and sought a connection. Was he falling in love with this young woman, or was James just looking to recapture a love he shared with Laura Palmer?

Just you and I. Just who and I?

James was a lonely soul, destined to stay that way. Maddy Ferguson suffered Laura's brutal fate, and James took off, leaving Donna and Twin Peaks behind. Out in the world, lost, James Hurley looked to be with someone "together, forever" but could never escape that moment in the Hayward living room. It haunts him still, decades later, as he plays the same old song, accompanied by surrogates of Donna and Maddy—lookalikes who embody a moment lost in time.

Renee, the woman whom James pined for in Part 2, watches from a distance and starts to cry. James' tragedy is undeniable, his loneliness palpable. His pain touches Renee, and she weeps.

Is James still cool? We want him to be. We are rooting for him. But James is stuck in the past, trapped in a memory and doomed to relive his heartache on the lonely Roadhouse stage. That's as cool as he's ever going to get.

Speaking of heartache, Part 13 ends in the dark offices of Big Ed's Gas Farm where Ed Hurley sits alone, eating soup from an "RR2GO!" carton. He stares through a window into the darkness outside.* He's thinking of Norma and the life they might have had. He's also thinking of Nadine and the life they can't escape. Ed Hurley sits alone, slurping his soup, and realizes his life is nothing but an endless now. Time crawls and nothing changes. As if to acknowledge his perpetual loneliness, Ed lights a match and sets a small, folded piece of paper on fire. He watches it burn and then drops it on his desk. What was on the paper? Was it a note to Norma that Ed lacked courage to deliver? We have to assume it was, and that Ed's decision to burn it is his way of accepting a hopeless future.

In *Twin Peaks: The Return*, time is a burden. It does not heal all wounds. It holds tight and suffocates.

---

* Attentive viewers have noticed that Ed's reflection in the window does not match Ed's movement at his desk (his reflection moves when Ed is sitting still). Some believe this movement implies another reality running parallel to the one we are watching. The truth is, Ed's reflection jumps because the editors were tinkering with the frame. To convey an empty darkness outside, they combined two different shots—one of the window and one of the back of Ed's head. Editor Duwayne Dunham is explicit: "If there was a reflection, there was nothing of value associated with it." Still, as I said in the text above, editing mistakes add to, rather than subtract from, the narrative. David Lynch has commented about happy accidents improving his work, and Ed's glitchy reflection is just such an accident.

<INTERLUDE 6>

WHAT'S GOING ON IN THIS HOUSE?

DAVID FOSTER WALLACE OBSERVED that David Lynch's movies "are not about monsters but about hauntings, about evil as environment, possibility, force.... [I]n his movies' world, a kind of ambient spiritual antimatter hangs just overhead." Nowhere is this more evident than in *Twin Peaks*, a story that is all about hauntings and evil environments. Look no further than the home at the center—the haunted house where ambient spirits dwell—the Palmer House.

A "haunted house," according to *The Encyclopedia of Fantasy*, is a dwelling where "the psychic disturbance of the inhabitants...or the impression of some powerful emotion has been absorbed...a place with a powerful flavor of *wrongness*." Fascinated by such dark and dangerous homes, David Lynch has explored this kind of setting again and again over the years. In *The Grandmother*, familial dysfunction plagues the grandson's house. In *Hotel Room,* distress echoes in room 603 of the Railroad Hotel. In *Lost Highway,* psychological disorder spreads through the halls and walls of Fred Madison's home. But in all of Lynch's work, one specific house is truly haunted. The Palmer House, a place of unspeakable trauma. The site of murder.

The disturbing nature of the Palmer House is signaled from the start. Early in the *Twin Peaks* pilot, a point of view shot lingers at the base of the stairs leading to Laura Palmer's room. This static image implies an ominous presence, a looming menace that has taken hold. Looking up the stairs, we are wary of what waits in the shadows above.

Sarah Palmer, gifted, damned (or both) is becoming aware of this presence. When the police ask about Laura's last night, she says, "She was going up the stairs. Those stairs right there," and we see again the same shot from earlier—the stairs leading up, the ceiling fan spinning—and we feel something corrupt in the house, something harmful and transgressive. Sarah's fear of this presence bursts forth in episode 2, when she confronts a distraught Leland and wails, "*What's going on in this house?!*"

Sarah's frantic plea (added by Lynch during filming; it was not part of the original script) confirms that David Lynch was intuitively aware of the Palmer House's dreadful nature early on. "I like to go deeper into a house," he explains, "and find things underneath things." Underneath Leland Palmer, we soon learn, is the demon, Bob, a haunting spirit that has resided within Leland (and within the house) for many years. Lynch signals this possession in episode 8, when Leland's hair turns suddenly white, as if Leland has turned into a ghost, an apparition of his former self. The wrongness in the house is manifesting, becoming bolder. It transforms Leland because it feels safe in the house. Free to act without penalty.

It will act again, decisively and brazenly, in episode 14, when Bob-as-Leland brutally murders Madeleine Ferguson (Laura's cousin) in, of all places, the "living" room. The Palmer House, already witness to the violation of Laura Palmer by her father, now witnesses death. It absorbs murder into its walls.

Contaminated by these traumas, the house festers for many years. When we see it again in *The Return*, it is decayed and disheveled. The lawn has gone to seed, the interior is dark and cluttered. (As Sarah Palmer describes in *Between Two Worlds*, "Lots of things are falling apart. That's for sure. Lots of things.") Sarah has surrendered to the "extreme negative force" of the dwelling. Yes, *The Return* posits that Sarah was infested by something awful at an early age, but this infestation needed the proper conditions in which to incubate. The haunted wrongness of the Palmer House has provided a diseased womb for it to flourish.

Like Sarah Palmer, the house has transformed, becoming a place of disembodied evil. Horrible scenes of animal carnage play on its television. Time flows erratically. It loops and repeats, destabilizing Sarah's already tenuous hold on reality. Poltergeists knock about, boldly making their presence known. Deputy Hawk hears one of these and is alarmed, but Sarah dismisses the sound as "something in the kitchen." Indeed, some *thing* is in the kitchen. Some "thing" occupies the entire house.

The Palmer House, haunted by the memories of violence and depravity, has become an entity unto itself, pulsing with electric menace. It's a "goddamned bad story" come to life, a scaffolding for a dark age.

This apparent "black lodge" at the heart of Twin Peaks attracts Mr. C, who seeks the negativity within. But it also beckons Agent Cooper, who brings Laura Palmer directly to it. The Palmer House is the place Laura must go to end the darkness within—and the darkness that remains.

David Lynch tells us, "A home is a place where things can go wrong." Things went terribly wrong in the Palmer House. The trauma inside grew unabated, inhabiting it, *haunting* it, until Laura Palmer confronted this dark energy and, in a cleansing scream of agony, brought the wrongness to an end.

PART 14:
WE ARE LIKE THE DREAMER

THE HINDU HOLY TEXT, the Yoga Vasistha, tells the story of a sage, a holy man, who entered the mind of another man and lived there:

> *"In the old days . . . I entered someone else's head and then I saw a universe with a sun and an ocean and mountains, and gods and demons and human beings. The universe was his dream and I saw his dream. Inside his head I saw his city and his wife and his servants and his son...*
>
> *"I had picked up his karmic memories along with his dream. I had become involved in that world, and I forgot my former life...*
>
> *"Time passed. A sage came to my house, and slept and ate, and as we were talking, he said, 'Don't you know that all of this is a dream? I am a man in your dream, and you are a man in someone else's dream....'"*

Dreams and dream imagery have been fundamental components of *Twin Peaks* since the very beginning. In the original series, FBI Special Agent Dale Cooper travels into the slippery territory of Twin Peaks full of dream-inspired deductive techniques, certain that his deep subconscious will unlock the mysteries of his investigation: "Let me tell you about the dream I had last night," he says, and then proceeds to tell Sheriff Harry Truman about a dream excursion to another realm where he, Cooper, encountered Laura Palmer. "My dream is a code waiting to be broken," he declares.

The Log Lady, too, recognizes the importance of dreams and embraces their evocations: "Some ideas arrive in the form of a dream," she tells us in one of her allusive introductions. She knows that Twin Peaks is a landscape fluctuating between physical and fantasy, between a natural world and the realm of the mind.

Jerry Horne, of all people, seems to grasp the elusive nature of reality when he asks, "Is it real, or some strange and twisted dream?" This line, added by director David Lynch while filming episode 9 of the original series (notably, it was not part of the shooting script), summarizes the confusion plaguing the residents of Twin Peaks: What is real? What is dream?

Twin Peaks will never supply easy answers. *Twin Peaks* and Twin Peaks are liminal spaces that straddle the real and the imaginary. So, when Jerry Horne wonders, "Is it real, or some strange and twisted dream?" maybe the answer is both. What we see is real and dream.

FRANK TRUMAN UPDATES Cole about the missing pages from Laura's diary, the ones that indicate two Coopers. "I thought you should know it," Truman says over the phone, "Maybe it means something to you." Indeed, it does. Cole remembers a case from long ago. A Blue Rose case.

Meanwhile, Albert explains the origin of the Blue Rose to Tammy: In 1975, Agents Gordon Cole and Phillip Jeffries encountered a woman, Lois Duffy, who had shot a twin version of herself—her exact double. Dying, the double uttered the words, "I am like the blue rose," and then vanished. Tammy listens carefully and concludes that the double, like a blue rose, was an unnatural entity. The double was a tulpa, a *conjured* being.

As I mentioned back in Part 7, a tulpa is a "thought form," a duplicate that takes the appearance of another person. The concept of tulpas finds its origins in Tibetan Buddhism, but the theurgical history and function of tulpas is not explored in *The Return*. Instead, the concept is given a cursory definition: In *Twin Peaks*, tulpas are copies of people into which basic programming can be installed. A tulpa lives its life as if a real human but can be triggered into certain behaviors when its background programming is activated. Unlike a doppelganger, a tulpa is not an opposite (or divided half) of a person, a tulpa is simply a duplicate. (How these duplicates are created is never fully explained.)

Only two tulpas explicitly appear in *The Return*: Diane (likely manufactured by Mr. C from the real Diane) and Dougie Jones (also likely manufactured by Mr. C). Dougie was flawed, prone to selfish and self-destructive behavior (prostitution, gambling, insurance fraud), because he was derived not from a whole Cooper, but from Mr. C, the impure half of Cooper. (Bushnell Mullins believes Dougie is "slow" because he was in a car accident, but Dougie's "car accident" is a pretext put in place by Mr. C to explain Dougie's limited and crude behavior.)

Gordon Cole interrupts Albert and Tammy and says, "I think I've got it." He's remembered a clue they've yet to ask Diane about. Before he can say more, however, he is assaulted by the excruciating sounds of a window washer. We don't see the washer (he is obscured behind a window shade), but we see his shadow working furiously with a squeegee. Cole winces at the rapid squeaking sounds and turns the volume down on his hearing aid. The sounds continue to assault and then suddenly disappear.

The border between Cooper and Cole's minds has thinned, and Cooper (manifesting as the window washer) makes a shadowy contact, prompting Cole to remember an important message. Cooper needs Cole to remember a dream he had just last night. Cole almost has it, but he's not there yet. He has other business on his mind.

The window washer retreats just as Diane arrives. (Note that the washer cleans only one of the two windows, his objective being to make sudden, provocative contact, not to wash windows.) Cole asks Diane about Cooper's visit years ago, specifically if Cooper mentioned Major Briggs. When she says yes, Cole nods to Albert, who explains that Briggs's body was recently found, and from it a ring was extracted, bearing the inscription: "To Dougie, with love, Janey-E."

Diane is astonished and reveals she has a half-sister in Las Vegas named Janey-E, married to man named Dougie Jones. Diane delivers this last bit of information with a sharp cut of her eyes toward Cole, as if she's exposed a crucial piece of the puzzle. Maybe she has. Maybe Diane's memory of Janey-E has only now emerged, having been suppressed by her tulpa programming.[*]

---

[*] Diane's curious connection to Janey-E is never mentioned again, and we are left to fill in the blanks. Could Janey-E be another version of Diane, a person with similar traits but reimagined (by Cooper, or by Diane) as another woman? Given how Cooper's world in Las Vegas has been evolving toward an idealized existence, I think this just might be the case.

Cole realizes they've made a breakthrough. He calls the FBI office in Las Vegas and orders the agents there to track down Douglas Jones.[*] (These agents, Wilson and Headley, are delightful caricatures: Wilson is innocent to the point of naiveté, while Headley is no-nonsense and gung-ho. In one of *The Return*'s funniest exchanges, Wilson wonders how he and Headley will locate Douglas Jones, and Headley screams: "Wilson! How many times have I told *you!?* This is what we do in the FBI!")

As Cole processes the Las Vegas lead, he suddenly recalls the vivid, revelatory dream he had the night before, the dream Cooper was prompting Cole to remember when the window washer appeared.

Dreams are a medium through which Cooper can visit other minds. He did it in *Fire Walk With Me* (when he warned Laura Palmer about the Owl Cave Ring), and he's done it again in *The Return*, appearing to Gordon Cole with disturbing information.

Cole describes his potent dream in detail, relating each part of the experience to Albert and Tammy:

At a sidewalk café in Paris, Cole waits for the actress, Monica Bellucci, to join him. As Bellucci approaches, Cooper appears, standing near Cole.[†] Bellucci sits, and Cooper vanishes. In effect, Cooper has now become Bellucci. He's using her as an avatar to communicate with Cole.

Bellucci (i.e., Cooper) looks directly into Cole's eyes, and a single tear rolls down her cheek. Cooper's emotions swell as he finally makes contact with his old friend. (As Cole recounts the dream, he pauses to ponder Bellucci's emotional response, as if he's just now become aware of it.)

Bellucci recites what Cole calls the "ancient" phrase, " *We are like the dreamer who dreams and then lives inside the dream.*" This statement, the core concept of *The Return*, originates from the Hindu holy

---

[*] A portrait of President Dwight D. Eisenhower hangs on the wall of the Las Vegas FBI office, another distinct call-back to the 1950s, David Lynch's favorite decade. U.S. Presidents haunt *The Return*. Johnny Horne smashes his head into a portrait of Eisenhower in Part 9 (the same portrait hanging in the Las Vegas office), President Franklin D. Roosevelt appears on a dime in Part 6, Abraham Lincoln appears on the penny in Part 8, and Albert shows Cole a picture of Mt. Rushmore in Part 4.

[†] Cooper is shown wearing his FBI pin, evidence that Cooper is appearing to Cole from the Red Room, the realm where Cooper's mind currently resides.

text, the Upanishads, and suggests that every human being perceives the world in his or her own way. Every person has a unique interpretation of reality, and these interpretations are analogous to dreams.[*]

Monica Bellucci looks at Cole and asks, "But who is the dreamer?"

This question troubles Cole. As soon as Bellucci asks it, he says, "A very powerful, uneasy feeling came over me." That's because Cole knows that no *single* mind can impose itself, no individual consciousness can be the dreamer. And yet that's what Cooper, through Bellucci, wants Cole to believe—that Dale Cooper is the dreamer. Cooper sees himself as the one and only.

As Cole ponders this worrisome idea, Cooper shifts the dream to another time and place, directing Cole to look back to an event from the past, to the day Phillip Jeffries visited the Philadelphia FBI offices in 1989.[†]

In a flashback from *Fire Walk With Me*, Jeffries dramatically enters Cole's office and confronts Cooper, pointing at him and asking, "Who do you think that is there?" Awake in Buckhorn, Cole ponders the question: Who does he think Cooper is? Up until now he's never had reason to ask. *Cooper is Cooper.*

Unless he isn't.

Jolted from his reverie by this new/old memory, Cole exclaims, "Now this is really something to think about!" Albert's mind clears at the same time. "Yes," he says, "I'm beginning to remember that, too." Phillip Jeffries' long ago appearance had faded from their minds (just as their encounter with the vortex did in Part 11), but Cole's dream has brought the memory back.

Cole assumes that the man he met at Yankton Federal Prison was Dale Cooper. He says as much to Albert in Part 4, "This business with Cooper, I don't like it." And in Part 9 he wonders why "Cooper has shown up in this neck of the woods." Cole is operating under the assumption that the entity we know as Mr. C is simply Dale Cooper, the agent who vanished long ago. But now clues from multiple sources

---

[*] We've already witnessed such character-specific realities: Bobby "sees" his mind reflected in the chaos of the Double R intersection (Part 11), and Audrey perceives a world concocted by her troubled psyche.

[†] Technically, this date should be 1988. I'll discuss the reasons for this mix-up in Part 15.

have Cole questioning this assumption. First, Frank Truman told Cole of "two Coopers," and then Diane connected the case to a "Dougie Jones" in Las Vegas, and now, Cole recalls Phillip Jeffries questioning the identity of Cooper way back in 1989. Cole indeed has "something to think about." He hasn't yet fit all the pieces together, but the idea of two Coopers, as crazy as it might be, is starting to make sense.

Dale Cooper has successfully contacted Gordon Cole. He's alerted Cole to danger and challenged him to reassess his perceptions of reality, but he's also left Gordon Cole uneasy and perplexed. "Two Coopers" is bad enough, but Gordon Cole knows tragedy looms if Dale Cooper believes his view of reality supersedes everyone else's.

AT THE TWIN PEAKS SHERIFF'S STATION, Andy, Bobby, and Hawk pack lunches for their upcoming hike to Jack Rabbit's Palace. Chad Broxford enters the conference room, and the officers quickly disarm and arrest him. Chad demands to know why he's being detained, but Truman simply replies, "I think you know, Chad." Nobody spells it out, but the police are savvy to Chad's involvement with the local drug trade. Maybe Bobby's surveillance cameras caught Chad coming down from Canada with a load of Sparkle, or maybe Miriam's confessions finally got through to the department. Either way, Chad's dirty dealings have landed him in the local lock-up. Truman grabs a sandwich from the table and gives Hawk a satisfied look.

A moment earlier, Bobby had placed four sandwiches on the table and listed the ingredients of each: turkey and cheese, ham and cheese, roast beef and cheese, and just cheese. Hawk asks who ordered "just cheese," and Andy says, "I did." This brief scene serves as a simple, humorous glimpse into the everyday lives of the deputies, but at the risk of over-analysis, I venture that the scene also holds a subtle clue. Andy is likely a vegetarian. His diet hints at a purer lifestyle, a refusal to harm life, even for sustenance. Yes, Andy's cheese sandwich may simply be an example of Andy's quirky behavior, but of the four officers who will soon venture into the supernatural, only Andy will be chosen to receive an otherworldly message. Harry Goaz, the actor who plays Andy Brennan, believes this is because Andy (and Lucy, too) is innocent and pure. He's right. Those traits are evident even in what Andy chooses to eat.

Truman and the deputies drive to a remote spot and hike deep into the forest. A faint electrical sound signals their incursion, hinting at supernatural forces nearby. Bobby recalls his boyhood visits with his father to these woods, and soon the group arrives at a tall, broken stump, sections of which reach high above their heads. The ragged stump resembles the ruins of a castle (or the otherworldly tower Cooper visited in Part 3, the home of The Fireman and Señorita Dido). Bobby smiles. This is Jack Rabbit's Palace.

Following Major Briggs's instructions, each man puts dirt in his pocket and begins hiking 253 yards to the east. They hike in a specific order: Hawk in front, followed by Truman, then Andy, with Bobby at the rear. They arrive at an eerie space among the trees. A bright light strobes within dense, coiled fog. Reality warps, and the laws of physics lose reliability. The men don't realize it, but their positions have completely reversed: Bobby arrives first, followed by Andy, then Truman, and lastly, Hawk. Encroachment into this place re-weaves the fabric of space. (This reversal of positions is not a mistake. In all the preceding shots, the men hike in the order they started. Only in the last shot, as they arrive at the supernatural spot, does their order change, and then it is an exact reversal, not some random shift.)

The body of a nude woman lies on the ground. This is Naido, the eyeless woman who guided Cooper in Part 3. When we last saw her, she was thrown into a void, and she plummeted away. She apparently ended up here, in the woods near Twin Peaks, 253 yards east of Jack Rabbit's Palace—just where Major Briggs knew she would be.

The men stare at Naido in confusion. Reality continues to warp. Hawk is shown in reverse, his head tilting unnaturally left and then down, as mist moves backward behind him.[*] The scene cuts to a pool of liquid stagnating in a small crater and then back to Hawk, whose earlier actions move forward (his head tilts up and to the right). Time is spiraling. Truman looks at his watch and announces that the time is 2:53. A vortex opens in the sky above the group. The men stare blankly into its core. And then Andy vanishes.

---

[*] This same type of reverse shot happened in Part 9, when the officers visit Betty Briggs.

Andy finds himself sitting in the realm of the Fireman, the same place Cooper sat during the opening minutes of Part 1.[*] The Fireman introduces himself, and Andy is suddenly holding a bizarre sculpture in his lap. Andy looks up at a white circle in the ceiling and watches as images play in this space, a sequence of events spanning past, present, and possible future.

Andy sees the dim visage of Experiment pulsing in darkness. He sees the Bob-cyst tucked into Experiment's vomited column of goo. He sees the exterior of the convenience store and the "Gotta light" Woodsman. Andy sees electric power lines and the nameless girl running through the high school courtyard. He sees red curtains and the smiling face of Laura Palmer between two angels. He sees Naido lying on the forest floor and the oscillating faces of Dale Cooper and Mr. C. And then, perhaps most disturbingly, Andy sees a shuddering vision of himself leading Lucy to the threshold of Sheriff Truman's office. Andy sees Naido again and, finally, multiple images of the #6 utility pole in Odessa, TX.

Andy is receiving vast amounts of data, a mind-full and then some. The Fireman is preparing Andy for an important role, providing him with information so that Andy will know what to do when the time is right.

The Fireman sat across from Agent Cooper in Part 1 and likely installed the same kinds of information into Cooper, preparing him for an important mission. The slippery nature of *The Return*'s chronology makes it hard to know exactly when The Fireman assigned Cooper this task, but whenever it was, Cooper has yet to complete his assignment. Now, worried that Cooper might not complete the mission, The Fireman initiates a backup plan. He presses Andy Brennan into service.

The Fireman puts context around what's at stake. He shows Andy Bob's escape and the existence of Experiment and the Woodsman. He conveys to Andy the angelic nature of Laura Palmer and her hidden location in Odessa.[†] In effect, The Fireman gives Andy a crash course

---

[*] The black and white imagery here suggests Andy has moved outside Cooper's observation. When Andy vanished before our eyes, he vanished before Cooper's, too.

[†] Andy becomes another in a small group of characters who is shown Laura Palmer's larger role. He glimpses Laura's divine nature and, deep down, realizes he has a small part to play in steering her toward her destiny.

on the whole cosmological conflict currently underway. He does this because Andy needs to understand, even if subconsciously, the dire nature of the game being played.

Memory being what it is in *Twin Peaks*, Andy will recall little of what The Fireman shows him. But that doesn't matter. Andy's mind becomes profoundly altered, and he subconsciously grasps the gravity of his task. When the time comes, Andy will act without hesitation, as if the very survival of the universe hangs in the balance. Because it does.

Why did The Fireman choose *Andy* for this role? Why not Truman (one of the "true men" The Log Lady describes), or Hawk (someone surely in touch with the larger forces of the universe)? Why does The Fireman choose Andy Brennan to perform this most crucial of duties? Like the purely good Cooper who manifests in Las Vegas, Andy is a figure of peace and kindness. His purity resembles the transcendent condition known as "moksha," a state of consciousness described by some Hindu scholars as "luminous," "serene," and "pure." That sounds like Andy Brennan—someone pure-of-heart, steadfast, and dedicated. When the inevitable show-down with Mr. C arrives, The Fireman needs someone every bit as reliable as Dale Cooper, and Andy Brennan fits the bill. Unlike Cooper, Andy is an unwavering agent. He will not allow personal desires to distract him.

"It's all about insurance." That's the motto for many in *The Return*'s intricate, unmappable narrative. By programming Andy, The Fireman ensures the coverage (the insurance policy) necessary to keep his plan on-track. (As we will soon see, Andy is not the first such individual to be drafted in this way.)

Andy proves his worth as soon as he returns to Earth. Back at Jack Rabbit's Palace, Bobby, Truman, and Hawk somnambulate into hazy positions, unsure of what just happened. Andy materializes among them, holding Naido in his arms, and immediately takes charge. "We need to get her down the mountain," he declares. "We need to put her in a cell where she'll be safe." Truman instinctively cedes to Andy's authority with a simple, "OK." The other men are confused, but Andy takes command. He orders them to keep Naido's presence a secret, and then confidently leads them out of the woods.

Later that night, Andy and Lucy situate Naido in a jail cell. While this is surely a safe spot, neither Andy nor Lucy question why they are depositing an ailing, distressed woman into what is, essentially, a cage. For that matter, Andy and Lucy are not dismayed by Naido's disfigurement, nor are they perplexed by Naido's inability to communicate. They hardly notice Naido's breathy sounds and high-pitched yelps. Andy has been programmed to put Naido here, and that's exactly what he does. Her unusual characteristics are of no concern.

It's quite likely that Andy and Lucy don't see Naido the way we do, which explains why they are unfazed by her appearance. To them, Naido exhibits no deformities or unnatural features. In fact, she probably looks like Diane. Indeed, in Mark Frost's *The Final Dossier*, Tammy Preston says that Diane Evans "was seen by more than twenty witnesses emerging from the jail cell in the [station's] basement." What's more, Tammy never acknowledges a character named Naido, suggesting that Naido was not part the original script. David Lynch added the character because that's who Cooper, watching from The Red Room, sees. (Cooper refuses, or doesn't know how, to see Naido the way she really appears. Not yet anyway.)

FREDDIE SYKES AND JAMES HURLEY, security guards at the Great Northern Hotel, are taking a break on the loading docks. Freddie tries to crack a walnut with his gloved hand, but every time he squeezes, the nut crumbles into powder. Freddie explains that the glove is part of him. When a doctor tried to take it off, Freddie started bleeding. James wants to know how Freddie ended up with the glove, and, after a little prompting, Freddie tells the tale.

One night, six months ago, Freddie decided he should spend his life helping people. In that moment, Freddie was sucked into a vortex and met The Fireman, who told Freddie to purchase a green glove from the hardware store, put it on, and go to Twin Peaks. There, The Fireman explained, Freddie would find his destiny. Freddie doesn't know what his destiny is, but he knows the green glove gives him "the power of a pile driver."*

---

* Freddie's glove finds its origins in Jean Cocteau's 1950 film, *Orpheus*. David Lynch has acknowledged the artistry of Cocteau, declaring him "the heavyweight of surrealism," and *Orpheus* is a major influence on Lynch's visual and textual conception of *Twin Peaks*. *Orpheus* focuses on dreams and dreamers and features

Freddie is another piece in the Fireman's long game, someone maneuvered to Twin Peaks and given the tools to perform a specific task. In this case, that task is to eliminate Bob.

James listens intently, but his is not the only mind taking in Freddie's story. Dale Cooper is listening, too, and paying strict attention. Cooper has some inkling of what Freddie's destiny might be. Later, Cooper will remember Freddie's story and find room in it to add a few embellishments of his own.

James leaves to check on the hotel's furnaces, and Cooper's observing mind follows. In the hotel basement, James hears the same high-pitched ringing noise Ben Horne and Beverly Paige heard back in Parts 7 and 9. James attempts to locate the source of the ringing, moving deeper and deeper into the bowels of the hotel until he comes upon a closed door. His gaze settles there, having traced the sound to this exact spot. James sees the door and hears the sound but (as far as we know) does not open the door. Cooper, however, has discovered a critical threshold, something his powerful imagination will repurpose later.

Cooper is gathering data, storing it away so he might later remember it the way he desires. Cooper is "the one and only" dreamer (that's what he believes anyway), and everywhere he looks, he finds new material to weave into his specific vision.

AS WE NEAR THE END OF PART 14, we arrive at the grisly end of Sarah Palmer's story. Few have suffered as much as Sarah. She was certainly the girl infested by an otherworldly parasite in 1956, a creature that lay dormant in Sarah for decades, waiting for the right conditions upon which to activate. When Experiment broke free from the glass box in New York City it found a host in Sarah, who was passive, inebriated, and awash in images of blood and carnage. On that terrible night, a malignancy blossomed inside Sarah and began leeching her humanity.

---

chevron-patterned floors, a liminal realm called The Zone, and a man guiding a woman out from the realm of death. When one character in *Orpheus* dons rubber gloves, he gains the ability to cross between worlds. In *The Return*, Freddie's glove has a cruder function, but Lynch's use of it is almost certainly an homage to Cocteau's film.

Sarah tried to resist. When the darkness exerted itself during her visit to the liquor store, she pushed back, reaching down and finding strength to deny its hold upon her. "Stop doing this!" she said out loud. "Leave this place."

Sarah bought herself some time. She pressed the evil back and reassured a concerned Hawk that she was fine. But the evil inside was unremitting. It tormented Sarah, subjecting her to endless cycles of despair in a house that conspired against her. Trapped inside the unnatural, chronic walls of her home, Sarah sank deeper into madness.

Now, Sarah reaches a breaking point. She leaves the confines of her haunted house to drink alone in the back room of a local tavern, The Elk's Point #9. But even here, Sarah cannot escape depravity. She is forced to contend with the most deplorable of men, a trucker who approaches Sarah and rudely imposes himself. He looms over her, spitting vulgarities.

When the man threatens violence, Sarah's resistance gives way, and she "opens" her face to reveal a landscape of roiling evil. Dark energies, deformed and depraved, lash within. Sarah bites the man's neck, tearing away chunks of flesh and ripping into arteries.

Just like the lion she watched on television, Sarah takes down her prey, savagely and efficiently.

Sarah knew this might be coming. She told us in *Between Two Worlds* that she's been vying against something alien. "Inside is one thing," she explained, "But step aside. Separate." In the back room of a seedy bar, Sarah Palmer finally separates and succumbs to the horrible thing inside. She gleefully attacks, becoming at last the victor instead of the victim.

The price of such aggression is that Sarah Palmer ceases to be. The darkness fully absorbs, transforming Sarah into something vile. In the Elk's Point bar, in a moment of brutal release, Sarah Palmer steps aside and her goddamn bad story comes to an end.

IT'S BEEN A LOT TO TAKE IN, Part 14, so much to collate and process. As usual, we end things at the Roadhouse, and, as we wait for the inevitable music to play over the credits, we're privy to another conversation in the Roadhouse booth. Although it may seem inconsequential, this brief exchange provides another peek into the mind of Audrey Horne.

We know Audrey is desperate to find someone named Billy, someone she believes might be at the Roadhouse. Audrey can't seem to get to the Roadhouse on her own, so she creates alter-egos who go there in her stead. This time, her alter-egos are two women named Sophie and Megan.

Sophie dominates the conversation with advice and demands. She accuses Megan of "hanging out at the nuthouse" and taking drugs. "Don't go in that nut place," she says (a possible acknowledgment from Audrey to herself that she is in a psychiatric facility). Before long, Sophie asks if Megan has seen Billy. Megan hesitates, but Sophie presses, "I heard you were the last person to see Billy."

Megan relents and describes how Billy, "bleeding from the nose and mouth," came into her kitchen with "this look in his eyes." He only stayed a moment and then bolted out the back. (Here, Audrey conflates Billy with Dale Cooper, the man who briefly came into her life before "bolting" out again. Dale Cooper, the man who assaulted her while she was trapped in a hospital bed, the man who had that strange look in his eyes and was bleeding from a self-inflicted wound.)

Megan says Billy and her mom "had a thing," which startles Sophie (indeed, Audrey has ventured into fraught territory). Cautiously, Sophie asks Megan the name of her mom (Audrey hopes to hear her own name, wants to believe she and Cooper shared a real love). There's tension in the conversation now, a palpable moment of revelation as Megan looks at Sophie and says her mom's name is Tina. Ominous music suddenly swells, a manifestation of Audrey's anxiety, an admission to herself that Cooper never really loved her. Sophie looks down and tightens her lip. Something essential has just been revealed, a confession, a concession. Megan says Billy just took off, "real fast and crazy." (Just like Cooper did all those years ago.)

Sophie and Megan have nothing left to say. Audrey has admitted hard truths to herself and has no further use for these avatars. Where does her mind go now? Does she retreat to her artificial world with Charlie? Or does she linger in this liminal Roadhouse a moment more, enough to hear the musical act, Lissie, perform? If Audrey does stay, maybe she finds reasons to keep pushing against her self-imposed boundaries. Lissie's confident lyrics proffer a better world, a world where "All that you lost, you get back; all that you want, you can have."

There's hope for Audrey here, hope in the message Lissie delivers: "I've been dancing in the moonlight. I've been laughing in the firelight. I'll be fine, fine. I'll be fine, fine. I'll be fine, fine."

PART 15:
THERE'S SOME FEAR IN LETTING GO

AS WE REACH THE END of Act 2, we get a better understanding of the narrative scheme Mark Frost and David Lynch have devised for *The Return*. Many characters, particularly those from the original series, make their last appearances in Part 15. Nadine, Big Ed, Norma, Shelly, Gersten, Carl Rodd, and, of course, The Log Lady, all take their final bows. None of these characters has had any distinct arc in the narrative, none has had a story with a traditional beginning, middle, and end. Instead, *The Return* has given them epilogs. Denouements twenty-five years in the making.

The denizens of Twin Peaks have drifted through the story, surfacing now and then as recurring figures in a complex milieu. The existence of all these wonderful characters provides texture, symmetry, and color-commentary to a grander pattern unfolding. They are part of something bigger, these local waitresses and cops, mechanics and cooks, these everyday small-town folk. They are pieces of a whole, a network of relationships comprising the town that is Twin Peaks. Their "stories" inform a wider tale of mood and setting.

But their time has come to an end. As Act 2 closes, much of the action in Twin Peaks comes to an end as well. (Yes, a major climax occurs there, in the sheriff's office, in Part 17, but that climax has more to do with Dale Cooper than it does with Twin Peaks.) In Part 15, we take our leave of the environs and the inhabitants of this mysterious little town in Washington State.

Our farewell to Twin Peaks will be highly charged. Part 15 is arguably the most emotional episode of *The Return*, full of love, anger, sadness, and fear. Where previous parts have sometimes been coolly distant, even in the midst of dramatic confrontations, Part 15 revels in emotion. It also deliberately—and extraordinarily—addresses us, the audience, and our passionate investment in the world of *Twin Peaks.*

IT'S A BRIGHT, BEAUTIFUL MORNING in Twin Peaks. The sun is shining, the birds are chirping, and the day is full of promise and purpose. Nadine has both on her mind. She marches down the road[*] proudly carrying a gold shovel on her shoulder. She has a mission today, a decades-old wrong she is determined to set right.

Nadine boldly marches up to her husband, Big Ed, who stands outside his gas station alarmed at her approach. Nadine gets right to the point: "Ed," she says, "I came to tell you I've changed." Nadine confesses her sins, admitting she has manipulated Ed all these years and kept him from his true love, Norma. Thanks to Doctor Jacoby, Nadine explains, she has transformed. She wants Ed to be free, to be happy. *To be with Norma.* "Run to her, Ed," Nadine exclaims, "Enjoy the rest of your lives together."

Ed is wary because he knows Nadine. He knows well that she can be flighty and confused. But something is different this time. When Ed receives a long hug from Nadine, he can sense the change in her, the truth of what she's saying. As Nadine turns and walks toward her new life, Ed senses hope. He takes a deep breath and feels the shackles of twenty-five years drop from his shoulders.

There's no time to waste. Ed hops in his old lime-green Chevy pickup and drives straight to the Double R. Hopping with excitement, he spies Norma and joyously tells her he is a free man at last. But Norma can't talk, she has a meeting with Walter Langford, her business (and possible romantic) partner, and she gently puts Ed off.

Devastated by Norma's cold shoulder, Ed sits at the counter, numbly processing the giant hole forming in his heart. He's at his lowest point, bitterly believing suicide would be preferable to this hurt. But he's too close to give up that quickly, too close to getting the life he's dreamed about for so long, and so, as if hoping to bend reality to

---

[*] A sign for Interstate 90 is visible over Nadine's left shoulder. I-90 runs through the middle part of Washington State (east from Seattle to Spokane) and would be nowhere near Twin Peaks, which is in the northeast corner of the state.

his will, Ed sits and meditates. Perhaps he asks God for the one good thing he believes he deserves, or perhaps Ed gives himself over to fate, trusts that the message he delivered to Norma will be as vital to her as it is to him. In these tense minutes, Big Ed Hurley puts his trust in the woman he loves and waits for her to see the open door they both believed had been shut forever.

Ed's news is, in fact, registering with Norma. As she sits across from Walter, her world changes. She tells Walter she's done with their business arrangement. She prefers to focus solely on close friends and family.[*] Maybe she was always going to break this news to Walter (she was hesitant about Walter's plans in Part 13), but maybe Ed's news has given her a new perspective, an escape from Walter's grand schemes. Norma's done with distractions. The life she's always wanted beckons just a few stools down the Double R lunch counter.

Ed remains sitting, stock-still, eyes closed. Walter walks past in the background, leaving the Double R, and Norma, for good.

The camera moves closer to Ed, and the soundtrack swells with the song, "I've Been Loving You Too Long" by Otis Redding. The lyrics underscore a swelling tension: "My love is growing stronger as our affair grows old." We know Norma waits somewhere just off screen, but we don't know how this affair will play out. For twenty-five years, we fans of *Twin Peaks* have mourned Ed and Norma's thwarted love, and we teeter upon an unexpected, agonizing precipice—Ed freed, Norma free.

Ed's face holds vigil for only a few seconds, but it feels like an eternity. Norma's hand appears from outside the frame and gently rests on Ed's shoulder. He turns to her and beams. "Marry me," he says. She kisses him and replies, "Of course I will."[†]

---

[*] Walter claims Norma told him she had no family, but Norma has a sister, and her name is Annie Blackburn—a character whose fate remains unknown within the text of *The Return*. (Hawk tells us in Part 7 that Annie escaped from the Black Lodge, but we never learn more about her story.) In *The Final Dossier*, Mark Frost reveals that Annie ended up in a private psychiatric facility in Spokane, WA. Why, then, would Norma tell Walter she has no family? Her sister is only a few hours south. Perhaps Norma, like *The Return* itself, has written Annie out of her story. (Or perhaps Cooper knows Annie's tragedy is partly his fault, and he'd rather not dwell on it.)

[†] This long-yearned-for reunion likely makes a strong impression on Dale Cooper's observing mind. He sees in Ed and Norma the kind of love he wishes he could have.

David Lynch honors Ed and Norma's powerful, cathartic reunion by cutting away to shots of sun-lit mountains and clouds dissipating in blue skies. The imagery is accompanied by Otis Redding's voice extolling a love unconstrained: "With heart and soul I love you. Good God almighty, I love you." Lynch could have moved on to other stories, but he doesn't. He could easily have left Ed and Norma embracing in the Double R, but he pauses in this joyous moment and basks in its beauty. With imagery and song, Lynch confirms Ed and Norma's union. They are together again, sharing a love as strong as ever.

A wave of transcendent goodness is moving across the community. It started in Part 13, when Doctor Jacoby and Nadine shared a moment of revelation and liberation. Nadine carried that freedom to Ed, releasing him from the burdens she had long imposed. Ed went to Norma and effectively liberated her from a profiteer's perilous path.

And now Ed and Norma's joy radiates to Shelly Briggs, who stands rapt and tearful as Ed and Norma recommit their love. Did this wave of hope wash over Shelly too? Shelly won't appear again in *The Return*, and we don't know the rest of her story (we leave her here, in the Double R, watching from the margins), but it's possible she finds inspiration in Ed and Norma and will find the strength to change her life. Given the domino effect we've seen so far (from Nadine to Ed to Norma) one hopes that Shelly can free herself from Red and rekindle her love with Bobby. If Ed and Norma can sustain a love once denied, surely Shelly and Bobby can rediscover their true romance.[*]

MR. C DRIVES DOWN DARK ROADS until he arrives at a rundown gas station,[†] the convenience store we saw in Part 8 around which the Woodsmen frantically paced after the atomic explosion. As if expecting Mr. C's arrival, a Woodsman waits outside the station and guides Mr. C to metal stairs attached to the side of the store. The two ascend, fading from view as they cross from this plane to another. Mr. C is moving into The Dutchman's, the space "above the convenience store,"

---

[*] Who knows? Maybe this liberating effect will pass from Shelly to her daughter, Becky, who will free herself from a stifling life with Steven. (I want to believe in the optimism of this scenario.)

[†] Edward Hopper's painting, *Gas* (1940) is a likely inspiration here.

a liminal world of dark rooms, labyrinthine passages, and menacing figures.

In the original series, Mike (the inhabiting spirit attached to Phillip Gerard) explained that he and Bob lived above a convenience store. In *Fire Walk With Me*, Phillip Jeffries said he had been to one of "their" meetings "above a convenience store,"[*] where he saw Bob and The Arm about to consume vast amounts of garmonbozia. Also present at this meeting were Mrs. Tremond and her grandson (two mysterious beings who typically manifest near places of extreme distress), a few Woodsmen, and a masked man who jumped onto a crate while holding a gnarled wand in his hand. This latter figure is known as The Jumping Man.

Mr. C has come to this realm in search of Phillip Jeffries, but we have to ask: Why would Jeffries be *here* of all places? The Dutchman's is the home of dark and dangerous beings, surely not a place where Phillip Jeffries would choose to dwell. And yet this is where Mr. C has come to find him.

Ray told Mr. C that the last he "heard," Jeffries was at The Dutchman's. Narratively speaking, this throwaway line serves to direct Mr. C to the next stage of his journey, but let's extrapolate: Ray's line implies that Jeffries was not always at The Dutchman's, but he's there now. A compelling argument can be made that Jeffries did not voluntarily go to The Dutchman's. He's a captive. He's being held there against his will.

This is all speculation but consider that Jeffries infiltrated the space above the convenience store yet again (like he did years earlier) and was caught by the Woodsmen and then incarcerated. When Mr. C goes looking for Jeffries, he is essentially visiting him in a supernatural prison. The Dutchman's is Jeffries' jail.

The prison scenario makes sense when you see the "security protocols" Mr. C must go through to get to Jeffries: The first Woodsman escorts Mr. C to a second Woodsman, who guards the threshold leading deeper into The Dutchman's. Mr. C says he wants to see Phillip Jeffries, and the sentry Woodsman pulls a lever on a machine, submit-

---

[*] Jeffries almost certainly infiltrated the meeting in the guise of a monkey, hidden behind a mask.

ting Mr. C's request to some unseen authority. There's a flash of light, and The Jumping Man flickers across the screen. A moment later, a third Woodsman appears to lead Mr. C through the "prison."

LET'S PAUSE HERE BRIEFLY for a few thoughts about The Jumping Man. In *Fire Walk With Me*, The Jumping Man was a background player, a last-minute embellishment added by David Lynch to provide texture to the convenience store scene. Carlton Lee Russell, the actor who plays The Jumping Man, says that Lynch described the character as a "talisman come to life." In other words, The Jumping Man was a piece of set-dressing that could move within the proscenium.[*]

Lynch redefined The Jumping Man for *The Return*, just as he did with other elements from *Fire Walk With Me* (such as the Owl Cave Ring). Where The Jumping Man was once simply a set piece, now he becomes a gatekeeper, a "dweller on the threshold," granting admission to darker recesses. In effect, The Jumping Man guards the passages that lead to Phillip Jeffries.

When The Jumping Man appears, we see an image of Sarah Palmer flash across his features. In Part 14, Sarah attacked the deplorable who accosted her and "opened" her face to reveal horrors roiling within. When she did, Sarah showed us the world of The Jumping Man, the point-of-view of the dweller upon the threshold. Here, in The Dutchman's, Lynch explicitly connects the two characters.

THE THIRD WOODSMAN escorts Mr. C deeper into The Dutchman's, steering him down a long hall, and up another flight of stairs. Mr. C passes through a door and finds himself in the nighttime courtyard of a dingy motel.[†] Woodsmen flank Mr. C as they escort him across the courtyard to room 8. The door to the room is locked, but a ghastly figure, the "Bosomy Woman," appears from the shadows and unlocks it. She is the custodian of keys, the final figurant Mr. C must pass in order to gain access to Phillip Jeffries.

---

[*] Lynch probably gave The Jumping Man little more thought than that. He was constantly tinkering with *Fire Walk With Me* as he developed it, and The Jumping Man was simply a last-minute addition.

[†] Mr. C is in the courtyard of the Red Diamond City Motel, the same place Leland Palmer planned to meet Teresa Banks and her "friends" in *Fire Walk With Me*. (Both scenes were shot at the same location: the Mt. Si Motel in North Bend, WA.)

Mr. C enters the cell in which Phillip Jeffries has been incarcerated, and, as if in a real-world prison, he waits for an audience with an inmate. As Mr. C watches, one wall of the room fades away, and Phillip Jeffries appears. Like Gordon Cole's audience with Mr. C at Yankton Federal Prison (in Part 4), a barrier is removed so a visitor can speak with a prisoner.

Phillip Jeffries, however, isn't human. Not anymore. As Gordon Cole explained, Jeffries "doesn't really exist, at least not in the normal sense." In Cole's dream (the flashback to *Fire Walk With Me*), Jeffries was an able (if slightly confused) man trying to deliver information to the FBI. Now, he's taken a new form. Jeffries manifests as a large metal canister, a clanking, hissing machine—a gigantic "tea kettle," issuing vapor from its "spout."

Mr. C is unperturbed by Jeffries' new appearance. He's got questions, and he wants answers. But Phillip Jeffries proves to be a tricky interlocutor. When Mr. C asks if Jeffries sent Ray to kill him, Jeffries acts surprised; he admits that he called Ray but won't say what they talked about. When Mr. C asks if Jeffries called a few days ago, Jeffries says, "I don't have your number." Neither answer is a definitive "no."

Jeffries changes the subject. He reminds Mr. C that the two of them "used to talk." Mr. C recalls their first meeting at the Philadelphia FBI offices in 1989,[*] when Jeffries mysteriously appeared but refused to talk

---

[*] What year is this? That line haunts *The Return* and, ironically, finds import here, because Mr. C's reference to Jeffries' appearance in 1989 is a mistake. According to the timeline established in the *Twin Peaks* pilot and in *Fire Walk With Me*, Jeffries appeared in Philadelphia in 1988.

Here are the facts: Laura Palmer was killed in 1989. In the *Twin Peaks* pilot, Dale Cooper reveals that Teresa Banks was killed almost exactly one year earlier (in 1988). At the beginning of *Fire Walk With Me*, Chet Desmond and Sam Stanley travel to Deer Meadow, WA in 1988 to investigate the Banks murder. At the same time, Jeffries appears in Philadelphia to deliver his message to the FBI, and Albert announces that Chet Desmond has disappeared from Deer Meadow. Days later, Dale Cooper travels to Deer Meadow to further investigate. He completes his report to Diane, and the story transitions to Twin Peaks in 1989 (a title card announces that the story has moved forward one year). By these established facts, there's no doubt Phillip Jeffries had been in Philadelphia in 1988.

But's here's the catch: The Phillip Jeffries scene in *Fire Walk With Me* was originally scripted to take place in 1989 (it would have occurred seven days prior to Laura Palmer's murder). David Lynch shot the Jeffries scene *as scripted* but, when editing the film, moved the sequence back a full year to coincide with the Teresa

about someone named "Judy." Back then, he emphatically declared: "We're not going to talk about Judy *at all*," and Mr. C wants to know why. More importantly, he wants to know who Judy really is.

True to form, Jeffries won't talk about Judy, but he does offer a tantalizing clue. He explains that Mr. C has "already met" Judy and provides coordinates to where Mr. C can find her. It takes a lot to elicit emotion from Mr. C (he didn't get angry when Darya double-crossed him, or when Renzo hit him in the back, or even when Ray brandished the Owl Cave Ring), but as Phillip Jeffries taunts him with vagaries and half-answers, Mr. C loses his cool. "Who is Judy?" he asks. *"Who is Judy?!"* But Jeffries is done speaking and withdraws once more behind the barrier wall.

A phone rings, and Mr. C moves to answer it. He lifts the receiver and is transported to a phone booth outside the convenience store. The receiver in his hand clicks. The line goes dead.

Whatever Mr. C was hoping to get from Phillip Jeffries, he's come away with more questions than answers. Yes, he apparently has coordinates that will lead him to Judy, but these are likely the same numbers he got from Ray, numbers that will probably lead to a trap. Mr. C is not going to trust the information Phillip Jeffries supplied, because if he didn't know before his visit to The Dutchman's, he knows now: Phillip Jeffries is an unreliable source.

AS I DISCUSSED IN PARTS 2 AND 13, someone pretending to be Phillip Jeffries has been in contact with Mr. C and Ray Monroe. (I believe that someone is Mike, the reformed Black Lodge spirit who inhabited Phillip Gerard.) But how much does the *real* Phillip Jeffries

---

Banks storyline. Lynch did this because he was rethinking the function of the Deer Meadow prologue within the overall narrative. (I've argued elsewhere that Lynch re-envisioned the prologue as a dream of Dale Cooper's, and I believe Lynch shifted the Jeffries scene back a year to strengthen this scenario.)

In the years between *Fire Walk With Me* and *The Return*, Lynch likely forgot he shifted the Jeffries scene back a year. Further complicating things, Lynch restored the original Jeffries scene for "The Missing Pieces" (available on *The Complete Mystery* Blu-ray), in which Jeffries explicitly notices the year on the calendar and says, "1989." In Lynch's mind this restoration to 1989 may have become *de facto* canon.

So, should we try to make sense of this odd discrepancy or just ignore it and move on? I'm sure Mr. C's reference to 1989 is wrong, the result of Lynch and Frost looking at the *Fire Walk With Me* script when they wrote Part 15. Still, there's a way to reconcile this error: In *Fire Walk With Me*, Dale Cooper was, indeed, dreaming events *from* 1988, but he was dreaming about them *in* 1989. And that's why Mr. C remembers it the way he does.

know about the machinations of Mr. C and players like The Fireman and Major Briggs? Is the real Jeffries even part of the scheme to stop Mr. C? There are no clear answers to these questions. Phillip Jeffries and his agenda remain unsolved mysteries.

And what about Judy? What secrets does Jeffries keep about whomever or whatever she is? Jeffries probably learned about Judy after he and Gordon Cole encountered the Lois Duffy tulpa (the first Blue Rose case). Jeffries felt compelled to find her and, during his search, learned sobering truths, enough to trigger a psychic overload which drove him a little bit crazy. (In *Fire Walk With Me*, Albert's instincts were right when he said Jeffries had "suffered a few bumps on the ole noggin.") Somewhere, somehow, Jeffries confronted the reality of Judy and was shaken to his core. He glimpsed the inescapable fact that all of humanity's distress manifests as a singular being, an entity of extreme negative force. Phillip Jeffries learned that Judy is the avatar of trauma.

Judy is a conundrum. We never definitively find out who or what she is. Does she exist as an external threat, an autonomous entity that *causes* pain and sorrow? Or was she conjured by man, existing as a *result* of man's pain and sorrow? Like the philosophical question, "Did God create man, or did man create God?", Judy (as *Twin Peaks: The Return* presents her) is impossible to solve. Trauma induces Judy, but Judy is trauma. This never-ending circle has sent Phillip Jeffries over the edge. If he could reduce Judy to a precise identity, define her as a singular being, he might be able to confront and combat her, but Jeffries cannot demote Judy to such simple terms.[*] It's no wonder he's lost his mind. These ideas are some serious bumps on the noggin.

In his search for Judy, it's likely that Jeffries repeatedly infiltrated The Dutchman's and was finally captured and imprisoned. By the time Mr. C arrives, Jeffries has become untethered to reality. He's even forfeited his human form. Jeffries literally spouts nonsense when Mr.

---

[*] Judy's dichotomous identity is the result, perhaps, of Mark Frost and David Lynch's conflicting narrative strategies. Frost wants to disclose Judy, calling her (in *The Final Dossier*) a Sumerian demon, or *utukku*: "I tried to pin it into some underlying concepts in a way that made sense...the idea of the interdimensional being that appears in the box was in play." But Lynch goes out of his way to keep Judy ambiguous. Gordon Cole simply describes Judy as an entity of "extreme negative force." What's more, Lynch explicitly labels the creature in the box as "Experiment" (not Judy).

C asks questions and then steers Mr. C toward an unreachable manifestation of Judy.

But maybe Jeffries is being as honest with Mr. C as he can. He gives him coordinates to a deadly trap, knowing that when Mr. C gets there, he'll certainly encounter an extreme negative force. When he does, Mr. C will have "found" Judy.

RICHARD, HOLDING A GUN, waits outside The Dutchman's for Mr. C. He calls Mr. C, "Cooper," believing he's the man in a photograph his mother, Audrey Horne, once owned. Mr. C realizes Richard is likely his son, but he has no time for Richard's games. He quickly disarms Richard and orders him to get in the truck. After what Phillip Jeffries just said about Judy, Mr. C knows Richard might prove useful to him very soon.

STEVEN AND GERSTEN SIT at the base of a tree in the forest. Steven, who is possibly suffering from a drug overdose, is having a panic attack. Breathing heavily, wracked by seizures, he babbles nonsensically. He claims he "did it," and, loading bullets into a gun, says he's going "to end it." Gersten frantically tries to talk him down, begging him to give her the gun. She thinks he's been deliberately overdosed: "What did she give you?" she asks. But Steven can't be reasoned with. He delivers an absurd good-bye to Gersten and then questions his imminent after-life: "Where will I be?" he wonders. "Will I be with the rhinoceros?"

A man walking his dog stumbles upon the couple and quickly retreats. Gersten screams at the interruption and runs to the other side of the tree. Sitting on the ground, wracked by fear, she hears a loud gunshot and dissolves into paroxysms of grief.*

So ends the story of Steven Burnett and Gersten Hayward—and Becky Burnett, too. Theirs was a sordid triangle of despair and anger. We don't know what drove Steven into the woods, making him think suicide was his only escape, but the details don't matter. We know

---

* I can't help but wonder about the key Gersten wears around her neck. It's one of those big, old-fashioned skeleton keys, the kind which opens treasure chests in pirate movies. She's wearing it here, and she was wearing it in Part 11 (when she stood in the stairwell with Steven). Does the key signify anything? Does Gersten, in fact, "hold the key" to a certain mystery? I don't have anywhere to go with this. I wish I could offer some keen interpretation about this curious, obvious key. It's a mystery. Like the Bosomy Woman at The Dutchman's, Gersten is simply another keeper of keys.

Steven was abusive, angry and lived a miserable life. He couldn't hold a job, he threatened his wife, and he betrayed her. We know that Becky was hot-headed, too, brazenly shooting through a door because of Steven's infidelity. What else was Becky capable of? Perhaps she poisoned Steven, gave him a dose of something so strong he was never coming back. But these are guesses. Becky's fate remains unknown. All we know for sure is that Gersten Hayward writhes in agony at the base of a tree, while a man with a dog rushes away to report the news.*

AT THE ROADHOUSE, James's schoolboy crush is about to bring Freddie one step closer to his destiny. James approaches Renee, who sits in a booth with her husband, Chuck.† Maybe it's the result of his motorcycle accident, but James doesn't know how to read the room. Tongue-tied and wearing his heart on his sleeve, James expresses his innocent feelings toward another man's wife.

That's all Chuck needs to hear. He punches James in the face and kicks him when he falls to the floor. Freddie steps in and with a quick tap of his green glove sends Chuck sprawling across the room. Knocked senseless, Chuck foams at the mouth.

James and Freddie can't simply walk away from a ruckus like this. Bobby and Hawk arrest the duo and lock them up at the station, but that's exactly where Freddie needs to be. It won't be long before Mr. C and Bob arrive at this same place. And Freddie will be waiting.

How many strings is the Fireman pulling? Did he somehow know that Freddie and James would become friends and that James's naïve behavior toward Renee would result in a trip to jail for both? The Fireman is a Grand Master on the fluid chess board of reality, planning moves, anticipating countermoves, and employing complex stratagems

---

* This man is Cyril Pons, a minor character who appeared briefly in the original series. Played by *Twin Peaks* co-creator, Mark Frost, Cyril Pons used to be a reporter for a local television station. At the time of *The Return*, he has retired to the environs around Twin Peaks. In fact, when he tells Carl Rodd what he saw in the woods, he knows to point at the trailer where Steven and Becky live, suggesting that Cyril is also a resident at the New Fat Trout Trailer Park.

† Names echo in *Twin Peaks*. There are multiple Chucks, Carries, Bills, Billys, Pauls, and, of course, Richards and Lindas. Simple names, recycled again and again by a mind that can't keep track of all the marginal players.

in preparation for the endgame. Part of that endgame is having Freddie in place for his upcoming encounter with Bob.

IN LAS VEGAS, Chantal kills Duncan Todd and Todd's assistant, Roger. In Part 2, Todd warned Roger not to get involved with someone like Mr. C, but now it's too late. Roger is a victim of two bullets from Chantal's silenced gun. As for Chantal, she's ready for her next target: Dougie Jones.

Speaking of Dougie…. Cooper sits contentedly at home while Janey-E brings him a piece of chocolate cake. Happier than ever, Janey-E kneels beside Cooper and says, "All our dreams are coming true." Cooper absently replies, "True."

The mind of Cooper, watching from the Red Room, knows time is running out. Freddie is in the Twin Peaks jail, Naido is just a few cells away, and Mr. C is getting closer. Events are rushing towards a climax, and all Cooper can do is watch his other self—his passive "Dougie Jones" persona—calmly eat chocolate cake.

But an opportunity arises. "Dougie" becomes captivated by the movie, *Sunset Boulevard*, playing on his television. One of the characters in the film says, "Get Gordon Cole," and Dougie becomes fully alert. He stares at the TV in recognition. The name means something.[*] As he struggles to make sense of this cue, his gaze wanders to the electric socket beside the TV.

Cooper lowers himself to the floor and attempts to insert the tines of his fork into one of the socket openings. When that doesn't work, Cooper reverses the fork and inserts the tapered handle into the socket.[†]

Electricity crackles, sparks fly, and a blinding flash illuminates the room. Cooper is knocked back, Janey-E screams, and all the lights go out.

This is just what the observing Cooper hoped would happen. He needs his corporeal self sidelined so that he, the one and only Cooper,

---

[*] There's a meta-fictional loop at play here: *Sunset Boulevard* was the source of the name "Gordon Cole" in the original series. Now, within the fiction of *Twin Peaks*, Cooper recognizes the name when he hears it on TV.

[†] Cooper pushes the fork into the socket's neutral slot, which might not result in any electric current. If Cooper had inserted the fork in the hot slot (the one on the right) he'd certainly get the electricity flowing.

can restore himself to the story and become the heroic figure who will save Laura Palmer (and "make all his dreams come true"). With "Dougie-Cooper" knocked out, this opportunity is imminent.

This is the last time we will see this version of Cooper.[*] Fittingly, his last scene as "Dougie" ends with the piercing scream of Janey-E and a sudden electrical blackout, foreshadowing the final scene of *The Return*, when another powerful scream darkens the light and ends the story.

AUDREY HORNE LITERALLY STANDS on the threshold of release, but her doubts hold her back. When Charlie consents to going to the Roadhouse, Audrey hesitates. She fears what might be outside her front door and so lashes out at Charlie, making him an impediment rather than a facilitator. He becomes a proxy for her own failures.

Not surprisingly, Charlie retreats. He's no longer interested in going to the Roadhouse.

Audrey explodes in anger and leaps on Charlie, putting her hands tightly around his neck. "How can you be like this?" she cries. "I hate you!" But it's not Charlie that Audrey hates, it's herself for being so weak.

Still, Audrey's angry release marks a breakthrough. By confronting the part of herself she hates, she's liberating a stronger, more confident persona. She's beaten her fear. Audrey's ready, at last, to go to the Roadhouse.

PART 15 HAS PULSED with emotion—so much energy, so much release—but the most emotional moment is yet to come.

The Log Lady makes her final call to Deputy Hawk to say farewell, but it's not just The Log Lady saying good-bye, it's Catherine Coulson, too. In a powerful, heart-wrenching scene, both Margaret Lanterman and Catherine Coulson bravely exhibit their battle with an unremitting cancer. In this moment, character and actor become one, a blending Part 15 acknowledges when, for the only time, *The Return*

---

[*] Yes, we *might* see him again in Part 18, but it's unlikely that the Cooper who returns to Las Vegas at the end of the story is the Cooper he was before (i.e., the Dougie Jones version of Cooper).

memorializes a character (Margaret Lanterman) in the end credits. (Catherine Coulson was acknowledged in the end credits for Part 1.)

The Log Lady and Catherine Coulson were fundamentally indistinguishable. They were shining representatives of both the fictional and real-life worlds of *Twin Peaks*. The Log Lady, with her wisdom and transcendent knowledge, was a vital component to the *Twin Peaks* mythology. Likewise, Catherine Coulson, with her kindness and faith, was a singular liaison between the fans and the creative forces behind the series. She was the conscience of the story and the show's biggest fan.

The Log Lady reminds Hawk that death "is just a change, not an end." She's still afraid, but she accepts the mystery of death and invites us, the fans who've known and loved her all these decades, to bear witness to her final moments. She gives herself to the audience in the boldest, most generous way possible. Her last words are, "My log is turning gold. The wind is moaning. I'm dying." Hawk says, "Goodnight," his final good-bye to Margaret…to Catherine. And so do we.

A moment later, Hawk gathers Andy, Lucy, Bobby, and Frank Truman in a conference room to announce the passing of Margaret Lanterman. Truman removes his hat. Lucy sheds a tear. Hawk stares gravely into the dark.[*]

The death of The Log Lady marks a crucial moment in *The Return*. Depicted here, near the end of Part 15 (and the end of Act 2), the passing of Margaret Lanterman signifies the end of Twin Peaks. Yes, there are a few loose ends to be tied up in the next few episodes, but the remaining story is about Dale Cooper and his exaggerated version of the world. It's no longer about Twin Peaks, a town defined by quirky residents, simmering melodramas, heavenly foods and spooky environs. That Twin Peaks is over in Part 15. With the death of The Log Lady, it's over for good.

---

[*] Kimmy Robertson described the emotional atmosphere on-set when she and her fellow actors were tasked with honoring Coulson and her character: "We had just heard about [Catherine Coulson passing away]. We shot that [scene] later in the week. David had to figure it out. He had the lights low. He made sure everyone out in the hall was quiet. Everyone had to stop working and stand up and focus their attention on Catherine. That was amazing. Not only was he filming us, but he was filming the entire crew thinking about her."

THERE'S A CODA TO PART 15, a last visit to the famous Roadhouse booth, the location of so many fragmented scenes. Gone are the usual twosomes, the duos sharing malaise and fugs of doubt and anger. Now, it's just Ruby, a young woman, lonely and alone, watching the band play and the people dance.

Two big men, bikers by the looks of them, loom over Ruby. She glances at them and, sensing their implicit demand, says she's waiting for someone. The bikers don't care. They want the booth, and they lift Ruby from her seat to get it.

Ruby doesn't resist. She's helpless under the strength of these overpowering men, who place her on the floor and appropriate her space.

For a long moment, Ruby sits facing the crowd. Then she crawls away, weaving a path between the legs of the revelers on the dance floor. The band is playing loudly. People are dancing and moving about. No one notices poor Ruby winding her way deep into the throng.

Ruby stops beneath the ceaseless crowd and screams. She screams uninhibitedly and utterly, and her scream becomes a denouement.

Ruby's scream releases all the emotion that has accumulated in Part 15. It channels the anger of Mr. C, powerless before the impenetrable Phillip Jeffries. It lets loose the agony of Steven and Gersten, suffering beneath an ancient canopy of trees. It releases the fear of Janey-E, bathed in a blinding electric flash. Ruby's scream unlocks an imprisoned Audrey Horne, and it affirms the long-denied love of Ed and Norma. Perhaps most importantly, Ruby's scream exorcises the overwhelming sadness of everyone living in Twin Peaks (and watching *Twin Peaks)* who mourns the passing of The Log Lady.

But her scream reaches deeper than that. It goes beyond Part 15 to release the emotional energy of all those suffering in Act 2. Ruby's scream is the shame of Bill Hastings, the brutality of Richard Horne, the revenge of Becky Burnett. It's the misery of Johnny Horne assaulted by the monotony of a child's toy. It's the confusion of Bobby Briggs amid the cacophony of an intersection. It's the despair of Sarah Palmer crushed by an unrelenting evil. Ruby's scream takes all the half-finished stories and unanswered questions and abandoned characters in *Twin Peaks* and gives them a single, astounding, unforgettable ending.

With Ruby's scream, it all comes out now, flowing like a river. All the stories and all the characters, surging forever into a larger universe....

Act III

"Who knows where or when."

PART 16:

NO KNOCK, NO DOORBELL

MR. C'S COORDINATES HAVE LED HIM to a remote spot among scrubby hills. He exits his truck and tells Richard to climb to a large rock sitting atop a slope. Gullible (or simply afraid), Richard follows Mr. C's instructions. When he reaches the rock, he is immediately electrocuted, his body disintegrated by a blast of light and sparks. Mr. C watches without affect. "Oh," he says. "Good-bye, my son." Mr. C has avoided another trap.

Mr. C told Richard that three people had provided him coordinates, but that's not correct. Only two sources have given him numbers (Ray Monroe and Phillip Jeffries). Diane will be a third source when she sends her information later, and that means Mr. C's comment about his three sources is a continuity error. The only coordinates Mr. C has right now lead to the trap on the rock.[*]

Mr. C's foes are closing in, and he knows it's time to activate Diane. He sends her a text that reads: ": -) ALL", a signal for her to kill Gordon Cole.

Meanwhile, on a nearby hilltop, Jerry Horne has been watching Mr. C through a pair of binoculars. He's extremely distressed by Richard's electrocution and blames his binoculars for the awful vision.

---

[*] If the imposter Jeffries was out to get Mr. C (and "be with Bob again"), then he likely provided coordinates to Ray to pass along to Mr. C. Later, Phillip Jeffries in The Dutchman's apparently provides the same numbers. It's possible the real Jeffries and the imposter are working together, but there's no evidence to support this conclusion. In the end, the coordinate backstory just doesn't add up.

Jerry Horne has been a curious presence in *The Return*. In Part 5, he wandered into the woods and watched one of Doctor Amp's videos on his phone. In Part 7, he called Ben Horne, complaining he was lost. Since then, he's wandered the woods, confused and frantic. Days have passed (possibly even weeks) since Jerry first set out. He couldn't have survived all that time in those dark, cold woods alone.

Jerry's long foray in the forest is obviously impossible, but it makes a kind of sense if we remember we're seeing it through Cooper's observing mind. Cooper is watching from the Red Room, a place where past, present and future occur all at once. As far as Cooper is concerned, Jerry is *always* lost in the woods, searching for a way home. Jerry won't appear again in *The Return*, and, in the end, his story becomes an ironic reflection of Dale Cooper's Red Room predicament.

COOPER'S BEEN HELPLESSLY WATCHING events in the real world, but now he's on the cusp of steering the story. He can't fully take control yet, however, until a few loose ends are tied up. One of those is the menace of Hutch and Chantal, who wait in their van in front of the Jones house on Lancelot Court. Cooper knows that Hutch and Chantal pose an existential threat to his physical well-being, and until their threat is eliminated, he does not dare let his mind wander into the story he *wants* to tell.

At "Memorial Hospital"[*] in Las Vegas, Cooper is attached to a ventilator and various monitors that beep and whirr. Hundreds of miles away, Gordon Cole stands in the FBI command center in Buckhorn and "hears" Cooper's machines. Cole senses something imminent, something just outside his frame waiting to break through, but, like the mystery of the window-washer who came and went so quickly, Cole can make no sense of it.

Outside the Jones household, Agent Wilson waits in his cruiser for Dougie to return. He watches the Mitchum Brothers arrive to deliver groceries and other goods. Across the street, Hutch and Chantal are watching, too, nonplussed by all the activity.

A car pulls up in front of Hutch and Chantal's van. The driver, a man named Zawaski (the "Polish Accountant"), insists that Hutch and

[*] This hospital name is an echo of Calhoun *Memorial Hospital* in Twin Peaks.

Chantal are blocking his driveway. When they refuse to move, Zawaski presses on his accelerator and slams his car into the front of the van. Hutch and Chantal attempt to drive away, but Zawaski pulls a gun and opens fire, brutally killing them both. Agent Wilson hops out of his car and orders Zawaski to drop his weapon, and Zawaski puts his gun on the ground and raises his hands in surrender.

Throughout *The Return*, forces associated with the letter "Z" have protected Cooper. These "Z agents" (for lack of a better term) include Tracey, who lured Sam away from the glass box long enough for Cooper to pass through unseen, and "Szymon's Famous Coffees," where Cooper bought the cherry pie that defused the bloodthirsty Mitchums. Add to this list Zawaski ("the Polish Accountant"), who eliminates Hutch and Chantal. He's another *deus ex machina*, arriving just in time to remove the last major threat to Cooper.

We'll never learn who (or what) is behind these intervening forces. Maybe it's Cooper, watching from the Red Room, pressing allies into service to protect his vulnerable physical body, or maybe it's the Fireman, commandeering the occasional agent to keep his plan on track. Whoever the entity is, it watches over Cooper and protects him when needed.

Hutch and Chantal were the last existential threat. With them gone, Cooper's otherworldly protection is no longer needed. As Zawaski surrenders to Agent Wilson, Lynch's camera rises above the action. It retreats, as if a supernatural observer (Zawaski's "operator," if you will) is taking leave, departing from the mortal plane.

An overhead shot like this is unusual; Lynch typically cuts away from his characters on static close-up or medium shots, and so when he raises the camera and moves it deliberately away, there's a sense of closure—of *completion*. The "powers that be" are leaving. Their work on Earth is done.

Now that all existential threats are gone, Cooper is free to take control. As soon as Hutch and Chantal are killed, the story shifts to Cooper lying in bed at "Memorial Hospital." His face twitches, and a humming noise, the same sound that permeates the Great Northern Hotel in Twin Peaks, is audible. Cooper wakes and sits up.

When Cooper awakens, the world immediately acquires a heightened, exaggerated quality, where everything is amplified. Phillip

Gerard appears and announces that Cooper is "awake," to which Cooper enthusiastically responds, "One hundred percent!" In this binary world, Cooper is switched to "ON." There's nothing half-way about him.

Cooper takes command. He tells Janey-E to get a doctor, and then he assertively removes his IV tubes from his arm. When the doctor[*] arrives, Cooper asks her to confirm he's "A-okay." She does and declares that she'll start preparing his release papers (she has no questions about why he is suddenly conscious, or if he has any lingering effects from being electrocuted). Cooper is in complete control of his surroundings. He knows exactly where his clothes are and asks Bushnell Mullins to fetch them. He also knows Bushnell carries a "32 snub nose in a shoulder holster under [his] left arm" and asks to borrow it. Bushnell doesn't hesitate. "Sure thing," he says and hands the gun over.

Cooper puts a plan into action: Over the phone he instructs the Mitchum brothers to prepare their private jet for a flight to Spokane, Washington. He gives Bushnell a message to read to Gordon Cole (whom Cooper knows will call). Conveniently, the message is already written on a piece of paper. Cooper simply pulls it from his pocket and hands it to Bushnell.

As Cooper bustles about giving orders, the classic theme from *Twin Peaks* ("Falling" by Angelo Badalamenti) plays on the soundtrack, underscoring the triumphant return of Dale Cooper to the world. But the music also calls attention to the artifice of what's happening: The exaggerated nature of Cooper's persona, the ease at which the world bends to his needs. The music is overt and invasive. It dominates as Cooper takes leave of the hospital (with Janey-E and Sonny-Jim in tow), as if highlighting the pretense of Cooper's "performance."

WHAT'S HAPPENING HERE? Why has the story shifted into such obvious exaggeration?

Cooper is imagining a hyperbolic version of himself, a persona that his troubled, impatient mind (still in the Red Room) has contrived. Up to this point, Cooper's been watching events as they occurred in the

---

[*] The doctor is played by Bellina Logan, the actress who played Louie, the Great Northern receptionist, in the original *Twin Peaks*. David Lynch has some affinity for the performer; Logan also appears in Lynch's *INLAND EMPIRE*.

real world, but now he's imposing himself on the narrative. He's telling the story he wants to tell, and the story he wants to tell features the dashing FBI Special Agent Dale Cooper. The star of the show. The hero who will save the day.

Here, Dale Cooper enters the story as an *apparition*, visible to all but nonetheless impotent. Indeed, as we see in the next episode, Cooper shows up, ready for action, but he never does anything. He has Bushnell Mullins's gun, but he doesn't use it. Other characters, (Andy, Lucy, and Freddie) dispatch Cooper's foes, while Cooper stands to the side and watches.

I want to be clear about what I think is going on: I contend that Cooper pierces the veil of the Red Room and "communicates" his presence into the world, steering the story toward a desired conclusion. But Cooper hasn't truly left the Red Room. He can't exit that realm simply because he wants to; he must be rehabilitated before he can get out. He must achieve a rebalancing of his good and bad sides, and that hasn't happened yet.

Cooper's impatience has gotten the better of him, and he enters the story as something ephemeral, a *spirit* who, like Phillip Jeffries when he appeared in Philadelphia long ago, was "never really there." (Cooper, like Jeffries, will vanish, and all who saw him will forget he had ever appeared.) Meanwhile, Cooper's body—the physical self who's been wandering Las Vegas all these many days—remains in the hospital recuperating[*] until Cooper *truly* wakes and returns home to Janey-E and Sonny Jim in Part 18.

This interpretation is difficult, I admit. It requires leaps-of-faith and a constructive reading of the text. *But the text demands such an interpretation.* We can't ignore that the next two chapters of *Twin Peaks* are distinctly different from what has come before. A new story-telling scheme is at play, a far more subjective scheme from what we've seen so far.

A romanticized Cooper exits Memorial Hospital. A larger-than-life character, complete with his own theme music. He's not simply a man or a detective, he's a savior, and he sees himself as mythic. "I *am* the

---

[*] Or "re-*Cooper*-ating." (Sorry. That was just too good to pass up.)

FBI!" he proclaims. More than a hero, Cooper is an institutional power. He's a *super*hero.

This isn't the first time David Lynch has positioned one of his characters in such an exaggerated, amplified way. The super heroic Dale Cooper finds precedence in Betty Elms, the protagonist from *Mulholland Drive.* There, Betty is presented as a cliché, an awestruck, plucky "every-girl" who takes Hollywood by storm and sweeps men off their feet. Betty is too good to be true. As scholars A.E. Denham and F.D. Worrell note, "there's something very contrived about Betty…everything [she] says is scripted, preordained by an idealized paradigm. Betty is an exaggeration, a hyperbole of the imagination." Such is the case with Special Agent Dale Cooper, who sets off to right the wrongs of the world. But this Cooper is a fantasy, an impossibility. Like Betty, he's "contrived," a "hyperbole of the imagination."

I understand that you might want to reject this complex, convoluted theory, and so, for argument's sake, let's consider some other possible interpretations of what's happening to Cooper.

Let's take everything we see at face value: Cooper really wakes up in the hospital. He's not a dream figure or wish-fulfilling alter-ego—he's Dale Cooper, assuming his role as FBI Special Agent and member of The Blue Rose Task Force. In this reading, Cooper travels to Twin Peaks, goes back in time, returns to the Red Room, and emerges in Glastonbury Grove. This is literally what happens. This is what we see.

As obvious (and tempting) as this interpretation might be, it fails to address many inexplicable happenings of the next episode: It can't explain the appearance of Cooper's omniscient, superimposed face, or the startling fade-to-black at "the moment of completion," or the transit through the Great Northern basement to otherworldly realms. A literal approach simply cannot encompass these (and other) confounding events. Even if we allow for a supernatural premise (one that allows, say, portals through time and space), a literal reading still runs into dead ends.

Let's consider a diametric theory: Let's say everything we see on screen is entirely a dream. Nothing about it is real, it's all being imagined by Dale Cooper. Admittedly, this theory is easier to support since we're told by Cooper, himself, that "we live inside a dream." The problem with such a theory (as I mentioned early in this book) is that it marginalizes all the supporting characters, the many rich and resonant figures who populate the story. Everything they experience—their joy, pain, loss and compassion—is rendered moot. The Log Lady's dying farewell, Ed and Norma's passionate reunion, Carl Rodd's selfless gestures—all of this (and more) is nothing but the whim of Cooper's subconsciousness. These stories have little value if they're nothing but reflections of Cooper's deeper psyche.

Okay, maybe we should simply reject all these theories. Maybe any effort to fit a template on *Twin Peaks* is a fool's errand. Maybe, as Kristine McKenna tells us in Lynch's biography-memoir, *Room to Dream, The Return* is not meant to be decoded. Cooper serves as a sub-jective artifact, a symbol of guilt, frustration, doubt—or anything else the viewer projects onto him. Any effort to further decipher the text is a lost cause. As David Lynch tells us, "There are no rules…it's a sensa-tion. I don't have the answers."

Still, even if Lynch refuses to draw boundaries around the work, there's an underlying mechanism at play. Lynch may not have the an-swers, but he insists *The Return* is "anchored in…the *Twin Peaks* that's gone before," and "is understandable, too, in an intuitive way."

My "Cooper-as-observer/Cooper-as-phantom-interloper" theory may not be correct, but it feels right (at least, to me). It feels "anchored" to the *Twin Peaks* that came before, and I believe it's the mechanism that drives the story….

NOW THAT COOPER'S MIND is steering the story and accommodat-ing his newly arrived presence, Cooper is no longer paying attention to the other characters he's been following. One of these is Diane, who sits alone at the bar in the Mayfair Hotel. As her scene opens, the *Twin Peaks* theme we heard in Las Vegas wafts into Buckhorn, echoing Cooper's mind as it drifts away.

The music abruptly stops when Diane reads the ": -) ALL" message.[*] Diane knows exactly what Mr. C's text means: It's an order to kill

---

[*] Close-up shots of Diane's phone reveal a slight continuity error. In the first (here, at the bar), Diane receives Mr. C's message at 16:44 (4:44 p.m.). In the second (shown later, when Diane is in the command center with Cole), we see Mr. C's message having arrived at 15:50 (3:50 p.m.).

Gordon Cole. As a tulpa created by Mr. C, Diane must follow orders; she's helpless to her programming. But that doesn't mean Diane is oblivious to the horror of the order. She knows what awful thing she must do, and it shocks her to the core. She physically reacts to the text, as if someone punched her in the stomach.

Something else happens, too. Something profound. When Diane realizes she must kill Cole, a deep memory surfaces. For a moment, the true Diane, the personality hidden all these years beneath the tulpa programming, regains control. She shudders and sighs as her new persona takes hold. An ambient hum grows louder. "I remember," she gasps and closes her eyes in relief. "Oh," she says. "Oh, Coop. I remember."

Diane regains agency. Her programming recedes, and she grabs her phone and sends Mr. C the coordinates.[*] "I hope this works," she says.

Way back in Part 7, Gordon Cole hinted that Diane knew something of Cooper's deeper plan, but he wouldn't elaborate. Now, in this moment of revelation, Diane remembers what Cole was referring to. She remembers "Coop" and the plan he concocted to find Judy and stop such evil entities as Bob. As the memory washes over her, Diane sends coordinates to Mr. C.[†]

Diane's liberation lasts only a moment. After she texts the numbers, her compulsory programming takes over. She looks up, shifts her eyes to the side, checks in her purse for a gun, and slowly walks toward her destiny with Gordon Cole. The oppressive chords of "American Woman" (last heard in Part 1 as Mr. C arrived at Buella's) accompany Diane as she makes her way to the elevator. Cooper's "*Twin Peaks*" theme may have opened the scene, but Mr. C's theme ends it.

Meanwhile, in the command center, Gordon Cole senses something imminent. He knows Diane is coming (and probably knows what's about to happen). Before Diane can knock, Cole calls for her to

---

[*] The coordinates Diane types are 48.551420 and 117.163956. When mapped, these coordinates designate a spot in northeastern Washington State—almost exactly where the fictional town of Twin Peaks would be.

[†] Some argue that when Diane says, "I remember" she is simply remembering she has the coordinates. If so, why didn't Mr. C prompt Diane for them earlier? And why does Diane sigh with relief and refer to Cooper as "Coop," a term of endearment? She is clearly relieved and she "hopes" sending the numbers will "work." Diane wants to see Mr. C defeated, and here, she emphatically expresses it.

enter. He will not be taken by surprise. He's asserting control from the start.

Diane sits and relates her long-ago encounter with Mr. C (whom she believed was Cooper).* She describes how Mr. C came to her home and raped her. The memories are vivid, and she sobs as she relives them. Diane describes how Mr. C took her to an old gas station (i.e., The Dutchman's), and as the memory comes back, the truth becomes clear. She realizes she is not really Diane; she's a tulpa. She also realizes that part of her, the Naido fragment, is in the Twin Peaks Sheriff's station. Fighting against her programming, Diane pleads this crucial truth to Gordon Cole. "I'm not me!" she cries, giving Cole a piteous look. She desperately wants Cole to know she's not responsible for her actions, that she's a victim, too. "I'm not me," she wails again and pulls the gun from her purse.

Before Diane can take further action, Tammy and Albert fire their weapons. Diane writhes amid a flurry of bullets and is suddenly whisked away, vanishing before the eyes of the three FBI agents.

Tammy is stunned; her voice shakes as she realizes she's just encountered a real tulpa. Albert is shocked, too; he gives Tammy a startled look. But Cole registers no surprise at all. He merely glances at the other agents and absently ponders what just happened. The only thing that puzzles him is Diane's mention of a "sheriff's station."

Gordon Cole has known Diane was a tulpa since Part 7, when he embraced Diane outside the Yankton Federal Prison ("I felt it when she hugged me," he tells Albert in Part 10), and he has not trusted her since. But Cole's lack of concern is odd. If he knew Diane was a tulpa, was he ever concerned about the *real* Diane? Was he worried about *her* welfare? Cordon Cole senses things no one else can. He knows about secret plans and invisible presences. For him, Diane's manifestation as a tulpa merely confirms deeper strategies at play. Cole can't keep all these secrets to himself. It's time he confesses a few to Albert (which he will, at the beginning of the next episode).

Meanwhile, the tulpa Diane finds herself deposited in the Red Room. Phillip Gerard tells her she has been manufactured, but Diane

---

*Diane says Cooper returned to her "about three or four years" after she last heard from him. If Cooper disappeared into the Black Lodge in 1989, that means Mr. C visited Diane sometime in 1992 or 1993.

knows all about it. Her body collapses, and a gold ball emerges from the raw material that once comprised her physical form. Her essence lingers here, in the Red Room, waiting for release.[*]

AT THE SILVER MUSTANG CASINO, Cooper says his farewells to Janey-E and Sonny-Jim, both of whom are startled by this new, confident Dougie. Cooper expresses his love and assures them that he will be back. Cooper misspeaks at first and says "Dougie" will be back, but then he corrects himself and says, "*I* will be back." Deep down, Cooper knows he will not see this family again. Despite his profound love for them, his destiny lies elsewhere.

But Dale Cooper will not break their hearts. He has arranged with Phillip Gerard to "make another" tulpa who can return to a life with Janey-E and Sonny Jim. Cooper says he'll "walk through that red door and be home for good," believing he can leave his Las Vegas family yet still provide a replacement. For him, both outcomes are possible. Janey-E easily accepts Cooper's bizarre farewell and expresses her gratitude: "Whoever you are, thank you." In this romanticized fantasy, Janey-E acquiesces to Cooper's narrative.

Cooper's idealized world also extends to the Mitchum brothers. He tells them they need not fear any reprisal from law enforcement because he can vouch for their characters. "I am witness to the fact that you both have hearts of gold," he says. That's all Bradley and Rodney need to hear. They smile widely and clap each other on the shoulder. Candie smiles too, confirming that the Mitchums "really do" have hearts of gold. It's all one big happy family in the Mitchum inner circle, a perfect world that will carry Cooper to Twin Peaks and his destiny.

AT LAST, AUDREY HORNE arrives at the Roadhouse. She and Charlie walk through the door just as singer Edward Louis Severson,[†] concludes his song, "Out of Sand." Because she arrives late, Audrey misses

---

[*] Interestingly, Phillip Gerard does not retrieve the gold ball "seed" from Diane's chair (at least we don't see him retrieve it). When the Dougie tulpa evaporated in Part 3, Gerard picked up the gold seed and pocketed it. This time, however, he lets it remain in the chair. I'd argue that Diane's persona (or soul) has some agency in the Red Room and is not subject to Gerard's control. Diane still has a mission to fulfill (as we will see in Part 17).

[†] The birth name of singer Eddie Vedder.

the song's prophetic lyrics ("I stare at my reflection to the bone/Blurred eyes look back at me"), but, then again, maybe she doesn't. Audrey has not arrived at the real Roadhouse (if there is such a place); this Roadhouse is imaginary, conjured by Audrey as a transitional space. If she can navigate her way through here, perhaps she can find freedom. If she can't—if she retreats and backs out the way she came—Audrey is likely to become trapped again. There's a lot at stake.

Audrey is on a threshold, a fact made startlingly clear when the Roadhouse band starts playing "Audrey's Dance" (the same music Audrey danced to on the Double R jukebox decades ago). The crowd disperses, offering her the dance floor, and Audrey becomes the center of attention. She dances, losing herself in the music. She moves slowly, *dreamily*, and as she does, her confidence grows.

But she's still afraid, and her fear manifests when one drunken man in the crowd accosts another. Audrey's idyll is shattered. She flees, grabbing Charlie and demanding he get her out of there.

And instantly Audrey "wakes" to another world. She is somewhere else, staring at herself in a mirror. Dressed in white and standing in a white space, she could be in a hospital or similar institution. She stares at her reflection in shock.

This is the end of Audrey's story, there is no more, but what we see here (and what Audrey sees) redefines all that came before. Everything up until now has been a product of Audrey's imagination, her mind finding refuge in fantasy. As David Lynch explains, "The mind is such a friend to us when it shuts off certain things. But there is a price for shutting off. It can fester. How big the mind is we do not know. It is a beautiful thing but sometimes it can be pitch-dark." Throughout her brief story in *The Return*, Audrey has been seeking release from her mental fugue. Her sudden appearance before the mirror implies that she has succeeded. She found a way out of the dark and into the light.

Despite being disconnected from the rest of that narrative, Audrey's story gives us insight into what is happening to Dale Cooper. Like Audrey, Cooper is paying a price for shutting things from his mind, insisting the world bend to his demands.

He can't bend reality forever. He, too, is due for an awakening.

<INTERLUDE 7>
MISSING PIECES: PUTTING "DIANE" TOGETHER

FEW CHARACTERS IN *TWIN PEAKS* are as elusive as Diane Evans, the longtime confidante and off-screen associate of FBI Special Agent Dale Cooper. After dwelling in the narrative margins for years, Diane finally takes the stage in *The Return*. She enters the story as an eldritch figure devised by Mr. C to do his bidding, but Diane is also enmeshed in Dale Cooper's secret plans, and her loyalties remain with him. Still, through most of the story Diane remains without agency, subject to the whims of powerful men. By the end, she's forgotten in the wake of Cooper's maneuvers. "Diane" may not even be her real name.

Diane's story is obscured, her character fractured, and it's easy to dismiss her as a narrative afterthought. But look deeper and you see a meaningful shape emerge. *The Return* provides ample clues to decipher Diane as a woman struggling to chart her own course, someone who eventually realizes that acquiescence will not culminate in "happily-ever-after." When her happy ending doesn't come—when her dreams are besieged by the preoccupations of Dale Cooper—Diane manages to save herself. In the end, she escapes the confines of Cooper's story and finds a story all her own.

Fragments

IN HER BOOK, *TELEVISION REWIRED*, Martha Nochimson observes that Diane "has too many bodies" and manifests within the narrative as four Diane "fragments." Nochimson argues that these fragments "neither fit together to form a whole, harmonious identity nor fit into any relationship or situation." She concludes that Diane is "not *really* anything." (Emphasis in the original.)

Nochimson's conclusion raises important questions. If Diane wasn't really anything, then why include her in the story? What was her function in the narrative? And what was the true nature of her relationship with Dale Cooper? There are no obvious answers to these questions. Diane remains inscrutable throughout. Still, if we study clues scattered within *The Return*, we can piece together a viable theory that clarifies Diane's presence. Nochimson is right that Diane is fragmented and cannot achieve a discernable, stable identity, but Diane is important to the story. She plays a unique and valuable role in how we ultimately interpret Dale Cooper.

David Lynch has been fascinated by dual identities and divided psyches for decades. In earlier works, Lynch depicts fractured identities as binary divisions, with characters either splitting into "good" and "evil" halves or seeking refuge in alternate identities: In *Lost Highway*, Fred Madison transforms into Pete Dayton to escape his perceived sexual impotence. In *Mulholland Drive*, Diane Selwyn fantasizes the persona of Betty Elms in order to escape a failed career and jilted love. I'd argue (I *have* argued) that Lynch explored dual identities in *Fire Walk With Me*, where Dale Cooper reimagines himself as another FBI agent (Chet Desmond) to relive his investigation of the unsolved murder of Teresa Banks.

Character fragmentation becomes more complex in *INLAND EMPIRE*, the last major film Lynch directed before working on *The Return*. As essayist Timothy William Galow observes, Lynch "discards the binary structure of the earlier films [in *INLAND EMPIRE*]" and "explores the relationship between trauma and fantasy through a multi-layered approach with more fluid boundaries." Laura Dern plays a character whose fractured identity shifts from one persona to another. "I thought of it as playing a broken or dismantled person," Dern explains, "with these other people leaking out of her brain." That description sounds like Diane Evans. Indeed, *INLAND EMPIRE* arguably establishes a template for interpreting how Diane is "distributed" throughout *The Return*. Like the character(s) in *INLAND EMPIRE*, Diane has been dismantled. The question is: Can she put herself back together?

(In an earlier chapter I used the *INLAND EMPIRE* template to analyze Audrey Horne, but such an analysis is equally valid when considering Diane. In fact, Lynch probably envisioned a fractured Diane long before he developed Audrey's story, which was added late in the production. It's not surprising that Lynch would apply themes of buried psychologies and multiple personalities to more than one character in *The Return*. These ideas are a constant throughout his work.)

Diane is devoted to Dale Cooper, and this devotion transcends the bounds of the forensic world. Throughout Cooper's journey in *The Return*, Diane is ever-present, repeatedly haunting Cooper as he moves along his path. To do this, Diane assumes multiple personalities, "fragments" (as Nochimson labels them) which take many forms. We see Diane in Naido, in Janey-E Jones, in three separate versions of the ostensible Diane, and in a final, rehabilitated Diane who is almost certainly the ambiguous figure known as Linda.

Naido

DURING THE FIRST STAGE of Cooper's journey, Cooper encounters Naido, a blind and unintelligible woman who inhabits the liminal space David Lynch calls "the Mansion Room." This Diane can hear Cooper, but she cannot see him. Naido must guess where Cooper is and hope he can decipher her breathy utterances and fitful gestures.

Naido personifies the "absent Diane," a figure who existed on the other side of Cooper's famous tape-recorder in the original series. Back then, Cooper shared his thoughts and observations with Diane through audio tapes. Cooper presumably mailed these tapes to Diane, who played them and heard his voice but never saw him. (If she replied, we don't know what she said or how she said it.) As the series progressed, Diane became less important to Cooper. He stopped recording messages and apparently forgot about her. Not surprisingly, this Diane—the one Cooper muted, blinded, and overlooked—manifests as Naido, the first Diane fragment.

Naido has been waiting to steer Cooper onto a specific path. After Cooper arrives, she pulls an inter-dimensional lever and reroutes him away from danger, an action which hurls Naido into a starry abyss. Ever faithful, Diane has sacrificed herself for Cooper, guiding him past the first barriers of his journey.

Naido falls to Earth, landing in the woods outside Twin Peaks. The sheriff's deputies rescue her and place her in a jail cell (ostensibly for her protection). Diane, as Naido, has inserted herself into the real world so she can intercept Cooper when he inevitably arrives.

Janey-E

IN THE MEANTIME, Cooper passes through the Number 3 socket in the Mansion Room and emerges in Las Vegas, exchanging places with Dougie Jones, a tulpa of Cooper. The newly arrived Cooper is purely good, a counterbalance to Mr. C's pure evil, but he lacks agency. Luckily for Cooper, Diane is there to guide him.

Diane appears as Dougie's wife, Janey-E Jones, the perfect domestic partner. Janey-E is loyal, affectionate, and protective. She values her relationship with Cooper and acts repeatedly to guard the life they've made together. Dale Cooper is a better version of her boorish husband, Dougie Jones, so it's easy for Janey-E to embrace him. She rises to his defense and protects him against loan-sharks and over-inquisitive law enforcement. In effect, Janey-E falls in love (true love) with Cooper.

It turns out, Janey-E is related to Diane. The two women are half-sisters. This biological connection is crucial because Janey-E is not some ephemeral avatar, she's Diane's flesh-and-blood surrogate. Unlike Naido—an aloof, impeded assistant—Janey-E becomes Cooper's intimate partner. She forms a spiritual and physical union with him, something the real Diane always wanted but was never able to do. In effect, Janey-E is a "pseudo-tulpa," conjured by Diane to achieve the "happily ever after" she has always dreamed about.

The Diane Tulpa (First Diane)

IN THE FIRST TWO SEASONS of *Twin Peaks*, Diane was discernable only through Dale Cooper's recorded messages, a blank slate onto whom we, the audience, projected certain traits. We knew Cooper relied on Diane, that he shared his feelings with her and even confessed to her, and so we imagined Diane as Cooper's "right-hand woman," his resourceful, dependable, *loyal* assistant. In *The Return*, when Gordon Cole and Albert Rosenfield request Diane's help, we expect her to enthusiastically agree, to become a stalwart ally of Cole and his team.

That doesn't happen. Instead, the Diane we see is bitter, angry, and rude. She's foul language and bad habits, world-weary and suspicious. When Cole and Albert explain that Cooper is in jail, her terse response is simply: "Good." This Diane is a far cry from the one we imagined.

That's because this Diane is not the true Diane, the one Albert and Cole knew and worked with long ago. This Diane is something else.

Diane's tragic backstory is revealed late in the story (in Part 16) when she reveals that, years ago, she was raped and captured by Mr. C (whom she assumed was Cooper). Mr. C removed Diane from the real world and took her to a place that resembled "an old gas station" (almost certainly the "convenience store" known as The Dutchman's). There, Mr. C created a "tulpa" of Diane—an exact replica with all the memories, emotions, and characteristics of the human Diane, but programmed to obey specific orders. This tulpa was installed back in the real world where it waited to be activated. Indeed, when Gordon Cole brings the Diane tulpa into the Blue Rose fold, Mr. C uses her as a spy to provide regular updates about the team's investigation into the reappearance of Major Briggs.

But there's more to Diane's backstory. Before he disappeared, Cooper told Diane of a secret plan he was concocting with Cole and Major Briggs—a plan to locate the entity known as "Judy" (and, most likely, a plan to stop Bob). Cooper shared the details of this plan with Diane, hoping she might someday help him.

By revealing the plan to Diane, Cooper placed her in great danger. When Mr. C escapes the Red Room, he targets and torments Diane in order to sabotage Cooper's plans. He creates a false version of Diane and puts her right back where he found the original. Mr. C, thinking like Dale Cooper (because he *is* Dale Cooper), knows Diane will be the perfect spy.

Oblivious to Mr. C's schemes, Gordon Cole believes Diane will be an asset to the Blue Rose Task Force. After questioning Mr. C in Yankton Federal Prison (in Part 4) Cole tells Albert, "We need one certain person to take a look at Cooper," and he assigns Albert to locate Diane. When Albert cannot convince her to cooperate, Cole tries to persuade her himself, but Diane is obstinate and refuses. Cole says something that changes her mind, however. He reminds Diane that she's part of Cooper's plan: "This is extremely important, Diane, and it involves something that you know about, and that's enough said about that."

Cole will say no more, but his generic nudge ("this involves something you know about") is enough to soften Diane. "Federal prison," she repeats resignedly, "South Dakota." She knows she has to go.

Cole obliquely references Cooper's plan again in Part 9, when he tells Diane the team needs to make an unexpected detour: "It could be of some interest to you," he says, "an old case involving a man Agent Cooper once knew." Diane knows exactly what Cole is talking about and responds by saying, "the Blue Rose case." Cole has been vague (he never mentions Major Briggs by name), but Diane knows about this specific case: *the* Blue Rose case. She remembers Cooper's partnership with Major Briggs and their "plan" to find Judy. Diane could only know these details because Cooper told her. She may not remember everything about the plan, but she remembers enough. *It's of interest to her.*

Shortly after arriving in Buckhorn, Diane receives a text from Mr. C ("around the dinner table the conversation is lively"), a coded message that activates her tulpa programming. She's helpless now but to spy on Cole and the team. Still, aspects of the real Diane lurk deep within. She's waiting for just the right moment to betray Mr. C.

That moment comes in Part 16, when she receives another coded command, this one directing her to kill Gordon Cole. Diane gasps when she sees it; she is physically jolted. Diane knows the command means her time on Earth is almost over. But something else happens, too. Memories flood back, memories of Cooper and his plan, and it takes Diane by surprise. "I remember," she whispers, and a deep rumbling pervades the scene. "Oh. Oh, Coop," she exhales deeply. "I remember."

Indeed, in this crucial moment Diane's purpose becomes clear. She grabs her phone and sends Mr. C the coordinates she surreptitiously gathered from Albert, the true coordinates, the ones Major Briggs made sure Bill Hastings and Ruth Davenport would find. These coordinates lead to a specific portal deep in the woods near Twin Peaks, a portal Cooper and Major Briggs (and quite likely The Fireman) have rigged to deposit Mr. C at the Twin Peaks Sheriff's station. "I hope this works," she exhales, knowing that the fragile plan Cooper developed years ago is no guarantee to stop Mr. C. Still, she knows this is what Cooper would have wanted. The real Diane has emerged, if only for a moment, while the rude, abrasive tulpa briefly recedes.

Diane's tulpa programming cannot be completely ignored, however, and she turns toward her destiny with Gordon Cole. She has no choice here—she must kill Cole—but before she does, she wants Cole to know the truth he asked about when they stood outside Yankton Federal Prison. Diane wasn't ready to reveal it then, but she is now. She tells Cole what "Cooper" did to her years ago, how he raped her and took her away from this world into some dark, supernatural realm.

As she tells Cole her darkest secret, new memories emerge, a realization of what Diane is and is not. For a moment she glimpses a refracted identity, her true self in pieces, scattered across the universe. "I'm in the Sheriff's station," she gasps, almost in disbelief. The staggering truth pours in: "I'm not me," she sobs. And in this elastic moment of compliance and compulsion, when she pulls her gun and is violently whisked away to the Red Room, Diane knows she is but a fragment of a greater whole, one piece of a larger "Diane" entity. "Someone manufactured you," Phillip Gerard tells the newly arrived Diane, but she's already way ahead of him. She stares into the distance and says, "I know."

The Diane tulpa in *The Return* parallels Nikki Grace, one of Laura Dern's many characters in *INLAND EMPIRE*. At one point in the film, when Nikki feels her identity slip away, her words resemble those of Diane in Part 16: "I'm remembering.... This whole thing starts flooding in, this whole memory...I don't know what it is." Nikki has a dawning realization: "It's me. It's me."

Nikki is an invented identity, an alter-ego. She's "Sue Blue's fantasy," according to author Bill Roberts, or, as essayist Todd McGowan theorizes, she's "the fantasmatic figure" originating from an absent character McGowan calls "The Lost Girl." By these readings, Nikki is no different than the tulpa "thought-form" that is Diane. Like Nikki, Diane glimpses another identity. "I remember," she exclaims when she reads Mr. C's text, and a deeper persona gains traction within her psyche.

Naido and the Idealized Diane (Second Diane)

BEFORE VANISHING, Diane realized that another version of herself was in the Twin Peaks Sheriff's station. She knew she was Naido, waiting for Cooper to arrive.

The events that transpire late in the narrative—those depicted in Part 17, in which Cooper returns to Twin Peaks—are highly subjective and open to many interpretations, but no matter how you read them, these events are heightened, as if presented through a skewed and biased point of view. Indeed, the reality we see in Part 17 is one Dale Cooper *imposes* on the world. He's not simply watching events; he's overtly narrating them to himself (and to us, the audience). Frustrated that things have not transpired as he hoped, Cooper attempts to steer the story in a different direction.

Despite Cooper's biased view of the world, Diane makes contact. A distillation of Diane's soul resides in the Red Room, a remnant of her tulpa form. This essence overlaps with Naido and transports itself into Cooper's fantasy. She knows that Cooper's idealized world calls for an idealized Diane, and that's exactly what she gives him. Naido transforms into a perfect Diane, someone who worships Dale Cooper and stands steadfastly by his side. Cooper and Diane share a passionate kiss, and Diane tells him what he wants to hear: "Cooper," she says admiringly, "the one and only." This "fantasy Diane" humors Cooper as she takes her place beside him.

This perfect Diane accompanies Cooper through the next stage of his mission. Attached now to Cooper's psyche, Diane (along with Gordon Cole) travels into the shadows of fantasy (a "never-never land," as Lynch calls it), emerging into an imaginary Great Northern basement. Diane can only get this far, though. Cooper takes his leave, parting from Diane and saying he'll see her again at "the curtain call."

Diane has done all she can. She has shepherded Cooper along his path and steered him clear of dangers and threats. There's nothing left to do. Cooper is determined to do the impossible, to somehow prevent Laura Palmer's murder and set the world back in order. Diane forlornly watches as Cooper steps across a threshold of hubris and into the unknown.

Diane has no choice but to simply wait for Cooper to appear again. Aware, now, of all her swirling fragments, the pieces she has scattered along Cooper's path, Diane reassembles herself into the true Diane, the autonomous Diane, the Diane who will do everything she can to save Cooper and bring him into her life. This is the Diane who waits for Cooper on the other side of the curtain.

The Real Diane (Third Diane)

AND SO, WE COME TO THE REAL DIANE (or the "realest" Diane) of *The Return*. Having shadowed Cooper throughout the tale, Diane waits for Cooper in the remote woods of Glastonbury Grove, standing before the ring of twelve sycamore trees, the Red Room curtains a membrane between one world and another. She stands there calmly, certain that Cooper will emerge at this moment, in this spot, and he does. Cooper parts the curtains and steps into the woods.

How did Diane come to be in this remote place at this exact time? We know that Diane was brought to the Dutchman's where Mr. C made a tulpa, but what happened to her after that? Presumably, Diane became trapped in her own Red Room, and, like Cooper, was stuck in a psychological realm of uncertainty and stasis. (The Red Room is not exclusive to Cooper, it's an abstraction, a variable realm that reflects each mind that enters. "It changes, depending on whoever walks into it," Lynch tells us. In other words, everyone, including Diane, has their own Red Room.)

Like Cooper, Diane could not leave her Red Room until she re-assembled her fragments. The demise of the tulpa, the transformation of Naido, and Diane's reconnection with Cooper—all contribute to making her whole again. Once restored, Diane is free to exit the Red Room and "find Cooper." (This is the same process Cooper had to undergo in order to get out.)

Cooper and Diane's greeting in Glastonbury Grove is markedly different than their exaggerated encounter in Part 17. Both are tentative. They cautiously inquire about each other as if they've been apart for many years. Indeed, when Lynch directed this scene, he told Kyle MacLachlan and Laura Dern, "You haven't seen each other for twenty-five years. Really and truly." His emphasis ("really and truly") proves that Diane—the real Diane—has finally found Cooper. Their reunion in Part 17 wasn't real, but this one is. *Really and truly.*

Diane searches Cooper's face, placing him in her memory. She touches his cheek, and he looks deeply into her eyes. "Is it really you?" they both ask each other, and both affirm their identities. Despite all their years apart, they share great affection for one another. Notably, they do not kiss; that kind of intimacy is rare. (Their kiss in Part 17 doesn't count. It was wish-fulfillment, Cooper's fantasy.)

Diane's appearance to Cooper proves a strong, unwavering commitment. She has traversed time, space and dimensional barriers to be with him. No one else, not even Gordon Cole, has managed to get this far.

Diane has given her body and soul to see Cooper to this endpoint. As Dern explains, "Diane is Cooper's true love because she understands the split in him that he's battling, and she's been the most victimized by it—perhaps more than Cooper himself." Fractured into pieces and cast upon interdimensional and psychological tides, Diane expects Dale Cooper to finally see her—to understand and appreciate all that she has done, all that she has sacrificed and endured to achieve her (their) "happily ever after." She needs to be *acknowledged*. It's time for them to start a life together. Time to drive off into the sunset.

Drive off they do, but not in the direction Diane had hoped. Cooper is not finished with his mission. He has more to do and fully expects Diane to accompany him, to faithfully support him as she always has. Cooper is determined to "find Laura."

Wearily, reluctantly, Diane remains with Cooper on this next stage of his journey, but she's not as committed as Cooper is. "You sure you want to do this?" she asks as they drive through barren landscapes toward some impossible destination. Cooper doesn't answer; he merely gives her a blank glance. Her apprehension doesn't register. He looks at her, but he doesn't see her.

Diane tries again. She gently challenges Cooper's judgment: "You don't know what it's going to be like once we—" but Cooper cuts her off. "I know that," he says, unmoved by Diane's concerns. He's focused on what's in front of him.

Diane tries a third time to steer Cooper onto a different path. As he's about to get out of the car, she puts her hand on his arm, and says, "Just think about it, Cooper," but Cooper doesn't look at her this time. He stares straight ahead and determinedly exits the car. Diane watches him go; dismay etched upon her face. As Cooper walks along the side of the road, Diane swallows hard. This may be her last chance to back out.

Cooper returns more determined than ever, but he notices Diane's hesitation. He wants to move forward, but he needs Diane to accompany him. And so, he relies on a shameful tactic. "Kiss me," he demands, playing upon her affection and love. Overwhelmed, torn, she gives him a pained look. She can't resist his spell, and with some hesitation she leans across and kisses Cooper. She's timid at first, but more passionate as the moment stretches. Finally, she relents. "Let's go," she says, summoning the courage to cross another threshold with this man who holds her in his thrall.

Cooper moves the car forward, and together he and Diane cross over into…something. Another time. Another reality. Maybe just another state of mind. Wherever of whenever they've gone, Diane has time to think. Cruising through the desert darkness, speeding along a highway lost in the night, Diane contemplates the new existence into which she has fallen. Cooper's kiss was a manipulation. He still doesn't see her. Not really.

After minutes, or hours, or some immeasurable amount of time, Cooper pulls into the lot of a roadside motel. He stops the car and says nothing; he simply exits and walks toward the motel's front office.

The camera stays on Diane as she watches Cooper walk away. This is Diane's story, her point-of-view (it has been since Cooper exited Glastonbury Grove). Sitting alone, thinking about what Cooper wants, she senses something imminent. She intuits that Cooper will ask her to sacrifice something sacred and precious, and it frightens her. No matter how much she gives to Cooper, it will never be enough. In these moments, alone in a dark car, Diane knows Cooper is beyond her reach.

She has been shattered and reassembled, Diane has, all for the love of Dale Cooper. Her identity has been entirely defined through him, through how she hopes he sees her. Now, she knows he can't see her. He won't see her. He will never see her. "It's really me," she assured Cooper. But who is Diane, really?

As these thoughts fill her mind, Diane sees another version of herself step out from behind one of the motel's brick pillars. Diane registers no shock or emotion at this other self, this apparition standing a few feet away, staring blankly at her. Light washes across Diane's face as she watches from the car. Shadows shift and flow over her features. In this moment, Diane relinquishes her identity. She lets go of the Diane who could not let go of Dale Cooper.

Cooper emerges from the office. (The Diane double has vanished.) He walks to the door of a motel room and stops, waiting stubbornly for Diane to come to him. She looks at him without affect and without hope. All that remains in this relationship are the mechanics of what Cooper demands. The Diane who once harbored expectation and aspiration has gone, and a different Diane, an empty Diane, exits the car and goes to Cooper.

Diane's glimpse of her double recalls a scene in *INLAND EMPIRE* where Laura Dern's character looks across a nighttime street and sees another version of herself glaring back. This moment is critical, for it signals that one aspect of Dern's core character (the one whose monologue anchors the film and from whom, Dern explained, "other people leaked") is confronting veiled identities in a search for a truer, more stable self. Shortly after the nameless woman sees her double, she enters a room and delivers the last of four monologues, her final confession in which she describes a man (perhaps her husband) who has kept things from her. "Men don't change," she says at one point, "[but] in time they reveal what they really are." In *The Return*, Diane sees her double emerge from behind the pillar and glimpses herself the way Cooper sees her—deferential and obedient. In this moment Diane recognizes Cooper for what he really is.

Diane follows Cooper into the motel room and turns on the light, forcing Cooper to see her. Cooper prefers to keep her in the dark and tells her to turn the light off. Maybe that's his last transgression, the final proof of Cooper's disregard, the moment when Diane makes the excruciating decision to leave. For too long her sense of self has been contingent upon Cooper's limiting gaze, and that must end. Only Diane can define herself.

Diane and Cooper kiss and soon engage in sexual intercourse, but Diane shows no joy in the act. She looks at Cooper's blank face and sees, even during this most intimate moment, that he still doesn't see her. He won't connect with her. As Diane moves rhythmically on top of Cooper, she kisses him and then kisses him again. She is saying good-bye, moving past him to something else.

Diane puts her hands over Cooper's face and covers his eyes, deny-ing his gaze, ensuring an untainted transformation to her new identity. Holding her hands firmly against his face, she blinds him, imposing upon Cooper the same sensory limitations she experienced as Naido. And then Diane breaks contact with him for good. She looks away and does not look at Cooper again.

The grief on Diane's face is obvious, but something else is there, too. A determination. A certainty. As traumatic as this break is, Diane has committed herself to the act. There will be no going back. She takes leave of her old identity and frees herself from Cooper. Crucially, she also frees herself from Cooper's story. Diane narrates her own life now. Hers is an independent story, sundered from the world of Dale Cooper.

Linda (Liberated Diane)

HINDU PHILOSOPHY ADVISES, "sometimes you have to sacrifice something or break a relationship to serve a greater cause." The Maharishi Mahesh Yogi (whose philosophy informs much of David Lynch's creative approach to *The Return*) explains, "The important thing is to be able…to sacrifice what we are for what we could become." Not all of Lynch's protagonists understand such counsel, but Diane arrives at this hard truth. For most of her life Diane had faith in Cooper, faith that he would eventually meet her halfway and they would make a life together. But it was not to be. Cooper was always the dominant figure, a presence who kept Diane from actualization. Now, at last, Diane has removed herself from Dale Cooper's "observer effect" and found a world where she can be her own self.

Diane has become Linda.

Fittingly, Linda immediately rejects Cooper's identity. In a farewell note, she labels him as "Richard," a name that means nothing to her. (This arbitrary taxonomy recalls the nameless woman's assertion in *INLAND EMPIRE*: "There was this man I once knew. His name was…it doesn't matter what his name was.") Diane and Cooper's roles have reversed. For years, Cooper wouldn't see Diane, now Diane no longer sees Cooper.

The next morning, Cooper wakes and reads the note but, blind to Diane's plight and subsequent emancipation, makes no sense of it. In the note, Linda tells Richard she has left for good: "Please don't try to find me. I don't recognize you anymore. Whatever it was we had together is over." Diane's choice of words here is important: "I don't recognize you anymore," means she's no longer acknowledging Cooper. She's not saying she sees Cooper differently or believes he has become someone else. Diane is telling Cooper: "I don't accept you. I don't *see* you. I disavow you." Cooper hasn't changed, Diane has.[*]

Diane's story has been one of disaffection and estrangement, but her story does not end in tragedy. She takes control and charts a new course. We may not know where she went as Linda or what her future holds, but her transformation—*and her agency to effect that transformation*—represents a triumph. As Rourke describes the nameless woman in *INLAND EMPIRE*, Linda in *The Return* "exceeds the limits of the fictional frame." Her story exists outside the narrative, inenarrable, impossible to follow. But it's enough. While we cannot continue with Diane (now Linda) on her journey, we know she found a way out.

Cooper Incomplete

THE STORY OF DIANE EVANS in *Twin Peaks: The Return*, like the character of Diane herself, is easy to dismiss as a tragic subplot adding little to the overall narrative. But there's another way to interpret it. Diane's story has value because it contextualizes the tragedy of Dale Cooper.

David Lynch weaves Diane's story around Cooper's in order to show that Diane represents a better path for Cooper, an opportunity for him to realize happiness with the woman who truly loves him. Tragically, Cooper is so focused on his mission, he fails to include Diane as part of it.

Cooper's disregard has consequence; it ultimately leads to confusion and despair. The Fireman warns Cooper (albeit cryptically): "Re-

---

[*] Diane's farewell note recalls Jean Cocteau's observation about failed relationships: "When a Frenchman has fallen out of a love with a woman and can't stand the sight of her, what he says, literally, is 'I can't see her anymore.'"

member Richard and Linda." The Fireman knows that the "Richard and Linda" scenario is the wrong outcome, and he tries to steer Cooper from a doomed path. In effect, he implicitly advises Cooper to value Diane, to elevate her, to acknowledge the strength she can bring to Cooper's life.

Diane tempers Cooper, she balances him. She is what Carl Jung calls the *anima*, the "personification of all feminine psychological tendencies in a man's psyche, such as feelings and moods, prophetic hunches, receptiveness to the irrational, capacity for personal love, feeling for nature, and—last but not least—his relation to the unconscious." Without his Diane anima, Cooper (as we see him in Part 18) is incomplete. He is humorless and harsh, unbending and obdurate. He doesn't see the world around him, only the goal in front of him. Cooper's choice to ignore Diane highlights the deficits of his character and the futility of his "go-it-alone" attitude.

Imagine if Cooper had invited Diane to come with him rather than demanding it. Imagine if he had treated her as a partner rather than a means to an end. With Diane by his side, Cooper might very well have found Laura and confidently delivered her to her true purpose. Then Cooper and Diane could have exited the narrative with grace and surety. But Cooper chooses to proceed without Diane (he still believes he is "the one and only") and ends up lost in the night. As Martha Nochimson notes, Cooper does not "accept Diane's offer to relationship...opting for a course of action that leads to nonbeing."

Diane was Cooper's missing piece. She completed him. With her by his side he might have found harmony. Instead, he withered and became lost in the night.

PART 17:
THE PAST DICTATES THE FUTURE

FOR SEVENTEEN EPISODES of *The Return*, David Lynch employs a careful storytelling strategy, one that subverts the kind of narrative we're used to seeing. Rather than have Dale Cooper move across the stage, Lynch positions Cooper outside the proscenium. He's a figure we, the audience, inhabit. As such, we must construct a profile of Cooper by how we experience him, not by how he performs.

Dale Cooper is haunted by truths he'd prefer to ignore. He believes he's a hero, a leader, "the one and only," but he's none of those things. Like everyone else, Cooper is irrational, compulsive, and selfish. He's also haunted by failure, guilty that he could not prevent the murder of Laura Palmer or the suffering of his friends. This guilt obsesses Cooper, and, as he watches the real world from a remove, he dwells in lives that suffer and strain.

Cooper is also impatient. He may be drawn to pain, but he's not interested in following where the pain leads. His curiosity about those he observes lasts only as long as their stories align with his. Cooper's impatience gets the better of him in Part 16, and he takes over the story. He stops watching and starts devising. He vaults himself onto center stage

Lynch has employed this storytelling tactic before. The story of *INLAND EMPIRE* is conveyed through the psychological musings of an absent character—Laura Dern's Monologue Woman—who tries to make sense of her tormented life by spinning a tale that's one part wish-fulfillment, one part truth, and one part folktale. As a result, fact and fiction become jumbled. As Brian Rourke notes, "Lynch subverts [...]

the distinction between real and imaginary characters, moving from
[…] implied dream to crystal images, in which *actual and virtual can
no longer be distinguished.*" (Emphasis added.) In trying to make sense
of her history, the Monologue Woman inserts herself into a story that
is both real and make-believe: "She is both puppet and puppeteer in
her own story."

Cooper, too, becomes puppet and puppeteer. He concocts a heroic
fantasy in which he can defeat the villain and save the girl. That's the
story he's been telling since he first drove into Twin Peaks all those
years ago. It's the story he wants people to see.

Deluded by this sense of superiority, Cooper drives his story toward
the impossible. He's determined to re-write history and change the very
course of the universe.

But Cooper can't escape an inevitable reality: He's not a superhero.
He's not all-powerful. *And he can't change the past.* Only after
reckoning with this hard truth can Cooper reorient himself and escape
his psychic fugue.

THE TULPA OF DIANE EVANS has just vanished before the eyes of
Gordon Cole, Albert Rosenfield, and Tammy Preston. Naturally, the
first thing these agents do is have a glass of wine. The Blue Rose Task
Force sure loves their vino.

A deflated Cole sits apart from the others, lamenting that he could
not fire his gun at Diane, despite her obvious threat and almost certain
supernatural provenance. Musing about what just transpired and
recognizing his dangerous encounter with otherworldly forces (the
existence of which Albert and Tammy take in stride), Cole is compelled
to confess to Albert a decades-old plan.

What follows is more lengthy exposition, Cole's revelation of
deeper schemes at play. The plan Cole describes is supposedly the engine that drives much of the story, and Cole attempts to clarify to
Albert (and to us) what the FBI's mission has truly been, but while Cole
sheds light on the motives and actions of various behind-the-scenes
players, his disclosures ultimately result in more questions than answers (for the viewer, at least).

According to Cole, twenty-five years ago, Major Briggs discovered an entity of extreme negative force known as "Jowday" (i.e., "Judy").[*] Briggs, Cole, and Cooper put together a plan that would lead them to Judy, but Briggs and Cooper disappeared (just like Phillip Jeffries had years earlier).[†]

Cole reveals that the last thing Cooper said to him was, "I'm trying to kill two birds with one stone," a colloquial way of saying that Cooper had two goals in mind when he went into the Red Room. The first was to find Judy (that's what the Briggs/Cole/Cooper "plan" was about). The second goal is harder to ascertain, but it probably had to do with stopping Bob from further plaguing the world. Cooper believed he understood what Bob was and could put an end to him.

Yes, we might assume Cooper's second goal was to reverse Laura Palmer's fate, to save her from being murdered (that's what he tries to do later in this episode), but a close reading of *The Return* challenges this assumption. When Cooper encounters the luminous "Laura" in Part 2, he emphatically states, "Laura Palmer is dead," confirming that he has accepted her death; he understands her fate has been sealed. It's only later, when Cooper believes himself super-heroic, that he attempts to change the past.

Before Cooper set out to enact his plan, he was prescient enough to alert Cole to his possible disappearance. "If I disappear," he told Cole, "Do everything you can to find me."

That begs the question: Has Gordon Cole really done everything he could to find Cooper? I think it's unlikely. In fact, Cole may have lost interest in Cooper's plight altogether. He didn't stay in touch with Diane, he was unaware of Albert's contact with Phillip Jeffries, and he had no knowledge of Mr. C's actions in Rio de Janeiro and in New York City. Cole has, apparently, done very little to find Cooper

---

[*] In the original series, Briggs revealed that he was part of an unofficial group within the Airforce seeking a place called The White Lodge. Briggs likely "discovered" Jowday when he disappeared around March 15, 1989 (as shown in episode 17). Upon his return, Briggs wondered if what he encountered in another realm had been meant "for [his] soul," and he remembered images of a hooded figure, an owl, and flames.

[†] It's worth noting here that Cole describes the disappearances of Briggs, Cooper, and Jeffries but never mentions the disappearance of Chet Desmond. This omission reinforces my theory that Chet Desmond is not a major player—and may not even exist—in the world Gordon Cole inhabits.

(although, to be fair, Cole has kept tabs on Ray Monroe, the FBI's confidential informant embedded within Mr. C's operation).

Throughout *The Return*, Cole has been struggling to make sense of events. He's confused from the start, telling Albert in Part 4, "I don't understand this situation at all." And now, thirteen parts later, he says, "I don't know at all if this plan's unfolding properly." That's a long time to be baffled.[*]

That's about to change. Cole receives a call from Las Vegas and speaks with Bushnell Mullins, who reads the note that Cooper gave him. At last, Gordon Cole gets a direct message from Dale Cooper: "I'm headed for Sheriff Truman's. It is 2:53 in Las Vegas and that adds up to a ten, the number of completion." There's a clear and definitive message here: Cooper is heading to Twin Peaks. But the rest is ambiguous. Cole remains confused about what Cooper is up to. Any plan Cole may have previously expected is now out the window. The only thing he can do now is pack up the team and head to Twin Peaks to find out what happens next.

IN TWIN PEAKS, Ben Horne receives a call from the police in Jackson Hole, Wyoming. They say they've picked up Jerry, who needs a ride home (and some clothes, because he's apparently naked). This brief scene gives us some closure on Jerry (he made it out of the woods), but not much on Ben. Throughout the story, Ben's been stuck behind his desk, taking calls, receiving visitors, dealing with the outside world from the confines of his office. That's where we leave him, static within the mournful chambers of the Great Northern, doomed to the

---

[*] Whether by accident or design, Cole's confusion about Cooper's plan serves as a meta-commentary on the story-telling sensibilities (and tensions) between Mark Frost and David Lynch. Frost has described how he and Lynch "mapped out" many aspects of the story while scripting the series but that Lynch later revised and expanded much of it. "[We] seemed in concert while we were writing, but I can't vouch for what [Lynch] was thinking or where he went with some of it afterwards." It's no wonder, then, that parts of the backstory of *The Return* simply don't add up. Lynch re-configured the careful tale he and Frost had developed, altering it from their original "plan" by adding elements like "Richard and Linda." While Lynch's final vision in *The Return* is sublime, his artistic whims result in a baffling, sometimes inconsistent narrative. Frost tried to clarify some of the story in his book, *The Final Dossier* ("I was trying to offer a little more perspective, clues about what it all might have meant"), but even he could not satisfactorily decrypt Lynch's esoteric vision. (Then again neither can Lynch, who admits, "I do not know the answers. There are many things I do not know.")

nostalgia of childhood memories and fearful of a broken world outside (his damaged children, his failed marriage). Poor Ben, he's literally gone nowhere since Part 1. Perhaps he never will. Perhaps, like the many spirits already roaming the halls of the Great Northern, Ben is fated to stay in the hotel forever, another ghost within its walls.

MR. C FINALLY ARRIVES in the forest outside Twin Peaks, and the vast and mysterious forces working against him spring their carefully orchestrated trap. The coordinates he received from Diane lead Mr. C to the spot 253 yards east of Jack Rabbit's Palace, the same place where Andy vanished into the vortex. Mr. C believes this location will bring him to Experiment, the creature that broke free from the glass box in Part 1, the entity Mr. C crudely drew on an ace-of-spades and showed to Darya. Experiment is what Mr. C "wants."

The portal in the woods can, indeed, convey Mr. C to Experiment (who currently resides within the Palmer house in Twin Peaks), but what Mr. C doesn't know is that The Fireman and Major Briggs have rigged the portal to force Mr. C somewhere else.

There is no ambiguity here. David Lynch is uncommonly explicit about what happens in the next few minutes. When Mr. C enters the portal, he is instantly caged inside the Fireman's "theater room" (where Major Briggs hovers nearby, monitoring Mr. C's entrapment). An image of the Palmer house appears on the theater screen, but the Fireman swipes his hand, causing the image to slide away and be replaced by another—the parking lot just outside the Twin Peaks Sheriff's station. Mr. C is sucked into a tube, the same mechanism that transferred the golden "Laura Palmer" orb to Earth in Part 8, which rotates and deposits him into the image. The meaning here is obvious: The Fireman and Major Briggs have forcibly rerouted Mr. C to a specific location, a place where they have positioned (and programmed) various players to defeat Mr. C.

Mr. C appears in the parking lot and is startled by his new location, "What is this?" he asks.[*] Nearby, Andy Brennan sees Mr. C and is delighted. Agent Cooper has returned at last!

---

[*] Mr. C originally had no dialog here. His line, "What is this?" originates from Part 13 (when he arrived at The Farm) and has been used again here, dubbed into a shot showing the back of Mr. C's head.

Andy introduces Mr. C to Frank Truman, and his programming (installed by the Fireman) activates. Andy pauses and stares into the distance, and then, when Mr. C declines a cup a coffee, Andy is fully triggered. He rushes out of Truman's office, stops beside Lucy's desk and says: "Very important, very important!" Andy hurries away to free James, Freddie, and Naido from jail. His role in all of this is simple, to put the key figures in place so that The Fireman's plan will proceed accordingly.

Truman looks at Mr. C and says the name, "Cooper" twice, acquiescing to the far-fetched concept of "two Coopers" (an idea he relayed to Gordon Cole in Part 14). When Truman receives a call from Dale Cooper (who is proceeding rapidly toward the station) Truman knows he is facing the "bad" Cooper.

Both Truman and Mr. C reach for their guns. There is loud bang, and Truman's hat pops up. Mr. C falls violently to the floor, shot in the chest by Lucy Brennan, who stands in the doorway holding a pistol.

Andy arrives with James, Freddie and Naido. He surveys the scene and intuitively knows what Lucy did. He walks to her side and gently, reassuringly, touches her.

Lucy, for her part, is liberated by her actions. The world coalesces around her, and she realigns with time and space. "I understand cellular phones now," she declares, an innocent acknowledgment that she is no longer mired in a static past.

Cooper rushes into Frank Truman's office, ready to act, but stops short of approaching Mr. C. Instead, he watches as Woodsmen emerge from the shadows to work over the body (the same way they did in Part 8). Cooper doesn't leap into the fray, or shoot Bushnell Mullins's gun, or use the power of the Owl Cave Ring to send Mr. C back to the Red Room. He merely stands to the side, grimacing as the Woodsmen set to work. Cooper has materialized in the real world, but he is not "really there." He's helpless as the action unfolds around him.

The Woodsmen remove the Bob cyst from Mr. C, and it floats into the air, hovering below the ceiling of Truman's office. Bob sees Cooper and attacks, but Freddie Sykes steps forward and draws Bob away. With the pile-driver strength of his gloved fist, Freddie punches Bob again and again, sending him flying across the room. Bob fights back, pummeling Freddie and knocking him to the ground, but Freddie rallies and, with one final blow, shatters the cyst and destroys Bob.

Wait.

Is that right?

Has Bob been destroyed?

Bob is an elusive figure. He may be a demon, or he may be an avatar for the darkest elements of humanity. *The evil that men do* (as implied by his "birth" during the atomic blast in Part 8). Maybe Bob's both. Is there really a difference?

Fire Walk With Me suggests that Bob is a psychological figment, a trick Laura Palmer uses to shield herself from the truth about her father and to disguise her own feelings of guilt. In this reading, Bob is a mask, one that Leland Palmer, himself, hides behind to avoid culpability for his actions. David Lynch endorses this interpretation: "[Bob] is an abstraction in human form. That's not a new thing, but it's what Bob was." Indeed, *Fire Walk With Me* hints that Bob becomes a demon only when you allow him to. Yes, he's "the evil that men do," but men are still responsible for that evil. By this interpretation, Bob is not physically real, he's *psychologically* real, manifesting when a person chooses to do bad things. If that's the case, Bob can never be destroyed.

"Everybody is a mix of good and evil," Lynch tells us. "Almost everybody has a bunch of stuff swimming in them, and I don't think most people are aware of the dark parts of themselves." In *Twin Peaks*, Bob is that "dark part." He was for Laura. He was for Leland. *And he is for Cooper.* Once again, Bob becomes a convenient scapegoat. As far as Cooper is concerned, "Bob" is the true source behind the evil that Cooper (as Mr. C) performed. Cooper had nothing to do with any of it.[*]

Indeed, Mr. C is a stark reminder of Cooper's "shadow self," the darkness and obscenity lurking within. Rather than acknowledge Mr.

---

[*] Ostensibly, Bob "hitched a ride" with Mr. C out of the Red Room and functioned as Mr. C's familiar (much the way he did with Mike when they were allies). Bob performed various tasks for Mr. C, such as disrupting the electrical system in Yankton Federal Prison in Part 5. Once Mr. C was incapacitated, Bob raged around Truman's office, tangled with Freddie, and then dissipated back into the world (just as he did after fleeing Leland Palmer's body in episode 16 of the original series). Bob's "destruction" in Truman's office is essentially performance art for Dale Cooper's sake. Cooper imagines Bob destroyed because he needs a satisfying and tidy ending.

C, or address his heinous actions, Cooper pretends he never existed. He places the Owl Cave Ring on Mr. C and banishes him to the Red Room and then turns his back as if it was all a bad dream, something he can forget. Mr. C must not threaten the heroic image Cooper wants to project.

No mention of Mr. C is ever made again, this horrific creature who dominated the story, this fierce and feral Cooper who murdered, raped, and pillaged his way across the narrative. Mr. C has simply been dispatched to the shadows. Dale Cooper neither acknowledges nor redresses the wounds Mr. C inflicted. Cooper refuses any culpability; his fantasy cannot encompass the enormity of Mr. C, and so Cooper essentially erases him. If ever Cooper exhibited a fatal flaw, it is here, when he entirely abrogates his connection to Mr. C.

With Mr. C gone, Cooper is ready for his perfect ending. The hero at last (even though he hasn't done anything), Cooper literally takes center stage, standing before his assembled friends and dictating to them the facts of the case. With their undivided attention, Cooper is the star of the show.

There's still one more thing Cooper needs: the adoring, faithful presence of his true love. As if on cue, Naido transforms into Diane, who beams when she sees Cooper and praises him as "Dale Cooper, the one and only"—the exact words Cooper wants to hear. Diane gives Cooper a passionate kiss (she's his fantasy, after all) and joins him by his side. Faithfull and attentive, this Diane is Cooper's ideal companion.

Watch closely, though. Just before Diane appears, Cooper falters and turns his face away, as if recognizing the artifice of his situation. He quickly restabilizes, but something shifts in his psyche. It is at this moment that *another* Cooper—an extreme close-up of Cooper's face—materializes over the scene. In a low monotone, Cooper's looming face says, "We live inside a dream." His words reverberate, but nobody in the office, not even the Cooper standing there, reacts. That's because Cooper's face is not speaking to the figures on screen. He is speaking to himself—and to us.

The covert narrator has revealed himself.

Expressionless and transparent, Cooper's face becomes a new component in the story, a third entity, hovering between the viewers and the characters.

Cooper's face is a rare, extra-diegetic conceit on the part of David Lynch. With it, Lynch gives us a glimpse inside the narrative mechanics of *The Return*. Dale Cooper—the *real* Dale Cooper—is watching events from a remove. His consciousness exists outside, and separate from, the story playing out. "It's slippery," Lynch says to Kyle MacLachlan and Laura Dern as he directs them in this scene, "Something's slippery." He's not explicit, but Lynch wants his performers to know they're playing in an unreliable, undefinable reality.

Awake in The Red Room, Dale Cooper has been watching a story unfold. Frustrated by his limited control over what he watches, Cooper inserted an aspect of himself into the world and attempted to bend reality to his will. Now, with his avatar standing in the Sheriff's department, Cooper believes he can dictate what will happen next. The world will be as he is.

In fact, Cooper is assembling his story from bits and pieces of what he's already seen: He remembers boxing ("Battling 'Bud' Mullins," and the boxing match looping on Sarah Palmer's television) and repurposes these memories as Freddie Sykes, his "pugilist-to-the-rescue." Cooper recalls the passionate kiss shared by Ed and Norma and ensures that he and Diane share something equally intense. Cooper remembers the Great Northern key Ben Horne gave to Frank Truman, and he retrieves it, planning to use it in the basement of the hotel, the place where he watched James Hurley discover a mysterious door. All the pieces are there for Cooper to manufacture his ideal ending.

Cooper is so confident in his prowess that he hints at what he's about to do: "Some things are going to change," he explains. "The past dictates the future." In this moment, a supremely overconfident Cooper thinks he is superhuman, that he has God-like powers, that he can travel back in time and right a terrible wrong. He believes he can prevent Laura's Palmer's death.

Dale Cooper never learns. He tried this gambit once before, sending his consciousness into the past to intersect with Laura Palmer's dreaming mind in *Fire Walk With Me*, warning her not to take the Owl Cave Ring. He was wrong then, and he is wrong now. In fact, the very foundation of Cooper's philosophy is faulty. *The past does not dictate the future.* If it did, all of us would be victim to our histories, our pasts forever defining who we are and what our futures will be. Under this philosophy what hope do we have for change? What chance is there to make life better?

Too many characters in *The Return* have submitted to this belief. They have given up their will to be anything different than what they were twenty-five years ago. James Hurley still pines for Donna Hayward and Maddy Ferguson, singing to their ghosts on the Roadhouse stage. Shelly Briggs is still trapped in the same job and the same kind of fraught relationship. Ben Horne mourns his past as he shelters within the walls of The Great Northern. Carl Rodd, as always, just wants to stay where he is. Even Bobby Briggs remains haunted by poor choices from long ago; he's still crying over an unrequited love.

It doesn't have to be that way. Some characters have found release. When Nadine accepts who she is—when she rejects a history of co-dependence and selfishness—she breaks free from a stifling life. Andy Brennan does not fret about the past; he's always in the moment, content with who he is. Characters like Andy and Nadine have come to terms with themselves and succeeded. This philosophy is the key to happiness. "It's the self knowing the self," David Lynch tells us. "Know thyself. This is the thing—and so many things get better when you experience that." Andy Brennan knows himself, but Dale Cooper does not. One succeeds. The other fails.

Cooper has deluded himself into believing he can fix the past and magically fix all the wrongs, mistakes, heartbreak, and tragedy of the present. The supremely confident, super-heroic Dale Cooper thinks it's all so simple.

There's just one catch: Where does Cooper go from here? How does he travel back in time if he's standing in Frank Truman's office? Cooper has come to a dead end. He cannot move from the reality he inhabits to the reality he needs to access. Diane looks to the clock on Truman's wall and sees it stuck at 2:53, signifying a threshold Cooper cannot cross. He's reached a barrier. There's nowhere else to go.

Reality breaks down at this point. Cooper's observing mind cannot maintain the illusion and, with no practical avenue to depart from the real-world, Cooper simply dims the lights and ends the scene. Literally.

The Cooper of Las Vegas—quickened into existence and implanted into the world at Memorial Hospital—has served his purpose. He exits the stage the same way Phillip Jeffries left Gordon Cole's office in *Fire Walk With Me*. *He was never there.*

The office fades to black. Only Cooper's transparent face remains. Cooper is retreating into the recesses of his own mind; he's no longer pretending he can steer his consciousness through the outside world.

From the start, Cooper has been moving through various layers of biased observation. First, he watched his physical self wander about Las Vegas. Then, he forced himself into the narrative in order to steer the story. Now, he's abandoned reality altogether.

Cooper's face fills the screen, gazing into the shadows of his mind, and three figures emerge from the dark: Diane, Gordon Cole, and the newly reconstituted "Agent" Cooper. They walk through a black void, untethered to any real-world setting, traversing what David Lynch calls a "never-never land," meaning (I presume) they inhabit a make-believe realm, a place entirely devised by Dale Cooper.

Unconstrained by the rules of the real world, Cooper envisions himself as an authority and an enforcer. He emerges from the shadows wearing his FBI lapel pin, something he's been without since his passage out of the Mansion Room. Cooper restores the pin because it symbolizes agency and identity. With this all-important talisman, Cooper reinstates himself as FBI Special Agent Dale Cooper.

Cooper also brings with him aspects of the two most important people in his life. He may think he is "the one and only," but Cooper requires the affirmation of Gordon Cole and Diane Evans. When he set out to enact his plan years ago, he confided in Diane, relying on her unwavering commitment to keep him going. Likewise, Cooper never strays far from Gordon Cole, to whom he's been sending dream messages and waking visions. Gordon Cole is more than Cooper's boss, he's a father-figure, someone whose approval Cooper needs.

Diane clasps Cooper's hand as they proceed through the dark. Cole walks right beside them. Diane and Cole provide emotional and psychological support to Cooper as he moves to the next stage of his journey.

LET'S PAUSE FOR A MOMENT and consider what may have happened to everyone left behind after Cooper "disappeared" from Truman's

office. We won't see Andy or Lucy or Bobby again. We won't learn the
fates of Truman or James or Hawk. As far as the narrative is concerned,
these characters (and all the others) are suspended in the dark.

After the lights went out, those who remained in Truman's office
likely succumbed to one of the mind-altering trances that frequently
occur in *Twin Peaks*. Like Gordon Cole and Albert Rosenfield forgetting Phillip Jeffries' visit in 1989, or the Twin Peaks Sheriff's deputies
forgetting their mysterious encounter in the woods, the people in
Frank Truman's office soon forget Dale Cooper and Diane were ever
there, their minds redacting all exposure to the supernatural. Mark
Frost describes this phenomenon in *The Final Dossier*. Tammy Preston
writes, "events are growing fuzzier and indistinct the more I stay [in
Twin Peaks]. I can feel a kind of mental lassitude physically advancing
on me." Tammy describes talking to the "good friends at the sheriff's
office" who "got a slightly dazed and confused expression on their
faces, as if they were lost in a fog." Memories of their supernatural encounter in Truman's office evaporate, leaving Dale Cooper nothing but
a distant, curious figment....

COOPER, COLE AND DIANE EMERGE from the darkness of "never-
never land" into a place that looks like the basement of the Great
Northern Hotel. (Cooper's omniscient, floating face fades from view.
Cooper's mind has successfully transitioned from one stage of the
journey to the next.) Cooper remembers James Hurley's exploration of
this basement and how James came to an old door. Cooper never saw
beyond the door, but the mystery and the urgency of what lay behind
it stayed with him. For Cooper, this insistent door becomes a threshold,
a portal that will lead him through time and space. "I'm going through
this door," Cooper declares. "Don't try to follow me."*

Before he leaves, Cooper provides a clue about where Diane might
find him next. "See you at the curtain call," he says, implying that all
that has just happened has been performance. Cooper has been putting
on a show. When it's over, he'll be backstage, ready to see Diane again.

---

* Cooper's farewell to Cole and Diane recalls his departure from Harry Truman at the
end of the original series. "Harry, I have to go alone," Cooper said, and then walked
away from Truman forever.

Cooper opens the door and, after stepping into a dark corridor, closes it firmly behind him.[*] He has broken free from any semblance of the real world. He's dimmed the lights, found a portal, and parted ways with the two most reliable people in his life. There's no stopping Cooper now.

In yet another pitch-black space, Cooper encounters Phillip Gerard, who recites his famous poem: "Through the darkness of future past/The magician longs to see/One chants out between two worlds/'Fire walk with me.'" Though credited as Phillip Gerard in Part 17, this character behaves a lot like Gerard's alter-ego, Mike: There's a know-ingness in his eyes, a certainty in how he navigates dark passages. Mike is arguably making his presence known, and his poem serves as a spell that transports both him and Cooper into the deeper regions of The Dutchman's (just as the Woodsman's machine did in Part 15).

Cooper follows Gerard through a metal door and into the motel courtyard Mr. C visited in Part 15. When Mr. C came here earlier, he passed through a wooden door, but now Cooper passes through a metal door, the same one, in fact, from Naido's Mansion Room, the door against which some menacing force pounded. (Both the Mansion Room door and the one Cooper passes through feature a "crossbar police lock"—two sliding steel bars which secure the door when closed.) Dale Cooper has plucked this door from his memory and used it as a portal.[†]

Rather than crossing the motel courtyard to room 8 (as Mr. C did), Gerard leads Cooper down a corridor to their right. Cooper and Gerard encounter no barriers on their way to Phillip Jeffries. No doors, gates

---

[*] In another eerie reverse shot, Diane and Cole awkwardly shift their heads toward the sound of the closing door. The column of steam behind Diane's head rushes downward, back into the furnace.

[†] Doors are crucial thresholds in *The Return*. In Las Vegas, a red door serves as beacon to guide Cooper home. In Twin Peaks, a farmer's opened door taunts with a trespassing presence. Elsewhere in Twin Peaks, a rival's impassable door elicits a fury of bullets from Becky Burnett's gun. In The Dutchman's, a motel door must be unlocked to gain access to Phillip Jeffries. And way back in Part 1, Marjorie Green summons the police to investigate an odor emanating from Ruth Davenport's locked door at 1356 Arrowhead Road, a door which stays locked until Marjorie remembers she has a key. (This incident leaves an impression on an observing Cooper: A locked door can be opened if you simply remember you've had a key all along.)

or sentries block their way. They emerge from the shadows into Jeffries' presence, as if Cooper simply wills it to happen.

According to Gordon Cole, Jeffries "doesn't really exist anymore," but Cooper recognizes Jeffries as a powerful figure who can steer Cooper to a desired destination.

Cooper barely knows Phillip Jeffries. He only met him once, fleetingly, in an encounter that has grown blurry over time, but for Cooper's fantasy to have validity, he needs the perfect mediator—an adjudicator who can grant access to the past. Cooper assigns that duty to Phillip Jeffries, an arcane player who can permit Cooper passage through time.

Cooper gets right to business. He provides Jeffries a date: February 23, 1989 (but, notably, no physical destination). Jeffries says he'll "find it" and sets to work. As he does, he makes some small talk. "It's good to see you again, Cooper," he says (even though he and Cooper don't really know each other). He assures Cooper that "Gordon will remember the unofficial version." (In other words, "Do what you want, Cooper; Cole will keep everything straight.") Such comforting proclamations ease Cooper's mind and give him tacit permission to cross the next threshold.

Jeffries works his magic. He generates a symbol—the number "8"— hovering in the air. A small sphere is visible, embedded in the lower right side of the contours of the 8. The 8 spins on its vertical axis, and the sphere moves around with it, rotating into a new position on the left. It only stays there a moment, however, before it rolls back along the curvature of the 8 to its original position.

This abstract, floating 8 is a baffling visual artifact. Some see it as representing an alternate timeline, others interpret it as a Möbius loop (an endless cycle of repetition), and still others see it as temporal map (something Jeffries uses to navigate time). The 8 symbol is infinitely decodable. It invites viewers to supply whatever meaning works for them.[*] In that spirit, I'll offer my own interpretation: We see the 8

---

[*] For example, Martha Nochimson suggests the sphere embedded in the 8 is the equivalent of Mr. C's "black dot"—the symbol Mr. C sent to Duncan Todd ordering the assassination of Dougie and Lorraine in Part 6. (Unfortunately, Nochimson doesn't elaborate. Why would Jeffries use Mr. C's code here? What message would it be sending to Cooper? Nochimson raises the questions but doesn't attempt the answers.)

invert itself, implying a mirrored view of the universe (or, as Cooper explained a moment ago, "some things having changed"), but as soon as the 8 flips over, the sphere inside rolls back to its starting point. The implication is: if you meddle with the universe, the universe will right itself. Cooper's subconsciousness is reminding him of his futility. It's telling him he's trying to alter what can't be altered.

Jeffries tells Cooper he can "go in now," and delivers a final directive: "Cooper…remember." In effect, Jeffries tells Cooper that the only *true* way to travel back in time is through memory. Cooper must recall what he knows about Laura Palmer in order to visualize a visit to her past.

Remember Cooper does. He closes his eyes and imagines the place he needs to go. The camera moves toward a close-up of Cooper's shut-eyed face, emphasizing his journey into memory. He's not traveling back in time; he's travelling deeper into his own mind. A black void fills the screen. Cooper has returned to never-never land.

DRAWING ON HIS KNOWLEDGE of the Laura Palmer case, Cooper inserts himself into the drama playing out hours before Laura's death. He materializes near a backwoods road, close to where James Hurley and Laura Palmer stand beside James's motorcycle. In black and white scenes (originally presented in *Fire Walk With Me*), Cooper sees James and Laura share an intimate moment. They kiss, but something isn't right with Laura. She struggles to balance her wildly oscillating good and bad selves. One minute Laura is experiencing a deep, uninhibited love for James, and the next she's slapping him across the face. Cooper watches all this from the cover of nearby trees.

After a moment, Laura tells James to take her home, and they drive away. A short distance down the road they stop at a light, and Laura jumps off the motorcycle and runs into the woods. She's on her way to rendezvous with Leo Johnson, Ronette Pulaski and Jacques Renault.

As Laura weaves her way through the trees, she is startled to come upon Cooper (who somehow knows exactly where to intercept her). Cooper stands confidently on a slope above Laura. (Notably, Lynch frames Cooper from below, accentuating Cooper's heroic view of himself. Cooper sees himself as Laura's savior. The champion who will set things right.)

Cooper stares at Laura and reaches out his hand, bestowing upon her the grace of his superhuman powers. Laura says she "knows" Cooper from a dream and puts her hand into his. Cooper turns and leads Laura deeper into the woods.

Once Laura places her hand in Cooper's, the story cuts to the image of Laura's dead body, wrapped in plastic, washed up on the beach. And then her body *dematerializes*—as if it was never there, as if Laura Palmer had not died. This is Cooper's goal. He has erased Laura's death. On February 24, 1989, Pete Martell never discovered the body of Laura Palmer, because Laura Palmer was never killed.

But it's all wishful thinking, all Dale Cooper's fantasy. As much as Cooper wants it to be true, he did not save Laura Palmer.

"Maybe it's only in his mind," Sheryl Lee says in a rare, unguarded comment about Dale Cooper's actions. Lee, who almost certainly received context from David Lynch about this scene,[*] provides valuable insight to what's happening between Laura and Cooper in the woods: "Agent Cooper wishes he could go back in time and rescue [Laura]. There's no proof that he did. Remember the whole thing about whose dream is…being told[.]"[†]

Cooper's encounter with Laura in the woods is a delusion. Distracted, missing the bigger picture, Cooper doesn't understand the importance of Laura's journey. He can't comprehend that Laura must come face to face with the evil in the train car. Only there, after experiencing pure despair, can Laura accept her inherent goodness. When that happens, Laura transcends and becomes something glorious.

"I am dead, yet I live," Laura tells Cooper in Part 2. If we take her literally (a dangerous thing to do, I admit, in a story like *Twin Peaks*),

---

[*] Lynch often contextualizes scenes for his actors. You can see him do so on various "Behind the Curtain" documentaries on the *Twin Peaks From Z to A* Blu-ray box set. For example, Lynch explicitly tells MacLachlan, "No time has passed for you," when Cooper returns to the Sheriff's station in Part 17, and he provides notes to MacLachlan, Dern, and Lee for various scenes in Part 18.

[†] Sheryl Lee is typically reserved when she discusses *Twin Peaks* and her role as Laura Palmer. "I have been told I'm not allowed to talk about what I think," she tells interviewer Scott Ryan in issue 8 of *The Blue Rose Magazine*, but when pressed about how *The Return* might alter the "legacy" of Laura Palmer, Lee opens up: "What was important…was that she got an angel. I feel like there is still truth in it because David is playing with time and stretching time. It doesn't negate Laura's journey…. If her body really did disappear, then she can't be in the Red Room to end the series."

this means Laura was killed but still has agency after death. Maybe Laura returned to life on Earth, or maybe she found refuge in an alternate reality. Either way, Laura Palmer died and then transformed into something else. She confirms this transformation in Part 2 when she reveals to Cooper a divine light within. Laura screams and is hurled from the Red Room, signaling her exit from the afterlife to a destiny elsewhere.

Now, in Part 17, that destiny infuriates the evil forces that still hope to prey upon Laura. In Twin Peaks, the monster inside Sarah Palmer wails in rage and agony, stabbing again and again at a framed picture of Laura Palmer. As much as she stabs, however, she cannot damage Laura's image. The glass in the frame shatters and jumps back into place, as if the picture is trying to restore itself. As Allister Mactaggart notes, "the photograph remains unbroken however much Sarah tries to destroy it—somehow it remains intact, smiling back at her failed, 'impotent' attempts to eradicate[.]" Laura defies destruction because her destiny cannot be altered. She is fated for grander things.

Cooper leads Laura through the woods, walking her out of a black-and-white world and into color (from a definite past to a subjective present), and he hears the same chirruping sounds he heard from The Fireman's phonograph in Part 1. The sounds are in Cooper's house now. They are back in his head, his programming reasserting itself. Maybe there's something else there, too, the sounds representing Cooper's subconscious admission that he cannot undo the past, his anxieties and regrets not so easily erased.

Time and again, Cooper carries his fantasies to the furthest point possible and bumps up against the impossible. It happened in the Sheriff's office, and it happens now as he leads Laura through the woods to…somewhere (Jack Rabbit's Palace? Glastonbury Grove?). Cooper says he's bringing Laura home, but what will happen after he does? Cooper doesn't know; he hasn't thought that far ahead. He's thinking only of his need to right past wrongs.

Sheryl Lee, privy to secrets about *The Return*, tells us unequivocally: "We know that something from his past is haunting him." Her comments provide a valuable glimpse into the psyche of Dale Cooper. He's a fraught soul, living in the past, wishing he could repair some long-ago damage. But he's on a fool's errand, and the chirruping sounds remind him of his folly.

Cooper reaches a dead end. Laura screams as she did in Part 2 (as she will in Part 18) and vanishes, leaving Cooper alone in the forest, looking back in confusion. His mind, still in the Red Room, has reached the final barrier.[*]

IT TOOK 17 EPISODES for *The Return* to reveal one of its greatest secrets, that Dale Cooper has been a constant presence, subtly hovering in a space between screen and viewer. Here, in Part 17, Cooper's transparent face fills the frame and provides a peek behind the curtain. At last, we see what Cooper's true role is.

Rather than a tangible, apprehensible protagonist who visibly occupies the stage, Cooper in *The Return* is a discursive presence through whom we, the audience, "see" the action. He is something *Kafkaesque*, a figure whose various psychoses, inhibitions, and emotions distort the story.

By showing Cooper in this way, David Lynch challenges us to reconsider who Dale Cooper really is. We may have thought him a man divided (as the last episode of the original series implied), his good and bad selves incomplete, both needing to recombine in order to restore balance. We may have thought Cooper the long-suffering hero who would eventually defeat his enemy and save the day. It's what heroes do, and it's what we expect from the Cooper we thought we knew.

But Cooper's blatant, superimposed face signifies something entirely different. It implies ubiquity. It challenges us to reevaluate Cooper, to take the story we've witnessed and derive from it a new and nuanced reading of Dale Cooper. When we do this, we end up seeing a static, flawed character, who, to our chagrin (most likely), is incapable of adjusting to a changing world. "There is a certain failing, a lack in

---

[*] In this moment, Julee Cruise appears superimposed over the forest singing "The World Spins." Though likely a piece of non-diegetic music used to signify the close of the episode, it's worth noting that Cooper once heard Cruise (i.e., "Roadhouse Singer") perform this song in the original series. It's not impossible that Cooper recalls the song as he ponders the impossibility of Laura's disappearance. (Cooper first heard "The World Spins" when, unbeknownst to him, Bob/Leland brutally murdered Madeleine Ferguson. As Cooper listened, he strained to perceive some deeper truth in the world. Now, just like then, the secrets of a larger universe elude him.)

me, that is clear and distinct but difficult to describe," Kafka wrote, "it is a compound of timidity, reserve...and half-heartedness.... This failing keeps me from going mad but also from making any headway." Like the long-suffering Franz Kafka, Dale Cooper wants to act but is trapped by his own mental fugue. The self has failed to know the self.

And because David Lynch positions us, the viewing audience, to experience the story through Cooper, we, too, feel a sense of uncertainty and distress. Perhaps even anger or betrayal. Lynch has lulled us into identifying with a flawed character. Like Cooper, we lack the tools to derive sense from what we see; we cannot distinguish between "what is and what is not." Cooper is doomed to fail, and, because we occupy his viewpoint, we (if unwary) fail too.

In *Twin Peaks: The Return*, Lynch asks us to divorce ourselves from preconceived notions of who we think Dale Cooper is, to move beyond our narrow, idealized view of him. If we can do this, if we can see past the stereotype of Cooper as the "one and only"—the savior, the knight-errant—then, perhaps, we can appreciate the deeper story at work.

<INTERLUDE 8>
I GOT IDEA MAN

IN SEPTEMBER 2018, the *Oxford English Dictionary* (*OED*) added the word "Lynchian" to its lexicon. The adjective, already in popular use for decades, presumably gained legitimacy when the *OED* defined it as: "juxtaposing surreal or sinister elements with mundane, everyday environments, and using compelling visual images to emphasize a dreamlike quality of mystery or menace." As good a definition as any, perhaps, but I'd submit that Lynchian is one of those slippery terms that resists the reductiveness of language. As admirable as the *OED* definition is, it attempts to solidify a very abstract concept the only way a definition can—by using other words. David Lynch, who believes that "once a name starts getting certain meanings attached to it, it can be good, or it can be really bad," would likely find all this effort to wrap language around his aesthetic rather ironic.

Lynch is notorious for being vague when he's being interviewed. It's not just because he wants to maintain mystery behind his creative process (certainly, he prefers to let the works speak for themselves), but also because he knows words are not enough to encapsulate his artistic sensibilities. In interview after interview (after interview), Lynch invariably resorts to the word "idea" to describe specific themes and topics in his films and his way of making them. On writing scripts, he says, "The script-making process involves getting ideas, writing them out and moving things about." On settings and world-building: "It's a film world, but it has its own reality, and things have got to be a certain way. And that 'certain way' comes from the ideas." On scenes and characters: "The ideas present a kind of flow of how it's going to unfold, and the ideas tell you each scene and each character. And you just follow the ideas." On *Twin Peaks*: "Ideas came, and this is what the ideas presented. Just focusing on *Twin Peaks*, these things came out for us, and there they were." On the importance of his work: "I strive to do something right, based on the idea, being sincere with the idea. Then, if I did my best and was faithful to the idea, I hope it will reach people, that they will feel its relevance." Ideas, ideas. Is there any interview in which David Lynch doesn't fall back on the term "idea" to describe his creative processes?

"Idea" is an imperfect word. Lynch probably knows this, but no other term works for him. That his films come from "ideas" makes perfect sense. Lynch uses the term because it's the closest he can come to expressing the inexpressible. When Lynch describes ideas, it's up to us, his audience, to figure out what he is saying.

Personally, when I hear Lynch use the word "idea," I think he's trying to convey abstract philosophical thoughts. Things that are fluid and dynamic. Notions akin to visions. There's almost a quantum physics component to how Lynch approaches ideas: If you define an idea too exactly (i.e., put it into precise words), the idea reduces to a single explanation and thereby loses its potential to be more than one thing. (In quantum terms, it's like a probability wave that collapses into a single state upon being observed.) For Lynch, an idea confined by a strict definition loses its mystery. As he explains: "A man tells a very abstract, very original story [to a group of people.] He finds himself compelled to explain what he wants to say in words more and more precise because they don't understand. By the time he's finished … the story has been reduced to one thing. There are no more harmonics."

David Lynch knows that even if he could perfect his message, crystallize a thought into flawless absolute prose, this message would still encounter the perceptual barriers and biases of his audience. He understands that everyone is going to see and hear things in their own way. "Every viewer, no matter what film they are looking at, has a different reaction than another viewer. It's just the way it is. Everybody is at a certain place, and they have so many internal things going on. The frames of the film are exactly the same [but] every individual reaction is different."

How do you overcome these barriers to understanding? How do you overcome this frustrating, imperfect mode of communication? If you're David Lynch, the answer is: *You don't.* You don't overcome the imperfect communication. You use it to your artistic advantage.

David Lynch embraces the notion of imperfect communication and incorporates it into the very essence of his stories, into the very way he makes films. For Lynch, the viewer is not a passive recipient for sound and picture; the viewer is a collaborator in the art David Lynch is putting forth. He wants his audiences to be their own creative force.

This attitude about the audience frees Lynch to *open* his texts, to embrace ambiguity, to invite viewers, each according to their own pre-dilections, to fill in the blanks. The viewer becomes an active participant in Lynch's art. It's an opportunity for viewers to use their imaginations. Lynch says he's "against the kind of film that would make absolutely one interpretation available." "The more abstract the film, the more audiences give—they fill in spaces, add in their own feelings."

Twin Peaks: The Return isn't for everyone, but for those viewers who can embrace a participatory narrative, one that offers multiple readings, one that hums with infinite possibility, then *The Return* is a rare gift, a piece of art that asks for engagement rather than muted acquiescence. *The Return*'s fragmentary structure is deliberate. David Lynch (and Mark Frost, too) understood that *Twin Peaks*, since its inception, encouraged viewers to engage with the show. If viewers saw in *Twin Peaks* ideas that neither creator intended, then those ideas were valid. As Mark Frost noted early on, "How do you know when something's in your work and when it isn't? If someone sees it there—I mean, if they *see* it there, it must *be* there. Because for them it *is* there. It gets into a strange kind of gray area where creativity is something that is shared, and the audience is using its own creativity in interpreting the material." (Emphasis in the original.) Put simply, what Frost is telling us is: whatever you, or I, or *anyone*, sees in *Twin Peaks* is a legitimate interpretation of the work.

Author David Foster Wallace once observed that our modern culture of mass-media consumption is "sort of lazy and childish in its expectations." Wallace decried the anesthetic effect of much of what we see on television and film, worrying that most popular entertainment fails to challenge the audience. Commercial entertainment, Wallace explains, "proceeds more or less chronologically...it eases you from scene to scene in a way that drops you into certain kinds of easy cerebral rhythms. It admits of passive spectation. Encourages it."

I would submit that the kind of mass media entertainment Wallace describes is exactly what David Lynch rejects. (Lynch bemoans the fact that "most films are designed to be understood by many, many, many, many people.") When Lynch set out to make *The Return*, he (and Frost, certainly) constructed the work to be open, to deliberately resist closure. In this way, watching *The Return* became a process of communication, one in which audiences could converse with the work and become, in effect, co-creators.

In *The Return*, Lynch is less concerned about where the story is going than he is in how the viewer makes sense of the story as it unfolds. This is what Lynch refers to, time and again, as "room to dream." Lynch's ideal is to create a work where there's "dialog between a picture and the audience. Watching a movie, we're like detectives—we only need a little bit of something and then we'll add in the rest, no problem."

We can list *The Return*'s many faults and complain about how it did not meet our expectations, but to appreciate it (not to love it, or to worship it, or to glorify it)—to really appreciate it—we need to approach the work on David Lynch's terms. If all we want is entertainment (or, as one critic demanded, "good television") then we're essentially asking Lynch to do the work for us. Lynch knows that's impossible, and so he asks us to take part in the story, to give some of ourselves to it. Those are his terms. It may not be for everyone, but that's what David Lynch's art is all about.

We should never forget that Lynch works with purpose and with deliberation. What he creates may be obscure, but just because it resists easy explanation does not mean it is meaningless. While Lynch wants to entertain with the stories he's telling, he also wants to convey the abstract and the ineffable. Since his earliest films, Lynch has been fascinated with how we make (or mistake) meaning from what we see and hear.

David Lynch's art is most alive when it occupies that liminal space between creator and audience, when the art, itself, becomes an amorphous entity available for the audience to shape. It's the journey, not the goal, that interests Lynch. It's what David Foster Wallace sees as "the story sharing its valence with the reader, [where] the reader's own life 'outside' the story changes the story."

Lynch refuses to deliver closure in his films because closure is static and final. It means the conversation between filmmaker and filmgoer is over, the potential for new discovery within the work is gone. Great storytellers know when and how to leave a tale, know that for a story to be art, the telling must be finite (even if the story, itself, is endless). Lynch is aware of how potent endings can be and so, in *The Return*, ends his tale on the brink of closure, balanced on the cusp of revelation but never tipping over the threshold.

In Part 17, Dale Cooper approaches "the moment of completion" (a moment that occurs at the exact time of 2:53), and although he's not told explicitly what this moment means, it is easy to surmise that the "moment of completion" is the end of the story, the conclusion to *Twin Peaks*. Lynch holds that moment in stasis. The clock on the wall clicks from 2:52 to 2:53 and back again, the minute hand never crossing that ultimate threshold. Time halts. The ending does not arrive.

In this moment, the story of Dale Cooper and *Twin Peaks* is suspended, existing forever on an asymptote of closure. As the distance toward an ending grows smaller, the story fades into darkness, and all the characters are left frozen in limbo, waiting for forward momentum to start again. (And perhaps, somehow, it will: We are told that 253 happens time and time again.)

And then the story jumps over this boundary of uncertainty to another story entirely. There, Dale Cooper emerges from the darkness to journey down another path, one that will strand him yet again, oscillating between revelation and confusion within the mystery that is Laura Palmer.

This is exactly how David Lynch wants to exit *Twin Peaks*, teetering on the edge of an ending but never quite dropping into one. By leaving his story suspended, Lynch ensures that his dialog with the viewer remains alive, a tale to be experienced again and again by those willing to participate. As far as Lynch is concerned, infinite interpretive paths are now available for viewers to discover.

Twin Peaks: The Return resists easy translations. Encrypted in a tangled language all its own, it tasks viewers to listen to sounds but not necessarily words, to look at pictures but to think outside the frame. *The Return* is a conjecture in search of a proof. It may not supply everything you want, but it gives you everything you need.

In the end, *The Return* leads us to a dramatically different definition of Lynchian: Something, yes, that contains menace, mystery, and the sinister wrapped within the mundane, but also something that hums with possibility: A story with the eternal inertia of uncertainty. A bounded infinity. A universe that exists at the chimerical intersection between artist and audience. A world as we are.

PART 18:

WHAT IS YOUR NAME?

AN ARGUMENT CAN BE MADE that *Twin Peaks: The Return* ended in Part 17. Cooper restored himself and then took his obsession to a conclusion, bumping up against the truth that no matter what he does, he cannot save Laura Palmer.

Standing baffled in the dark woods, the idealized Dale Cooper—the Cooper who believed he could accomplish the impossible—comes to an endpoint. Laura has screamed and vanished, leaving Cooper alone in the night with no idea of where to go next. The mysteries of Laura Palmer and the universe elude him.

Although what we are about to see in Part 18 looks like a continuation of Cooper's quest to find Laura Palmer, it is, in many ways, a retelling of the same story we saw in Part 17. Cooper will cross thresholds. He will take Diane with him part of the way. He will travel across dimensions to find Laura and guide her into darkness. Laura will scream at the end, and Cooper will be left in the night with no idea of where—or when—he is.

Despite these similarities, there is a distinct difference between Part 18 and Part 17. Up until now, we've seen the story play out as Cooper sees it, his skewed, idealized version of reality. In Part 18 we see Cooper unfiltered. We see him as he is, not as the biased version he believed himself to be.

It took 17 parts to get here, to the point where we see a truer Cooper (and perhaps a truer world) than we saw before. If we can make an argument that *Twin Peaks* ended in Part 17, we can make an equally valid argument that *Twin Peaks* doesn't really begin until Part 18.

Cooper has lived his fantasy, witnessed the failure of his idealized self, reintegrated the darker aspects of his personality, and found escape from the stagnation that plagued him for so long. In Part 18, Cooper is free to move to a more important story. He is ready to fulfill a role he once told The Fireman he "understood."

Cooper is no longer obsessed with saving Laura Palmer or undoing her death; his role here, in Part 18, is to guide Laura to where she can complete The Fireman's grand plan. Cooper is sidelined into a supporting role. He's not a savior, he's simply an escort.

While Part 18 depicts Cooper's journey into another world, it's fundamentally about Laura Palmer performing a cosmic role for which she has been designed. Strip away all the set dressings—the motels, diners, living rooms, and nighttime roads—and you're left with two souls who must journey together to an all-important endpoint.

This is what happens in Part 18. With the backstory over, everything is reduced to Dale Cooper and Laura Palmer executing a plan. Both characters experienced journeys of self-discovery (neither of which turned out the way they expected) and made it to "the other side." Cooper submits to his programming, unerringly seeking Laura Palmer (the little girl who lives down the lane) in order to guide her to the one place she must eventually "return." Laura, meanwhile, acquiesces to Cooper and allows him to bring her to a specific location where she can "complete the circle" (as The Log Lady foretells in Part 10).

This simple connection, this basic journey, is what Part 18 is about. It's what *Twin Peaks* is about. There's no point trying to map the boundaries of this last chapter because reality breaks down in Part 18. It's impossible to say definitively where Cooper has gone (or where Laura ostensibly lives). In a story that asks us to distinguish between "what is" and "what is not," one thing is true: Cooper escorts Laura into the dark, out of the world and to the end of time.

Dale Cooper. Laura Palmer. Their destination. These are the only things that matter.

BEFORE WE GET TO THE STORY PROPER, Part 18 begins with some housekeeping, a few loose ends that need tying up. The episode opens in The Red Room with Mr. C engulfed in flames. A black column of smoke consumes him, leaving no question about his demise. Mr. C, the autonomous evil half of Cooper, has been eliminated. Or, perhaps more precisely, he's been *reconstituted*. Mr. C is part of Dale Cooper's psyche once again.

Cooper now has the power of "combined opposites." As David Lynch explains, "To reconcile those two opposing things is the trick. In order to appreciate one, you have to know the other—the more darkness you can gather up, the more light you can see too." Without his Mr. C aspect, Cooper remains trapped in the Red Room. Reintegrated, Cooper can leave.

After Mr. C has been dealt with, Phillip Gerard makes a tulpa. He squeezes together the Dougie Jones gold "seed" and Cooper's lock of hair and speaks the word, "Electricity"—a galvanic spell that conjures a new Dougie Jones/Dale Cooper into existence.

This Dougie Jones looks nothing like the man who found himself in The Red Room in Part 3, the overweight, unkempt boor who had just spent an afternoon with the prostitute, Jade. He *does* look like the man who blissfully drifted through the environs of Las Vegas between Parts 3 and 15. But with a crucial difference. This time he is awake and aware.

The moment Dougie corporealizes, he engages with his environment. He delightedly looks around the Red Room and asks Phillip Gerard, "Where am I?" This "Dougie" exhibits genuine, unabashed curiosity. He's the Dale Cooper who marveled at trees and ducks and home-cooked food during his original visit to Twin Peaks.

We only glimpse the new Dougie for a moment, but we know he's not the same blank Cooper who wandered into the lives of Janey-E Jones and The Lucky 7 Insurance Agency. This Cooper is alive, alert, and grounded. He's the Cooper-equivalent of Andy Brennan, assuming a life of love and happiness back in Las Vegas with his wife and son.

That's exactly where we leave him, standing in the doorway of 25140 Lancelot Court embracing Janey-E and Sonny-Jim. An aspect of Dale Cooper (Dougie) has reunited with an aspect of Diane Evans (Janey-E*), and both characters, freed from their psychoses, find their happily-ever-after. Kyle MacLachlan explains, "He's not Dougie 'complete,' and he's not Cooper 'complete.' He's an entity that's a perfect

---

* Who's to say Diane didn't create Janey-E Jones out of her own lock of hair and golden seed and then insert her into a "happily-ever-after" scenario with Dale Cooper?

choice—the perfect person—to be with Janey E. They've found each other." If we wanted a happy ending for *The Return*, this is it: Dale Cooper embracing his family and acknowledging he's found the one place he's always wanted to be: "Home."[*]

Meanwhile....

COOPER LEADS LAURA through the woods. Crickets chirp, the wind blows, and Cooper occasionally looks back to make sure that Laura is okay. Suddenly the nighttime sounds cease, and Cooper hears the scratching sound of the Fireman's phonograph. He looks back again, but Laura is gone. Her scream pierces the night.

A moment passes, and the crickets start singing again. Cooper stands numbly in the dark, baffled by what just happened.

I wrote in Part 17 that when Cooper stands alone in the woods, "his mind has reached a barrier." Indeed, before he can even process his arrival at this boundary, the forest vanishes, and Cooper is back in the Red Room sitting across from Phillip Gerard.

Watch closely during Cooper's final seconds in the woods. He stares into the night, searching for some clue about what happened to Laura. He hears a sound—the "odd reverberation" of the Red Room—and turns his head to his left. When he does, his face is bathed in a red light. (If you blink, you'll miss it, but it's there.) Cooper sees the light and is instantly back in The Red Room.

This deliberate sound and lighting effect suggests that Cooper's mind never left the Red Room. In Part 2 "Laura Palmer" told Cooper he could "go out now," but when Cooper tried to physically leave the Red Room, he encountered a barrier. Cooper then experienced a

---

[*] This happy ending is welcome, but it doesn't answer a few questions: How did Dougie/Cooper get from the Red Room back to Las Vegas? Did he have to travel through another electric socket (like he did in Part 3)? David Lynch leaves those questions unanswered, but the implication is that Dougie somehow transferred out of the Red Room back into the real world. There's a lot of missing narrative here, and its absence risks making this ending read like an afterthought. Consider this possibility, though (one I mentioned in an earlier chapter): The body of Dougie Jones never left Memorial Hospital in Part 16. When Cooper's idealized, imaginary self hijacked the story, the physical body of Dougie/Cooper remained comatose in bed. Later, a "new" Cooper awakens in the hospital (in his already existing physical form) and finds his way back to Lancelot Court. (This explanation is simple and elegant, and I like it.)

strange phenomenon—he watched the Red Room divide into overlapping images, as if two Red Rooms were drifting apart, splitting into separate paths. As I detailed in Part 2, this divergence resulted in two narrative lines. In one, Cooper's physical body found its way to the real world (eventually, to the empty home in Rancho Rosa), and in the other, Cooper's mind remained in the Red Room, a passive observer of his real-world counterparts. As we saw, the physical Cooper who left the Red Room in Part 2 is *still* in Las Vegas. Now, in Part 18, the observing Cooper snaps out of his fugue and finds himself in the Red Room, the place his mind has never left.

Cooper sits across from Phillip Gerard just as he did in Part 2, and, like then, Cooper has blinked into existence: Absent one moment, he's there the next. In Part 2, Cooper and Gerard became separated, but now they are reconnected, as if someone pressed a "reset" button to start Cooper's odyssey all over again.

Cooper studies the chair across from him—the chair "Laura Palmer" sat in when he started his journey. The chair is empty, Laura is not present, a fact Lynch reinforces by moving the camera (i.e., Cooper's point-of-view) slowly toward the chair and holding it there.

On first viewing we might presume Laura is not there because Cooper intercepted her in 1989 and prevented her murder. If Laura isn't dead, she certainly can't be in the Red Room to encounter Dale Cooper. But, as I discussed in Part 17, *everything* Cooper does after "waking up" in Las Vegas is highly subjective. His grand performance in Truman's office, his failure to guide Laura "home," and the fact he ends up back in the Red Room strongly suggests Cooper's 1989 encounter with Laura was Cooper's wishful thinking. He didn't save her. She really *did* die.

So, why is she not sitting across from Dale Cooper, as we (and he) expect? "Laura Palmer" is not there because she exited the Red Room in Part 2: She whispered something to Dale Cooper, screamed, and was hurled into a black void. "Laura" had a destiny elsewhere.

Cooper wasn't ready to follow Laura out of the Red Room then, but he is now. The reconstitution of Mr. C with Dale Cooper's psyche and the installation of a new Dougie Jones into the real world completes his rehabilitation. Cooper is potent again. He has agency.

Restored, he can at last execute the mission assigned to him by The Fireman.

Phillip Gerard and The Evolution of the Arm waste little time steering Cooper in the right direction. Gerard guides Cooper to another room where The Evolution of the Arm impels Cooper to action, asking, "Is it the story of the little girl who lived down the lane?"

When Cooper hears these words, something unlocks. The phrase, "The little girl who lived down the lane" triggers him, and he remembers Laura Palmer whispering in his ear. He remembers her scream, and her sudden exit from the Red Room. Cooper puts these clues together and sees again Leland Palmer imploring Cooper to "Find Laura." Now, Cooper knows exactly what he needs to do. He must locate the girl who lived down the lane—Laura Palmer[*]—and take her to a specific time and place. This is what the Fireman was hinting at in the opening minutes of Part 1.

Cooper hears a ringing sound and purposefully walks away from Leland and down an adjoining Red Room corridor. He twists his hand in the air, divining the exact spot where he needs to exit. A section of curtain flutters at the end of the hall, and Cooper steps through...

...into what looks like Glastonbury Grove, the place where, twenty-five years earlier, Dale Cooper entered a portal in pursuit of Windom Earle and Annie Blackburn. But this is not the same Glastonbury Grove Cooper disappeared into all those years ago.[†] Cooper emerges into a liminal space, a threshold between the psychological trappings of The Red Room and the "real world." It's a place not unlike Naido's Mansion Room, which also linked one world to another. Cooper is passing through a peripheral realm as he makes his journey outward.

And just like he did in the Mansion Room, Cooper encounters Diane.

Cooper is relieved, as if he hoped to see her standing there. Diane, for her part, can't quite believe her eyes. "Is it you?' she asks. "Is it *really* you?"

---

[*] Audrey Horne realized the same thing in Part 13: "The little girl who lived down the lane" was Laura Palmer. (And her story was all that mattered to Dale Cooper).

[†] If it were, one might expect Cooper to pay a visit to nearby Twin Peaks and check in on his friend, Harry Truman, or find out how Annie is faring after all this time, but he doesn't. In this Glastonbury Grove, Twin Peaks is nowhere to be found.

Throughout *The Return*, we've accompanied Cooper on his journey and have some idea of what he's been through, but we know far less about Diane. Why is she here in these woods at this specific time?

Although we don't see it play out on-screen, Diane Evans has likely been on a journey much like Cooper's. Forced into an otherworldly realm by Mr. C, Diane was fractured into pieces and has, over the years, been reassembling herself. She succeeded; Diane has reconstituted and rebalanced herself and exited her own Red Room to wait for Cooper. (And, perhaps, left part of herself in Las Vegas, just like Cooper did.)

Cooper and Diane greet each other delicately. Both recognize what the other has been through. When Diane asks, "Is it really you?" she seeks assurance from Cooper that he has put himself back together. That he's been restored. Cooper is looking for the same thing. Aware that Diane was probably fractured into many selves, he wants to know if she is whole again.

Cooper and Diane's meeting in Glastonbury Grove is the first time they have seen each other in a very long time, probably decades. Their reunion in Part 17 was artificial, Dale Cooper's mind arrogating the story. (It bears repeating that David Lynch tells Kyle MacLachlan and Laura Dern when directing them in Glastonbury Grove: "You haven't seen each other in twenty-five years. Really and truly." This almost certainly means that Cooper and Diane's reunion in Part 17 was a fantasy. It wasn't real, and it wasn't true.)

Despite finding each other at last, Cooper and Diane are not done with their journey. They are still suspended in a peripheral world and must cross at least one more threshold to get out. Cooper seems to know what they need to do. He remembers The Fireman's clue about "430" and, inexplicably, interprets that to mean 430 miles. He also knows (somehow) which direction to go, because in the very next scene he and Diane are driving through a barren landscape toward a specific endpoint. Electric towers loom in the desert, crackling with energy. Cooper looks at the odometer and announces they've driven "exactly 430 miles."

How much does Cooper really know about where he's going? He tells Diane, "This is the place, all right," and seems to know he's arrived at another threshold, but can Cooper *choose* where he wants to go next?

Can he cross out of this interstitial dimension to a specific time and place? Diane's dialog suggests that they may have some say in where they go next. "Are you sure you want to do this?" she asks. Later, she says, "Just think about it, Cooper."

Diane is not as invested in the mission as Cooper is. As far as she's concerned, her journey is over. She's back with Cooper and happy to leave the supernatural investigations behind, but when Cooper exits the car and stands under the pulsing electric towers, Diane knows he will not be dissuaded. He only sees his mission and where he wants to go.

Cooper moves the car forward across an electric boundary. There is a powerful transition, and suddenly he and Diane are racing through the dark on a desert road. They've crossed another threshold, routed onto a new path.

COOPER AND DIANE do not speak as they hurtle through the night, and neither seems surprised by their sudden shift in reality. Cooper drives as if on autopilot. When he spies a small motel just off the road, he pulls into the parking lot, parks the car, and stares out the windshield. He exits the car and walks purposefully toward the motel office. He doesn't look at Diane or tell her what he's planning. Cooper has his own agenda.

Diane is dismayed by Cooper's behavior and afraid of what he expects. Her fears manifest when, alone in the car, she sees another version of herself appear in the motel parking lot. Diane's commitment to Cooper is wavering, her identity destabilizing. In this moment Diane realizes she has no future with Cooper.[*]

Cooper emerges from the motel office with a room key. He walks past the car to the door of the room and turns to stare at Diane. He's following a predetermined plan and expects Diane to follow along.

Cooper's "programming" is never more evident than when he stands inside the motel room with Diane. She turns on the light, but he tells her to turn it off. She asks, apprehensively, "What do we do now?" and he says, "You come over to me." Cooper behaves as if he is

---

[*] For a deeper analysis of Diane's journey, see the chapter, "Missing Pieces: Putting 'Diane' Together."

reciting instructions from a manual. He's listing the steps he and Diane must follow to achieve a certain outcome.

Cooper kisses Diane and sets in motion a joyless, perfunctory sexual intercourse. Diane rhythmically moves atop Cooper, who stares at her without emotion or intimacy. He touches her mechanically—not for pleasure, but because the act requires it. For Cooper, this sex is procedural, another step to be checked off the list.

Diane and Cooper's sexual encounter is part of a long line of third-act sex scenes in David Lynch films that propel narratives into portentous, unsettling territory: In *Eraserhead*, Henry's fantasy sex with the woman across the hall sets in motion Henry's mental breakdown and eventual murder of the baby. In *Fire Walk With Me*, Laura's sex with Bob/Leland leads to a horrible revelation and Laura's spiral into despair. In *Lost Highway*, Pete and Alice's sex transforms Pete back into Fred Madison and dooms him to a Sisyphean future. In *Mulholland Drive*, Betty and Rita's sex opens a path to the ominous space known as Club Silencio. Sex in Lynch's films transforms worlds or changes how characters perceive reality, so it's not surprising that Cooper and Diane's sex in *The Return* has similar consequence: Diane takes permanent leave of the story (implicitly transforming into someone named Linda), and Dale Cooper crosses yet another threshold.[*]

Cooper wakes the next morning and finds himself alone in the motel room. He calls for Diane, but she's gone. He reads a farewell note from "Linda" (addressed to "Richard") but makes no sense of it. Apparently, he can no longer recall the Fireman's advice, the clues he remembered just the previous evening (i.e., 430 "miles"). This is the first sign that Cooper is failing to grasp his new reality.[†] In fact, Cooper soon forgets about Diane, as if she's nothing but a remnant of a fast-fading dream.

Cooper has emerged into another world. He has completed his journey out of the Red Room and across all its adjacent zones. He's

---

[*] Diane and Cooper's sex parallels the beginning of *INLAND EMPIRE*, where, after a man and a woman engage in sexual intercourse in a hotel room, identities blur, and the woman emerges from the encounter alone, possibly as someone else.

[†] As I argued in the Diane essay, had Cooper understood the Fireman's "Richard and Linda" clue as a warning, he may have treated Diane better and included her in his plans. Instead, Cooper marginalizes Diane and loses her.

passed through the "Glastonbury Grove zone" and the "motel zone" to awaken in an ostensibly real world, but, right from the start, this world feels different from the ones Cooper has travelled before.

No mind mediates the story now. No psyche sifts what we see and hear. With this filter gone, the warmth of the earlier sequences (Twin Peaks and Las Vegas) has been replaced by a colder, desaturated palette. The sounds are different, too; the ambient hums and pulses, the ethereal echoes, the occasional background music—all are gone in this new reality. It's a flat world in which Cooper finds himself. Doleful. Charmless. A world where there's no room for heroes.

Cooper exits his room into the parking lot of an entirely different motel than the one he and Diane arrived at the night before. This lot is paved instead of dirt. What's more, this motel has two stories instead of one. Cooper's car has also changed. The previous night it was a 1963 Ford 300, now it's a 2003 Lincoln Town Car.[*] Cooper pauses for a moment, subconsciously registering the changes, but he dismisses them and drives away. Like his memory of Diane, Cooper's memories of the recent past are fading. He's looking only forward now, driven by a compulsion, the commands of his programming.

COOPER DRIVES THROUGH the industrial landscape of Odessa, Texas,[†] passing warehouses, shipping containers, and tractor-trailer trucks. He stares ahead, driving instinctively, until his attention is caught by a roadside diner, a place called "Judy's." A coin-operated rocking horse sits outside the diner. It's a white horse, and Cooper looks at it for a long moment before looking back at the diner's sign. Perhaps it's the name of the diner, or perhaps it's the obvious white horse, but Cooper is compelled to turn into the parking lot and enter the restaurant.

Cooper walks into a large open space where a small number of patrons are eating breakfast. An elderly couple sits at a table. A trio of

---

[*] The same make, model, and year of the car Mr. C drove in Part 2 (and in which Cole, Albert and Tammy rode from the airport in Part 4).

[†] Odessa is a reference to Homer's *The Odyssey*, which Mark Frost explicitly mentions as an influence on *The Return*.

men wearing cowboy hats sits in a booth. A waitress makes her rounds, refilling mugs with coffee.

Cooper sits in a booth, and the waitress, Kristi, pours him coffee. Cooper knows he's close to finding Laura (the clues have led him here), but he doesn't see her. He asks Kristi if there is another waitress working, and she confirms that, yes, another woman works at the diner but hasn't been in for the past three days. As Cooper processes this information, the cowboys in the nearby booth start harassing Kristi, grabbing at her and pulling her close.

Cooper tells them to stop, and the cowboys let Kristi go. Angry at the interruption, they approach Cooper, and the first cowboy threatens Cooper with a gun. Cooper springs into action. He grabs the gun, kicks the man in the groin, and shoots the second man in the foot. He orders the third man to surrender his gun and to sit on the floor.

Cooper gathers the men's guns and slowly walks across the room, levelling his own weapon at the surroundings, sweeping it past the elderly couple. Cooper moves like an automaton, as if surrendering to a programmed routine. He has no concern for how his loaded gun might traumatize the innocent bystanders. He's senseless to the power he wields.

Moving deliberately to the hot oil fryer, Cooper carefully drops the guns into the bubbling oil.* In a monotone voice, Cooper instructs Kristi to write the address of the absent waitress on a piece of paper. Although he reassures her that he's with the FBI, his affectless behavior shows he has no empathy for anyone who just witnessed his violence. Cooper's goal is to obtain the next clue that will lead him to Laura.

Cooper's behavior recalls Mr. C and his remorseless drive to obtain what he "wants" no matter who gets hurt. Cooper mildly warns the cook to be wary of the bullets in the hot oil, but he doesn't seem to care what happens after that; the cook is responsible for his own safety. This version of Cooper—an amalgamation of his good and bad selves—cares less for his fellow man than the Cooper we thought we knew (or the hero Cooper wanted us to see). With the filter gone, we're seeing

---

* There's a continuity error here; Cooper takes *two* guns from the cowboys but drops *three* guns into the oil. Clearly, Cooper was supposed to retrieve three guns from the floor, but for the final cut, the editors used a take in which Cooper picked up only two.

Cooper as he is. According to MacLachlan, "He's a slightly harder version of the Cooper we remember."

To emphasize this new view of Cooper, Lynch repeatedly cuts to the elderly couple watching from across the room. These two people are unbiased observers of everything that transpires in Judy's. They have nothing to do with the waitress (who's frustrated at having to work the shift by herself) or the three cowboys (who crudely impose their will on others), and so they serve as reliable arbiters of Cooper's behavior. Their viewpoint confirms Cooper as a frightening, threatening force, a vigilante who never lowers his gun.

A SHORT WHILE LATER, Cooper arrives at the address Kristi provided. He parks and surveys a small, rundown house. The scrubby front yard is littered with flowerpots, plastic buckets and knotted lengths of rope. It's not the most promising locale.

Cooper notices the "#6" utility pole just outside the house (the same pole that appeared in the Fat Trout Trailer Park in *Fire Walk With Me* and in Andy's vision in Part 14). Like the white horse outside Judy's, the pole is another clue that Cooper has arrived at the right place.

Cooper looks at the pole and hears a crackling electric hum. As we've seen throughout *The Return*, electricity is the lifeforce pulsing through the universe. It's the energy that allows a transition between worlds (or perhaps more accurately, between states of mind). Electricity is the force that permeates the entirety of reality. It's the medium upon which the world operates.

The Log Lady tells Hawk in Part 10, "Electricity is humming. You hear it in the mountains and rivers. You see it dance among the seas and stars and glowing around the moon." She describes electricity as a positive force, using words like "glowing" and "dancing" to describe its movement. She says that electricity is everywhere in nature, but its glow is dying, and soon there will be only darkness. After this dark age ends, one figure will "complete the circle." About this, The Log Lady is explicit: *Laura is the one.*

Laura is the one whom The Fireman created and sent to Earth. Laura is the one "who will be in the darkness that remains." Laura is the analog of the Hindu avatar, Kalki, the figurant who rides a white horse and was dispatched by the deity, Vishnu to end the dark age.* She is a cosmic being, glowing with divine purpose. Laura is the one Dale Cooper has been sent to find.

Cooper knocks on the door, and a woman who looks almost exactly like Laura Palmer answers.

When Cooper first sees her—sees *Laura Palmer* alive and in the flesh—his programming recedes, and he responds with genuine surprise. "Laura," he stammers, as if he can't believe his eyes. He's found the little girl who lives down the lane.

The woman gives Cooper a quizzical look and tells him he's got the wrong house, but Cooper persists. This has to be Laura Palmer. He asks her name, and she tells him, "Carrie Page."

As Cooper presses Carrie about her possible alter-ego as Laura, Carrie's identity destabilizes. At first, she proffers the name "Carrie Page" to enforce the identity, to make it real, but when Cooper asks if the name Laura Palmer means anything, Carrie doesn't answer directly. She says, "I don't know what you want, but I'm not her," and you can almost hear the implied "anymore" at the end of her sentence.

Carrie wants Cooper to go, but Cooper refuses to leave, and he tells her more about Laura. He mentions Laura's father, Leland, but the name means nothing to Carrie. Then he mentions Laura's mother, Sarah, and Carrie falters. With a wavering voice, Carrie repeats the name and closes her eyes, steadying herself in the doorframe. "What's going on?" she asks as the world spins around her. Something is unlocking deep inside. Tumblers are falling into place. The name "Sarah" has had an impact.

Carrie's reaction strongly suggests that she is, indeed, Laura Palmer and that the name "Carrie Page" is an alias. But how do we explain this change of identity? Carrie isn't consciously trying to fool Cooper—she's just as confused as he is—but her sense of identity crumbles when she is confronted with an undeniable truth.

Laura Palmer is exhibiting traits of Dissociative Identity Disorder (once known as multiple personality disorder). According to the Mayo Clinic, "Dissociative disorders usually develop as a way to cope with

---

* See the chapter, "Ten is the Number of Completion," for more about how Laura's role maps to Hindu theology.

trauma. The disorders most often form in children subjected to long-term physical, sexual or emotional abuse or [...] a home environment that's frightening or highly unpredictable." Laura has suppressed her memories. All the trauma and abuse and heartache from her life in Twin Peaks has been pushed so deep she has forgotten it.

How did Laura end up here, in this dismal house in Texas? We might think that Cooper changed the timeline (in Part 17) and allowed Laura to escape death and leave Twin Peaks. We would therefore surmise she fled to Odessa and developed the alternate personality known as Carrie Page. Mark Frost confirms this scenario (he says Cooper's actions "ended up hurling both Cooper and Laura into a sideways, alternate dimension"), but David Lynch's discourse complicates—and possibly contradicts—this reading.

After Laura vanished in the woods in Part 17, Cooper immediately returned to the Red Room, a place his mind probably never left. It was in the Red Room (in Part 2) that Cooper encountered an otherworldly Laura, who (it's obvious now) looked "almost exactly like Carrie Page." This Laura tells Cooper, "I'm dead yet I live," then screams and is thrown from the Red Room. Though not explicit, the scene suggests that Laura returned to Earth *after* death and assumed the persona of Carrie Page. She started over. She erased Laura Palmer and developed a new identity.

Cooper, standing at her door, accepts that Carrie doesn't remember who she is, and tries to reorient her. He provides an abbreviated summary of why he's there: "As strange as it might sound, I think you're a girl named Laura Palmer. I want to take you to your mother's home. It's very important." Notably, Cooper refers to Laura as a "girl," even though he is looking at a woman who is over forty years old. He can't think of her any other way. She was seventeen when she was killed, and Cooper still sees her as a "girl."

Cooper doesn't explain why "it's very important" to take Laura home. If Cooper's goal had to be to alter the past and save Laura from death, he should be relieved to see he has succeeded. Laura Palmer is standing right in front of him, alive and (reasonably) well, having lived decades of life she had once been denied. Shouldn't that be enough? Why does he need to take her home?

The answer is simple. Cooper's role here is to follow the directives installed by The Fireman. He must take Laura home. He doesn't know why; he just has to do it.

Cooper enters Carrie's house and immediately sees the body of a dead man sitting stiffly in a chair. The man has been shot through the head. Carrie's home is a murder scene. Something violent and horrible happened here.

The dead man is a tantalizing piece of Carrie's backstory. When Carrie opened her door, she breathlessly asked, "Did you find him?" implying that she is afraid of some unidentified man likely connected to the grisly murder in her living room. Carrie assumes the FBI is investigating the crime, but when she realizes Cooper knows nothing about it, she realizes she's in danger. (Which is why she accepts Cooper's offer to leave Odessa. Under "normal" circumstances, she'd tell Cooper to leave, but, as Carrie explains, "right now I've got to get out of Dodge." In other words, Carrie needs to get away from the threat of a dangerous man.)

"Men are coming," Sarah Palmer warned a look-alike Laura (the checkout girl) in Part 12, a premonition, perhaps, of Carrie Page's predicament in Part 18.* The story has already shown us the kind of men who threaten Carrie, rough men, threatening men, men like Gene and Jake, who stalked Dougie Jones through Rancho Rosa, or the bikers who forcibly removed Ruby from her Roadhouse booth, or the loan sharks who confronted Janey-E in the park. These men are emblems of the dark age Janey-E decried.†

While Cooper waits for Carrie to pack, he glances around, taking in the crime scene. The dead man dominates the space, and Cooper, disturbed by his presence, struggles with his sense of duty to investigate. He examines the rest of the living room and spies a small statue

---

* I'm convinced Sarah mistook the checkout girl for Laura. Sarah's memories are jumbled, and perhaps she intuits that Laura is still alive (somewhere "different") and is compelled to warn her. (Surely, it's no coincidence that the grocery store where Sarah sees the checkout girl is named "Keri's," a variation of "Carrie's.")

† Narratively speaking, of course, the man Carrie fears serves as story-telling expediency. It's easier for us to accept that Carrie would hastily leave with Cooper if we see her situation as dire. (*Normally*, she wouldn't; but *right now* driving away with Cooper is her safest bet.)

of a white horse on Carrie's mantel. He stares at it for some time, enough for him to forget the dead man across the room.

What is Cooper thinking when he sees the statue? Is he remembering the white horse he saw in the Red Room just after Laura was whisked away? Cooper knows the white horse is connected to Laura, and its presence here in Carrie's living room confirms he has come to the right place.* The foreboding figure of the dead man threatens to divert Cooper, but seeing the white horse restores his intent. Yes, Carrie has been missing from work for the past three days and is likely involved in something dire, but Cooper can't take the time to investigate or ask questions. His compulsion to take Laura home supersedes all other instincts. (Indeed, when Kyle MacLachlan asks about the dead man during rehearsal, Lynch explains, "We're not going to stop and worry about those things," confirming that Cooper has other priorities.)

COOPER AND CARRIE LEAVE ODESSA, and what follows is a surreal drive deep into the blackness of night. Cooper travels along back roads, off any main highway. The only thing visible is the dimly lit road in front of the car. For all intents and purposes, Cooper and Carrie drive through a void, traversing another of Lynch's "never-never lands." The world drops away and only these two journeying souls remain. (Cooper and Carrie do stop for gas, but the gas station seems to float in the darkness, disconnected from any fixed location.) Cooper is not simply taking Carrie away from Odessa, he's taking her away from the world as she knows it.

The passage of time becomes suspect, too. Lynch uses long point-of-view shots of the road passing beneath the car (and extended close-ups of Cooper and Carrie) to convey their journey out of the normal flow of time. A drive from Odessa to northeast Washington State would take about thirty hours, but Cooper and Carrie never stop to rest, nor do they change their clothes. They seemingly drive through the night to Twin Peaks, but what they're really doing is driving to the end of the universe. Cooper needs to take Laura Palmer to the end of The Dark

---

* As I discussed in the chapter, "Ten is the Number of Completion," Lynch deliberately connects the white horse to Laura. The horse symbolizes her new role.

Age, and that's exactly where he's going. Just as he crossed into this world with Diane, he's travelling back out with Laura.[*]

Time passes, and after a long while Carrie ruminates on her life, giving voice to some quiet thoughts: "I tried to keep a clean house...keep everything organized." These brief lines are easy to dismiss, but a closer look reveals their import. "I was too young to know any better," Carrie says, talking to herself rather than Cooper. She's reminding herself that she's a good person. She's lived a good life, and the mistakes of her youth do not define the person she is now. (In effect, she's acknowledging that the past does not dictate the future.)

This dialog also humanizes Carrie. Until now she's been a bit of a caricature, an obstinate, superficial "Southern gal," who's involved in sordid wrongdoings. As she reflects on her past, however, she becomes a more realized character. The complex persona of Laura Palmer is surfacing.[†]

The farther Carrie travels from Odessa, the more her identity shifts and re-shapes. Carrie senses the change, even if she can't quite articulate it. She is not going back to Odessa—that part of her life is gone. She's a on a one-way trip to an inevitable destiny. "It's a long way," she says, as she adjusts to shifting landscapes, her movement through space, time, and consciousness. Carrie is on the cusp of releasing her earthly identity and assuming a larger role.

After an unknowable amount of time, Cooper and Carrie reach Twin Peaks. They cross a bridge leading into town, and a subtle, ominous music cue is audible when they do. (This crossing echoes a similar scene in David Lynch's *The Straight Story* where Alvin Straight crosses a bridge between Iowa and Wisconsin. Lynch alerts us to the importance of this crossing by cutting to an aerial shot of the bridge and introducing a foreboding music cue. The very next shot shows

---

[*] The symmetry of this episode is impossible to ignore. Part 18 begins with Cooper driving through the dark with Diane and ends with Cooper driving through the dark with Carrie. In fact, the editors use some of the same driving footage in both sequences. A careful look at the two scenes shows that Cooper drives *in* with Diane on the exact same road he drives *out* with Carrie. (The traffic signs, distant lights, and road markings are identical.)

[†] Carrie's lines are a reminder of Laura's realization at the end of *Fire Walk With Me* that she is a good person, that she can resist and deny the oppressive forces around her.

Alvin in a graveyard, implying that Alvin will not return from his journey. If he has not already died, he will do so before he can return home. Likewise, the dark music cue as Cooper crosses the bridge into Twin Peaks suggests his visit is a one-way trip. Cooper and Carrie won't be coming back.*)

Cooper and Carrie have reached the boundary of the universe, the end of time and space, a territory devoid of all living things. It might look like they've arrived in Twin Peaks, but no cars drive on the streets, no people walk on the sidewalks, no faces watch from inside the homes. This is a hollow realm, a facsimile of a world they once knew.

The Double R Diner is proof. As Cooper and Carrie drive through the heart of Twin Peaks, they pass a vacant, darkened diner. The parking lot is empty, the lights are off, and the banners welcoming customers for "RR2GO!" are gone. The Double R Diner, once the vibrant, bustling hub of Twin Peaks, is a husk of its former self. Cooper asks if Carrie recognizes anything, but she says, "No." This pseudo-Twin Peaks means nothing to her.

At long last, Cooper arrives at his destination, the Palmer House, the childhood home of Laura Palmer, the great haunted house of Twin Peaks. It looms atop a rise, looking down upon Cooper and Carrie as they exit their car. Lights blaze from almost every window, but there's no sign of life within.

Cooper and Carrie climb the long steps, and Cooper knocks on the front door. He's unsettled that Carrie recognizes nothing of this place, and he gives her an anxious glance. Carrie, for her part, looks all around, as if grasping for an answer just out of reach. She's not afraid; she's in a state of wonder. Her eyes widen as she looks at Cooper and then into the distance and then back at the door. There's a mystery here, and she's trying to solve it.

After a moment, a woman Cooper doesn't recognize opens the door. Cooper asks to see Sarah Palmer, but the woman doesn't know the name. She explains that she owns the house and bought it from someone named Mrs. Chalfont. Cooper, doing his best to hide his confusion and mounting dismay, asks for the woman's name. She tells

---

*Such bridge crossings recall one of Kafka's aphorisms: "From a certain point on, there is no more turning back. That is the point that must be reached."

him: "Alice. Alice Tremond." Cooper thanks her and reluctantly says goodnight.

"Tremond" is not a new name in the story (in fact, it's a name Cooper has heard before, he just doesn't remember it). Mrs. Tremond has haunted the periphery of *Twin Peaks* since Season 2 of the original series, and her presence here, living in the "Palmer house," is a sign that inscrutable forces remain at play, even this late in the story.* It's impossible to say who (or what) Alice Tremond is, but she's certainly an otherworldly character, one of the many Kafkaesque observers who populate the *Twin Peaks* narrative. In the past, Mrs. Tremond was associated with evil inhabitants of the Black Lodge. In *Fire Walk With Me*, she appeared "above the convenience store," watching Bob and The Arm prepare to consume a large amount of garmonbozia, and her presence there suggested that she, too, was a dark figure.

In *Fire Walk With Me*, Mrs. Tremond delivered a framed painting to Laura, a trap designed to lure Laura's dreaming mind into the Red Room and force Laura to confront The Arm. Clearly, Mrs. Tremond (who, as *Fire Walk With Me* hints, might use the alias, "Chalfont") is another entity who would do Laura harm.

What is Mrs. Tremond doing in the Palmer house at the end of time and space? As she stands in her doorway, blocking Cooper from crossing one more mysterious threshold, she carefully glances at Carrie, cutting her eyes away from Cooper as if measuring Carrie's intent.

She's been haunting Laura for ages, Mrs. Tremond has, and she's doing so now. Mrs. Tremond and her compatriots (Bob, The Arm, the Woodsmen) have long known that Laura is "not what she seems," that she is a divine being created by The Fireman and sent to Earth to end The Dark Age. Now, Mrs. Tremond is doing everything she can to

---

* Most *Twin Peaks* fans know that Alice Tremond is played by Mary Reber, the real-life owner of the "Palmer house" in Everett, WA. Some fans speculate that because David Lynch chose Mary Reber for this role, he was signaling that Cooper had entered *the real world*, that Cooper had crossed from the fictional world of *Twin Peaks* into the world we, the viewers, inhabit, but if that's the case, why didn't Cooper encounter a homeowner named *Mary Reber*? Surely that's who would have opened the door to Cooper's knock. (Of course, equally baffling under this scenario is why Cooper would have driven to Everett, WA, instead of Twin Peaks. The whole "real world" theory falls apart the more you think about it.)

postpone the inevitable. If she can turn Cooper and Carrie away, maybe she can extend The Dark Age further.

It appears she has succeeded. Stymied and dispirited, Cooper and Carrie descend the steps and linger in the street. Cooper's program has run its course. He found Laura and brought her home, yet he seemingly failed. Now, Cooper has nowhere else to go, and he buckles in confusion, his certainty slipping away. (According to Kyle MacLachlan, "As I was playing it, I felt a slow draining of confidence…. It was seeping from [Cooper's] pores.")

It's clear in this moment that Cooper never understood why he was bringing Laura home. He walked her to the front door and asked for Sarah Palmer, but he doesn't explain his intent. Earlier, he told "Carrie" it was very important that she go home, but he said no more. You might think that during their long drive from Odessa, Cooper would have elaborated on his reasons for bringing her home, but (as far as we know) he doesn't. That's because he doesn't know himself.

And he probably never will. His participation in The Fireman's grand scheme never required his autonomy, only his acquiescence. He was merely a courier, encoded to deliver Laura Palmer to the end of time. He drove through an endless space and arrived at a cosmic ghost town and never questioned the chronic anomalies around him. As he slumps in the street, Cooper loses his temporal bearings. He has no idea "when" he is. His place in the universe is so incomprehensible he lacks the language to investigate, and he resorts to the simplest of queries: "What year is this?" But there is no answer, because there are no years.

Carrie Page watches Cooper and realizes he can do nothing else for her. He was her ticket out of Odessa and away from trouble, but now she's on her own. Carrie looks back at the house on the hill and takes it all in again and senses something imminent. Lynch's camera floats around her, conveying an instability in the air.

She's close now, close to the answer, close to the reason she needs to be there. There's a faint voice in the night. A memory. An echo of a spirit trapped within the walls of the house. It's her name, sounding across the ages. The voice of her mother calling out…

"Laura!"

Carrie Page ceases to be. Laura Palmer stands alone, balanced on the very edge of The Dark Age, and *screams*. She screams because that's her purpose. She screams because only she can erase the evil that permeates the world. She screams to complete the circle. And when Laura Palmer screams the universe goes dark.

"What will be in the darkness that remains?" asked The Log Lady. We don't know, and we can't know. We are Dale Cooper sitting in the Red Room, baffled as Laura Palmer whispers in his ear, stymied by the secrets she reveals. We cannot grasp the universe she heralds, cannot cross the threshold she evokes.

"We're in a Dark Age," David Lynch tells us. "If we lived in The Golden Age today, we would be there at the end of *Twin Peaks*. But we don't live there, we are in front of the Palmer house."

In front of Laura Palmer's house.

A woman screams.

ACKNOWLEDGEMENTS

WHEN I STARTED WRITING A BOOK about the eighteen-hour *Twin Peaks: The Return*, I imagined it would be a relatively simple task: I'd write my way through the story and provide commentary about what I was watching. I had reams of notes from the many times I'd viewed the series, and I'd simply pepper these observations throughout. Writing such a book wouldn't be much different than how I engaged with social media, tweeting comments about interesting and obscure discoveries I'd made.

How naïve I was! It became apparent early on that a "running commentary" was not going to do *The Return* justice. The work demanded a deeper, more critical analysis.

I had written an essay for *The Blue Rose Magazine* about Dale Cooper's hidden presence in *The Return*, and I wanted that theory to occupy the core of the book. *The Return* is about Cooper and his frustrated, paralyzed mental state, and I could not stray too far or for too long from that central thesis. I knew also that I had to explore the way Laura Palmer has been repositioned in the story. The events of Part 8 demanded a new evaluation of Laura, and, though she was not a prominent character in *The Return*, the story was crucially connected to her.

All that to say, *Ominous Whoosh* became a bigger task than I first expected. What I thought would take about a year to write ended up taking the better part of four years.

Fortunately, along the way, I benefitted from the encouragement, guidance and expertise of many talented people, all of whom are devoted *Twin Peaks* fans.

From the start, Jeff Lemire provided motivation and energy. Jeff read some of the earliest version of my essays, and his positive, enthusiastic feedback buoyed me at times when the material threatened to overwhelm. Thanks, Jeff, for your encouraging words.

I am also lucky for the support from Ben Durant and Bryon Kozaczka (hosts of the podcast, *Twin Peaks Unwrapped*). During one of our conversations in early 2019, I lamented that despite having amassed many pages of notes I didn't know where to start writing. Ben and Bryon gave me valuable advice: "Just start writing. Don't overthink it. Just do it." That was the nudge I needed, and the writing started in earnest after that.

It's no secret that Jeff Jensen is a big *Twin Peaks* fan. He and co-host Darren Franich deliver a lively, savvy exploration of *The Return* on their *Entertainment Weekly* podcast, *A Twin Peaks Podcast: A Podcast About Twin Peaks*. I am grateful for the many kind words Jeff has sent my way over the years. It was a privilege to have him review chapters from this book.

Scott Ryan believed in me long before I started *Ominous Whoosh*. One day, he told me he was going to publish a new *Twin Peaks* magazine and insisted I become part of it. As a result, I was writing about *Twin Peaks* again, this time for *The Blue Rose Magazine*, ten years after I last put pen to paper for *Wrapped In Plastic*. The seeds for this book took root in *The Blue Rose*, and if it weren't for Scott, I might never have tackled this larger project. Thanks for lighting the fire, Scott!

It's been a delight to collaborate with Josh Minton over the past few years. Josh has been my co-host on the podcast, *In Our House Now*, and he has expertly administered that forum, giving me an opportunity to talk about *The Return*. My conversations with Josh have helped me fine-tune much of went into this book. Thanks, Josh, for your continued support and enthusiasm (and for patiently listening to me talk about *Twin Peaks*).

I owe a special thanks to Christian Hartleben, who read early drafts of the book's first six chapters. Christian provided serious, constructive feedback and steered me onto a clearer path during those tentative, beginning days.

My deepest thanks to Courtenay Stallings, who took on the challenging task of copy-editing all the words I wrote about *The*

Return. Courtenay knows *Twin Peaks*, and she knows how to write (see her excellent book, *Laura's Ghost: Women Speak about Twin Peaks*). Her expertise and advice made this a better book, and I'm grateful for her input.

When you're writing a book like this, you need to have reliable resources. I frequently consulted the home video version of *The Return* to check dialog, but, thanks to the tireless effort of Bo Monarch, I also had *scripts* of *The Return* to reference. Bo took the official "Combined Dialog and Continuity Lists" for *The Return* and reconfigured them into script format. As a result, I have two big binders containing the scripts for Parts 1-18. I probably consulted these binders more than any other resource. You worked a miracle, Bo. My hat's off to you!

Andreas Halskov is a gentleman and a scholar and, of course, a great fan of *Twin Peaks*. It was a privilege to meet Andreas in London in 2018. Back then, Andreas and I made tentative plans to write something together—and then I promptly took a four-year detour to write this book. Thanks for understanding, Andreas, and for your generous review of my theses here.

Over the years, I've had many long conversations about *Twin Peaks* with Joel Bocko. It was during one of those talks Joel suggested that "Judy" in *The Return* could be defined as "trauma." I latched onto that idea and wrote an essay about it, but the idea originated with Joel. I'll always be grateful for Joel's insights and his careful thinking about *Twin Peaks*.

Meaningful conversations about *Twin Peaks* are essential, and I'm thankful for the many friends who spent time with me on the phone (or in person) chatting about *The Return*. Greg Olson (author of the indispensable *David Lynch: Beautiful Dark*) patiently listened to many of my ideas and provided valuable feedback. I also benefitted from lively conversations with Brad Dukes, Nick Hyman, Karl Reinsch, Jubel Brosseau, Karl Eckler, Andrew Grevas, Travis Blue, David Bushman, and Robert Wolpert. I am fortunate to be friends with these smart, creative people.

Over the years, I've met or spoken with many *Twin Peaks* fans who have been positive forces in the community (and by extension, my work), including Keith Gow, Steven Miller, Rob King, George Griffith, Josh Eisenstadt, Brian Kursar, Aaron Cohen, Scott Prendergast,

Douglas Baptie, David Milner, Daniel Lambert, John Bernardy, Micah Harris, Ethan Harper, and many, many others. *Twin Peaks* fans are the best!

ON MAY 3, 2017, I was astonished to receive an email inviting me to the world premiere of *Twin Peaks: The Return* in Los Angeles. Thanks to the generosity of Mark Frost, I was able to attend the screening and the party that followed. Truly, it was one of the greatest experiences of my life. Thank you, Mark, for your kindness and the wonderful work you've created over the years.

LATER IN 2017, Mary Reber graciously hosted a *Twin Peaks* "watch party" in her home, the real-life Palmer House. I, along with a few other lucky fans, watched Part 12 of *The Return* in the house where some of that very episode had been filmed. As I mentioned elsewhere in the book, it was an unforgettable evening. Thanks, Mary, for hosting us. And thanks for your continued support of *Twin Peaks* fandom.

THANKS, OF COURSE, TO DAVID LYNCH for his indelible art. (Thanks also for mentioning *Wrapped In Plastic*, Craig Miller, and myself, in your book, *Room to Dream*.)

LAST, BUT NOT LEAST, I thank my family for their support and their contributions to this book. My wife, Laura, read every chapter and provided constructive, essential feedback. My daughter, Sarah, spent many hours designing the front cover. And my son, Daniel, provided a "civilian" perspective on *Twin Peaks* (which came in very handy). Thanks for tolerating my many obsessions over the years. *I'm witness to the fact that you all have hearts of gold.*

Notes

PRELUDE: THE DARKNESS OF FUTURE PAST

"We ought to read only books that bite and sting us" Kafka, letter from January 27, 1904, quoted in Ruefle, *Planet on the Table: Poets on the Reading Life,* p. 52

"as dead as a doornail" David Lynch, *The Complete Lynch,* (Hughes), p. 164

"Ever since we began" Craig Miller & John Thorne, *Wrapped In Plastic* 35, p. i

"The thing that folks" Mark Frost, "Expanding the Twin Peaks Universe," *Electric Lit* (www.electricliterature.com), Dec 27, 2016

"It's hard to believe that someone looks" Lynch, *Eraserhead, The David Lynch Files: Volume 1,* 2020 (Godwin, ebook)

"Somebody has got to intellectualize stuff" Ibid.

PART 1: MY LOG HAS A MESSAGE FOR YOU

"spaceframe" David Sylvester, *Looking back at Francis Bacon,* p. 37

"There's nothing like a beautiful, contained space" Lynch, *Room to Dream,* p. 325

"Fragments of things are pretty interesting" Lynch, *Lynch on Lynch* (Rodley), p. 26

Despite the severity… Kristine McKenna, *Room to Dream,* p. 483

"I cut myself" Grace Zabriskie, *Wrapped In Plastic* 40 (Miller & Thorne), p. 5

"I cut my hand; I still have a scar" Ray Wise, speaking at a screening of *Fire Walk With Me* at the Alamo Drafthouse, Richardson, TX, November, 17, 2019

"powerless individual who" Christina Nicolae, "Franz Kafka's Metamorphic Prison: The Door and the Window," in *Studia Universitatis Petru Maior – Philologia,* Vol. 18, # 1, p. 143

"He thrills me with every sentence" Lynch, *Twilight Zone Magazine* (Vernier), October 1988, Vol. 4, No. 8, p. 50

"The one artist that I feel" Lynch, *David Lynch Interviews* (Barney, ed.), p. 38

"I am memory come alive" Kafka, October 15, 1921, *Diaries,* Schocken Books, p. 392

DAMN! THIS IS REALLY SOMETHING INTERESTING TO THINK ABOUT

"Almost all of . . . the dream" Thorne, *Wrapped In Plastic* 60, p. 6

"threatens to render" Tim Kreider, "But Who is the Dreamer?", http://quarterly.politicsslashletters.org/dreamer-twin-peaks-return/, May 28, 2018

"Cooper is a critical player" Thorne, *Wrapped In Plastic* 60, p. 11

"One of the most important scriptures" Paul Corazza, "Mathematics of Pure Consciousness," *International Journal of Mathematics and Consciousness* Vol. 3, 2017, p. 2

"The world is as you are" Lynch (translated from French), *Cahiers Du Cinema* (Delorme & Tessé), 739, December 2017, p. 13

He expresses it to Martha Nochimson Lynch, *David Lynch Swerves* (Nochimson), p. 182

"If you have dark green dirty glasses" Lynch, *David Lynch Interviews* (Barney), p. 261

"That which is rendered by the senses" *Little Book of Philosophy* (Buckingham), p. 112

"There is no world" George Saunders, *A Swim in the Pond in the Rain*, p. 283

"Overlapping deliria" Brian Rourke, "A Man I Once Knew," sensesofcinema.com, July 2016, #79

"Remembering that the images" Ibid.

"Someone who speaks of events" Seymour Chatman, *Story and Discourse*, p. 197

"Projectionists once in a while" Lynch, *New York Times Style Magazine* (Battachargi), April 12, 2017

"Mental entries" Chatman, p. 216

"Thinking is itself the plot" Ibid.

"I think people's memories are different" Lynch, *Room to Dream*, p. 299

"Even if you get the whole thing" Lynch, *Lynch on Lynch Revised Edition* (Rodley), p. 288

"positioned story material" Thorne, *Wrapped In Plastic* 60, p. 12

PART 2: THE STARS TURN AND A TIME PRESENTS ITSELF

"a long period" Frost, thefilmstage.com, November 7, 2017

"It's the pilot and the Red Room" Lynch, *Room to Dream*, p. 278

"anything can happen" Lynch, *Lynch on Lynch* (Rodley), p. 19

"[In] the Red Room…time doesn't exist" Sheryl Lee, *The Blue Rose* 8 (Ryan), November 2018, p. 5

"some abstract elements" Lynch, *Lynch on Lynch Revised Edition* (Rodley), p. 288

"once had some sort of intelligible shape" Kafka, "The Cares of a Family Man," *The Complete Stories*, p. 428

"pretending to be Phillip Jeffries" Frost, *Conversations With Mark Frost* (Bushman), p. 270

a place beyond cosmic law… Norman W. Brown, "The Creation Myth of the Rig Veda," *Journal of American Oriental Society,* Vol. 63, No. 2, p. 88

"I think the show" Frost, "The Mark Frost Guide to The Pilot" (Marrone), *The Blue Rose* #13, p. 10

PART 3: CALL FOR HELP

"the Mansion Room" Lynch, "Impressions: A Journey Behind the Scenes of Twin Peaks—The Number of Completion," Disc 8, *Twin Peaks: A Limited Event Series* Blu-ray

"embodies the ideal" Todd McGowan, *The Impossible David Lynch*, p. 131

"symbolizes the exact traits" Siobhan Lyons, "David Lynch's American Nightmare," *Approaching Twin Peaks: Critical Essays on the Original Series* (Hoffman & Grace), p. 134

"In this story" Lynch, *Cinefantasique* (Godwin), Vol. 14, 4/5, September 1984, p. 46

"That there's a mystery" Lynch, *Lynch on Lynch* (Rodley), p. 26

"Many dots can be connected" McKenna, *Room to Dream*, p. 491

"Everybody has theories" Lynch, *Room to Dream*, p. 503

"in the confusion of our senses" Kafka, *The Blue Octavo Notebooks* (Third Octavo Notebook) (ebook)

SOUL SURVIVOR

"almost inhuman, lacking any remorse" Kyle MacLachlan, Monte Carlo TV Festival, 2017

"No time has passed for you" Lynch, "A Very Lovely Dream: One Week in Twin Peaks," Disc 8, *Twin Peaks: A Limited Event Series* Blu-ray

"would only be half-a-person" Miller & Thorne, *Wrapped In Plastic* 53, p. 12

"a sort of super-being" Ibid.

"literally comes apart" Thorne, *The Essential Wrapped In Plastic*, p. 241

"In order to appreciate one" Lynch, *Lynch on Lynch* (Rodley), p. 23

PART 4: ...BRINGS BACK SOME MEMORIES

"the greater the amount of 'watching,'" Weizmann Institute Of Science, "Quantum Theory Demonstrated: Observation Affects Reality," www.sciencedaily.com/releases/1998/02/980227055013.htm

PART 5: CASE FILES

"Coop wasn't occupied by Bob" Lynch, *Lynch on Lynch* (Rodley), p. 183

"managed to take a picture of himself" Lynch, speaking at 2017 Festival of Disruption, as quoted in *Twin Peaks Blog*, https://twinpeaksblog.com/2019/03/03/twin-peaks-film-location-lucky-7-insurance-building-exterior/

"total fulfilment in infinite bliss" Lynch, *David Lynch Swerves* (Nochimson), p. 182

PART 6: DON'T DIE

"When you see this red light" Lynch, *Lynch on Lynch* (Rodley), p. 170

"There were moments where Cooper" MacLachlan, *Twin Peaks Unwrapped*, (Durant & Kozaczka, eds.), p. 277

David Lynch re-wrote... Actor Jeremy Lindholm confirmed the re-writing of this scene at the 2017 Twin Peaks Fan Festival.

"[Lynch] added the Richard and Linda" Frost, *Conversations with Mark Frost* (Bushman), p. 268

"In the Hindu religion" Lynch (translated from French), *Cahiers Du Cinema* (Delorme & Tessé), 739, p. 13

"It is a dark time" Ibid.

"I know that Laura wrote that down" Lynch, *Lynch on Lynch* (Rodley), p. 187

LEAVE HER OUT OF IT

"She fits into a cyclical pattern" Thorne, *Wrapped In Plastic* 75, p. 32

"[Phillip Jeffries] was down there" Robert Engels, *Wrapped In Plastic* 58 (Miller & Thorne), p. 8

"In Lynch's mind" Thorne, *Wrapped In Plastic* 75, p. 34

Judy to be a "bad entity" Lynch (translated from French), *Cahiers Du Cinema* (Delorme & Tessé), 739, p. 12

"He never explained why" Martha Nochimson, *Television Rewired*, p. 288

"You might think your script" Lynch, *Wrapped In Plastic* 65 (Miller and Thorne), p. 4

"According to her parents" Frost, *The Final Dossier*, p. 136

"I've never heard that term before" Frost, *Conversations with Mark Frost* (Bushman), p. 256

"Wandering demon that thrives" Frost, *The Final Dossier*, p. 122

"A lot was left unsaid" Lynch, *Lynch on Lynch Revised Edition* (Rodley), p. 223

PART 7: THERE'S A BODY ALRIGHT

"It was a scene that I hadn't seen" Robert Forster, *A Twin Peaks Podcast*, 19:51, June 30, 2017

a presence "identified with camera" Alice Kuzniar, *Full of Secrets* (Lavery), p. 128

"There is another picture" Lynch (translated from French), *Cahiers Du Cinema* (Delorme & Tessé), 739, p. 18

He once took two of the show's actors vulture.com, "10 Quirky David Lynch Stories," (Ivie), Sept. 6, 2017

"I don't seem to be getting any nearer" Kafka, "The Burrow," *The Complete Stories*, pp. 344 & 347

Mark Frost describes Part Seven... "A Conversation with Mark Frost," *On Story*, Season 8 Episode 9, www.pbs.org/video/a-conversation-with-mark-frost-ti8nwn/

"It's just one of those things" Duwayne Dunham, *The Blue Rose* 12 (Stallings), p. 21

"We did nine movies in one year"   Ibid.

PART 8: GOTTA LIGHT?

"a beautiful medium for going back"   Lynch, *Wrapped In Plastic* 65 (Miller & Thorne), p. 5

"There are different ages"   Lynch (translated from French), *Cahiers Du Cinema* (Delorme & Tessé), 739, p. 10

"the young Sarah Palmer"   Tikaeni Faircrest, *Twin Peaks Unwrapped* (Durant & Kozaczka, Eds.), p. 224

TEN IS THE NUMBER OF COMPLETION

"I was in love with the character"   Lynch, *Lynch on Lynch* (Rodley), p. 184

"Lynch is asking viewers to assess"   Thorne, *The Essential Wrapped In Plastic*, p. 297

"moral order will continue to decline"   Amrutur V. Srinivasan, *Hinduism for Dummies*, p. 122

"[Lynch] did tell me about that"   Frost, *Conversations with Mark Frost* (Bushman), p. 136

"What is real never ceases to be"   *The Bhagavad Gita*, Chapter 2, Verse 16

"his method of telling stories"   Nochimson, *David Lynch Swerves*, p. xv

"are born into human life"   Srinivasan, *Hinduism for Dummies*, p. 114

"I work for David Lynch."   Laura Dern, "Impressions: A Journey Behind the Scenes of Twin Peaks—The Number of Completion," Disc 8, *Twin Peaks: A Limited Event Series* Blu-ray

"Lynch couldn't let go"   Frost, *Conversations with Mark Frost* (Bushman), p. 251

"Fire Walk With Me is very important"   Lynch, *Room to Dream*, p. 503

"Things have harmonics"   Ibid.

"I knew my life was over"   "Between Two Worlds," Disc 10, *Twin Peaks: The Entire Mystery* Blu-ray

"The presence of the angel"   Nochimson, *The Passion of David Lynch*, p. 190

"They [angels] destroy"   Luce Irigaray, *The Passion of David Lynch* (Nochimson), p. 252

"capacitor: storing a huge"   David Auerbach, "Twin Peaks Finale: A Theory of Cooper, Laura, Diane, and Judy," https://www.waggish.org/2017/twin-peaks-finale/

"through his deep concern"   Ken Volante, "Dale Cooper, Buddhist Mystic," *Wrapped in Plastic* 67, p. 3 & p. 8

"Lynch's cinematic zeitgeist"   Nochimson, *David Lynch Swerves*, p. xvi

"alludes to the wheel"   McKenna, *Room to Dream*, p. 140

"When will all the new universes"   Lynch, *Ronnie Rocket* screenplay, p.182, https://docs.google.com/document/d/10krnH87f4zJc6_wuT5QHU93NVqnar-VMa5gBqBvPkmQ/edit

PART 11: THERE'S FIRE WHERE YOU ARE GOING
a Jack Russell Terrier that he called "the love of [his] life"   Lynch, "Lynch dives within," (Chonin), SFGate.com, February 7, 2007

PART 12: LET'S ROCK
"the sound of doors closing"   Andrew T. Burt, "The Thread Will be Torn," *Music in Twin Peaks* (Wissner & Reed), p. 112

"[Lynch] didn't pursue it"   Frost, *Conversations with Mark Frost* (Bushman), p. 245

"a couple of times"   Ibid.

"perfect balance"   Lynch, *Wrapped in Plastic* 75 (Miller & Thorne), p. 4

"When you talk about things"   Lynch, *Lynch on Lynch* (Rodley), p. 27

"No one really knows"   "Between Two Worlds," Disc 10, *Twin Peaks: The Entire Mystery* Blu-ray

"The town's houses are rife"   Richard Martin, *The Architecture of David Lynch*, p. 87

I'M NOT SURE WHO I AM, BUT I'M NOT ME
"It was just bad"   Sherilynn Fenn, "Days of the Dead: Sherilynn Fenn Walks Through Fire," fox59.com

"We got in a fight"   Fenn, Twin Peaks Panel at SpaCon 2017, https://www.youtube.com/watch?v=6IVPJPEmqWk

"the Battered Woman"   Greg Olson, *Beautiful Dark*, p. 671

"the abused woman"   Nochimson, *David Lynch Swerves*, p. 146

"the nameless woman"   Rourke, "A Man I Once Knew," sensesofcinema.com, July 2016, # 79

"a standalone thing"   Lynch, *Room to Dream*, p. 234

"holds the key to everything"   Ibid. p. 343

"Everything in the film"   Olson, *Beautiful Dark*, p. 672

"Gone was Audrey's original"   Nochimson, *The Passion of David Lynch*, p. 92

"Names are weird things"   Lynch, *Lynch on Lynch* (Rodley), p. 26

"I picture it like a white room"   Lynch, *Catching The Big Fish*, pp. 49-50

"My delusion has gone"   Jack Hawley, *The Bhagavad Gita: A Walkthrough for Westerners*, (ebook)

PART 13: WHAT STORY IS THAT, CHARLIE?
"I did this drawing based on Gogol"   Lynch, *The Air is On Fire*, p. 23

"People still made sense"   Lynch, *New York Times Style Magazine* (Battacharji), April 12, 2017

"If there was a reflection"   Dunham, *The Blue Rose* 11 (Stallings), p. 21

WHAT'S GOING ON IN THIS HOUSE?

"are not about monsters" Wallace, "David Lynch Keeps His Head," *A Supposedly Fun Thing I'll Never Do Again*, p. 204

"a psychic disturbance" David Langford and John Grant, "Haunted Dwellings,' *The Encyclopedia of Fantasy* (Clute & Grant), p. 455

"I like to go deeper" Lynch, *Lynch on Lynch* (Rodley), p. 18

"Lots of things are falling apart" "Between Two Worlds," Disc 10, *Twin Peaks: The Entire Mystery* Blu-ray

"A home is a place" Lynch, *Lynch on Lynch* (Rodley), p. 10

PART 14: WE ARE LIKE THE DREAMER

Harry Goaz believes Andy is innocent Harry Goaz, personal conversation with the author, Richardson, Texas, September 16, 2017

"was seen by more than twenty witnesses" Frost, *The Final Dossier*, p. 131

"the heavyweight of surrealism" Lynch, *The Complete Lynch* (Hughes), p. 24 (original citation: *Ruth, Roses and Revolvers*, BBC Television, 1987)

PART 15: THERE'S SOME FEAR IN LETTING GO

"talisman come to life" Carlton Lee Russel, "Moving Through Time: Fire Walk With Me Memories," *Twin Peaks: The Entire Mystery* Blu-ray

"I tried to pin it into some underlying concepts" Frost, *Conversations with Mark Frost* (Bushman), p. 248

"We had just heard about" Kimmy Robertson, appearing at a panel at the Dallas Comic Show, September 16, 2017

PART 16: NO KNOCK, NO DOORBELL

"there's something very contrived" A.E. Denham and F.D. Worrell, "Identity and Agency in Mulholland Drive," *Mulholland Drive* (Giannopoulou), p. 22

"There are no rules" Lynch (translated from French), *Cahiers Du Cinema* (Delorme & Tessé), 739, p. 12

"anchored in...the *Twin Peaks*" Lynch, *Room to Dream*, p. 502

"The mind is such a friend to us" Lynch, *Lynch on Lynch Revised Edition* (Rodley), p. 289

MISSING PIECES: PUTTING "DIANE" TOGETHER

"has too many bodies" Nochimson, *Television Rewired*, p. 254

"Not really anything" Ibid., p. 256.

Lynch explored dual identities... Thorne, "Dreams of Deer Meadow," *The Essential Wrapped In Plastic*

"discards the binary structure of the earlier films" Timothy William Galow, "From Lost Highway to Twin Peaks," *Critical Essays on Twin Peaks: The Return* (Sanna), p. 203

"explores the relationship between trauma and fantasy" Ibid. p. 212

"I thought of it as playing a broken or dismantled person," Dern, *The Man from Another Place* (Lim), p. 172

"Sue Blue's fantasy" Bill Roberts, *Unlocking INLAND EMPIRE*, p. 22

"the fantasmatic figure" McGowan, "The Materiality of Fantasy," *David Lynch: In Theory* (Gleyzon, ebook)

"never-never land" Lynch, "Impressions: A Journey Behind the Scenes of Twin Peaks—A Bloody Finger in Your Mouth," Disc 8, *Twin Peaks: A Limited Event Series* Blu-ray

"It changes, depending" Lynch, *The Passion of David Lynch* (Nochimson), p. 251

"You haven't seen each other" Lynch, "Behind The Curtain, Part 18," A Limited Event Series Disc 10, *Twin Peaks from Z to A* Blu-ray

"Diane is Cooper's true love" Dern, *Room to Dream* (Lynch & McKenna), p. 479

"sometimes you have to sacrifice" Srinivasan, *Hinduism for Dummies*, p. 348

"The important thing is to be able...to sacrifice" Maharishi Mahesh Yogi, *Between the Sabbats: The Magick and Mystery of the Interpora* (Case), p. 143

"exceeds the limits" Rourke, "A Man I Once Knew," sensesofcinema.com, July 2016, # 79

"personification of all feminine" M. L. von Franz, *Man and His Symbols* (Jung), p. 186

"When a Frenchman" Jean Cocteau, "Cocteau on Orpheus," excerpted from *The Art of Cinema*, as excerpted in "Orpheus," Criterion Blu-ray booklet, p. 20

"accept Diane's offer" Nochimson, *Television Rewired*, p. 256

PART 17: THE PAST DICTATES THE FUTURE

"Lynch subverts...the distinction" Rourke, "A Man I Once Knew," sensesofcinema.com, July 2016, # 79

"She is both puppet" Ibid.

"[We] seemed in concert" Frost, *Conversations with Mark Frost* (Bushman), p. 263

"I was trying to offer" Ibid. p. 270

"I do not know the answers" Lynch (translated from French), *Cahiers Du Cinema* (Delorme & Tessé), 739, p. 14

"[Bob] is an abstraction in human form." Lynch, *Lynch on Lynch* (Rodley), p. 178

"Everybody is a mix" Lynch, *Room to Dream*, p. 228

"Something's slippery" Lynch, "Behind The Curtain, Part 17," disc 10, *Twin Peaks from Z to A* Blu-ray

"It's the self knowing the self" Lynch, *David Lynch Interviews* (Barney), p. 257

"never-never land" Lynch, "Impressions: A Journey Behind the Scenes of Twin Peaks—A Bloody Finger in Your Mouth," Disc 8, *Twin Peaks: A Limited Event Series* Blu-ray

"black dot" Nochimson, *Television Rewired*, p. 263

"Agent Cooper wishes" Lee, *The Blue Rose* 8 (Ryan), p. 5

"I have been told" Ibid. p. 4

"the photograph remains unbroken" Allister Mactaggart, "I am dead yet I live": Revealing the Enigma of Art in *Twin Peaks: The Return, NANO (New American Notes Online)*, nanocrit.com/issues/issue15

"We know that something" Ibid. p. 5

"There is a certain failing" Kafka, *Diaries*, p. 411

I Got Idea Man

"Once a name starts getting certain meanings" Lynch, *Lynch on Lynch* (Rodley), p. 29

"The script-making process involves getting ideas" Lynch, *Conversations at the American Film Institute with the Great Moviemakers* (Stevens, ebook)

"It's a film world but it has its own reality" Lynch, *Wrapped In Plastic* 65 (Miller & Thorne), p. 4

"The ideas present a kind of flow" Lynch, deadline.com, May 19, 2017

"Ideas came, and this is what the ideas presented" Ibid.

"I strive to do something right" Lynch, (translated from French), *Cahiers Du Cinema* (Delorme & Tessé), 739, p. 13

"A man tells a very abstract, very original story" Lynch, *David Lynch Interviews* (Barney), p. 114

"Every viewer, no matter what film they are looking at" Lynch, *Wrapped In Plastic* 65 (Miller & Thorne), p. 4

"against the kind of film" Lynch, *David Lynch Interviews*, (Barney), p. 138

"The more abstract the film, the more audiences give" Lynch, *David Lynch Interviews*, (Barney), p. 203

"How do you know when something's in your work and when it isn't?" Frost, *Teleliteracy: Taking Television Seriously* (Bianculli), p. 283

"sort of lazy and childish in its expectations" Wallace, *Conversations With David Foster Wallace*, (McCaffrey) p. 22

"proceeds more or less chronologically" Ibid.

"most films are designed to be understood by many" Lynch, *Lynch on Lynch* (Rodley), p. 228

"dialog between a picture and the audience" Lynch, *David Lynch Interviews*, (Barney), p. 209

"good television" Brad Dukes, "A Love Letter to Twin Peaks: The Return," *The Blue Rose* 12, p. 4

"the story sharing its valence with the reader" Wallace, *Conversations With David Foster Wallace*, (McCaffrey) p. 40

PART 18: WHAT IS YOUR NAME?

"To reconcile those two opposing things is the trick" Lynch, *Lynch on Lynch* (Rodley), p. 23

"He's not Dougie 'complete,' and he's not Cooper 'complete'" MacLachlan, "The Envelope's Emmy Contender Series," *Los Angeles Times*

"You haven't seen each other" Lynch, "Behind The Curtain, Part 18," A Limited Event Series Disc 10, *Twin Peaks from Z to A* Blu-ray

Odessa is a reference to Homer's *The Odyssey*... Mark Frost discusses *The Odyssey* on the *Talkhouse Podcast*: "Sam Esmail (*Mr. Robot*) Talks with Mark Frost (*Twin Peaks*)," 11/16/17

"He's a slightly harder version of the Cooper we remember." MacLachlan, "The Envelope's Emmy Contender Series," *Los Angeles Times*

"Dissociative disorders usually develop as a way to cope with trauma." https://www.mayoclinic.org/diseases-conditions/dissociative-disorders/symptoms-causes/syc-20355215

"ended up hurling both Cooper and Laura into a sideways, alternate dimension" Frost, *Conversations with Mark Frost* (Bushman), p. 271

"We're not going to stop and worry about those things" Lynch, "Behind The Curtain, Part 18," Disc 10, A Limited Event Series, *Twin Peaks from Z to A* Blu-ray

"From a certain point on, there is no more turning back." Kafka, *Aphorisms*, p. 7

"As I was playing it, I felt a slow draining of confidence" MacLachlan, "Toast of 2017: Kyle MacLachlan Shares the Secrets of 'Twin Peaks: The Return'" Yahoo TV, 12/18/17, Yahoo.com

"If we lived in The Golden Age today, we would be there at the end of Twin Peaks." Lynch (translated from French), *Cahiers Du Cinema* (Delorme & Tessé), 739, p. 10

Sources

BOOKS:

Alexander, John; *The Films of David Lynch*; (Charles Letts and Co. Limited, 1993)

Alison, Jane; *Meander, Spiral, Explode: Design and Pattern in Narrative*; (Catapult, 2019)

Anderson, Melissa; *Inland Empire*; (Fireflies Press, 2021)

Ball, Philip; *Beyond Weird: Why Everything You Thought About Quantum Physics is Different*; (University of Chicago Press, 2018)

Barney, Richard A. (Ed.); *David Lynch: Interviews*; (University Press of Mississippi, 2009)

Bianculli, David; *Teleliteracy: Taking Television Seriously*; (Continuum, 1992)

Boulègue, Franck; *Supernatural Studies Special Issue: Twin Peaks*; Vol 5, Issue 2; (Supernatural Studies Association, 2019)

Breskin, David; *Inner Views: Filmmakers in Conversation*; (Faber and Faber, 1992)

Bryon, Sharon and William Olson; *Planet on the Table: Poets on the Reading Life*; (Sarbande Books, 2003)

Buckingham, Will, (et al.); *The Little Book of Philosophy*; (DK Publishing, 2011)

Bulkeley, Kelly (Ed.); *Among All These Dreamers: Essays on Dreaming and Modern Society*; (State University of New York Press, 1996)

Burn, Stephen J.; *Conversations with David Foster Wallace*; (University Press of Mississippi, 2012)

Bushman, David; *Conversations with Mark Frost*; (Fayetteville Mafia Press, 2020)

Capra, Fritjof; *The Tao of Physics: An Exploration of the Parallels between Modern Physics and Eastern Mysticism*, 5th Ed.; (Shambhala Publications, 2010)

Case, L.; *Between the Sabbats: The Magick and Mystery of the Interpora*; (L. Case, 2019)

Chatman, Seymour; *Story and Discourse: Narrative Structure in Fiction and Film*; (Cornell University Press, 1978)

Chion, Michel; *David Lynch*; (BFI Publishing, 1995)

Clute, John and John Grant (Eds.); *The Encyclopedia of Fantasy*; (St. Martin's Griffin, 1999)

Devlin, William J., and Shai Biderman; *The Philosophy of David Lynch*; (The University Press of Kentucky, 2011)

DiPaolo, Amanda and Jamie Gillies (Eds.); *The Politics of Twin Peaks*; (Lexington Books, 2019)

Durant, Ben and Bryon Kozaczka; *Twin Peaks Unwrapped;* (Scott Ryan Productions, 2020)

Dyer, Geoff; *Zona: A Book About a Film About a Journey to a Room*; (Vintage books, 2012)

Frost, Mark; *The Secret History of Twin Peaks*; (Flatiron Books, 2016)

——; *Twin Peaks: The Final Dossier*; (Flatiron Books, 2017)

Gabbert, Elisa; *The Unreality of Memory*; (FSG Originals, 2020)

George, Stevens, Jr. (Ed.); *Conversations at the American Film Institute with the Great Moviemakers: The Next Generation*; (Knopf, 2012)

Giannopoulou, Zina (Ed.); *Mulholland Drive*; (Routledge, 2013)

Gleyzon, Francis-Xavier (Ed.); *David Lynch: In Theory*; (Litteraria Pragensia Books, 2010)

Godwin, Kenneth; *Eraserhead, The David Lynch Files: Volume 1*; (Bear Manor Media, 2020)

Gogol, Nikolai (translated by Ronald Wilks); *Diary of a Madman and Other Stories*; (Penguin Books, 1972)

Grossman, Julie, and Will Scheibel; *Twin Peaks*; (Wayne State University Press, 2020)

Hawley, Jack (Ed.); *The Bhagavad Gita: A Walkthrough for Westerners*; (New World Library, 2001)

Hayes-Brady, Clare; *The Unspeakable Failures of David Foster Wallace: Language Identity and Resistance*; (Bloomsbury Academic, 2016)

Hoffman, Donald; *The Case Against Reality: Why Evolution Hid the Truth from Our Eyes*; (W.W Norton & Company, 2019)

Hoffman, Eric and Dominick Grace; *Approaching Twin Peaks: Critical Essays on the Original Series*; (McFarland & Company, Inc., 2017)

Hughes, David; *The Complete Lynch*; (Virgin Publishing, 2001)

Jung, Carl G. (Ed.); *Man and His Symbols*; (Dell Publishing, 1964)

Kafka, Franz; *Aphorisms* (translated by Willa and Edwin Muir and Michael Hoffmann); (Schocken Books, 2015)

——; *Blue Octavo Notebooks;* https://docs.google.com/document/d /1gD981HZ190BUJF-3czZNX3DsFWvqp3cq-Z4QS4d-9gw

——; *The Castle* (translated by Mark Harman); (Schocken Books, 1998)

——; *Complete Stories* (Nahum N. Glatzer, Ed.); (Schocken Books, 1971)

——; *Diaries* (Max Brod, Ed.); (Schocken Books, 1948)

——; *The Metamorphosis* (translated by Susan Bernofsky); (W.W Norton & Company, 2014)

——; *The Trial* (translated by Breon Mitchell); (Schocken Books, 1998)

Lavery, David (Ed.); *Full of Secrets: Critical Approaches to Twin Peaks;* (Wayne State University Press, 1995)

Levin, Gail; *Edward Hopper: The Art and The Artist*; (W.W Norton & Company, 1980)

Lim, Dennis; *David Lynch: The Man from Another Place*; (New Harvest, Houghton Mifflin Harcourt, 2015)

Lynch, David; *The Air is on Fire*; (Fondation Cartier pour l'art contemporain, Paris, 2007)

——; *Catching the Big Fish*; (Jeremy P. Tarcher/Penguin, 2007)

——; *The Prints of David Lynch*; (Tandem Press, University of Wisconsin-Madison, 2000)

Lynch, David and Kristine McKenna; *Room to Dream*; (Random House, 2018)

Mactaggart, Allister; *The Film Paintings of David Lynch: Challenging Film Theory*; (Intellect, The University of Chicago Press, 2010)

Martin, Richard; *The Architecture of David Lynch*; (Bloomsbury Academic, 2014)

Mayo Clinic Staff; "Dissociative disorders"; https://www.mayoclinic.org/diseases-conditions/dissociative-disorders/symptoms-causes/syc-20355215

McGowan, Todd; *The Impossible David Lynch*; (Columbia University Press, 2007)

Miller, Matt (Ed.); *NANO (New American Notes Online) Special Issue 15: Twin Peaks: The Return*; nanocrit.com/issues/issue15

Nieland, Justus; *David Lynch*; (University of Illinois Press, 2012)

Nochimson, Martha P.; *David Lynch Swerves: Uncertainty from Lost Highway to Inland Empire*; (University of Texas Press, 2013)

——; *The Passion of David Lynch: Wild at Heart in Hollywood*; (University of Texas Press, 1997)

——; *Television Rewired: The Rise of the Auteur Series*; (University of Texas Press, 2019)

Olson, Greg; *David Lynch: Beautiful Dark*; (Scarecrow Press Inc, 2008)

Radin, Dean (PhD); *Real Magic: Ancient Wisdom, Modern Science, and a Guide to the Secret Power of the Universe*; (Harmony Books, 2018)

Rhodes, Richard; *The Making of the Atomic Bomb*; (Simon and Schuster, 2005)

Roberts, Bill; *Unlocking INLAND EMPIRE*; (Createspace, 2020)

Rodley, Chris (Ed.); *Lynch on Lynch*; (Faber and Faber, 1997)

——; *Lynch on Lynch Revised Edition*; (Faber and Faber, 2005)

Sanna, Antonio (Ed.); *Critical Essays on Twin Peaks: The Return*; (Palgrave MacMillan, 2019)

Saunders, George; *A Swim in the Pond in the Rain*; (Random House, 2021)

Sheen, Erica and Annette Davison (Eds.); *The Cinema of David Lynch: American Dreams, Nightmare Visions*; (Wallflower Press, 2004)

Srinivasan, Dr. Amrutur V.; *Hinduism for Dummies*; (John Wiley & Sons, Inc, 2011)

Stallings, Courtenay; *Laura's Ghost: Women Speak about Twin Peaks*; (Fayetteville Mafia Press, 2020)

Sylvester, David; *Looking back at Francis Bacon*; (Thames and Hudson, 2000)

Thorne, John; *The Essential Wrapped In Plastic*; (John Thorne, 2016)

Wallace, David Foster; *A Supposedly Fun Thing I'll Never Do Again*; (Little, Brown & Co., 1997)

Weinstock, Jeffrey Andrew and Catherine Spooner (Eds.); *Return to Twin Peaks: New Approaches to Materiality, Theory, and Genre on Television*; (Palgrave MacMillan, 2016)

Wissner, Reba A. and Katherine M. Reed (Eds.); *Music in Twin Peaks; Listen to the Sounds*; (Routledge, 2021)

ESSAYS, ARTICLES, AND INTERVIEWS

Auerbach, David; "Twin Peaks Finale: A Theory of Cooper, Laura, Diane, and Judy"; *Waggish*; waggish.org, September 7, 2017

Battacharji, Alex; "25 Years Later, David Lynch Returns to 'Twin Peaks"; *New York Times Style Magazine*, April 12, 2017

Beaver, Jeremiah; "Days of the Dead: Sherilynn Fenn Walks Through Fire," *Fox 59*; fox59.com, July 4, 2019

Bradley, Ryan W.; "Expanding the Twin Peaks Universe"; https://electricliterature.com/expanding-the-twin-peaks-universe/; 2016

Brown, Norman W.; "The Creation Myth of the Rig Veda." *Journal of American Oriental Society,* Vol. 63, No. 2, June 1942

Chonin, Neva; "David Lynch dives within"; *SFGate*; www.sfgate.com/entertainment/article/Lynch-dives-within-The-cult-director-discusses-2651144.php, February 7, 2007

Chute, David, "Out to Lynch"; *David Lynch: Interviews*; (University Press of Mississippi, 2009)

Church, Margaret; "Time and Reality in Kafka's The Trial and The Castle"; *Twentieth Century Literature*, Vol. 2, No. 2

Ciment, Michael and Hubert Niagret; "Interview with David Lynch"; *David Lynch: Interviews*; (University Press of Mississippi, 2009)

Cocteau, Jean; "Cocteau on Orpheus"; excerpted from *The Art of Cinema*, as excerpted in "Orpheus" Criterion Blu-ray booklet, 2011

Corazza; Paul; "Mathematics of Pure Consciousness"; *International Journal of Mathematics and Consciousness,* Vol. 3, 2017

Daniel, Adam; "Kafka's Crime Film: Twin Peaks—The Return and the Brotherhood of Lynch and Kafka"; *Critical Essays on Twin Peaks: The Return*; (Palgrave MacMillan, 2019)

Delorme, Stéphane and Jen-Phillipe Tessé; "Mystery Man: Interview with David Lynch;" *Cahiers Du Cinema,* #739, December 2017

Denham, A.E., and F.D. Worrell, "Identity and Agency in Mulholland Drive"; *Mulholland Drive*, (Routledge, 2013)

Dijkstrajuly, Nadine; "The Fine Line Between Reality and Imaginary"; nautil.us/the-fine-line-between-reality-and-imaginary-9884/; July 28, 2021

Dukes, Brad; "A Love Letter to Twin Peaks: The Return (Straight from my Heart)"; *The Blue Rose Magazine*, Vol. 1, No. 12

Eidizadeh, Hossein; "When You See Me Again It Won't Be Me: The Metamorphosis, Franz Kafka and David Lynch's Life-long Obsession"; *Senses of Cinema*; sensesofcinema.com, October 2018, #88

Galow, Timothy William; "From Lost Highway to Twin Peaks"; *Critical Essays on Twin Peaks: The Return*; (Palgrave MacMillan, 2019)

Godwin, Kenneth; "Eraserhead: The Story Behind the Strangest Film Ever Made and the Cinematic genius Who Directed It"; *Cinefantasique* Vol. 14, #4/5, September 1984

Hall, Simon; "Sentiment, Mood, and Performing the Past: James Hurley's Re-enactment of 'Just You' in Twin Peaks: The Return"; *NANO (New American Notes Online)*; nanocrit.com/issues/issue15

Ivie, Devon; "10 Quirky David Lynch Stories"; vulture.com; www.vulture.com/2017/09/david-lynch-10-quirky-stories.html

Kreider, Tim; "But Who is the Dreamer?"; quarterly.politicsslashletters.org/dreamer-twin-peaks-return/, May 28, 2018

Kuzniar, Alice, "Double Talk in Twin Peaks"; *Full of Secrets: Critical Approaches to Twin Peaks;* (Wayne State University Press, 1995)

Lončar, Karla; "The Trial and Tribulations in Twin Peaks: The Return"; *NANO (New American Notes Online)*; nanocrit.com/issues/issue15

Lynch, David; *Ronnie Rocket* screenplay, https://docs.google.com/document/d/10krnH87f4zJc6_wuT5QHU93NVqnar-VMa5gBqBvPkmQ/edit

Lyons, Siobhan, "David Lynch's American Nightmare"; *Approaching Twin Peaks: Critical Essays on the Original Series*; (McFarland & Company, Inc., 2017)

Mactaggart, Allister; "'I am dead yet I live': Revealing the Enigma of Art in Twin Peaks: The Return"; *NANO (New American Notes Online)*; nanocrit.com/issues/issue15

Marrone, Matt; "The Mark Frost Guide to The Pilot"; *The Blue Rose Magazine*, Vol. 2, #13, April 2020

McCaffrey, Larry; "An Expanded Interview with David Foster Wallace"; *Conversations with David Foster Wallace*; (University Press of Mississippi, 2012)

McGowan, Todd; "The Materiality of Fantasy"; *David Lynch: In Theory*; (Litteraria Pragensia Books, 2010)

Mejia, Paula; "Dreaming the Big Dream: A Conversation with David Lynch"; *Spin*; spin.com, June 28, 2013

Miller, Craig and John Thorne; "The Kaleidoscopic Talent of Grace Zabriskie"; *Wrapped In Plastic* #40, April, 1999

John Thorne

———; "We're Gonna Talk About Judy and a Whole Lot More: An Interview with Robert Engels"; *Wrapped In Plastic* #58, April, 2002

———; "An Interview with David Lynch: The Mind Inside the Mind Inside Eraserhead"; *Wrapped In Plastic* #65, June, 2003

———; "Perfect Balance: David Lynch on Movies and Meditation"; *Wrapped In Plastic* #75, September, 2005

Miller, Steven, "Twin Peaks Film Location – Lucky 7 Insurance Building Exterior"; *Twin Peaks Blog*, twinpeaksblog.com/2019/03/03/twin-peaks-film-location-lucky-7-insurance-building-exterior/

Newman, Nick; "Mark Frost on 'Twin Peaks,' Realistic Endings, and David Lynch's Consciousness"; *The Film Stage*, thefilmstage.com, November 7, 2017

Nicolae, Christina; "Franz Kafka's Metamorphic Prison: The Door and the Window"; *Studia Universitatis Petru Maior – Philologia*, Vol. 18, #1

Rourke, Brian; "A Man I Once Knew: Old Tales and Bad Time in David Lynch's Inland Empire"; *Senses of Cinema*; sensesofcinema.com, July 2016, #79

Ruefle, Mary, "Someone Reading a Book is A Sign of Order in the World"; *Planet on the Table: Poets on the Reading Life*; (Sarbande Books, 2003)

Ryan, Scott; "Sheryl Lee: The Dream Interview"; *The Blue Rose Magazine*, Vol. 1, #8, November 2018

Sragow, Michael; "I Want a Dream When I Go to a Film"; *David Lynch: Interviews*; (University Press of Mississippi, 2009)

Stallings, Courtenay; "The Editor: Duwayne Dunham (Part 1)"; *The Blue Rose Magazine*, Vol. 1, #11, August 2019

———; "Duwayne Dunham Interview (Part 2)"; *The Blue Rose Magazine*, Vol. 1, #12, November 2019

Thorne, John; "Dreams of Deer Meadow"; *Wrapped In Plastic* #60, August, 2002

———; "Fire Walk With Me: Three More Observations"; *Wrapped In Plastic* #75, September, 2005

Vernier, James; "David Lynch: American Primitive"; *Twilight Zone Magazine*, October 1988, Vol. 4, No. 8

Volante, Ken; "Dale Cooper, Buddhist Mystic"; *Wrapped in Plastic* #67, October 2003

Weizmann Institute Of Science; "Quantum Theory Demonstrated: Observation Affects Reality"; www.sciencedaily.com/releases/1998/02/980227055013.htm

Wise, Damon; "David Lynch Travels Back To 'Twin Peaks': The Story Was Not Over"; deadline.com, May 19, 2017

VIDEO AND AUDIO RECORDINGS

de Lauzirika, Charles; "A Very Lovely Dream: One Week in Twin Peaks"; *Twin Peaks: A Limited Event Series* Blu-ray, 2017

——; "Moving Through Time: Fire Walk With Me Memories"; *Twin Peaks: The Entire Mystery* Blu-ray, 2014

Fenn, Sherilynn; "Twin Peaks Panel w/ Sheryl Lee and Sherilyn Fenn - SpaCon 2017, Hot Springs, AR"; https://www.youtube.com/watch?v=6IVPJPEmqWk; 2017

Franich, Darren and Jeff Jensen; *A Twin Peaks Podcast*; https://podcasts.apple.com/us/podcast/robert-forster-joins-the-podcast/id1219263074?i=1000389377995; June 30, 2017

Frost, Mark; "A Conversation with Mark Frost"; *On Story*, Season 8 Episode 9, www.pbs.org/video/a-conversation-with-mark-frost-ti8nwn/; 2018

——; "Sam Esmail (Mr. Robot) Talks with Mark Frost (Twin Peaks)"; *Talkhouse Podcast*; https://www.talkhouse.com/sam-esmail-mr-robot-talks-mark-frost-twin-peaks-talkhouse-podcast/; 2017

Lynch, David; "Between Two Worlds"; *Twin Peaks: The Entire Mystery* Blu-ray, Disc 10; 2014

MacLachlan, Kyle; "57th Monte Carlo TV Festival"; https://www.youtube.com/watch?v=Y64MhWDCK8w; 2017

——; "Kyle MacLachlan from the TV series 'Twin Peaks'"; *The Envelope's Emmy Contender Series, Los Angeles Times*; https://www.facebook.com/watch/live/?ref=external&v=10155860123361185; 2018

——; "Toast of 2017: Kyle MacLachlan Shares the Secrets of 'Twin Peaks: The Return'"; *Yahoo TV*; https://www.yahoo.com/entertainment/toast-2017-kyle-maclachlan-shares-secrets-twin-peaks-return-150028926.html?fr=sycsrp_catchall; 2017

S., Jason; "Impressions: A Journey Behind the Scenes of Twin Peaks"; *Twin Peaks: A Limited Event Series* Blu-ray; 2017

——; "Behind The Curtain, Part 17"; *Twin Peaks from Z to A* Blu-ray; 2019

——; "Behind The Curtain, Part 18"; *Twin Peaks from Z to A* Blu-ray; 2019

ABOUT THE AUTHOR

John Thorne has a Bachelor of Science from Clarkson University in Potsdam, New York, and a Master of Arts in TV/Radio/Film from Southern Methodist University in Dallas, Texas. (His thesis was on the narrative structure of the television series, *Homicide: Life on the Street.*) For thirteen years, John was co-editor and co-producer of *Wrapped In Plastic* magazine where he wrote extensively about *Twin Peaks* and the works of David Lynch and Mark Frost (as well as other film and television). In 2017, he joined the editorial staff at *The Blue Rose* magazine where he continues to write about *Twin Peaks: The Return.* John is author of the book, *The Essential Wrapped in Plastic: Pathways to Twin Peaks* and is co-editor and contributor to the Kindle book, *Twin Peaks in the Rearview Mirror: Appraisals and Reappraisals of the Show That Was Supposed to Change TV.* John is co-host of the podcast, *In Our House Now.* You can follow him on Twitter: @thornewip.

"The correct understanding of a matter and misunderstanding the matter are not mutually exclusive."

– FRANZ KAFKA

Made in the USA
Monee, IL
21 December 2022

23065991R00215